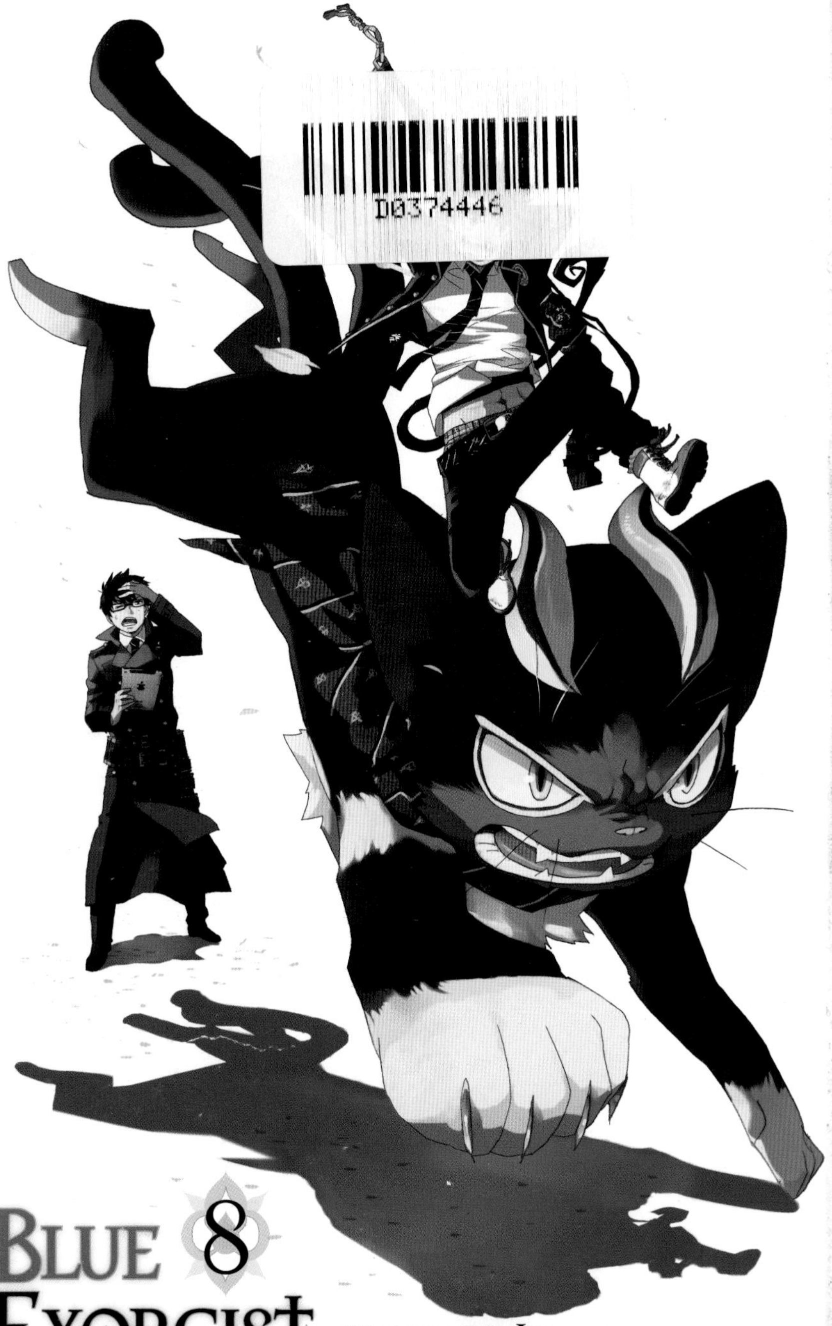

BLUE 8 EXORCIST

KAZUE KATO

BLUE EXORCIST

Contents 8

CAST OF CHARACTERS

KNIGHTS OF THE TRUE CROSS

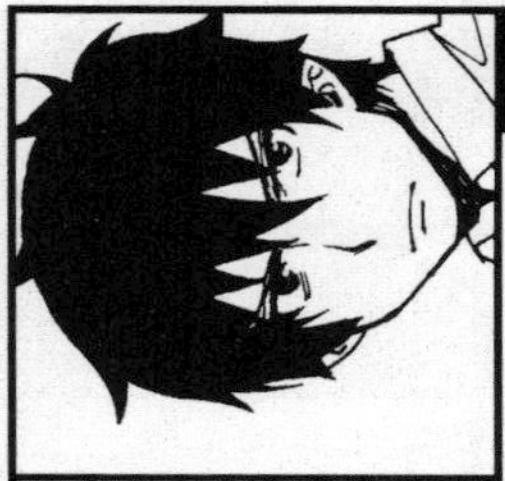

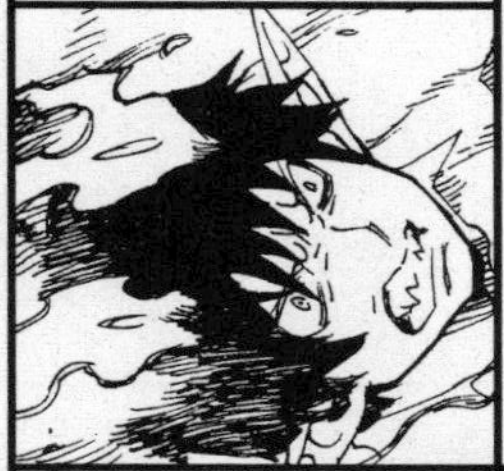

RIN OKUMURA

Born of a human mother and Satan, the God of Demons, Rin Okumura has powers he can barely control. After Satan kills Father Fujimoto, Rin's foster father, Rin decides to become an Exorcist so he can someday defeat Satan. Now a first-year student at True Cross Academy and an Exwire at the Exorcism Cram School, he hopes to someday become a Knight. When he draws the Koma Sword, he manifests his infernal power in the form of blue flames. The Order forbade him to use his flames, but he did anyway, and he is now being held in solitary confinement. After raging out of control with his flame, he lost confidence and now can't draw his sword.

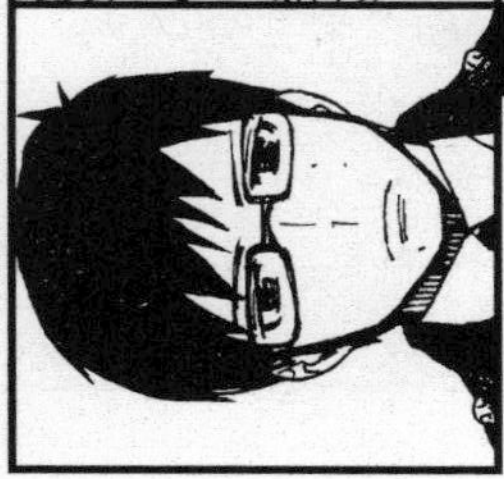

YUKIO OKUMURA

Rin's brother. Hoping to become a doctor, he's a genius who is the youngest student ever to become an instructor at the Exorcism Cram School. An instructor in Demon Pharmaceuticals, he possesses the titles of Doctor and Dragoon.

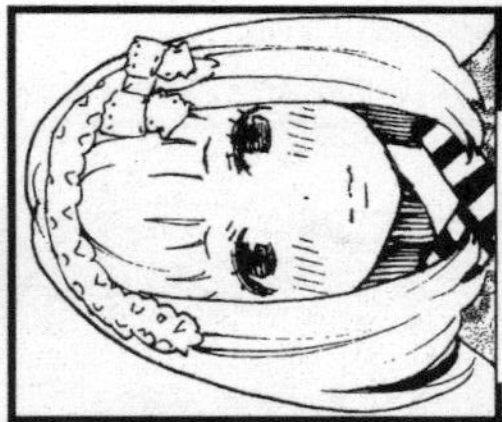

SHIEMI MORIYAMA

Daughter of the owner of Futsumaya, an Exorcist supply shop. Inspired by Rin and Yukio, she became an Exwire and hopes to someday become an Exorcist. She has the ability to become a Tamer and can summon a baby Greenman.

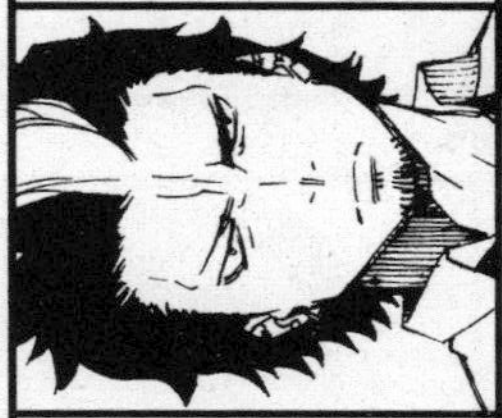

RYUJI SUGURO

Heir to the venerable Buddhist sect known as Myodha in Kyoto. He is an Exwire who hopes to become an Exorcist someday so he can reestablish his family's temple, which fell on hard times after the Blue Night. He wants to achieve the titles of Dragoon and Aria.

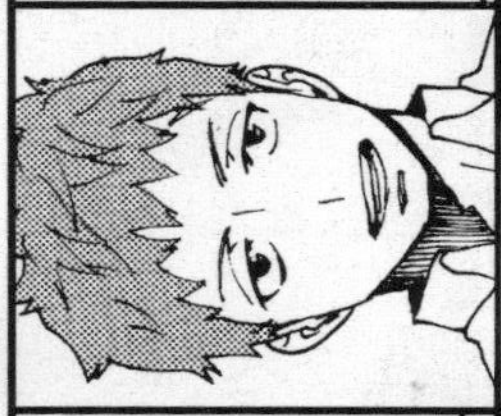

RENZO SHIMA

Once a pupil of Suguro's father and now Suguro's friend. He's an Exwire who wants to become an Aria. He has an easygoing personality and is totally girl-crazy.

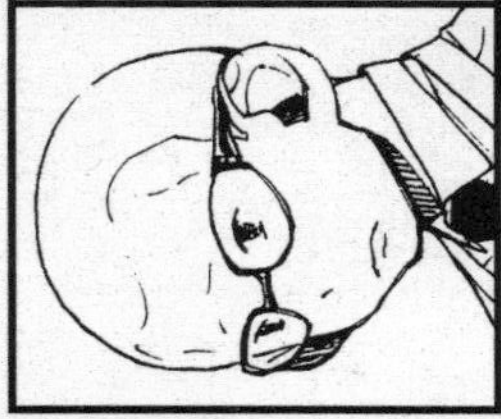

KONEKOMARU MIWA

Like Shima, he was once a pupil of Suguro's father and is now Suguro's friend. He's an Exwire who hopes to become an Exorcist someday. He is small in size and has a quiet and composed personality.

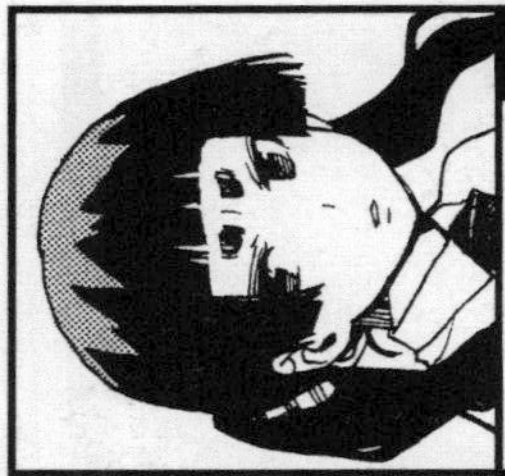

Izumo Kamiki

An Exwire with the blood of shrine maidens. She has the ability to become a Tamer and can summon two white foxes.

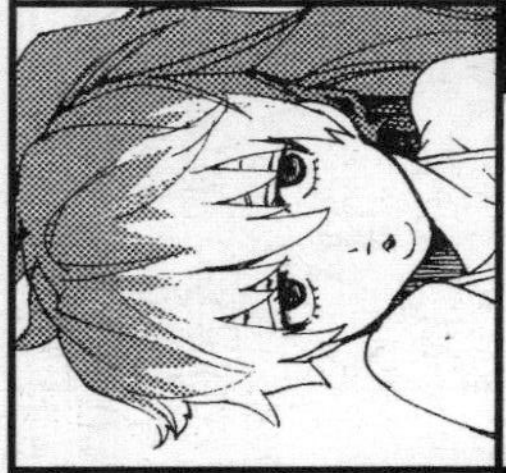

Shura Kirigakure

An upper-rank special investigator dispatched by Vatican Headquarters to True Cross Academy. A Senior Exorcist First Class who holds the titles of Knight, Tamer, Doctor and Aria.

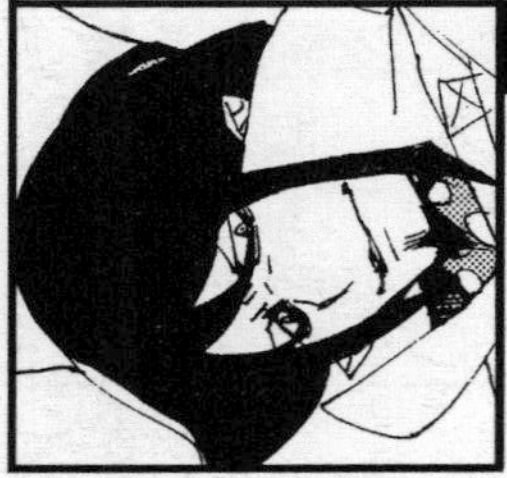

Mephisto Pheles

President of True Cross Academy and head of the Exorcism Cram School. He was Father Fujimoto's friend, and now he is Rin and Yukio's guardian. He plans to turn Rin into a weapon to use in the fight against Satan.

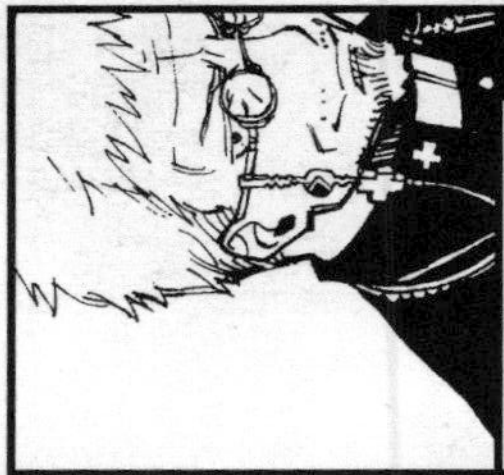

Shiro Fujimoto

The man who raised Rin and Yukio. He held the rank of Paladin and once taught Demon Pharmaceuticals. Satan possessed him and he gave his life defending Rin.

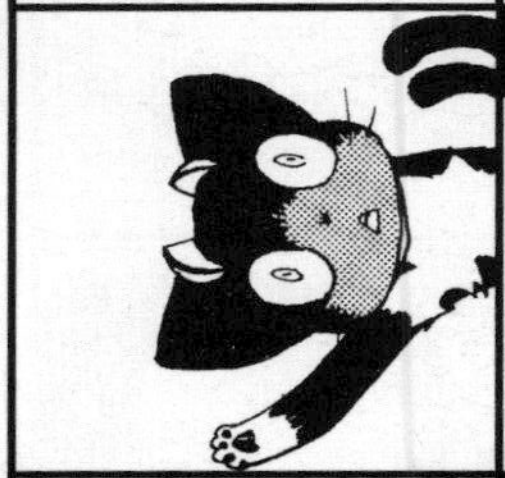

Kuro

A Cat Sídhe who was once Shiro's familiar. After Shiro's death, he began turning back into a demon. Rin saved him, and now the two are practically inseparable. His favorite drink is the catnip wine Shiro used to make.

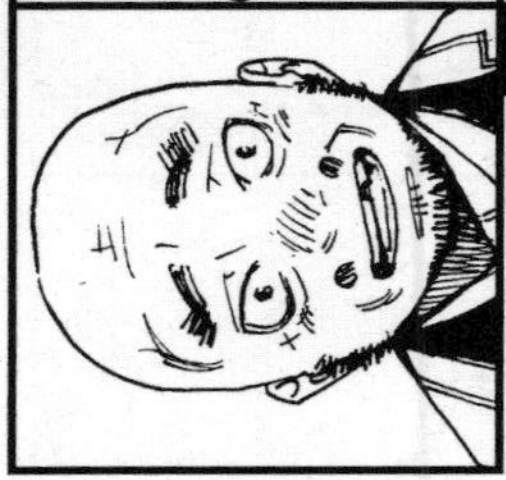

Tatsuma Suguro

Ryuji's father and the leader of Myodha. While keeping the secret that was the price of his contract with Karura, he developed the Aeon Wave Flame technique for defeating the Impure King. He has transferred the flame to Ryuji and asked him to destroy the Impure King.

Torako Suguro

Ryuji's mother. She runs the Toraya Inn and secretly uses the proceeds from it to prop up the family temple.

Yaozo Shima

Renzo's father. A Senior Buddhist Exorcist First Class holding the classifications of Knight and Aria. In Myodha, he is an archpriest, one rank beneath Tatsuma.

Juzo Shima

Second son of the Shima family. A Senior Buddhist Exorcist Second Class holding the classifications of Knight and Aria. He looks cool and collected on the outside but is actually short-tempered.

Kinzo Shima

The fourth son of the Shima family. An Intermediate Buddhist Exorcist Second Class holding the classifications of Knight and Aria. Like Juzo, he's always ready for a fight.

Uwabami Hojo

A Senior Buddhist Exorcist First Class holding the classifications of Tamer and Aria. Like Yaozo, he is an archpriest and helps lead the Myodha sect.

Mamushi Hojo

An Intermediate Buddhist Exorcist First Class holding the classifications of Tamer and Aria. Todo took advantage of her worries about the future of Myodha and tricked her into cooperating with him.

Demons

Saburota Todo

Todo comes from an honorable family that has supplied the Order with Exorcists for generations. But now he has joined the demons and awakened the Impure King. What is his goal now that he has stolen Karura from Tatsuma?

⬟ THE STORY SO FAR ⬟

UNKNOWN TO RIN OKUMURA, BOTH HUMAN AND DEMON
BLOOD RUNS IN HIS VEINS. IN AN ARGUMENT WITH HIS
FOSTER FATHER, FATHER FUJIMOTO, RIN LEARNS THAT
SATAN IS HIS TRUE FATHER. SATAN SUDDENLY APPEARS
AND TRIES TO DRAG RIN DOWN TO GEHENNA BECAUSE RIN
HAS INHERITED HIS POWER. FATHER FUJIMOTO FIGHTS TO
DEFEND RIN, BUT DIES IN THE PROCESS. RIN DECIDES TO
BECOME AN EXORCIST SO HE CAN SOMEDAY DEFEAT
SATAN AND BEGINS STUDYING AT THE EXORCISM CRAM
SCHOOL UNDER THE INSTRUCTION OF HIS TWIN BROTHER
YUKIO, WHO IS ALREADY AN EXORCIST.

HOWEVER, DURING SUMMER VACATION FOREST TRAINING,
EVERYONE LEARNS THAT RIN IS THE SON OF SATAN, AND
HE APPEARS AS EVIDENCE AT THE QUESTIONING OF
MEPHISTO BY THE KNIGHTS OF THE TRUE CROSS. THE
COURT LETS RIN GO ON THE CONDITION THAT HE PASS THE
EXORCIST CERTIFICATION EXAM IN SIX MONTHS. UNDER
THE SUPERVISION OF SHURA AND YUKIO, HE BEGINS
LEARNING TO CONTROL HIS FLAME.

THEN, THEY LEARN THAT SOMEONE HAS STOLEN THE LEFT
EYE OF THE IMPURE KING FROM THE ACADEMY'S DEEP
KEEP.

◉ THE STORY SO FAR ◉

RIN AND THE OTHERS GO TO THE KYOTO FIELD OFFICE OF THE KNIGHTS OF THE TRUE CROSS TO ASSIST DEFENSE OF THE RIGHT EYE OF THE IMPURE KING. WHEN THEY ARRIVE, THEY LEARN THAT ALMOST HALF OF THE COMBATANTS THERE BELONG TO A RELIGIOUS SECT NAMED MYO-O DHARANI AND THEIR LEADER IS RYUJI'S FATHER, GREAT PRIEST TATSUMA SUGURO.

TODO, A FORMER EXORCIST, STOLE THE LEFT EYE AND THEN TRICKED MAMUSHI, WHO BELONGS TO THE HOJO FAMILY OF MYODHA ARCHPRIESTS, INTO GIVING HIM THE RIGHT EYE. TODO THEN USES THE EYES TO AWAKEN THE IMPURE KING AND SEIZE THE POWER OF TATSUMA'S FAMILIAR, KARURA.

MEANWHILE, RIN USES HIS FORBIDDEN FLAME, CAUSING THE ORDER TO IMPRISON HIM. AFTER HIS FRIENDS BREAK HIM OUT, THEY ALL PREPARE TO FACE THE IMPURE KING, BUT FOR SOME REASON RIN CAN'T DRAW THE KOMA SWORD. THE IMPURE KING IS SWELLING TO GIGANTIC PROPORTIONS AND IS ABOUT TO SPEW POISONOUS GAS OVER KYOTO. THE CASUALTIES COULD BE MASSIVE...

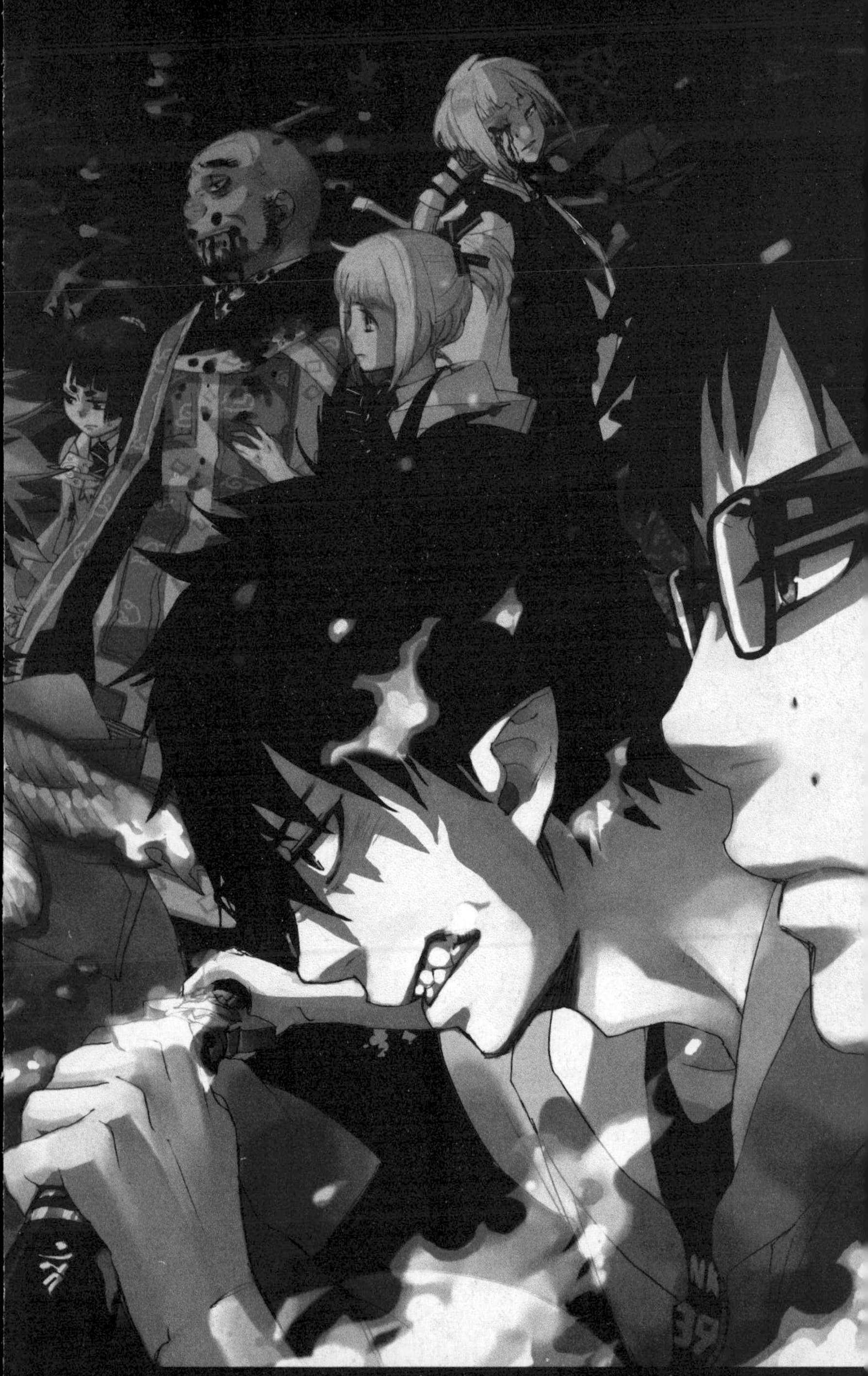

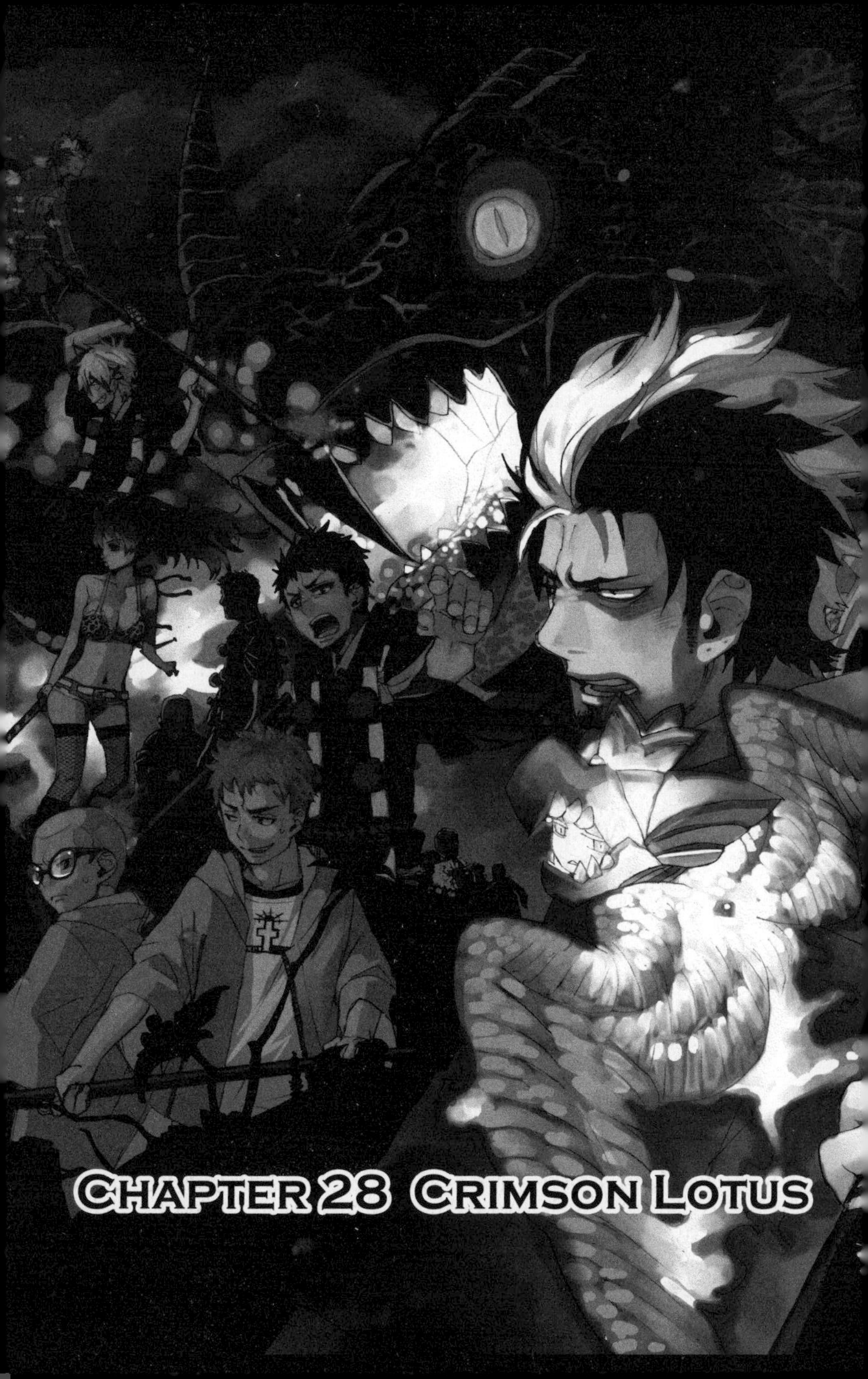
CHAPTER 28 CRIMSON LOTUS

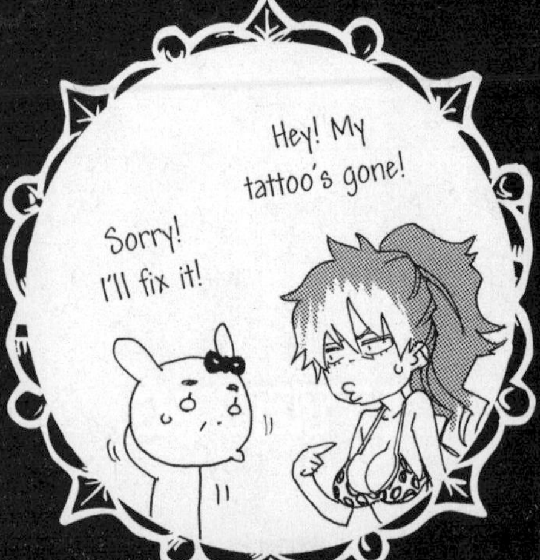
Hey! My tattoo's gone!
Sorry! I'll fix it!

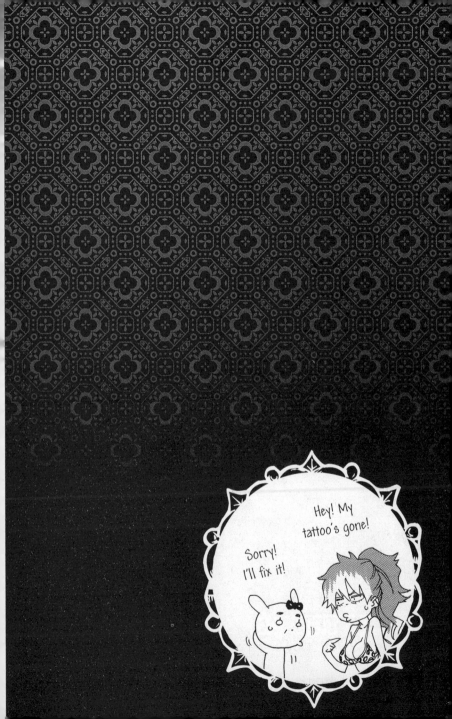

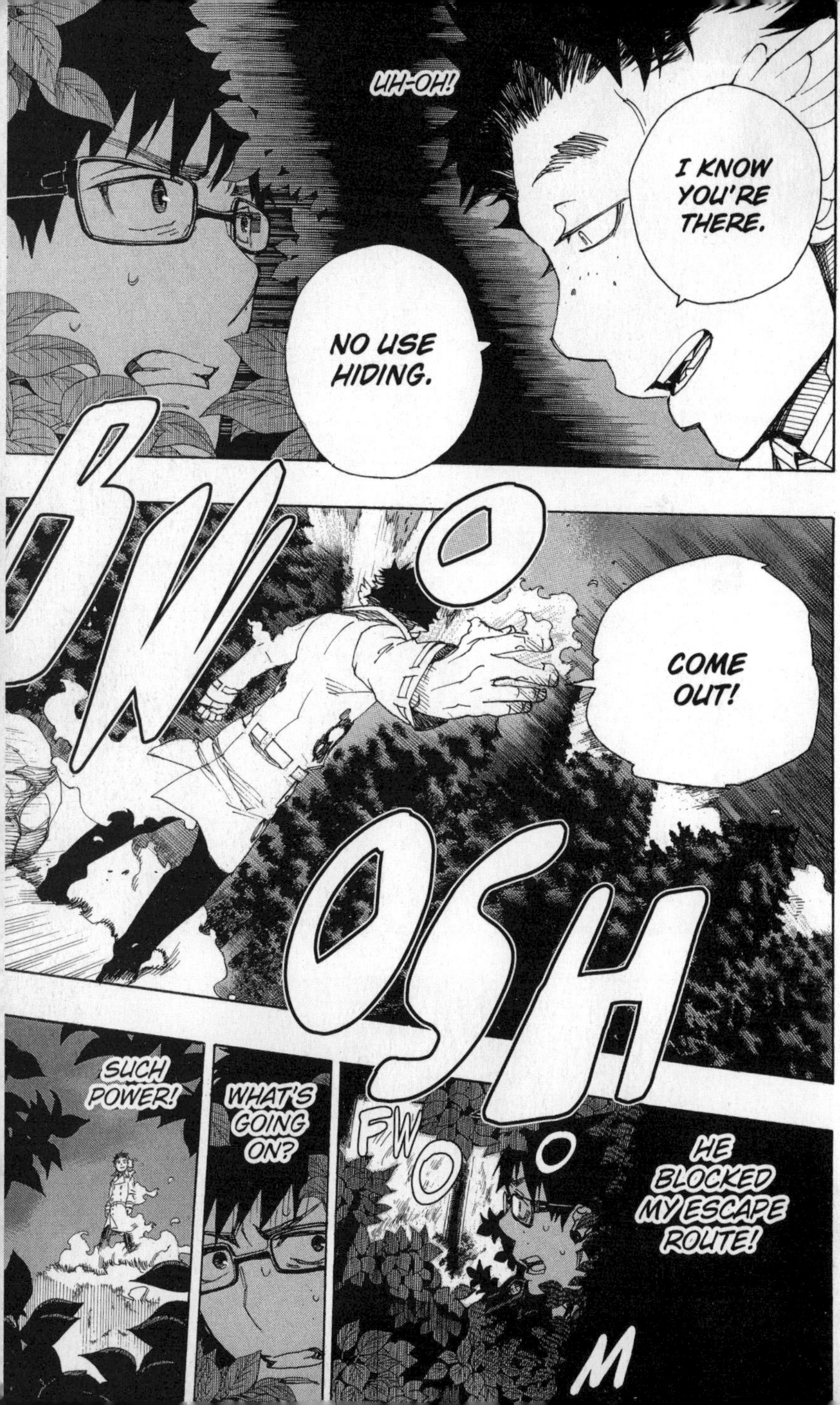
I KNOW YOU'RE THERE.
NO USE HIDING.
UH-OH!
BWOOSH
COME OUT!
FWOOM
HE BLOCKED MY ESCAPE ROUTE!
WHAT'S GOING ON?
SUCH POWER!

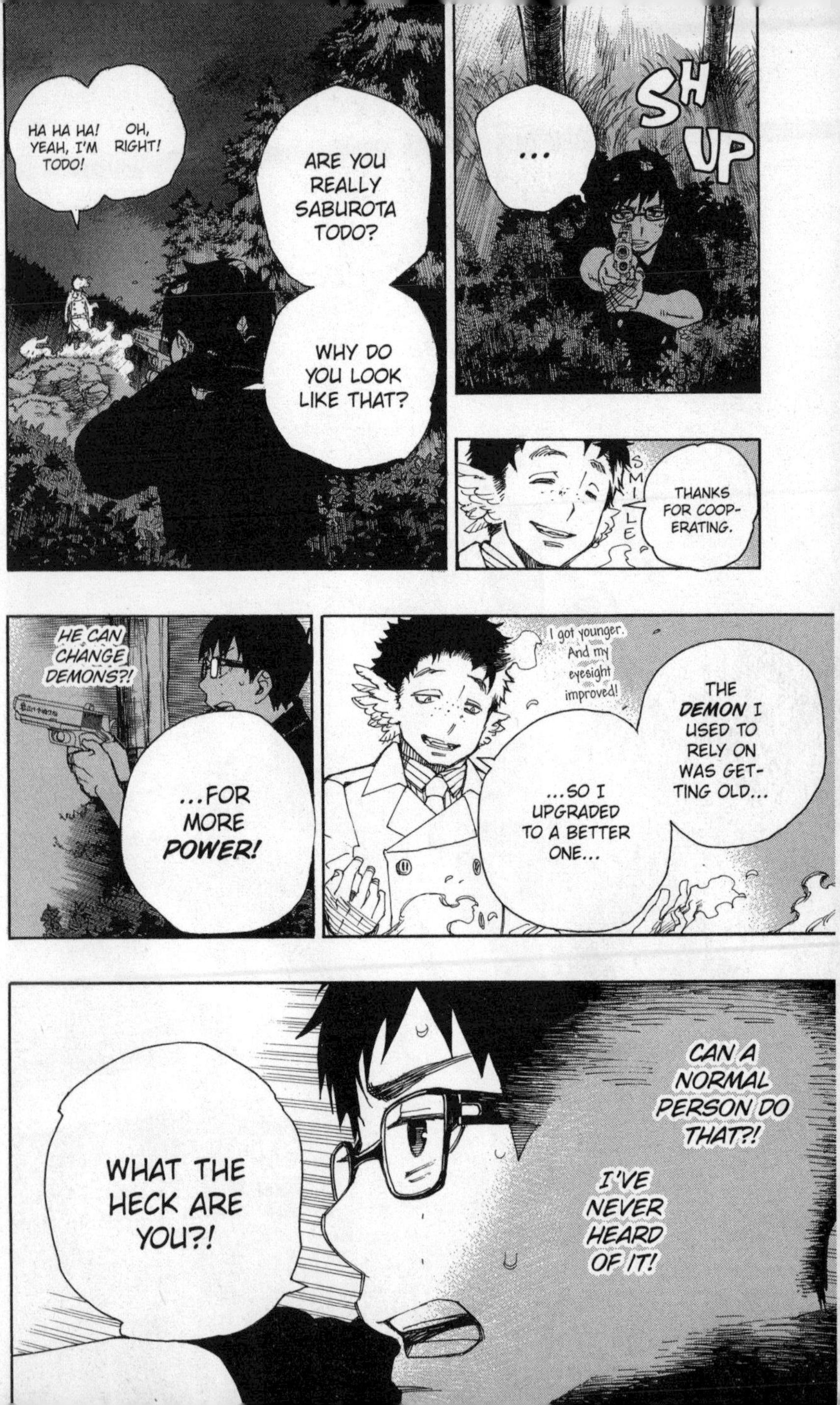
...
SH UP
SMILE
THANKS FOR COOPERATING.
ARE YOU REALLY SABUROTA TODO?
WHY DO YOU LOOK LIKE THAT?
OH, RIGHT!
HA HA HA! YEAH, I'M TODO!
I got younger. And my eyesight improved!
THE DEMON I USED TO RELY ON WAS GETTING OLD...
...SO I UPGRADED TO A BETTER ONE...
HE CAN CHANGE DEMONS?!
...FOR MORE POWER!
CAN A NORMAL PERSON DO THAT?!
I'VE NEVER HEARD OF IT!
WHAT THE HECK ARE YOU?!

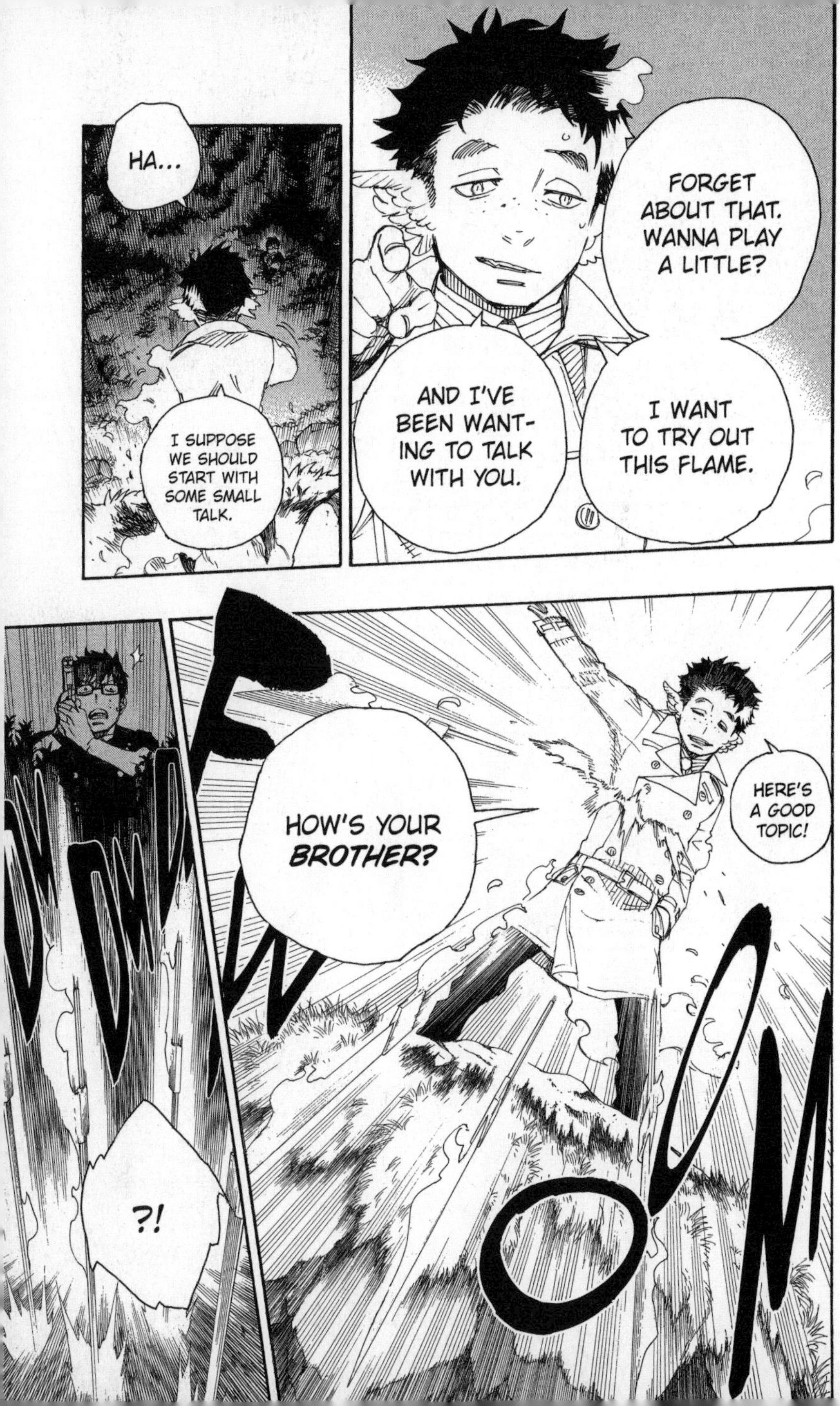
FORGET ABOUT THAT. WANNA PLAY A LITTLE?
I WANT TO TRY OUT THIS FLAME.
AND I'VE BEEN WANTING TO TALK WITH YOU.
HA...
I SUPPOSE WE SHOULD START WITH SOME SMALL TALK.
HERE'S A GOOD TOPIC!
HOW'S YOUR ***BROTHER?***
?!

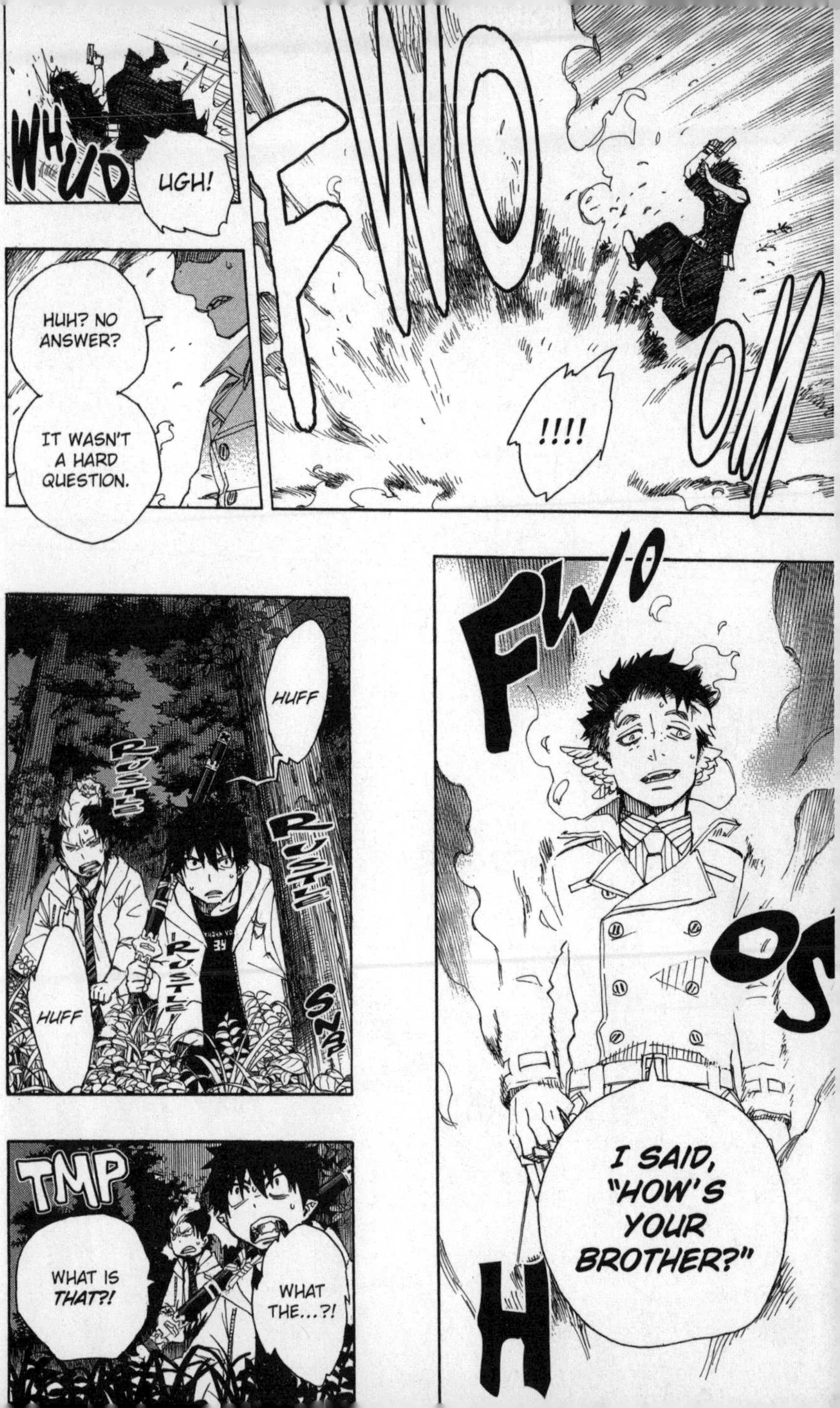
FWOOOM
!!!!
WHUD
UGH!
HUH? NO ANSWER?
IT WASN'T A HARD QUESTION.
FWOOOSH
I SAID, "HOW'S YOUR BROTHER?"
HUFF
RUSTLE
RUSTLE
RUSTLE
SNAP
HUFF
TMP
WHAT THE...?!
WHAT IS *THAT?!*

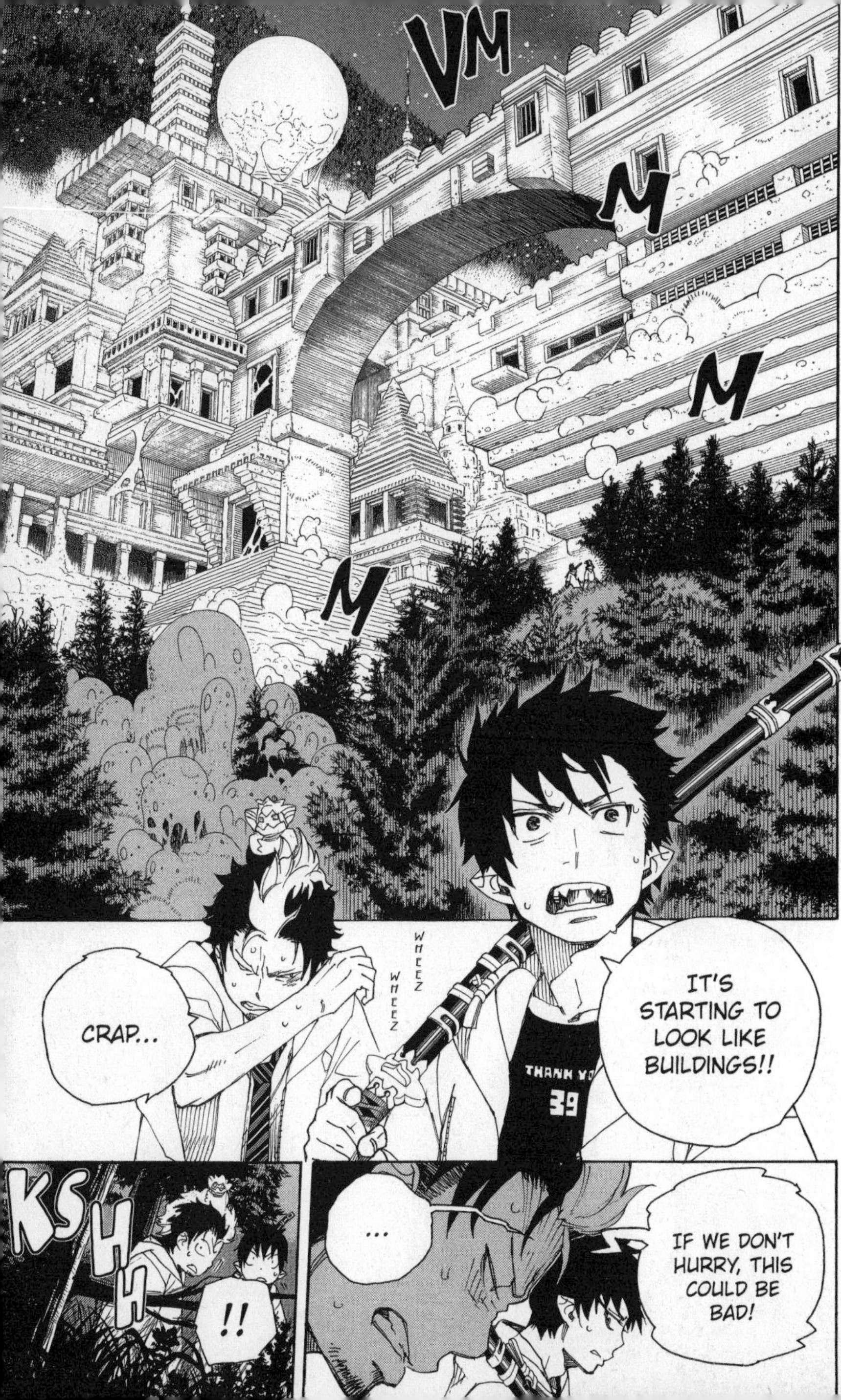
VMMMM
IT'S STARTING TO LOOK LIKE BUILDINGS!!
THANK YO
39
WHEEZ WHEEZ
CRAP...
IF WE DON'T HURRY, THIS COULD BE BAD!
...
KSHH
!!

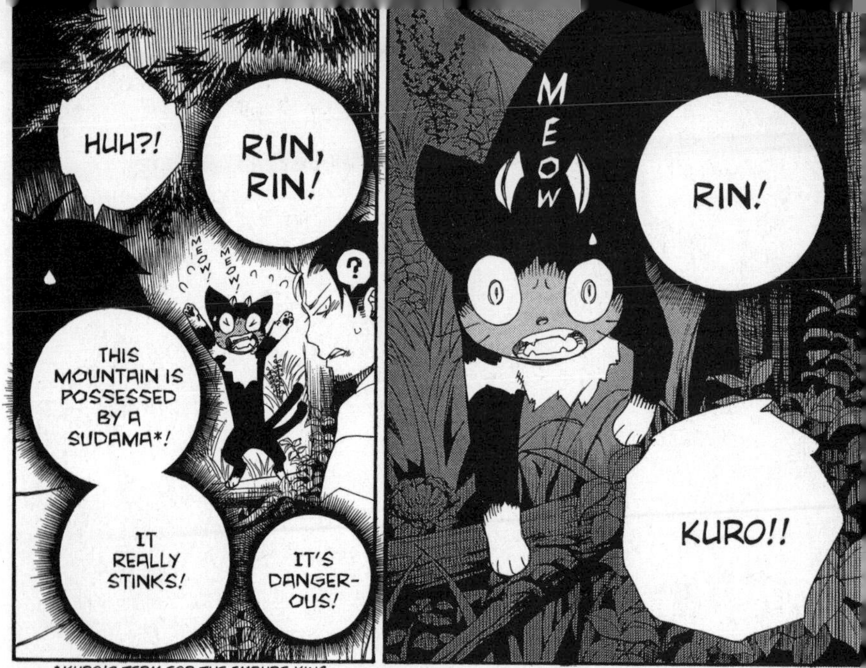
MEOW
RIN!
KURO!!
RUN, RIN!
HUH?!
MEOW! MEOW!
?
THIS MOUNTAIN IS POSSESSED BY A SUDAMA*!
IT'S DANGEROUS!
IT REALLY STINKS!

*KURO'S TERM FOR THE IMPURE KING, MEANING THE SOUL OR SPIRIT OF THE MOUNTAIN.

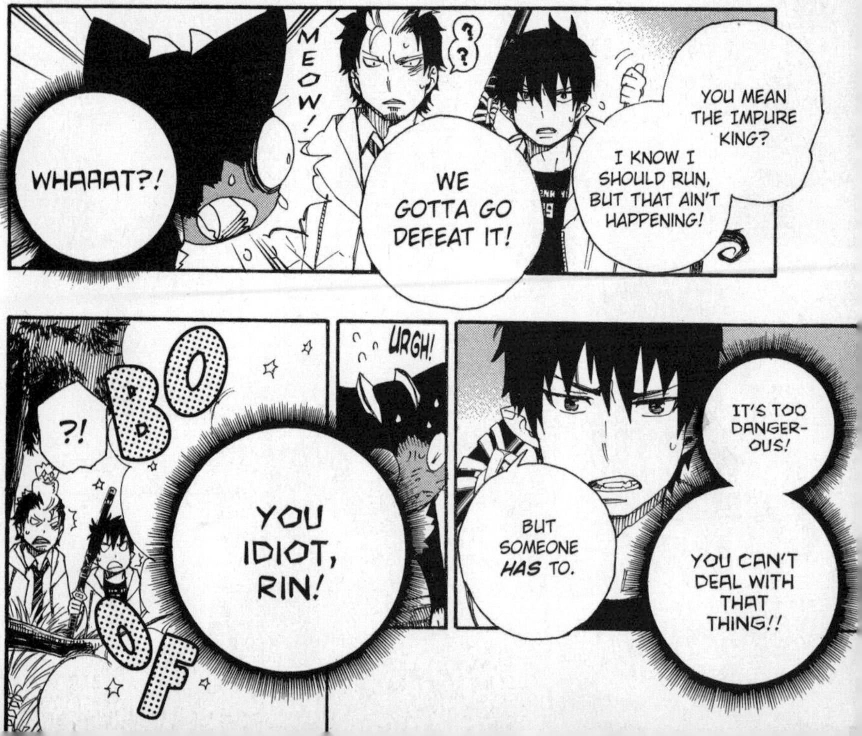
YOU MEAN THE IMPURE KING?
I KNOW I SHOULD RUN, BUT THAT AIN'T HAPPENING!
WE GOTTA GO DEFEAT IT!
??
MEOW!
WHAAAT?!
IT'S TOO DANGEROUS!
YOU CAN'T DEAL WITH THAT THING!!
BUT SOMEONE *HAS* TO.
URGH!
BOOF
?!
YOU IDIOT, RIN!

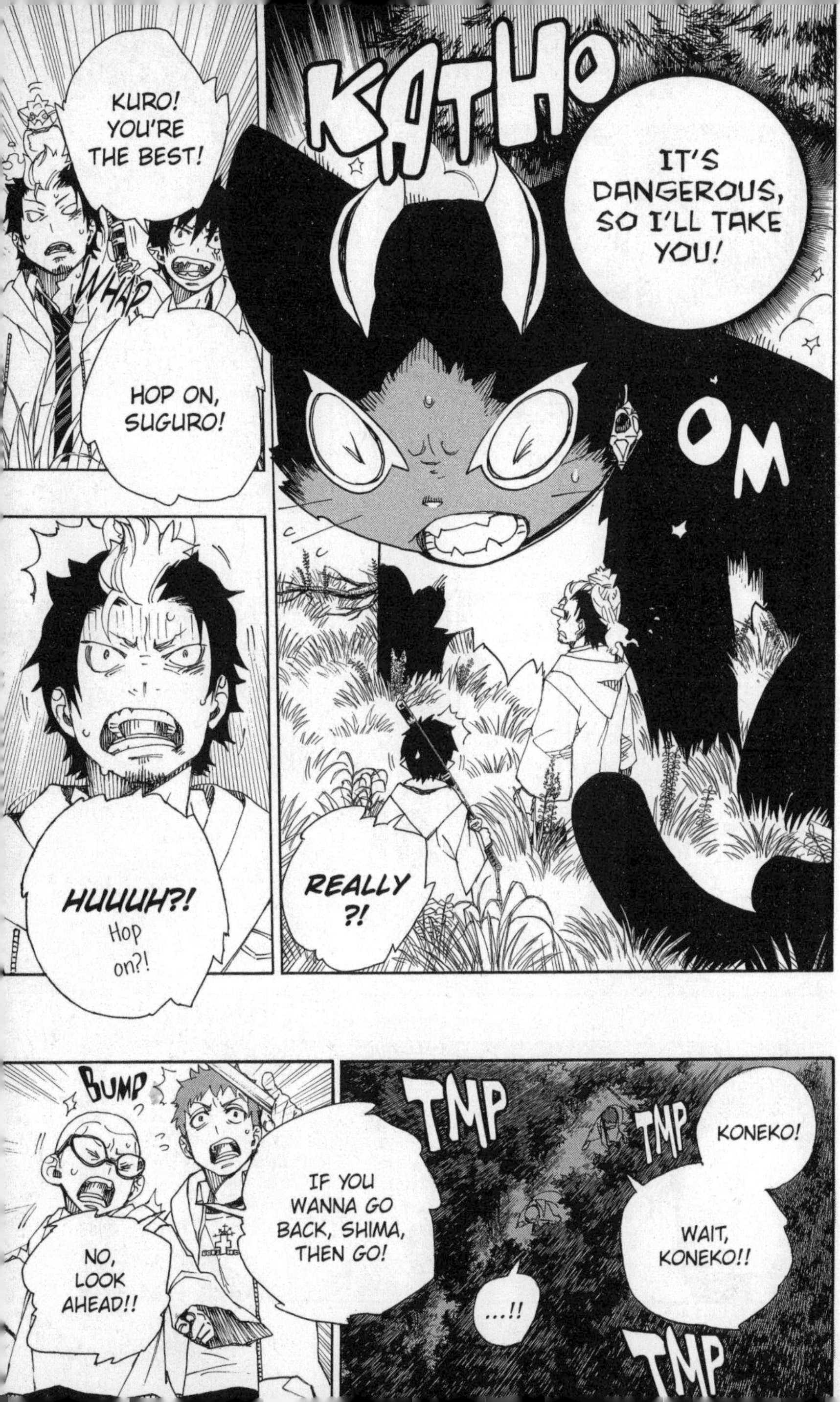
KATHO
IT'S DANGEROUS, SO I'LL TAKE YOU!
OM
REALLY ?!
KURO! YOU'RE THE BEST!
WHAP
HOP ON, SUGURO!
HUUUH?! Hop on?!
TMP
TMP
KONEKO!
WAIT, KONEKO!!
...!!
TMP
BUMP
IF YOU WANNA GO BACK, SHIMA, THEN GO!
NO, LOOK AHEAD!!

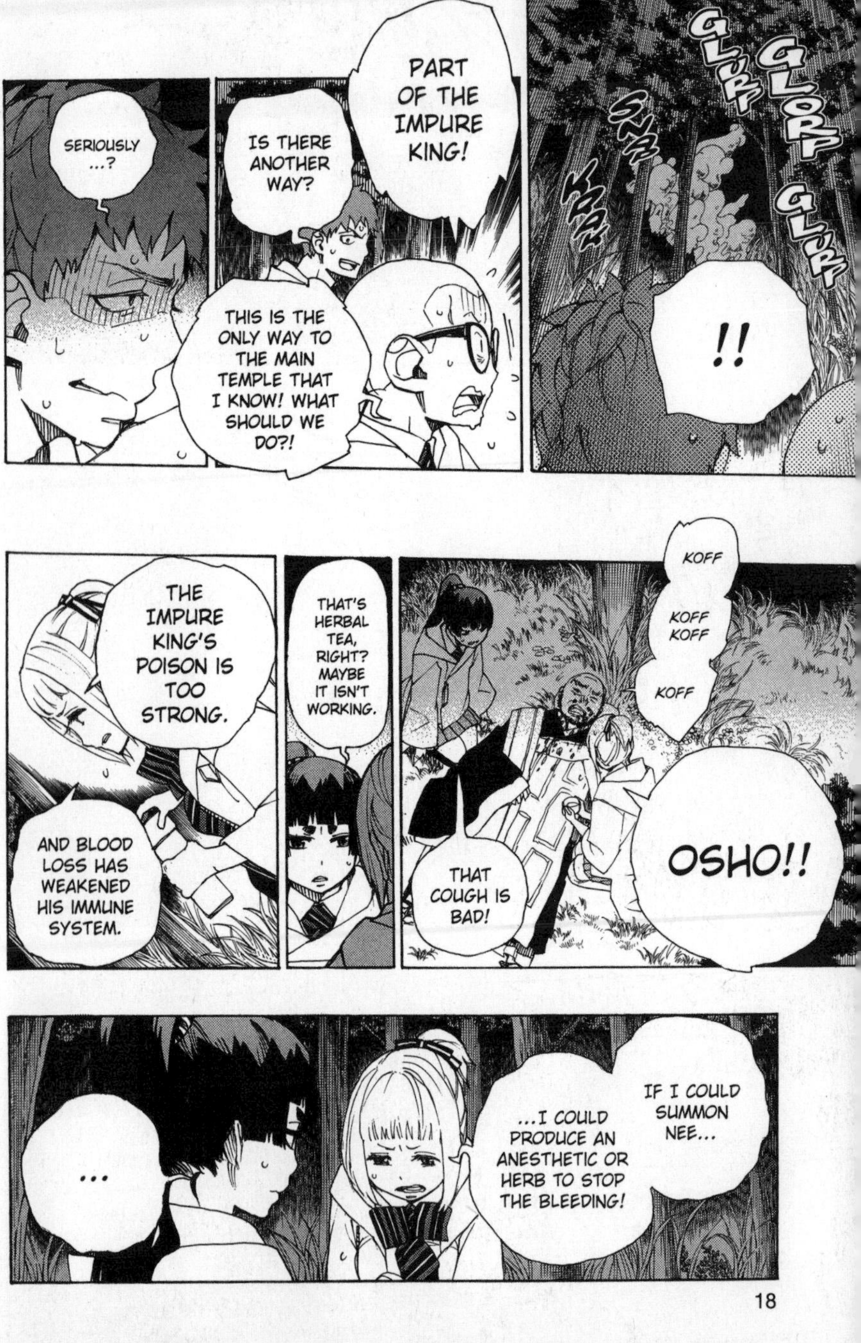
GLORP
GLURP
GLURP
!!
PART OF THE IMPURE KING!
IS THERE ANOTHER WAY?
THIS IS THE ONLY WAY TO THE MAIN TEMPLE THAT I KNOW! WHAT SHOULD WE DO?!
SERIOUSLY ...?
KOFF
KOFF KOFF
KOFF
OSHO!!
THAT COUGH IS BAD!
THAT'S HERBAL TEA, RIGHT? MAYBE IT ISN'T WORKING.
THE IMPURE KING'S POISON IS TOO STRONG.
AND BLOOD LOSS HAS WEAKENED HIS IMMUNE SYSTEM.
IF I COULD SUMMON NEE...
...I COULD PRODUCE AN ANESTHETIC OR HERB TO STOP THE BLEEDING!
...

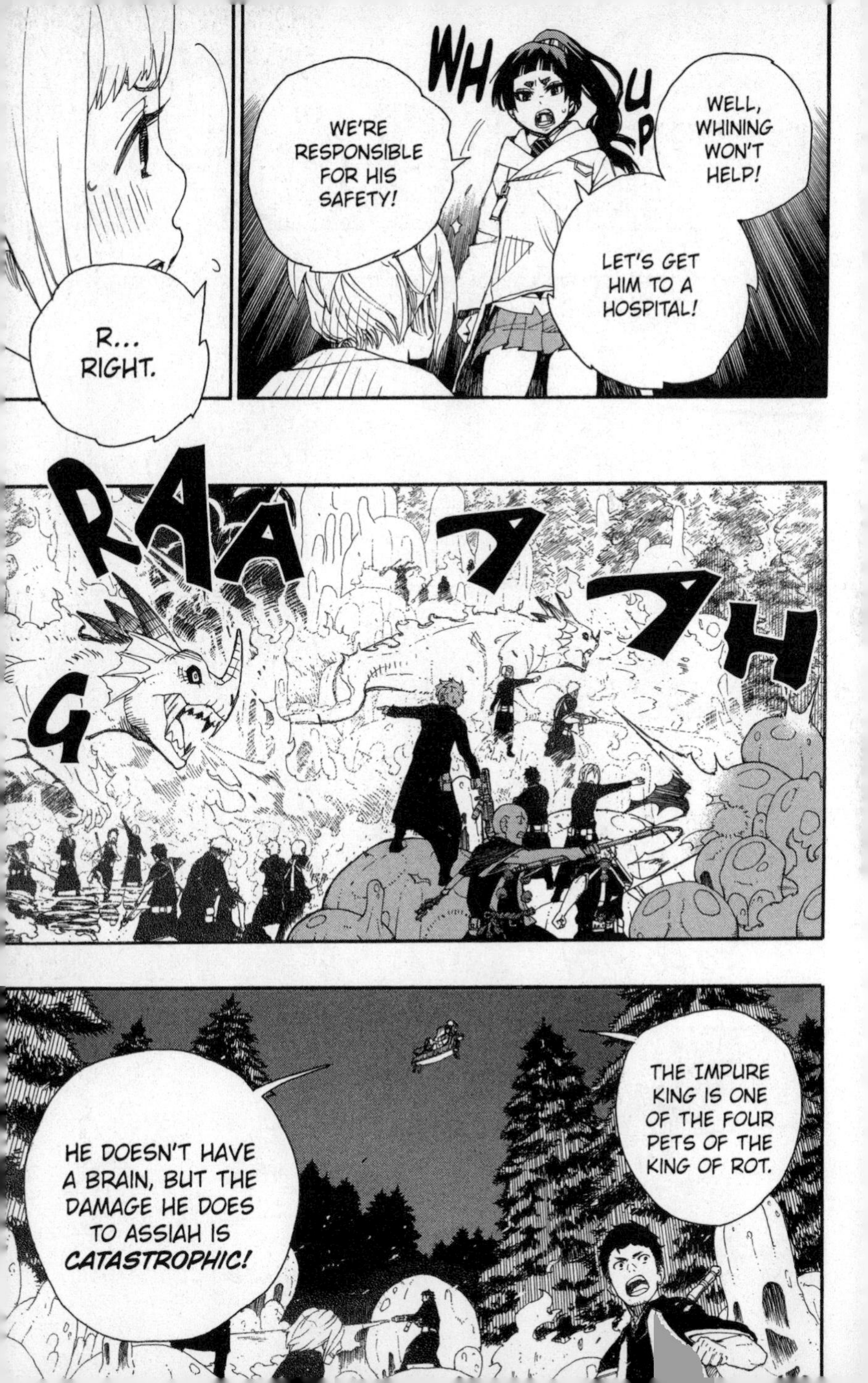
WHUP
WELL, WHINING WON'T HELP!
WE'RE RESPONSIBLE FOR HIS SAFETY!
LET'S GET HIM TO A HOSPITAL!
R... RIGHT.
RAAAAH
G
THE IMPURE KING IS ONE OF THE FOUR PETS OF THE KING OF ROT.
HE DOESN'T HAVE A BRAIN, BUT THE DAMAGE HE DOES TO ASSIAH IS *CATASTROPHIC!*

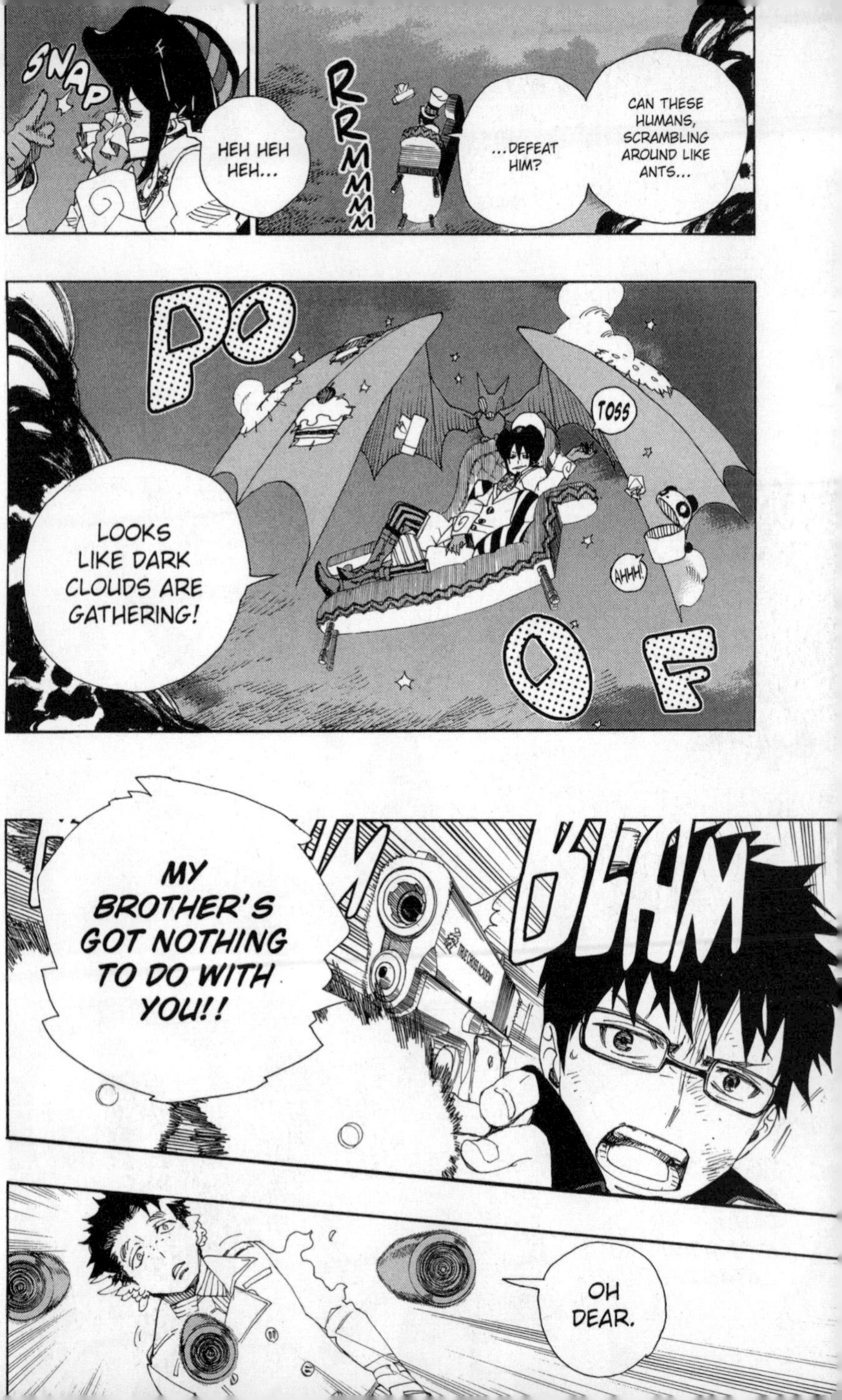
CAN THESE HUMANS, SCRAMBLING AROUND LIKE ANTS...
...DEFEAT HIM?
RRMMMMM
SNAP
HEH HEH HEH...
POOF
TOSS
AHHH!
LOOKS LIKE DARK CLOUDS ARE GATHERING!
BLAM
MY BROTHER'S GOT NOTHING TO DO WITH YOU!!
OH DEAR.

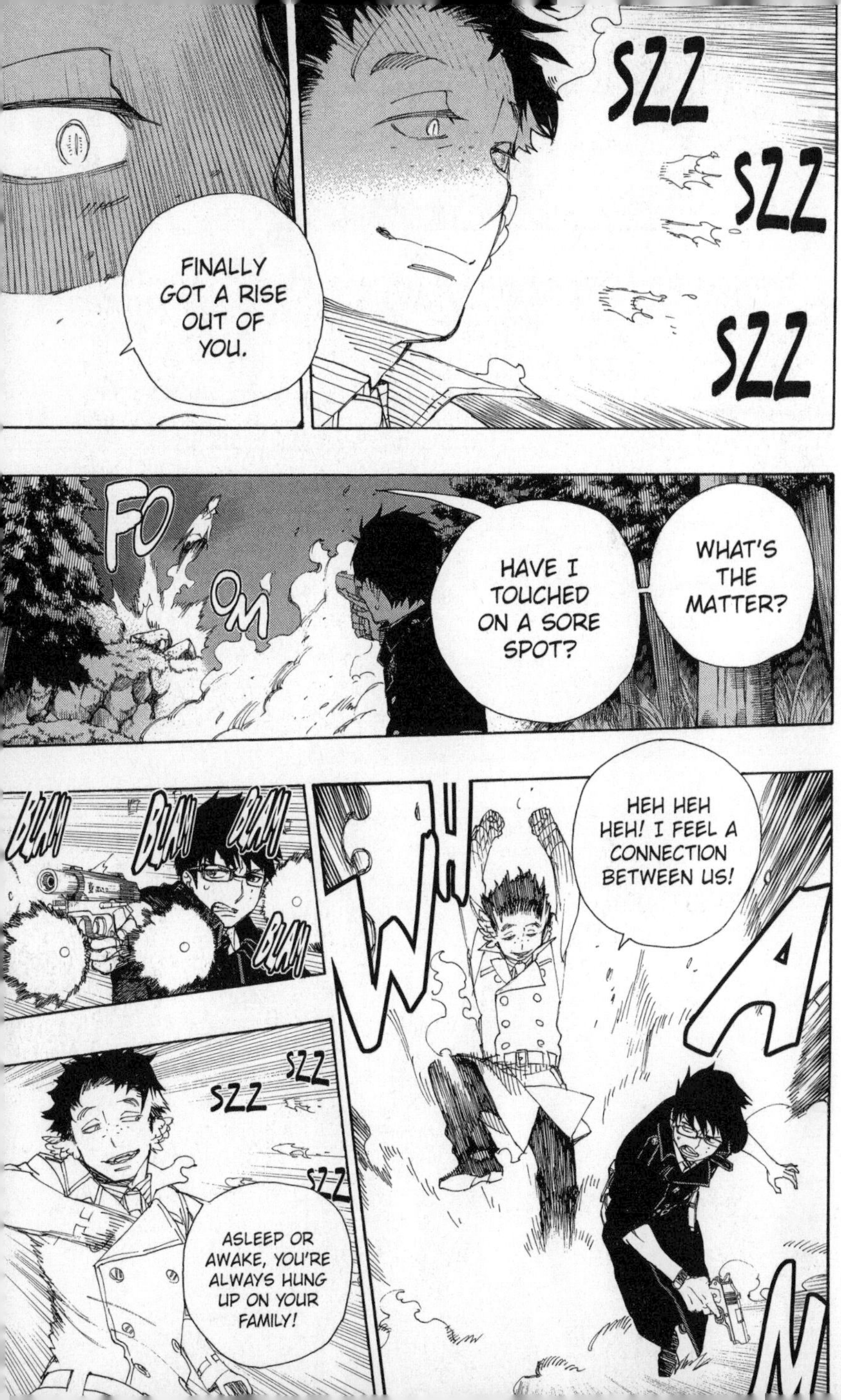
SZZ
SZZ
SZZ
FINALLY GOT A RISE OUT OF YOU.
WHAT'S THE MATTER?
HAVE I TOUCHED ON A SORE SPOT?
FOOM
HEH HEH HEH! I FEEL A CONNECTION BETWEEN US!
WHAM
BLAM
BLAM
BLAM
BLAM
SZZ
SZZ
SZZ
ASLEEP OR AWAKE, YOU'RE ALWAYS HUNG UP ON YOUR FAMILY!

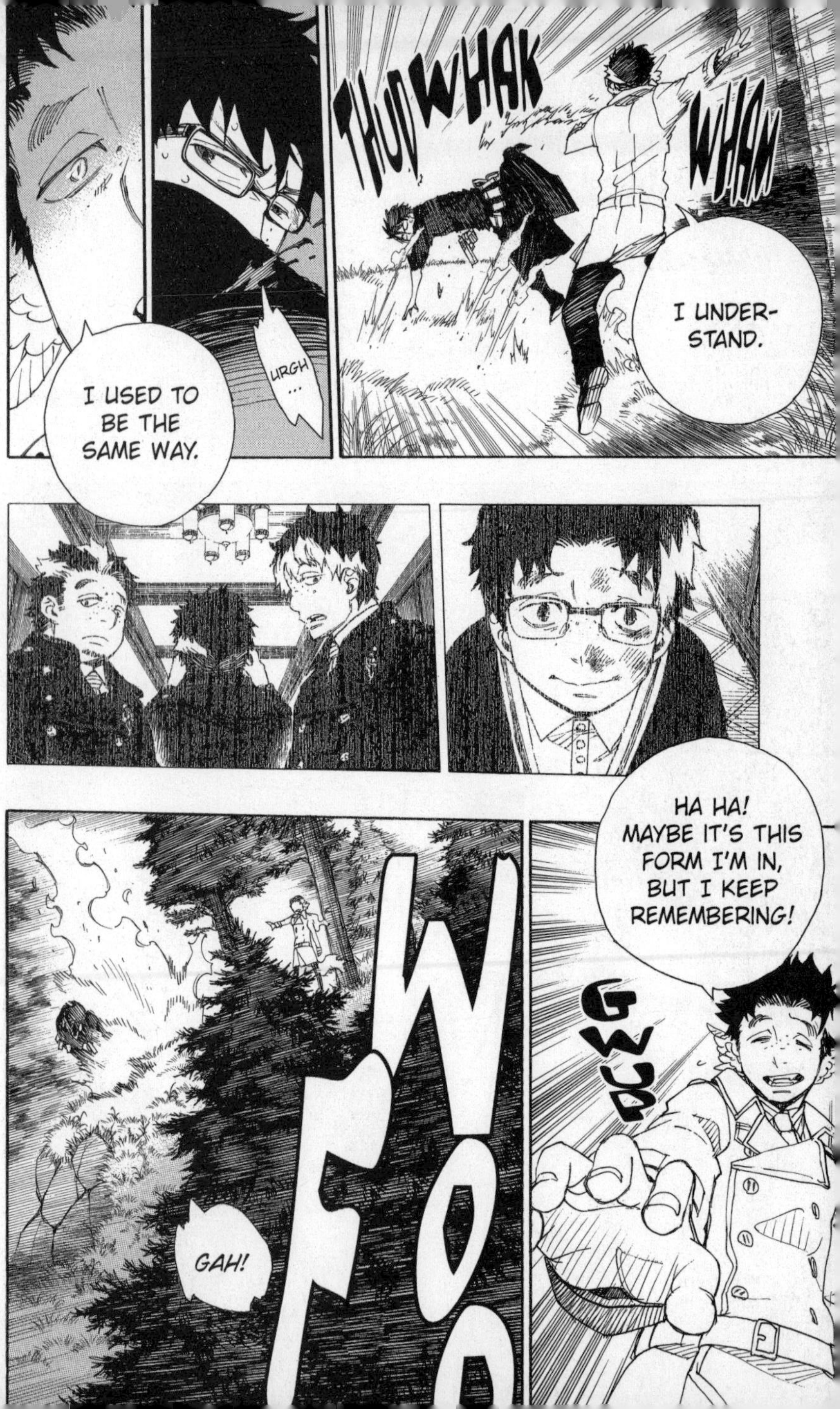
WHAM
I UNDER-STAND.
THUD WHAK
URGH...
I USED TO BE THE SAME WAY.
HA HA! MAYBE IT'S THIS FORM I'M IN, BUT I KEEP REMEMBERING!
GWUD
WFOO
GAH!

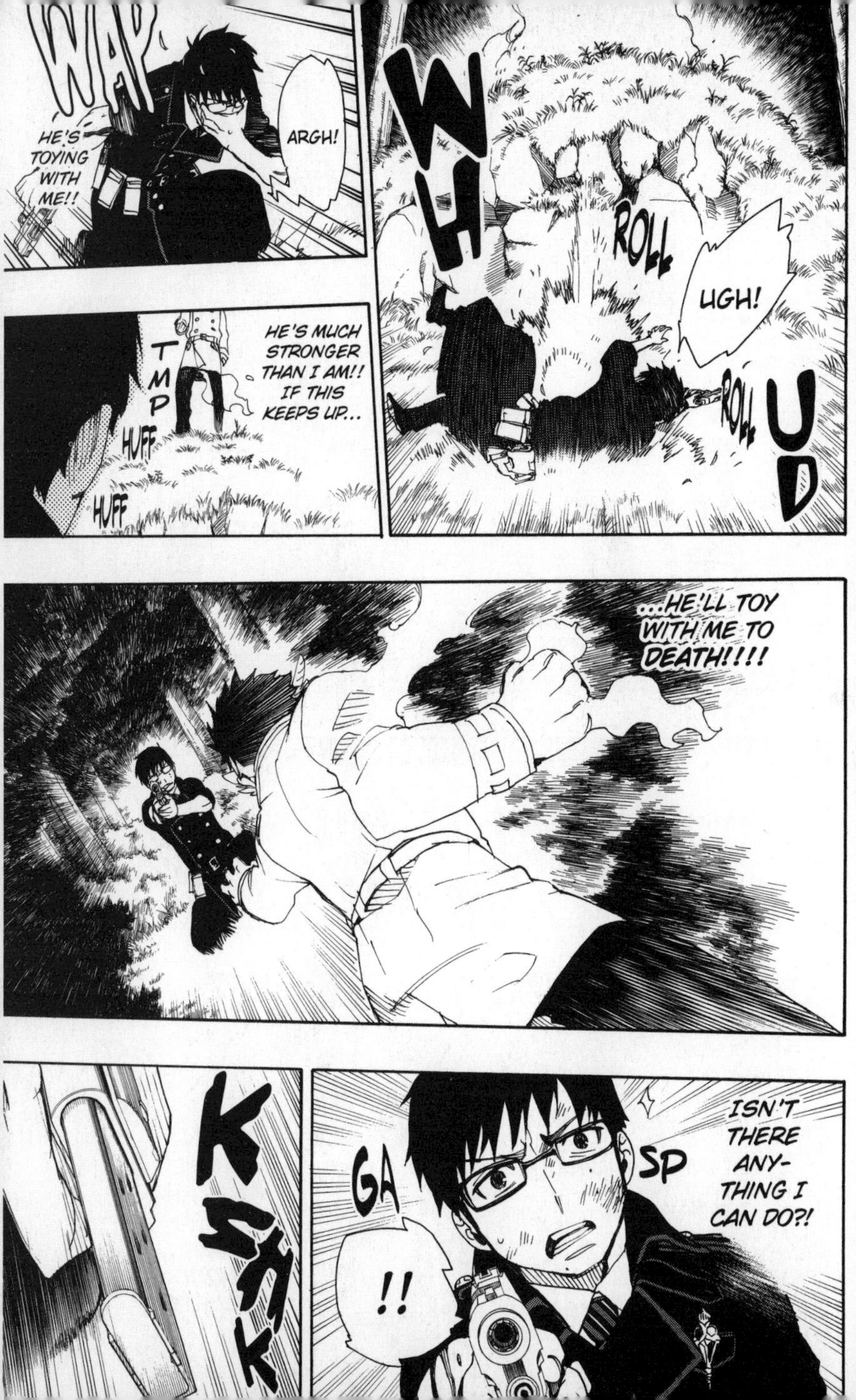
WHUD
ROLL
UGH!
ROLL
ARGH!
WAP
HE'S TOYING WITH ME!!
HE'S MUCH STRONGER THAN I AM!! IF THIS KEEPS UP...
TMP
HUFF
HUFF
...HE'LL TOY WITH ME TO DEATH!!!!
ISN'T THERE ANY-THING I CAN DO?!
GASP
!!

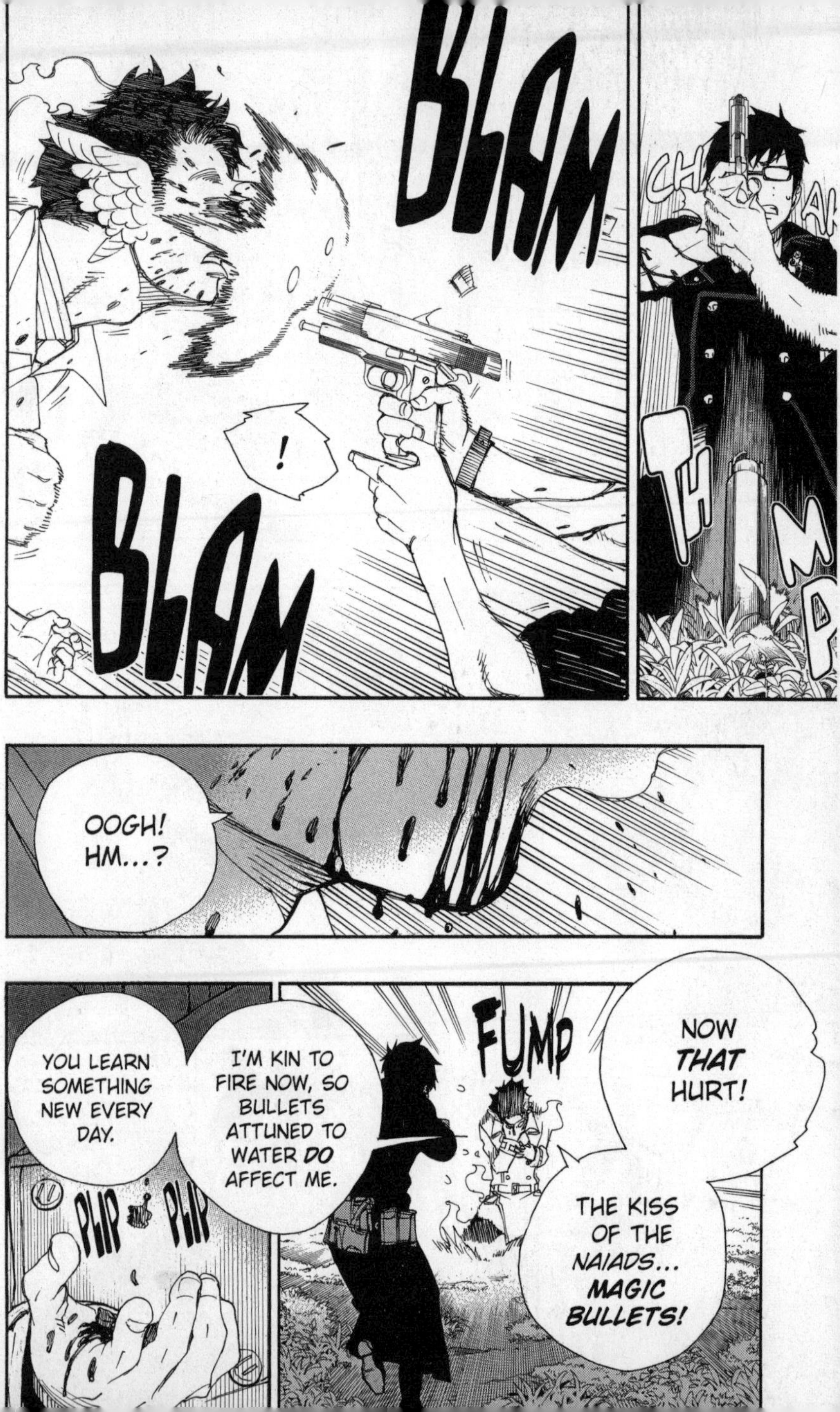
THMP
BLAM
BLAM
!
OOGH! HM...?
FUMP
NOW *THAT* HURT!
THE KISS OF THE NAIADS... ***MAGIC BULLETS!***
I'M KIN TO FIRE NOW, SO BULLETS ATTUNED TO WATER ***DO*** AFFECT ME.
YOU LEARN SOMETHING NEW EVERY DAY.
PLIP PLIP

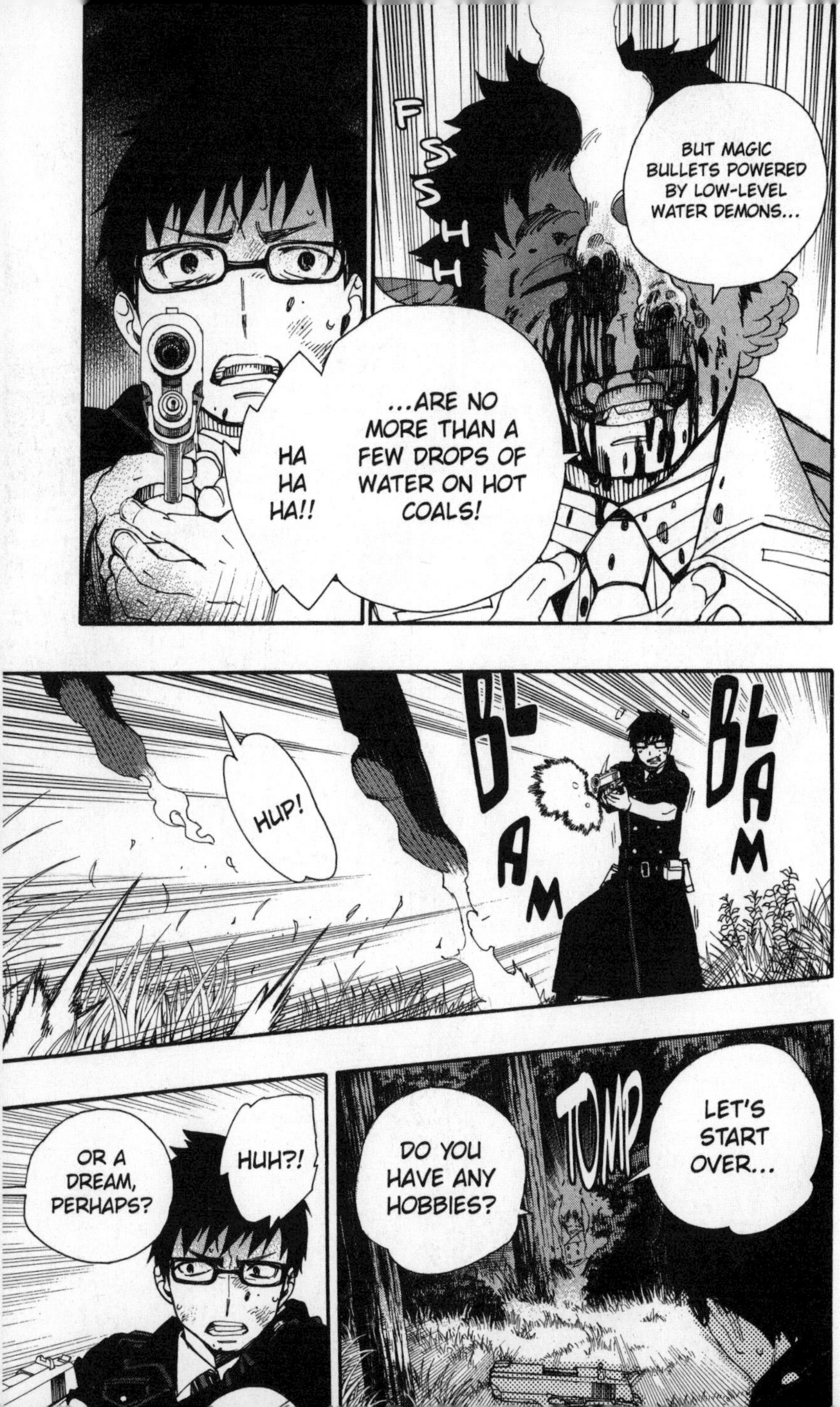

BUT MAGIC BULLETS POWERED BY LOW-LEVEL WATER DEMONS...
FSSHH
...ARE NO MORE THAN A FEW DROPS OF WATER ON HOT COALS!
HA HA HA!!
BLAM
BLAM
HUP!
LET'S START OVER...
TOMP
DO YOU HAVE ANY HOBBIES?
HUH?!
OR A DREAM, PERHAPS?

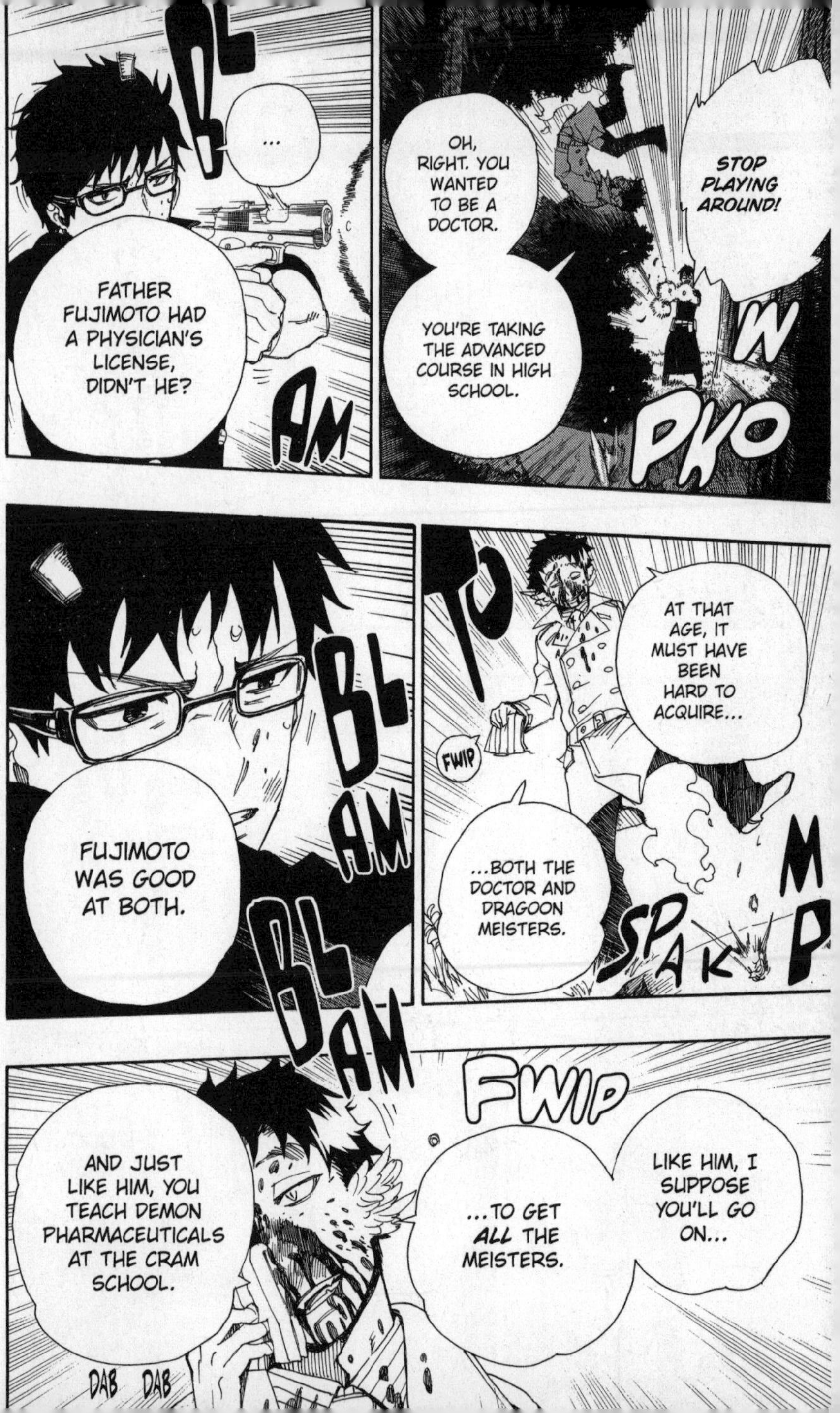
STOP PLAYING AROUND!
OH, RIGHT. YOU WANTED TO BE A DOCTOR.
YOU'RE TAKING THE ADVANCED COURSE IN HIGH SCHOOL.
PKOW
...
FATHER FUJIMOTO HAD A PHYSICIAN'S LICENSE, DIDN'T HE?
BLAM
AT THAT AGE, IT MUST HAVE BEEN HARD TO ACQUIRE...
FWIP
...BOTH THE DOCTOR AND DRAGOON MEISTERS.
SPAK
BLAM
FUJIMOTO WAS GOOD AT BOTH.
BLAM
FWIP
LIKE HIM, I SUPPOSE YOU'LL GO ON...
...TO GET *ALL* THE MEISTERS.
AND JUST LIKE HIM, YOU TEACH DEMON PHARMACEUTICALS AT THE CRAM SCHOOL.
DAB DAB

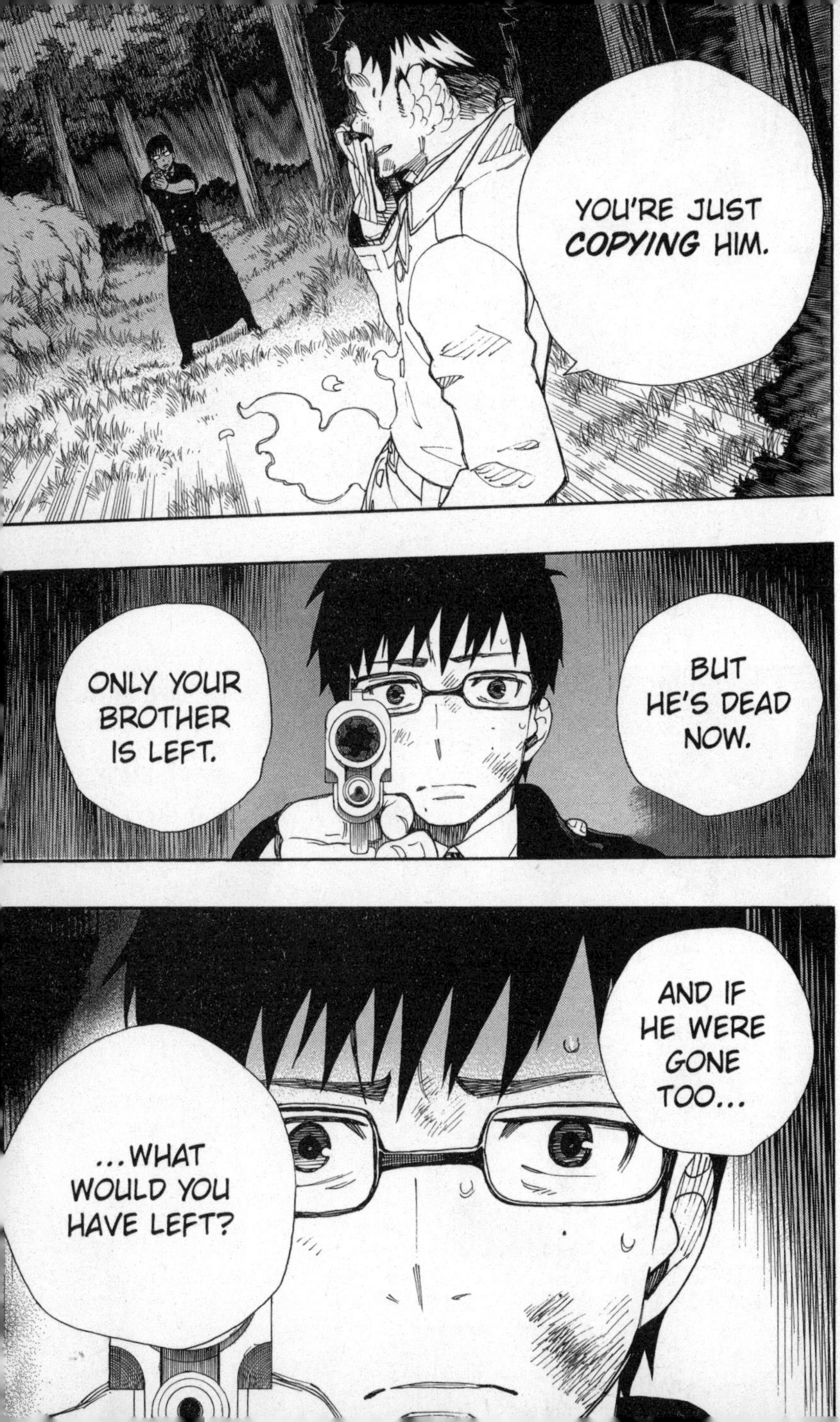
YOU'RE JUST COPYING HIM.
BUT HE'S DEAD NOW.
ONLY YOUR BROTHER IS LEFT.
AND IF HE WERE GONE TOO...
...WHAT WOULD YOU HAVE LEFT?

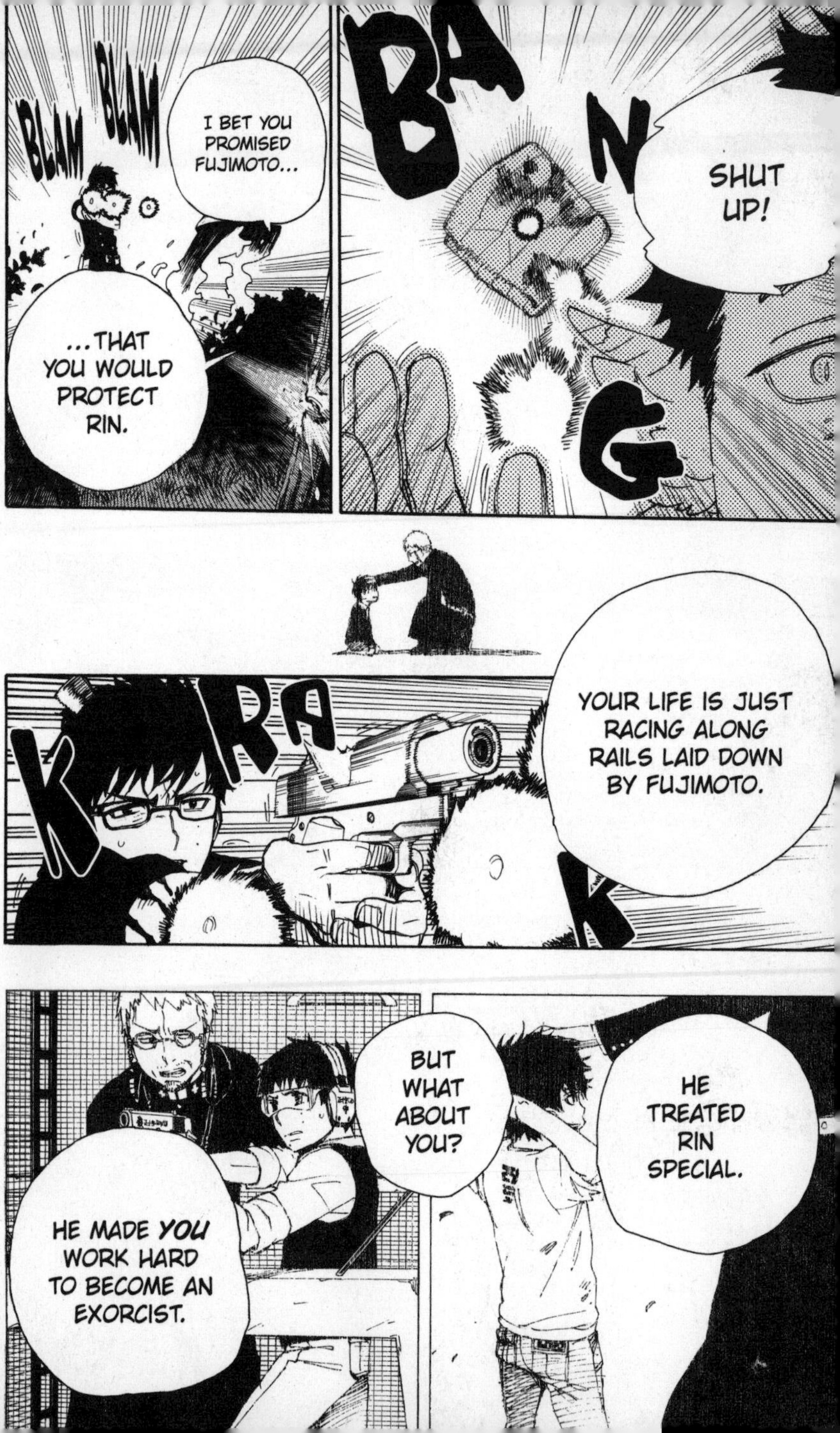
BANG
SHUT UP!
BLAM BLAM
I BET YOU PROMISED FUJIMOTO...
...THAT YOU WOULD PROTECT RIN.
YOUR LIFE IS JUST RACING ALONG RAILS LAID DOWN BY FUJIMOTO.
KRAK
HE TREATED RIN SPECIAL.
BUT WHAT ABOUT YOU?
HE MADE *YOU* WORK HARD TO BECOME AN EXORCIST.

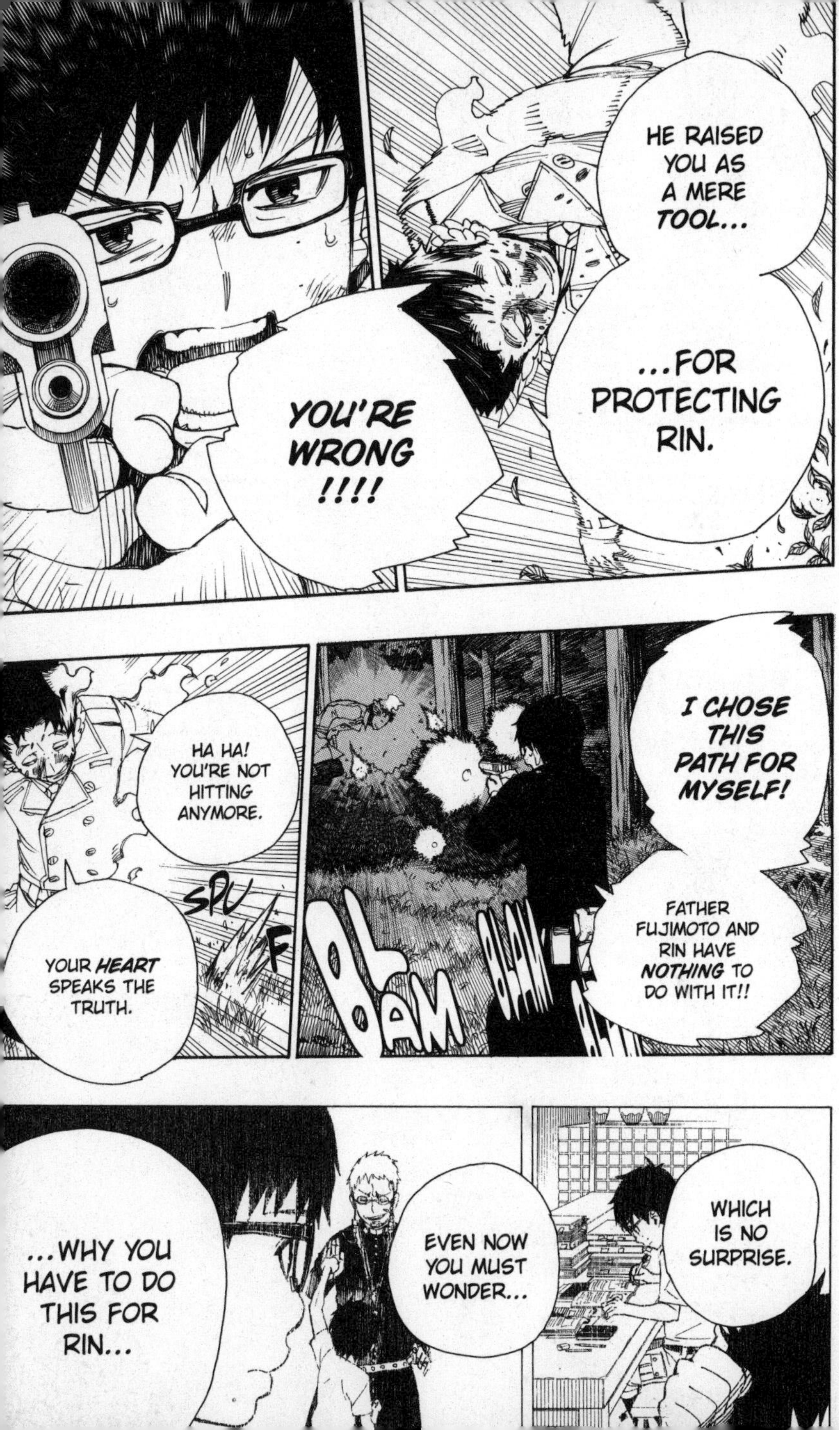
HE RAISED YOU AS A MERE *TOOL...*
...FOR PROTECTING RIN.
YOU'RE WRONG !!!!
I CHOSE THIS PATH FOR MYSELF!
FATHER FUJIMOTO AND RIN HAVE *NOTHING* TO DO WITH IT!!
BLAM
HA HA! YOU'RE NOT HITTING ANYMORE.
SPUF
YOUR *HEART* SPEAKS THE TRUTH.
WHICH IS NO SURPRISE.
EVEN NOW YOU MUST WONDER...
...WHY YOU HAVE TO DO THIS FOR RIN...

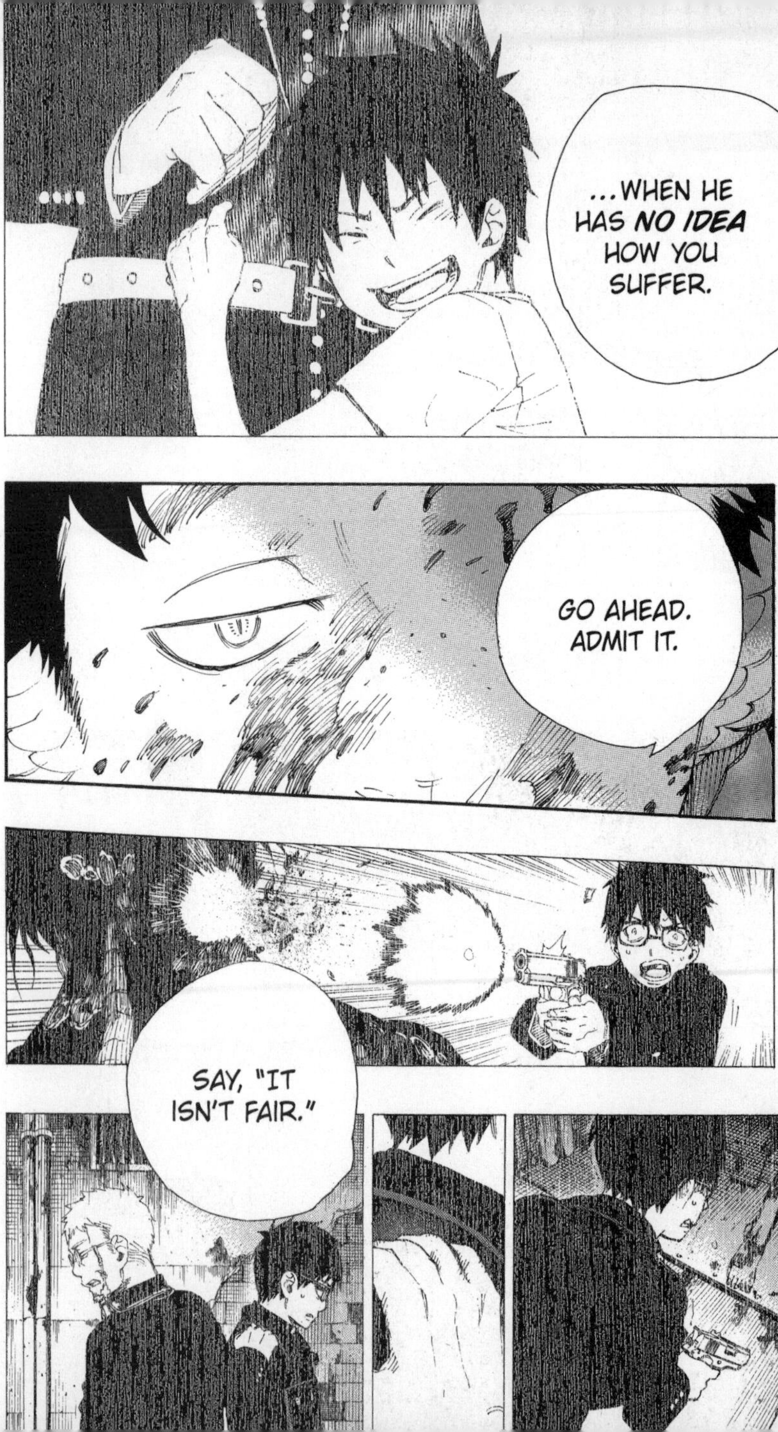
...WHEN HE HAS NO IDEA HOW YOU SUFFER.
GO AHEAD. ADMIT IT.
SAY, "IT ISN'T FAIR."

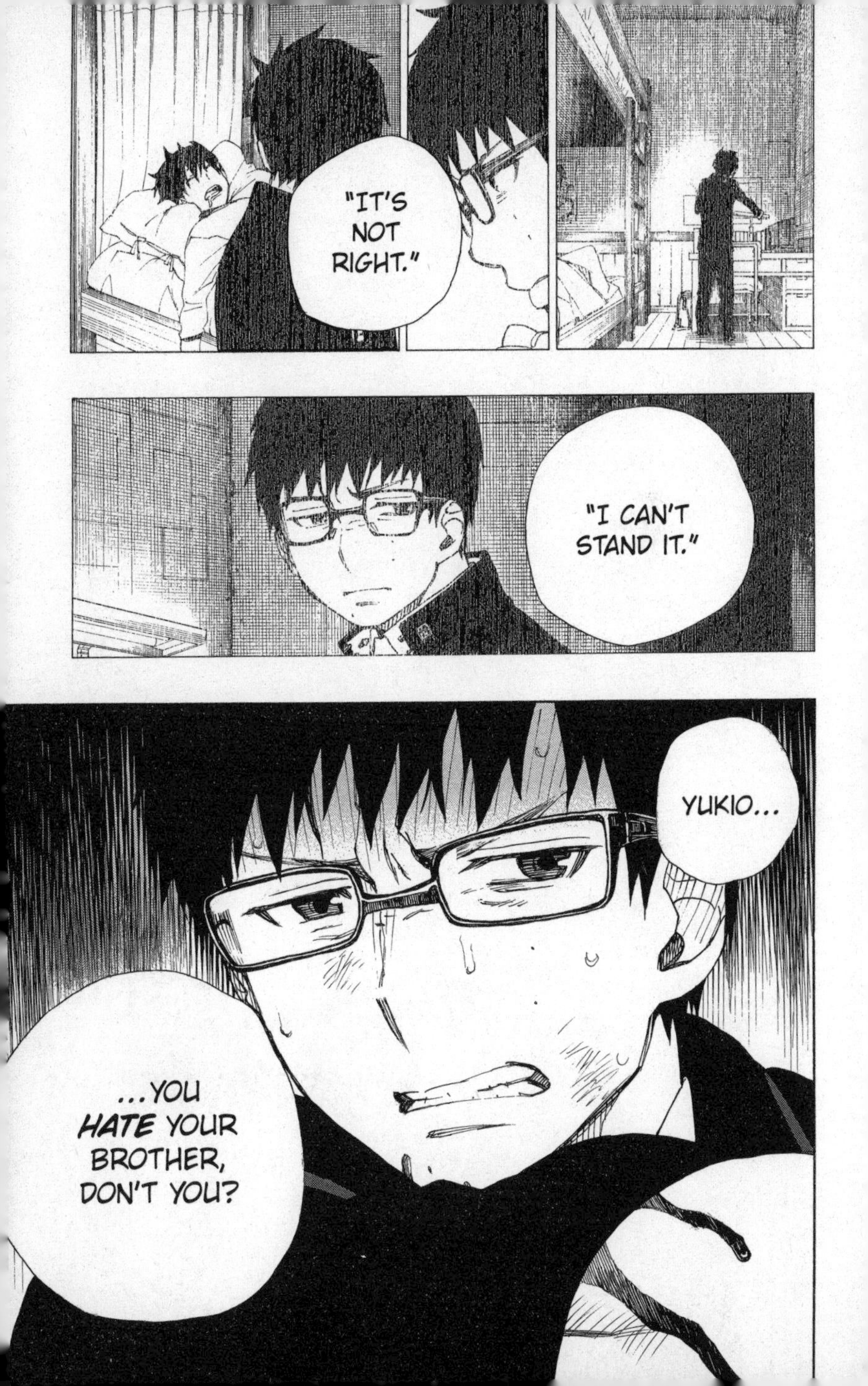
"IT'S NOT RIGHT."
"I CAN'T STAND IT."
YUKIO...
...YOU HATE YOUR BROTHER, DON'T YOU?

Blue Exorcist Chapter 28 Crimson Lotus

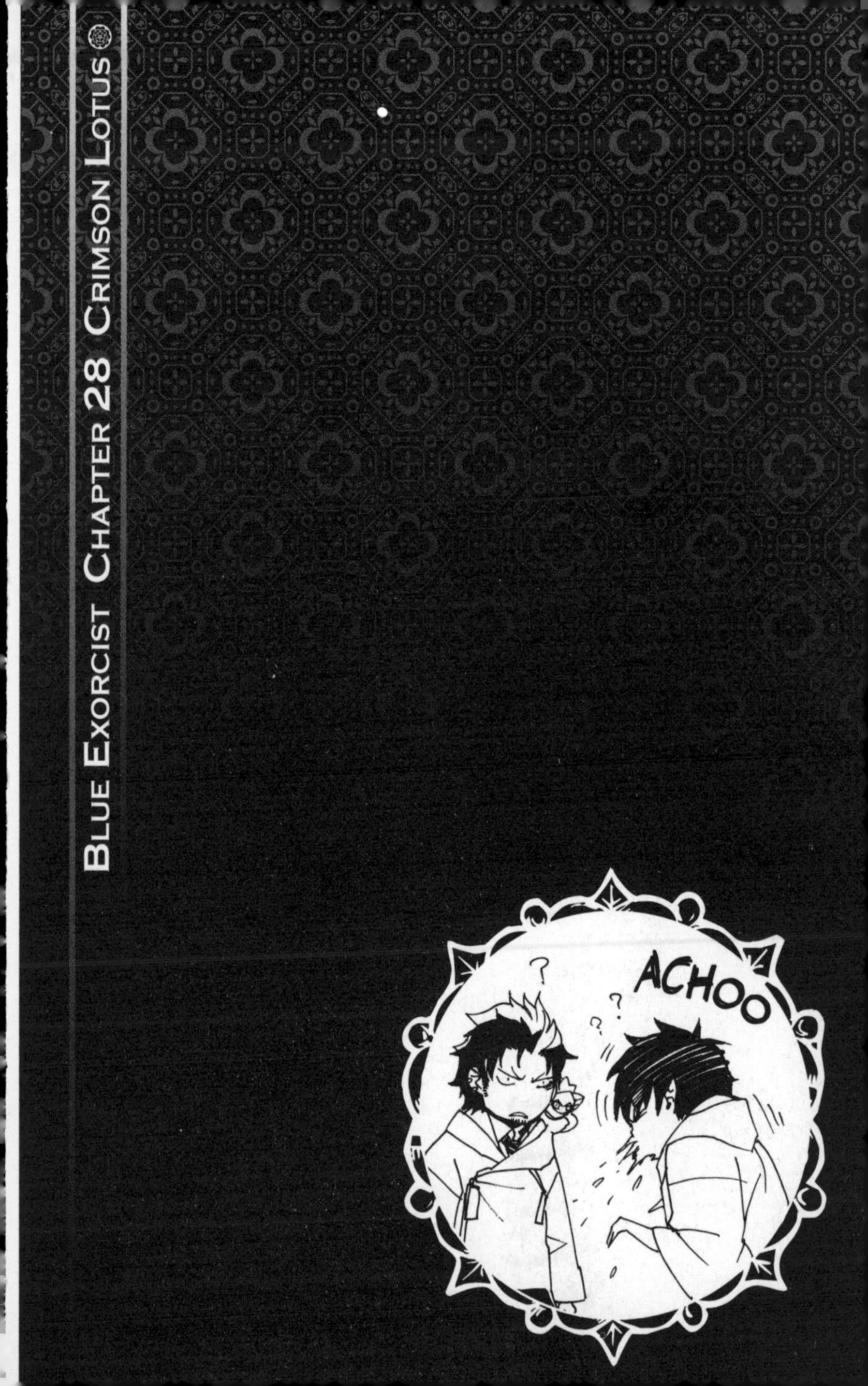
ACHOO

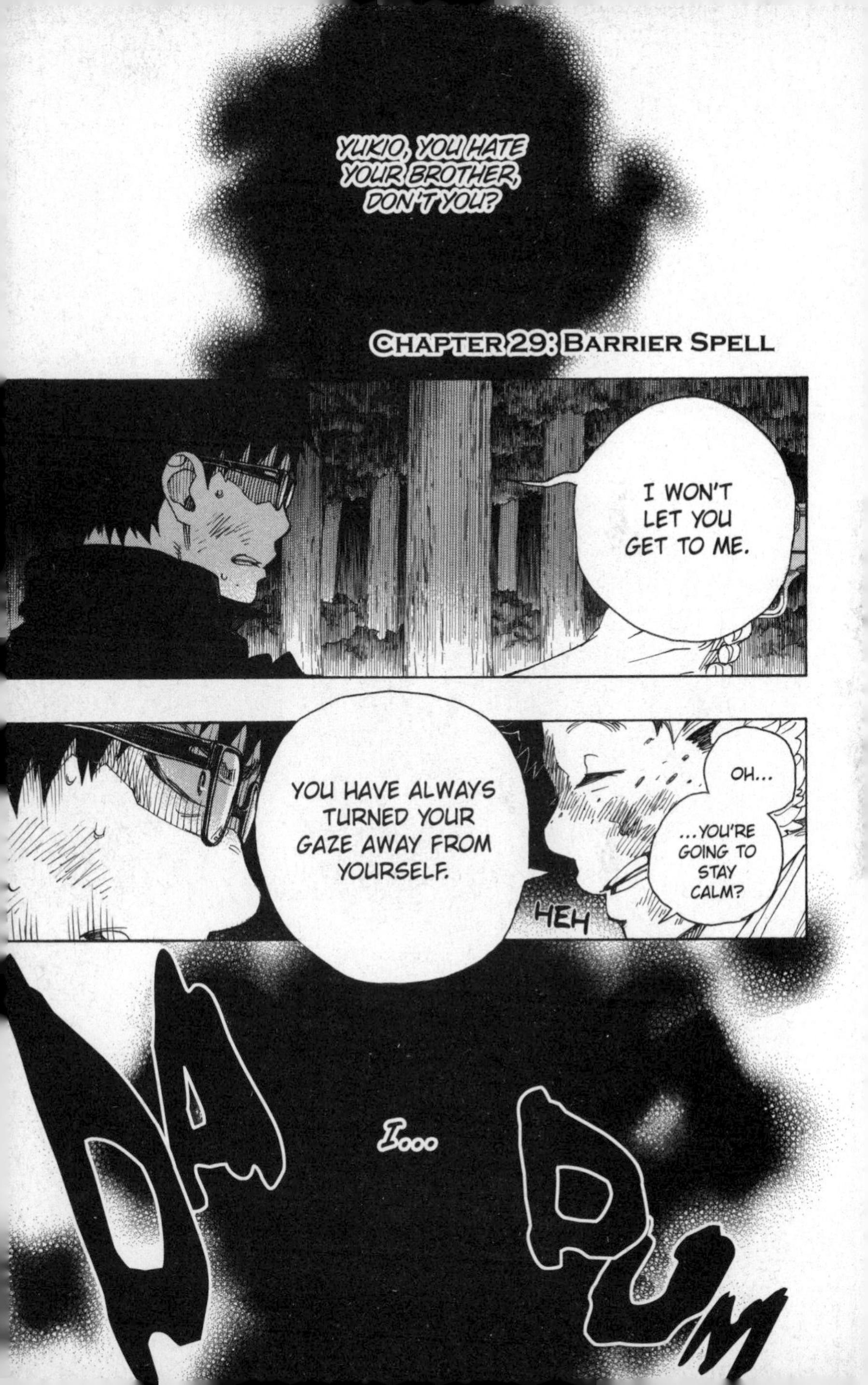
YUKIO, YOU HATE YOUR BROTHER, DON'T YOU?
CHAPTER 29: BARRIER SPELL
I WON'T LET YOU GET TO ME.
OH...
...YOU'RE GOING TO STAY CALM?
HEH
YOU HAVE ALWAYS TURNED YOUR GAZE AWAY FROM YOURSELF.
DA
DUM
I...

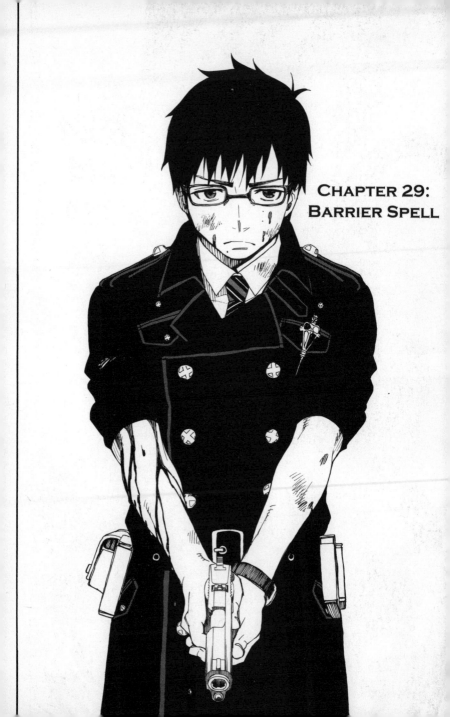

Chapter 29: Barrier Spell

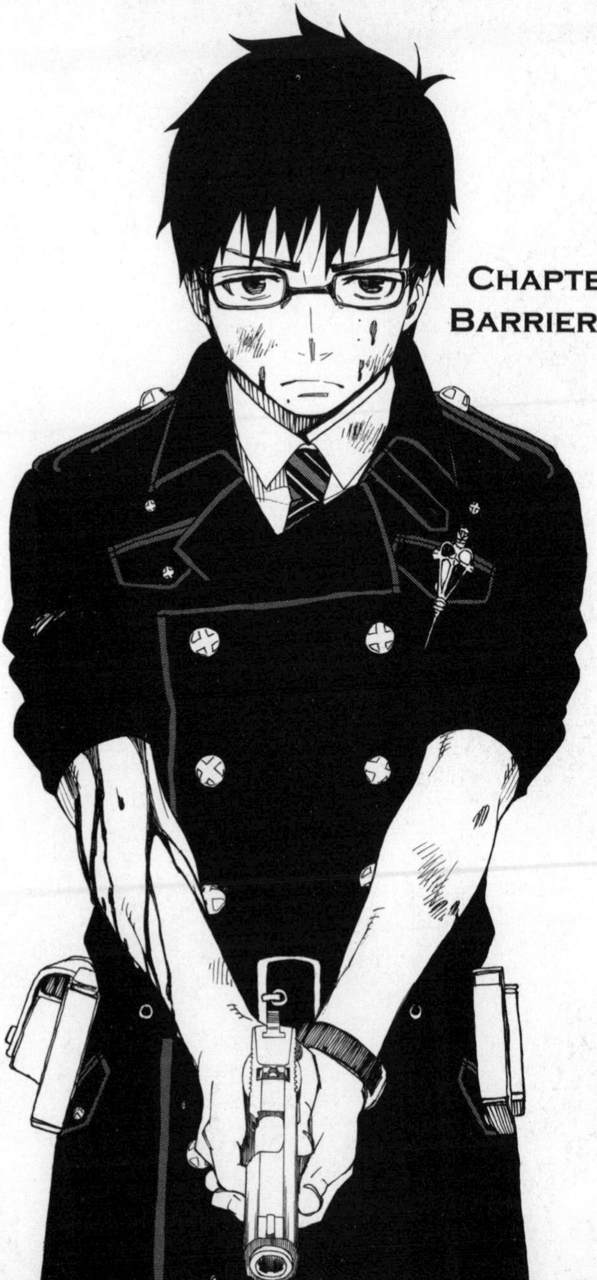

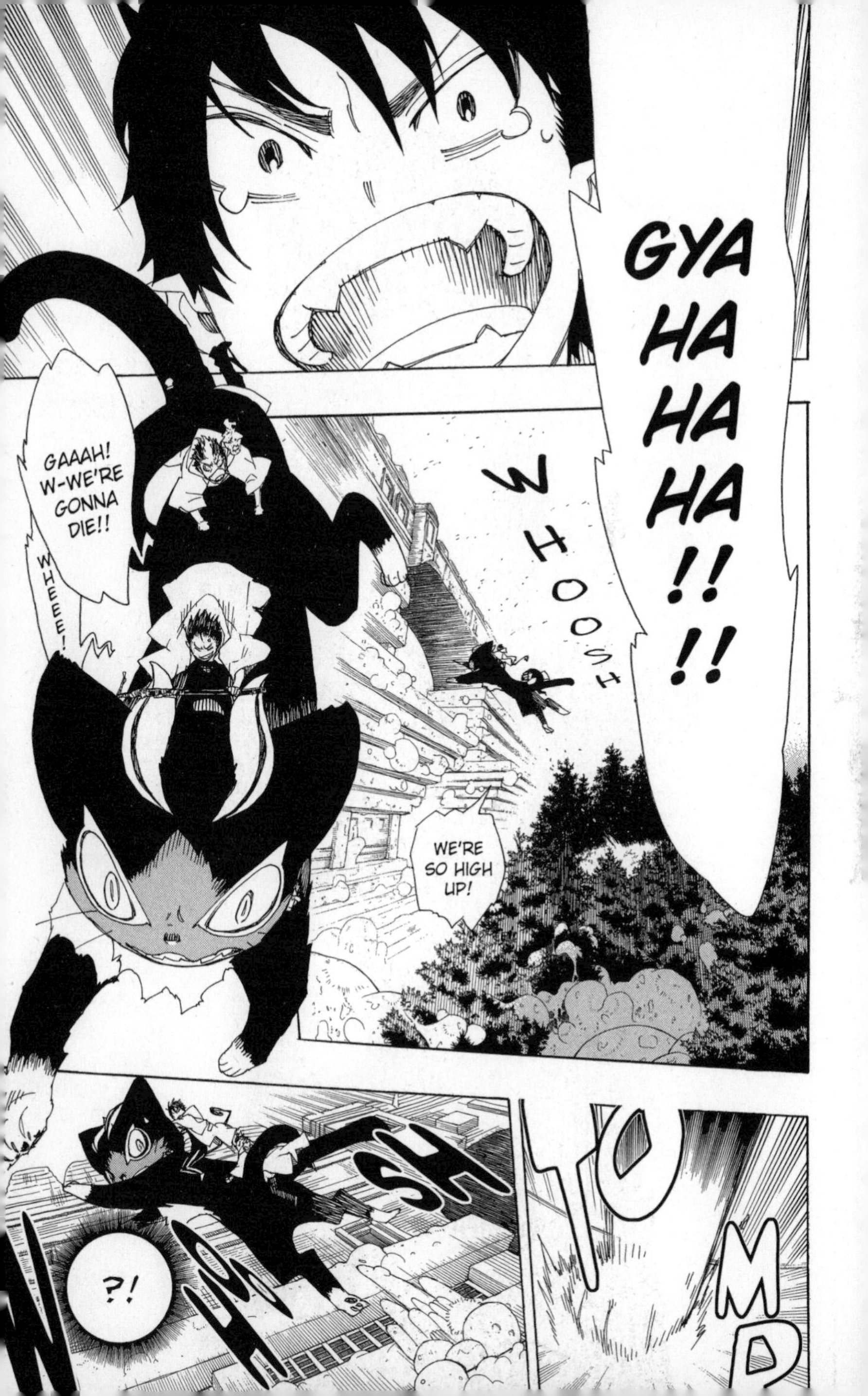
GYA HA HA HA!!!!
WHOOSH
GAAAH! W-WE'RE GONNA DIE!!
WHEEEE!
WE'RE SO HIGH UP!
?!

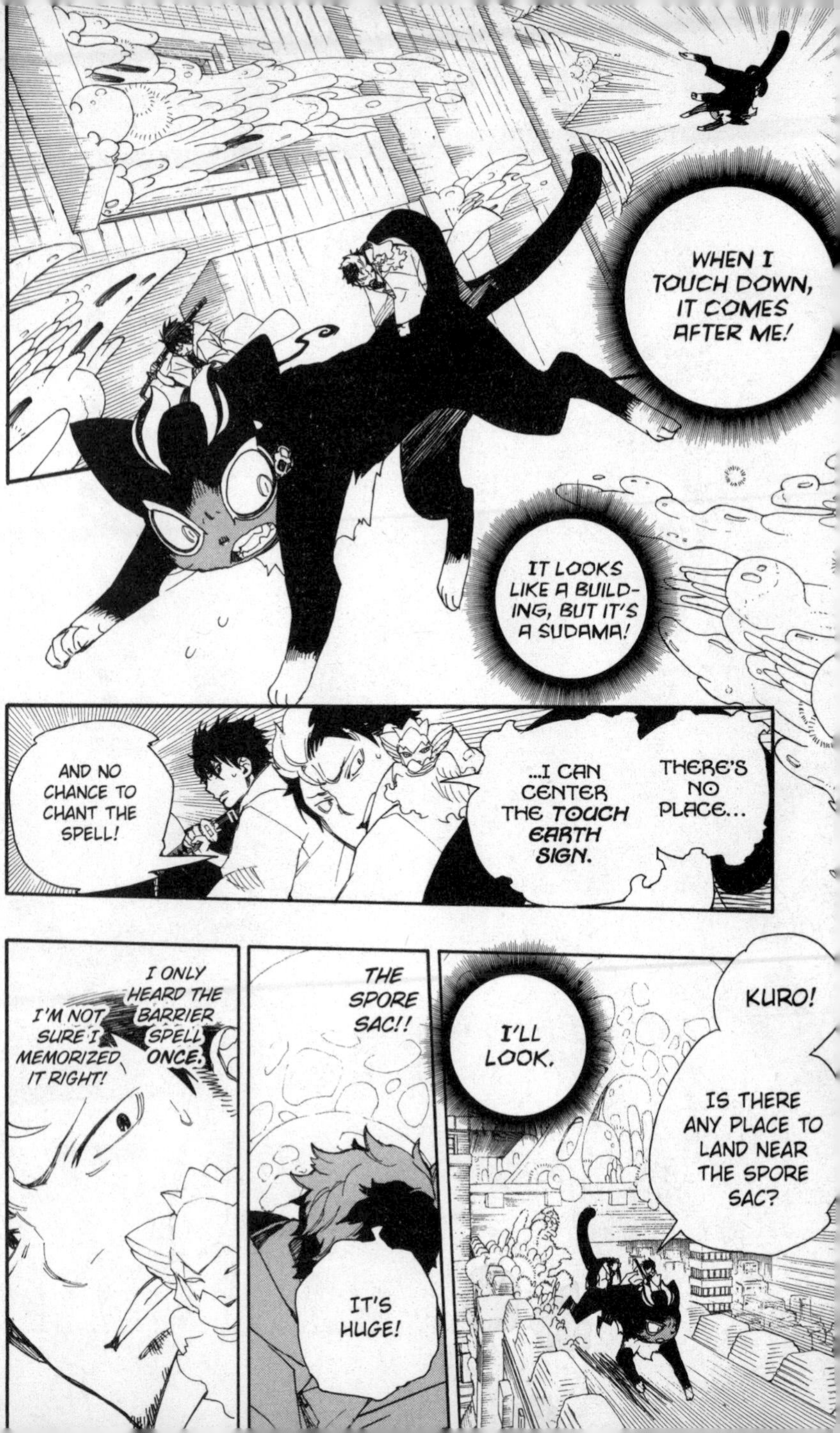
WHEN I TOUCH DOWN, IT COMES AFTER ME!
IT LOOKS LIKE A BUILDING, BUT IT'S A SUDAMA!
THERE'S NO PLACE...
...I CAN CENTER THE TOUCH EARTH SIGN.
AND NO CHANCE TO CHANT THE SPELL!
KURO!
IS THERE ANY PLACE TO LAND NEAR THE SPORE SAC?
I'LL LOOK.
THE SPORE SAC!!
IT'S HUGE!
I ONLY HEARD THE BARRIER SPELL ONCE.
I'M NOT SURE I MEMORIZED IT RIGHT!

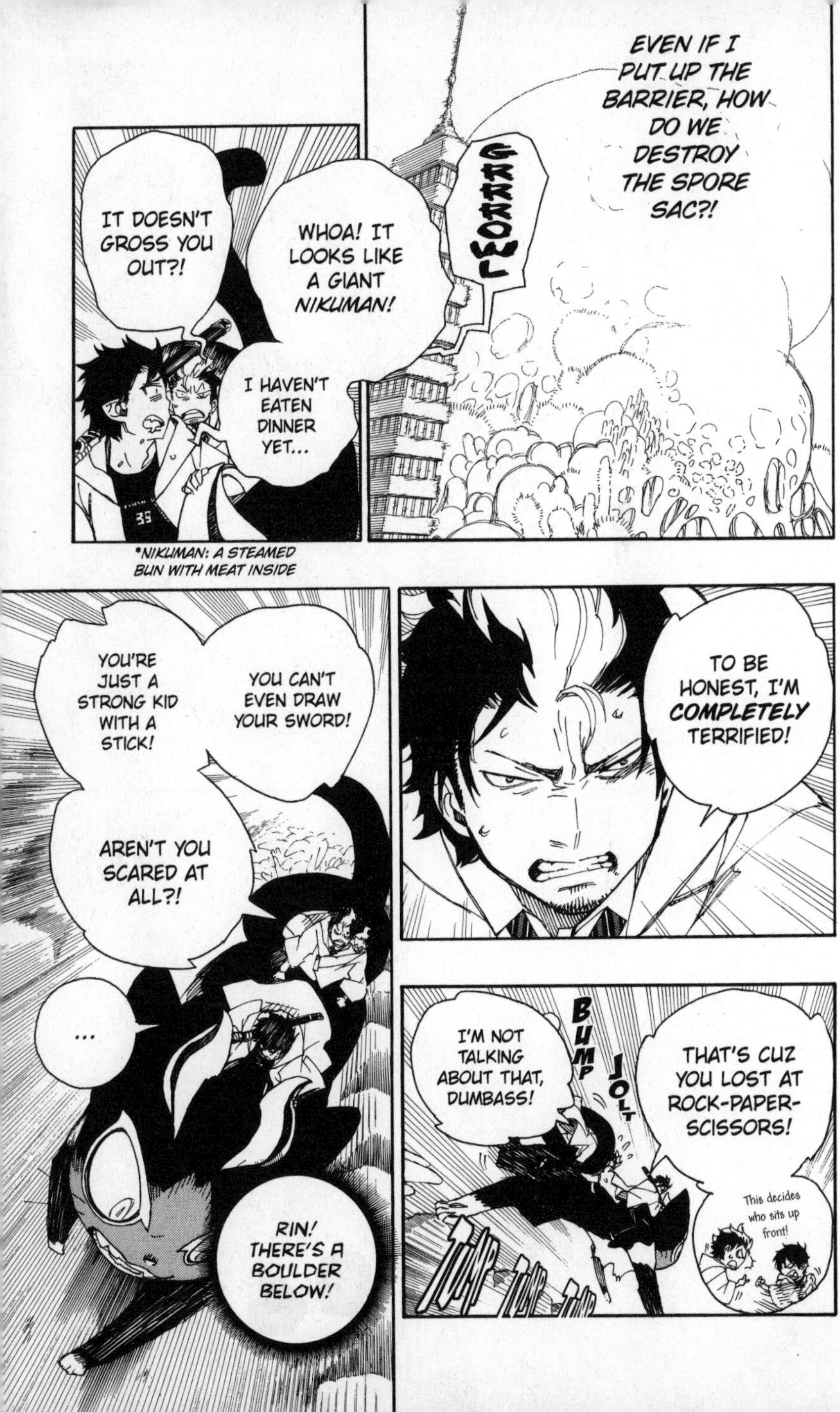
EVEN IF I PUT UP THE BARRIER, HOW DO WE DESTROY THE SPORE SAC?!
GRRROWL
WHOA! IT LOOKS LIKE A GIANT NIKUMAN!
IT DOESN'T GROSS YOU OUT?!
I HAVEN'T EATEN DINNER YET...
TO BE HONEST, I'M COMPLETELY TERRIFIED!
THAT'S CUZ YOU LOST AT ROCK-PAPER-SCISSORS!
This decides who sits up front!
JOLT
BUMP
I'M NOT TALKING ABOUT THAT, DUMBASS!
YOU CAN'T EVEN DRAW YOUR SWORD!
YOU'RE JUST A STRONG KID WITH A STICK!
AREN'T YOU SCARED AT ALL?!
...
RIN! THERE'S A BOULDER BELOW!

*NIKUMAN: A STEAMED BUN WITH MEAT INSIDE

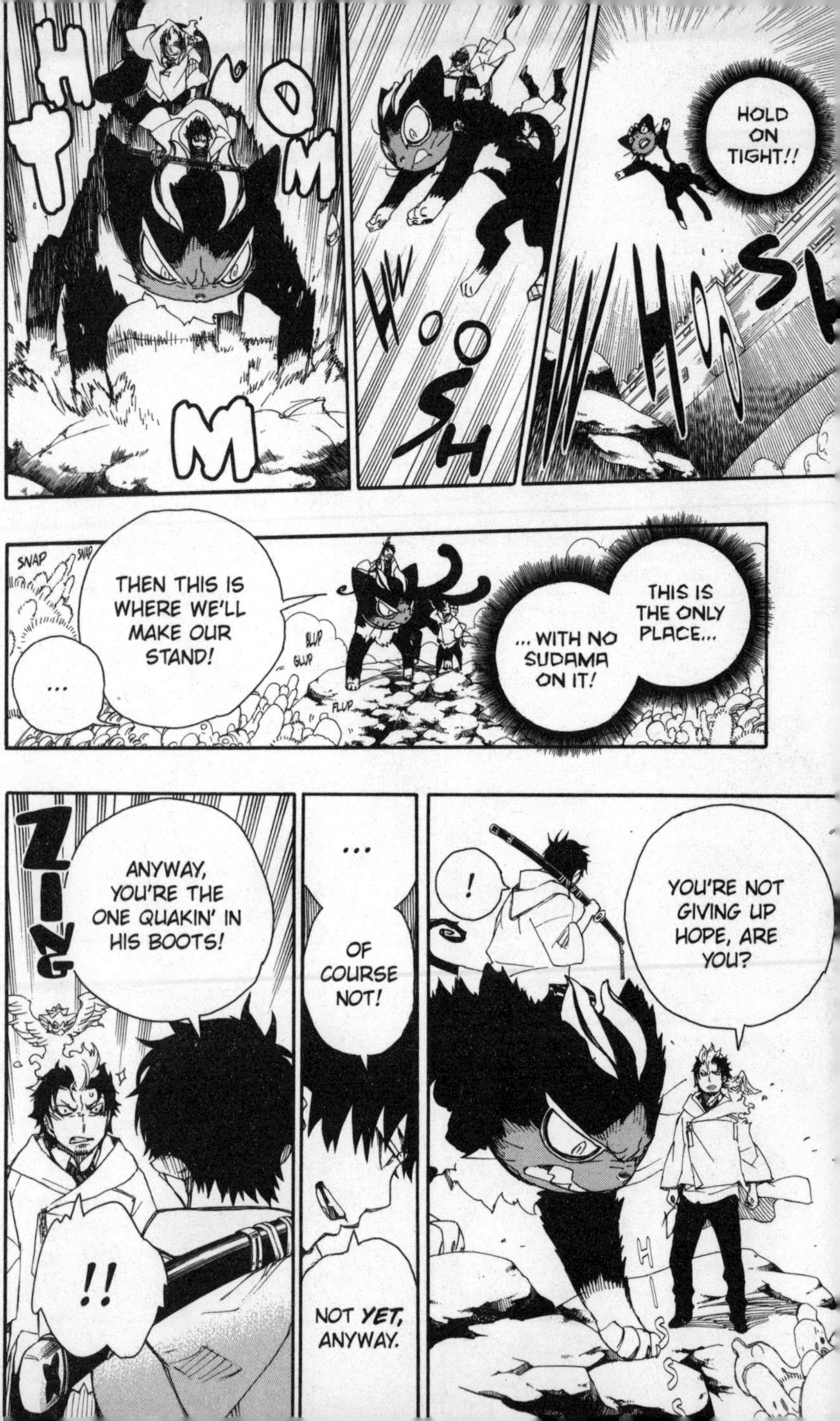
HOLD ON TIGHT!!
WHOOSH
WHOOSH
THOOM
THIS IS THE ONLY PLACE...
...WITH NO SUDAMA ON IT!
BLUP
GLUP
FLUP
THEN THIS IS WHERE WE'LL MAKE OUR STAND!
...
SNAP
SNAP
YOU'RE NOT GIVING UP HOPE, ARE YOU?
!
HISS
...
OF COURSE NOT!
NOT YET, ANYWAY.
ZING
ANYWAY, YOU'RE THE ONE QUAKIN' IN HIS BOOTS!
!!

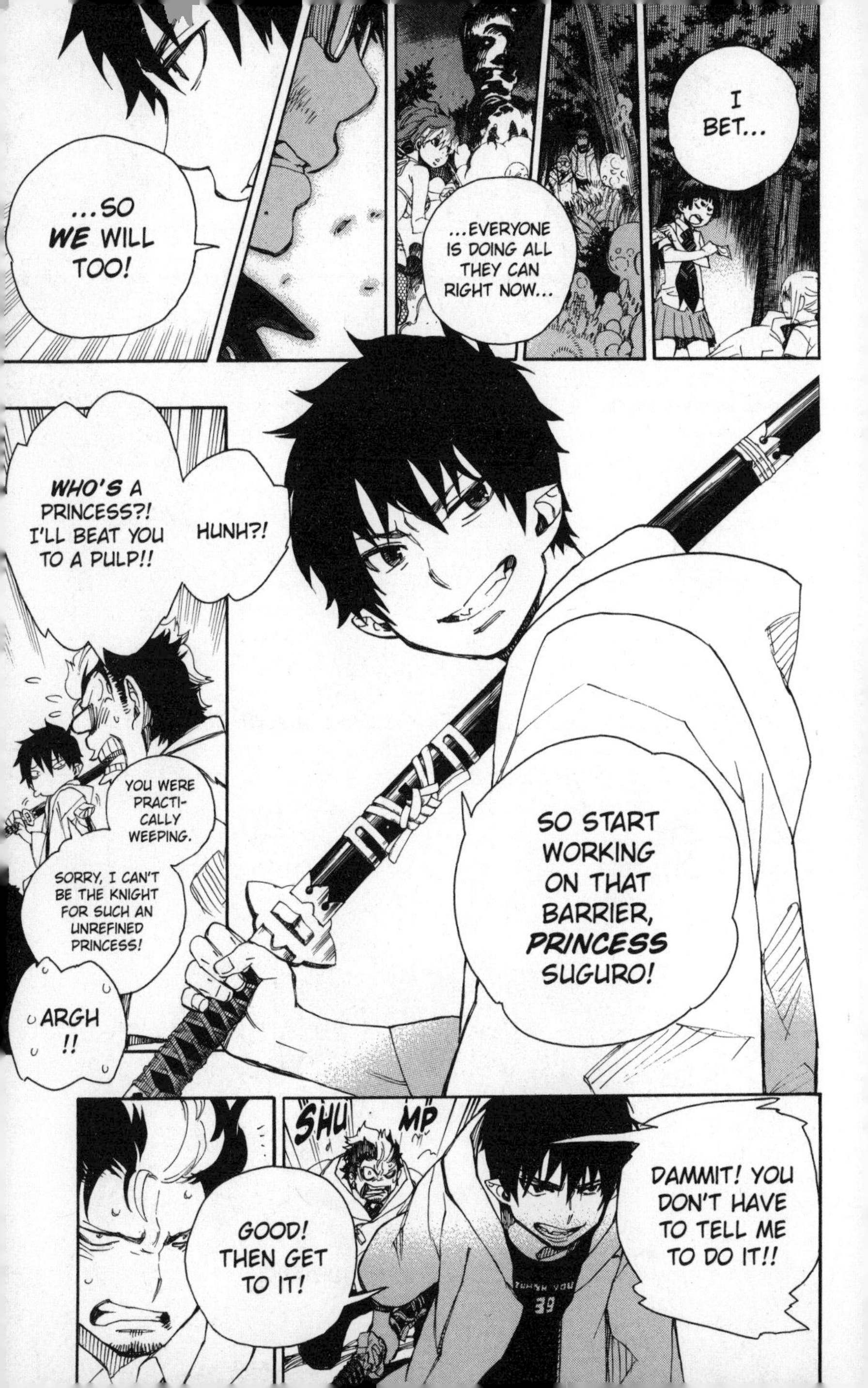

I BET...
...EVERYONE IS DOING ALL THEY CAN RIGHT NOW...
...SO WE WILL TOO!
SO START WORKING ON THAT BARRIER, PRINCESS SUGURO!
HUNH?!
WHO'S A PRINCESS?! I'LL BEAT YOU TO A PULP!!
YOU WERE PRACTI-CALLY WEEPING.
SORRY, I CAN'T BE THE KNIGHT FOR SUCH AN UNREFINED PRINCESS!
ARGH!!
SHUMP
DAMMIT! YOU DON'T HAVE TO TELL ME TO DO IT!!
GOOD! THEN GET TO IT!

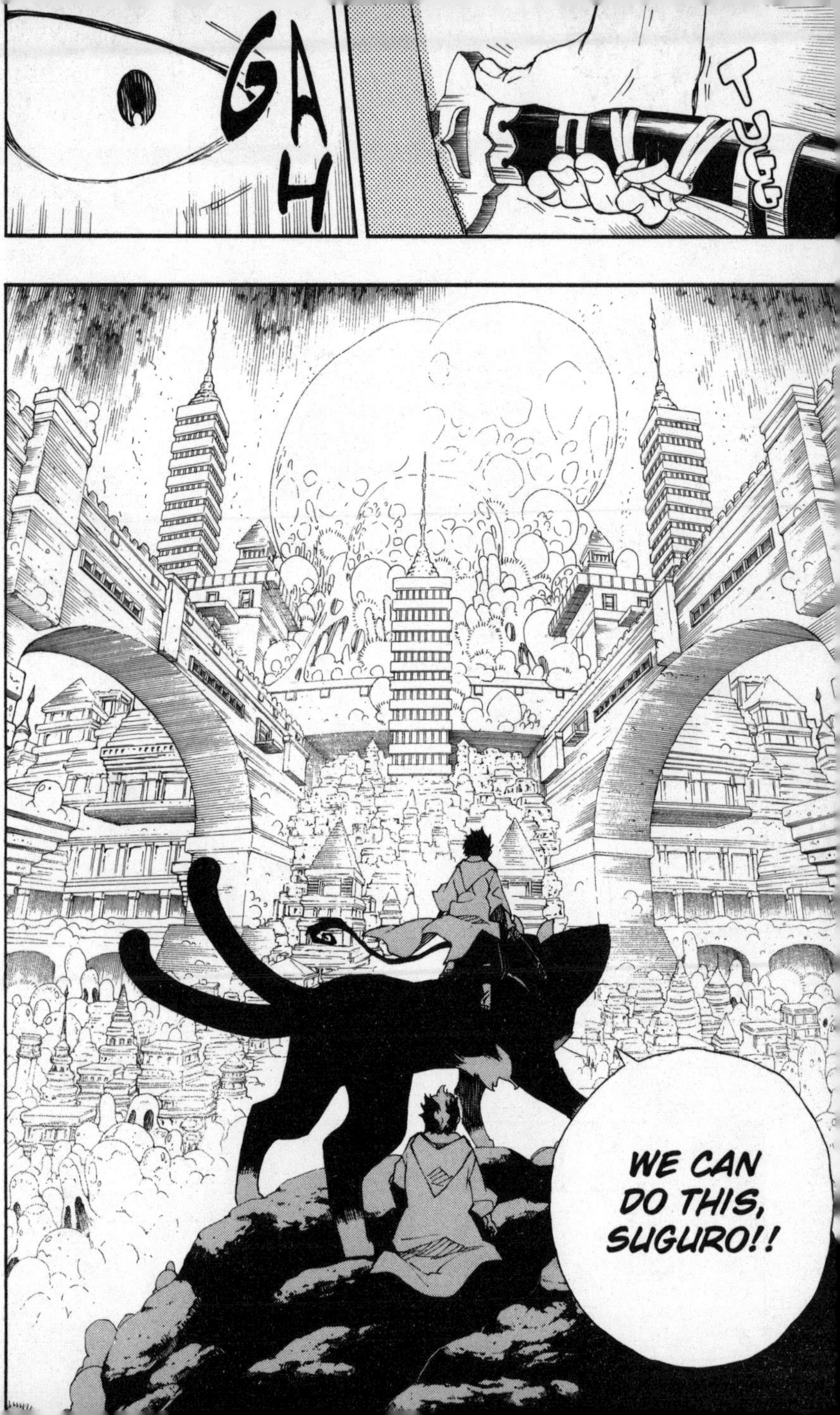
TUG
GAH
WE CAN DO THIS, SUGURO!!

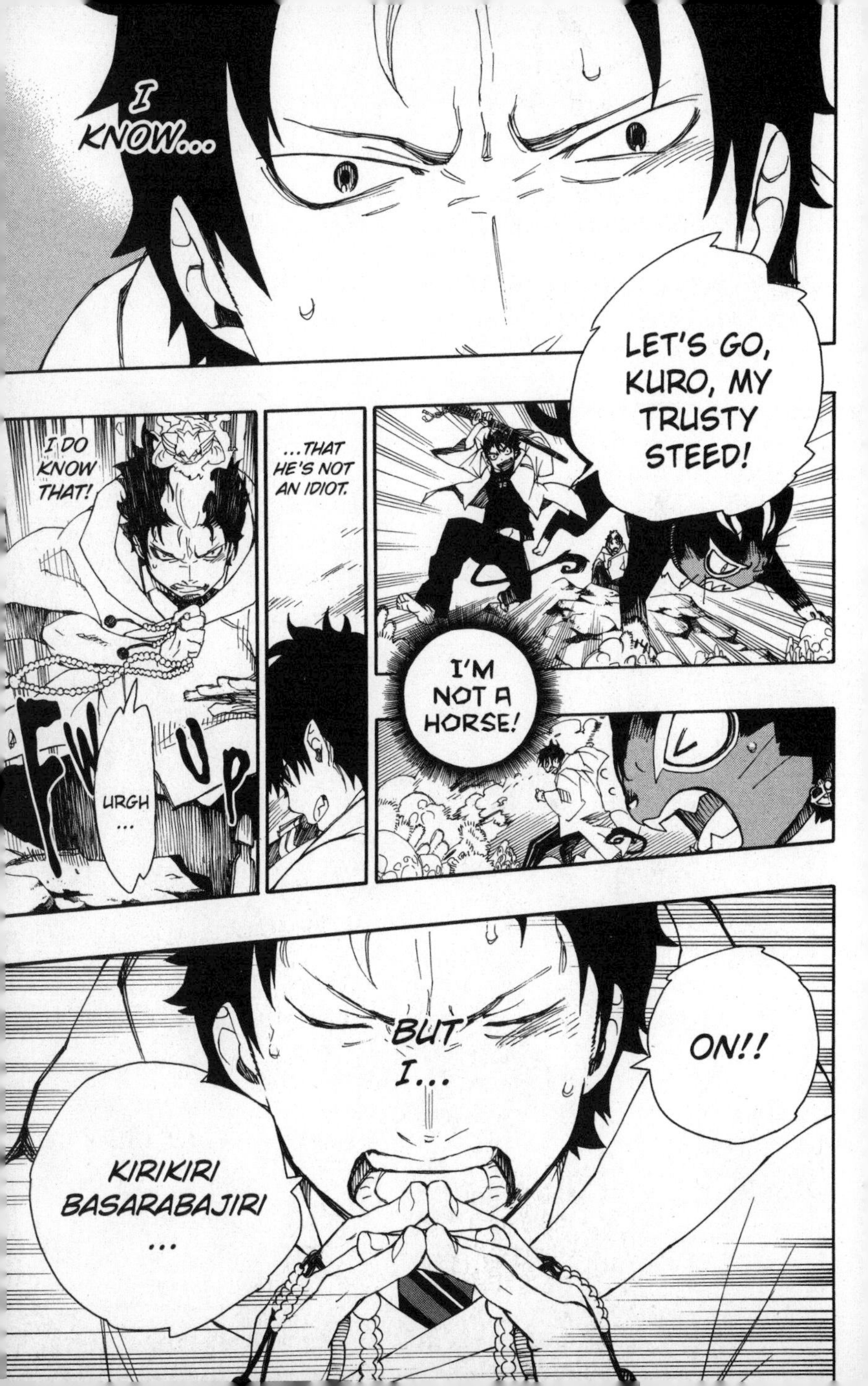
I KNOW...
LET'S GO, KURO, MY TRUSTY STEED!
I'M NOT A HORSE!
...THAT HE'S NOT AN IDIOT.
I DO KNOW THAT!
FWUP
URGH ...
BUT I...
ON!!
KIRIKIRI BASARABAJIRI ...

I...

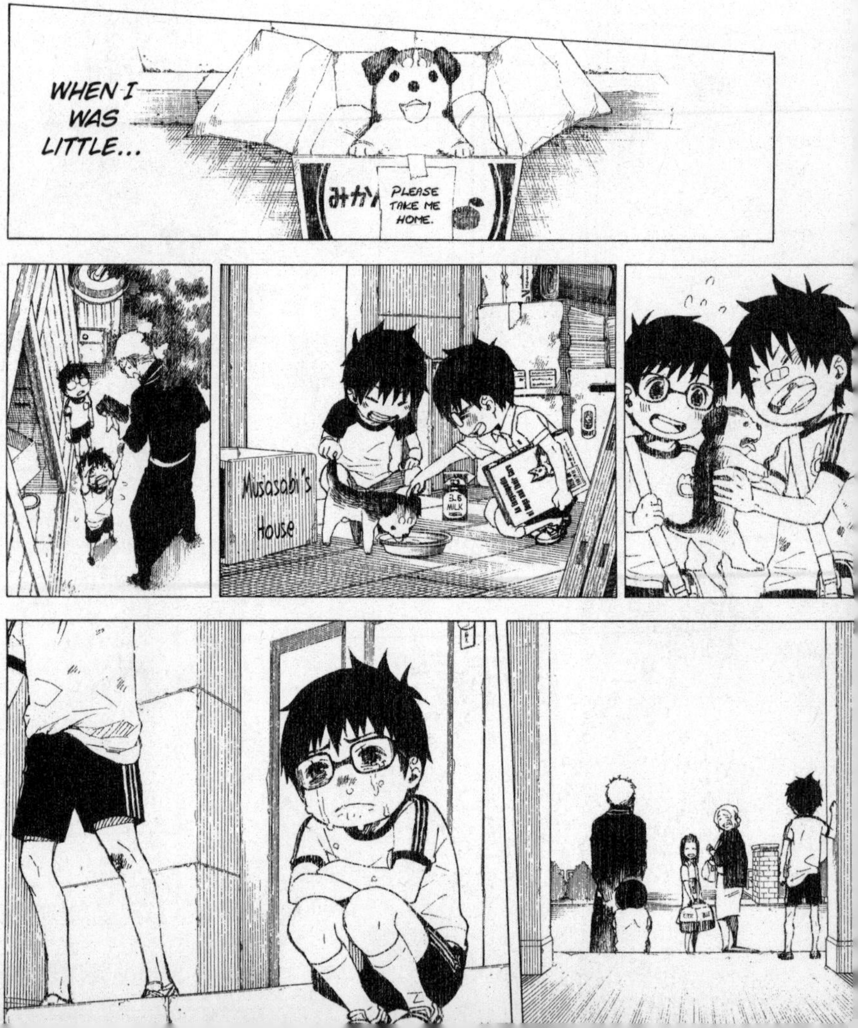
WHEN I WAS LITTLE...
PLEASE TAKE ME HOME.
Musasabi's House
3.6 MILK

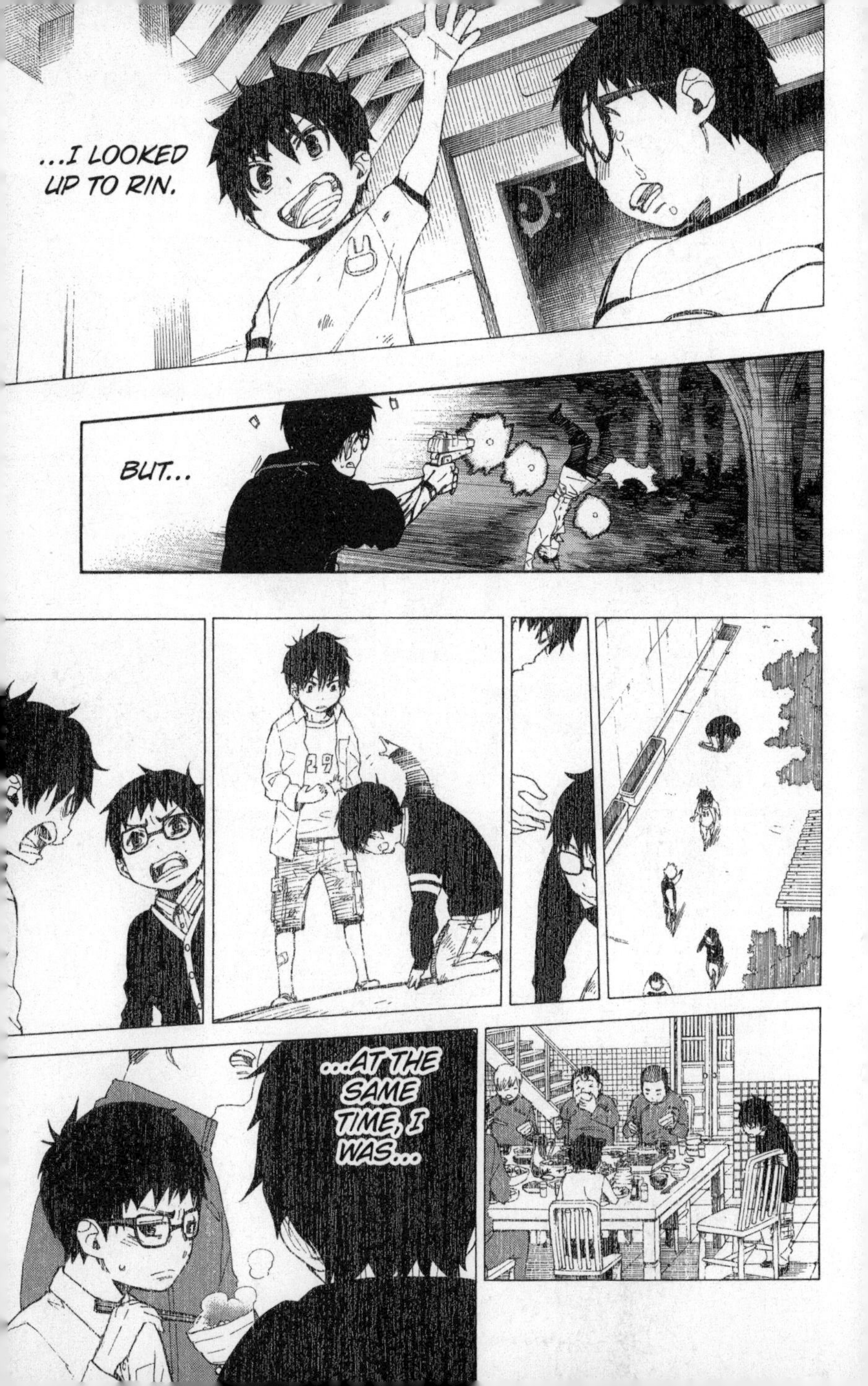
...I LOOKED UP TO RIN.
BUT...
...AT THE SAME TIME, I WAS...

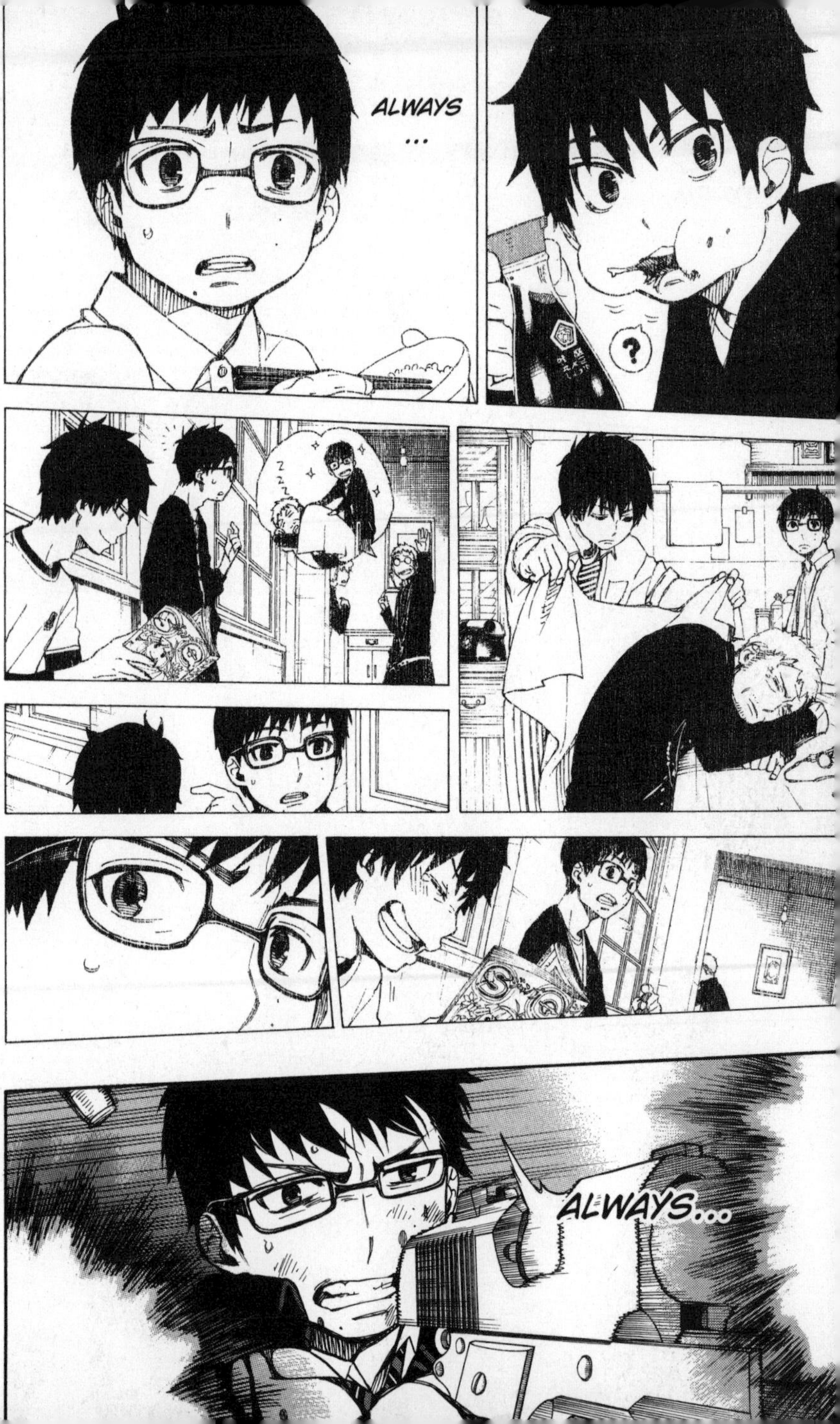
?
ALWAYS ...
ALWAYS...

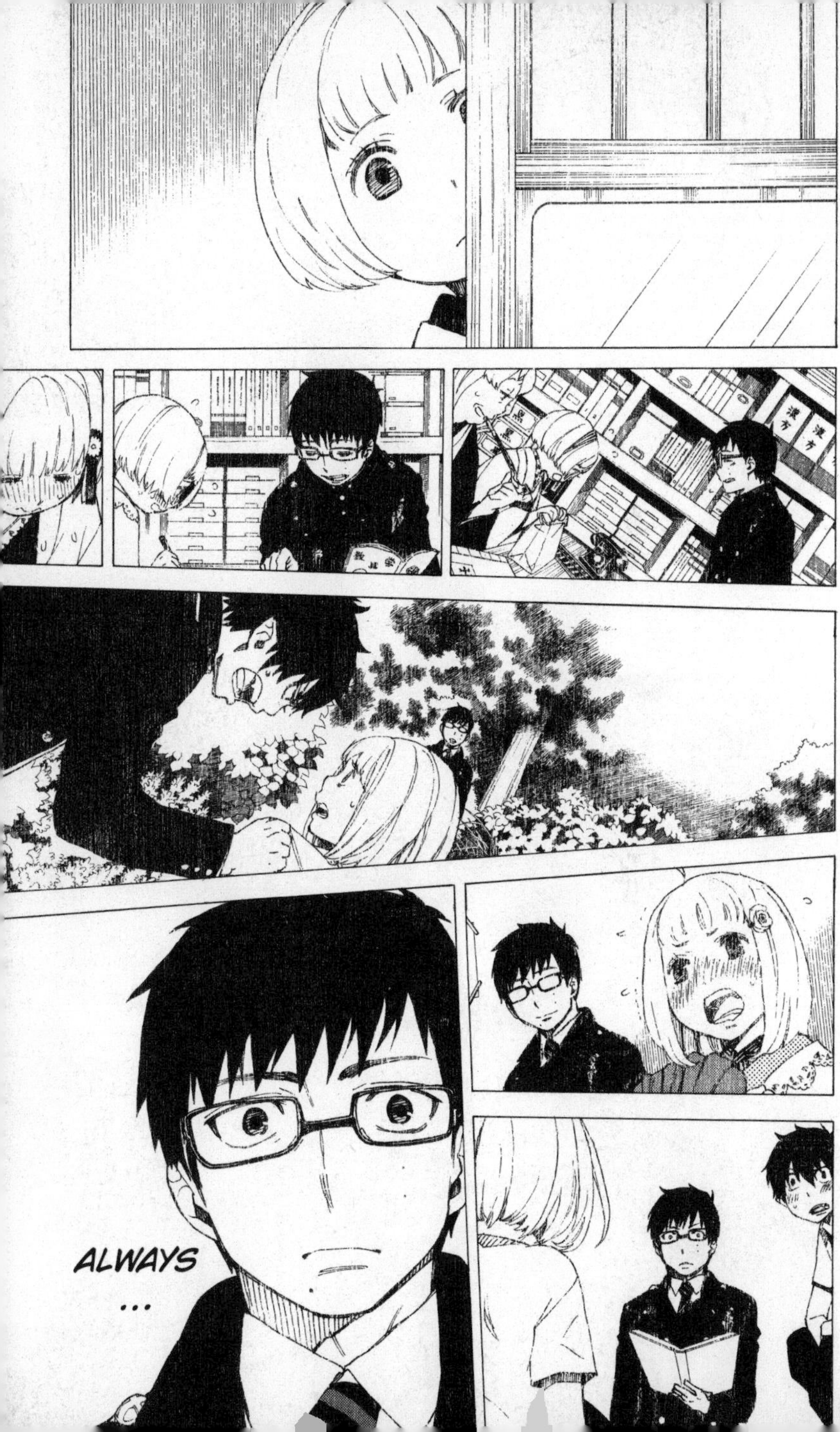
ALWAYS
...

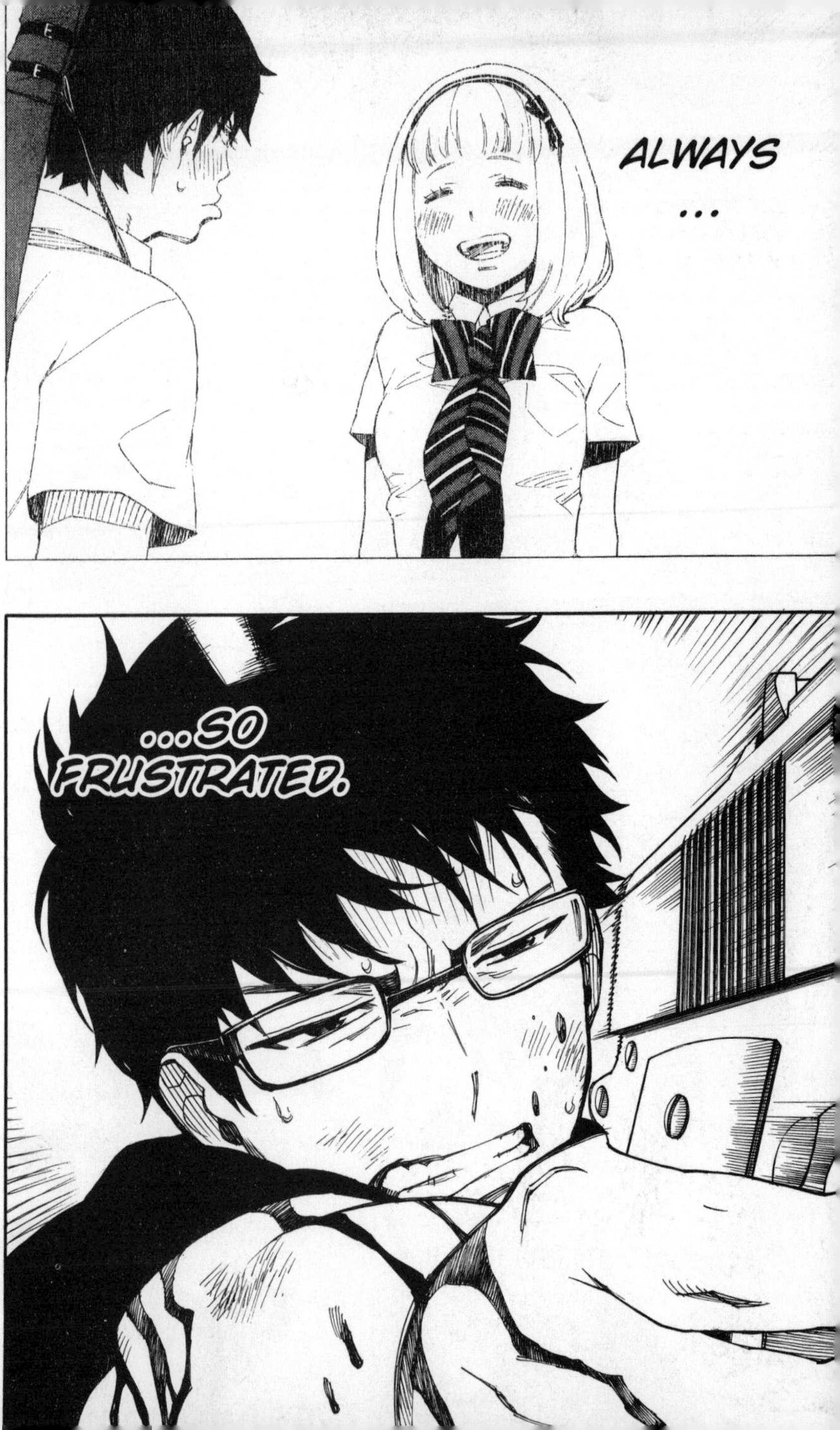
ALWAYS
...
...SO
FRUSTRATED.

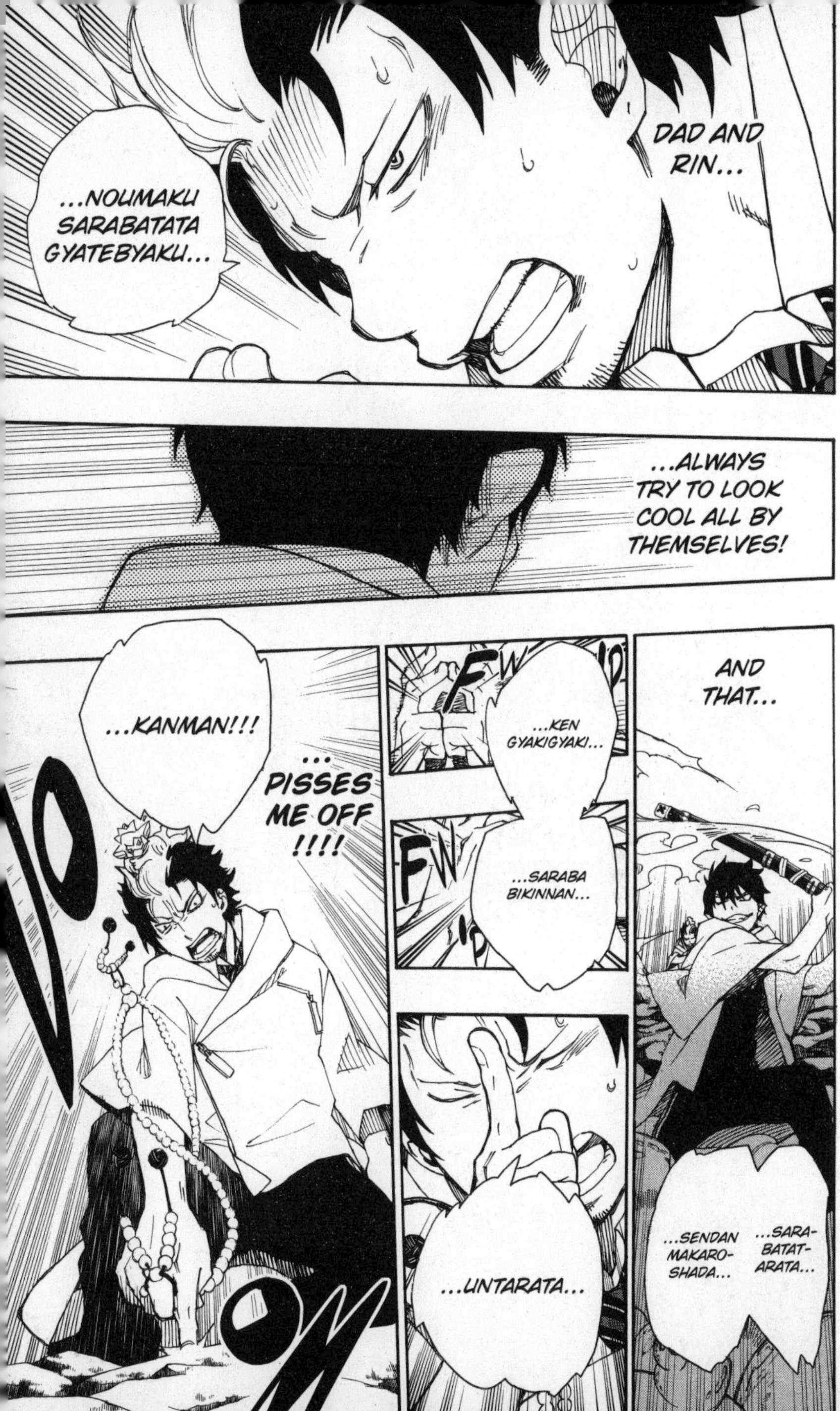
DAD AND RIN...
...NOUMAKU SARABATATA GYATEBYAKU...
...ALWAYS TRY TO LOOK COOL ALL BY THEMSELVES!
AND THAT...
...SARA-BATAT-ARATA...
...SENDAN MAKARO-SHADA...
FW
...KEN GYAKIGYAKI...
FW
...SARABA BIKINNAN...
...UNTARATA...
...KANMAN!!!
... PISSES ME OFF !!!!

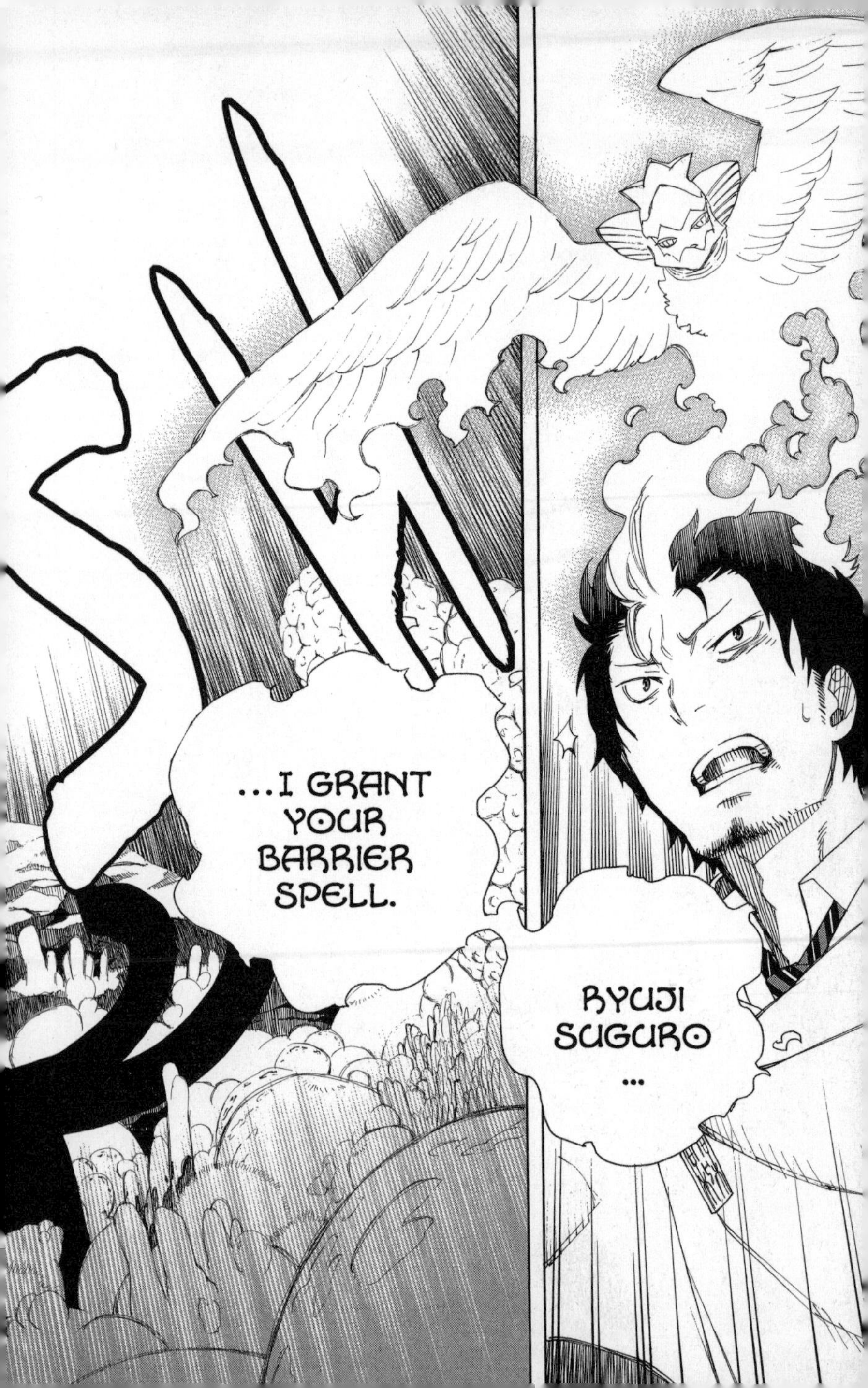
RYUJI SUGURO ...
...I GRANT YOUR BARRIER SPELL.

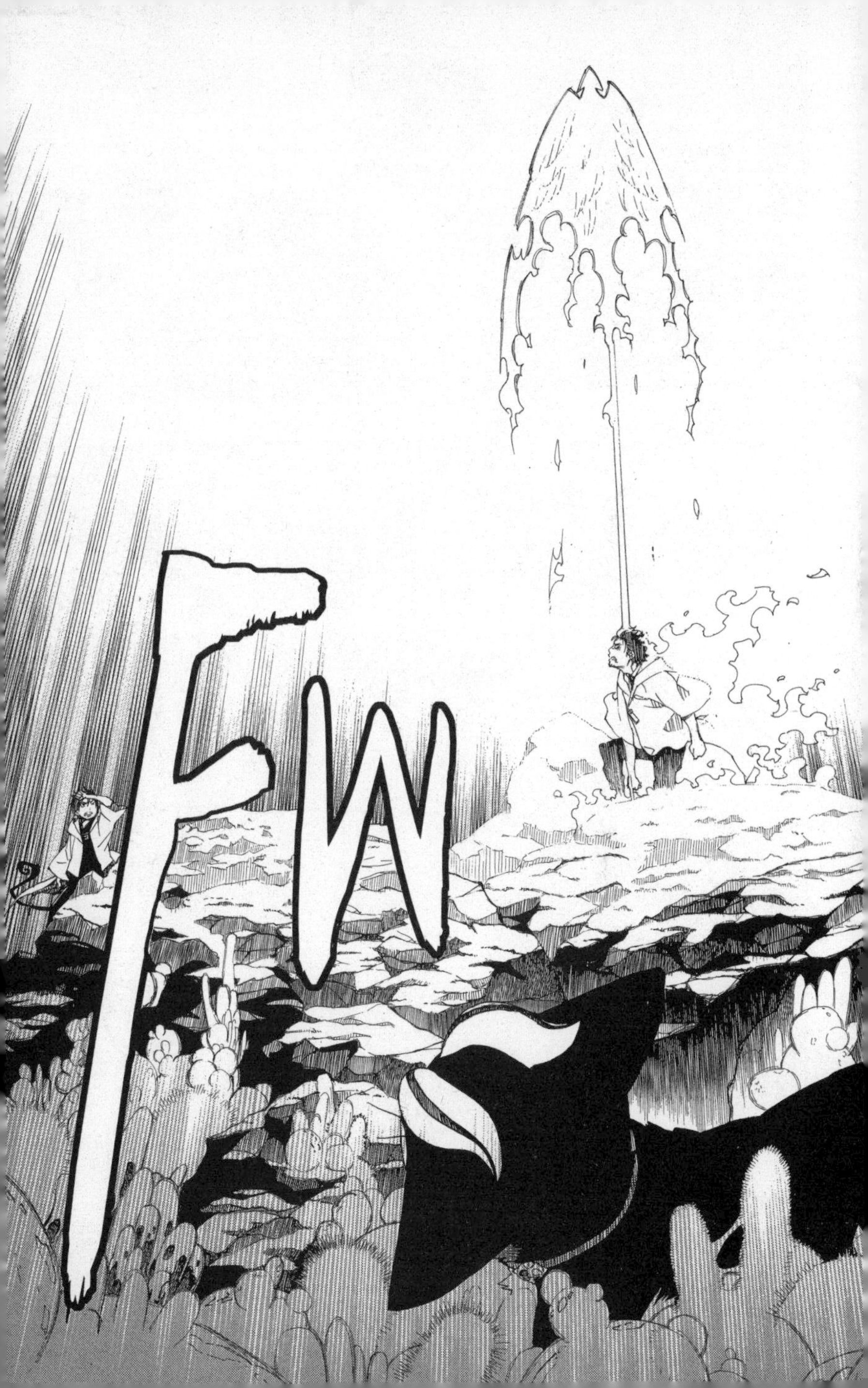
FW

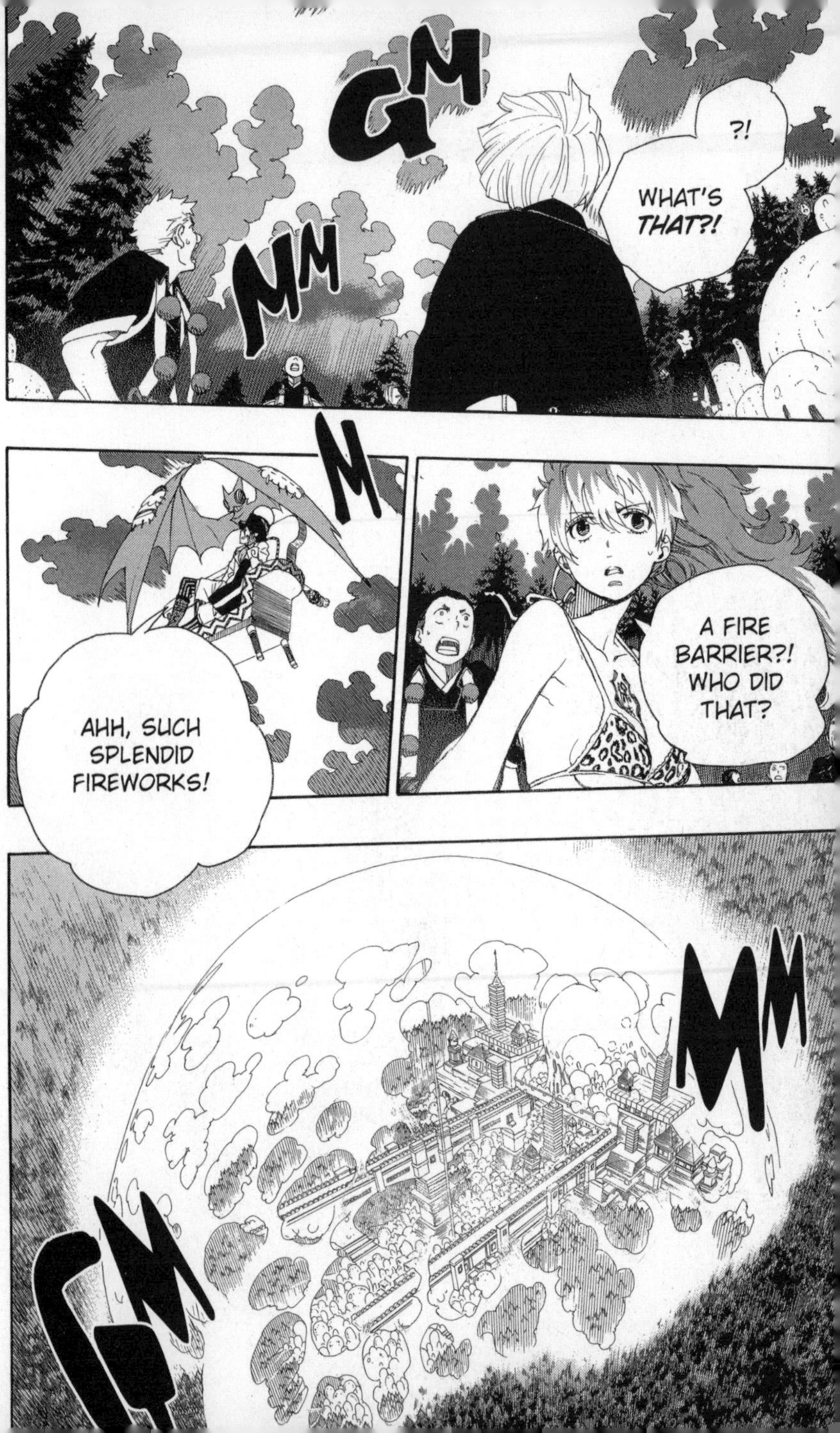
?!
WHAT'S *THAT?!*
GM
MM
A FIRE BARRIER?! WHO DID THAT?
M
AHH, SUCH SPLENDID FIREWORKS!
MM
GM

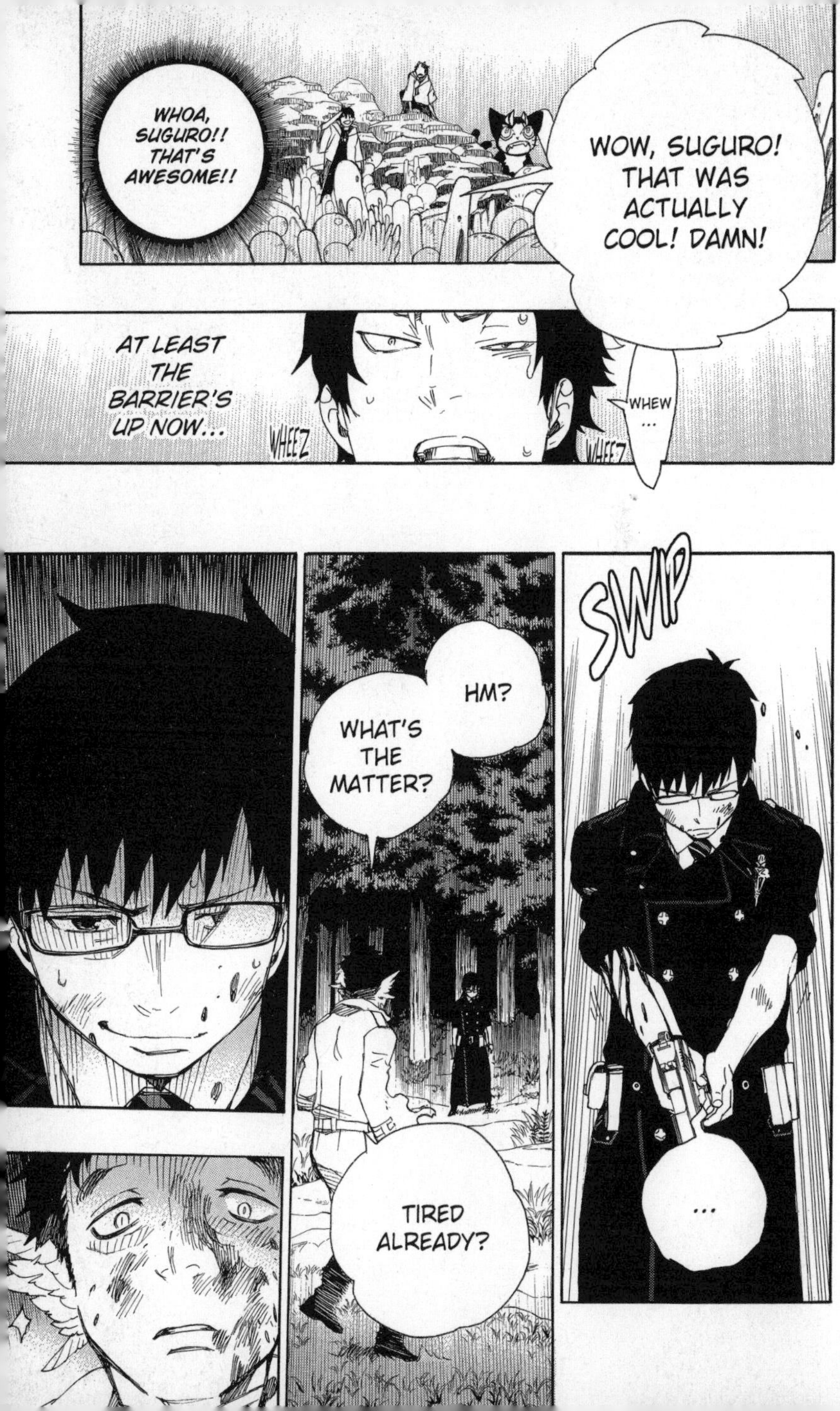
WOW, SUGURO! THAT WAS ACTUALLY COOL! DAMN!
WHOA, SUGURO!! THAT'S AWESOME!!
WHEW...
WHEEZ
WHEEZ
AT LEAST THE BARRIER'S UP NOW...
SWIP
...
HM?
WHAT'S THE MATTER?
TIRED ALREADY?

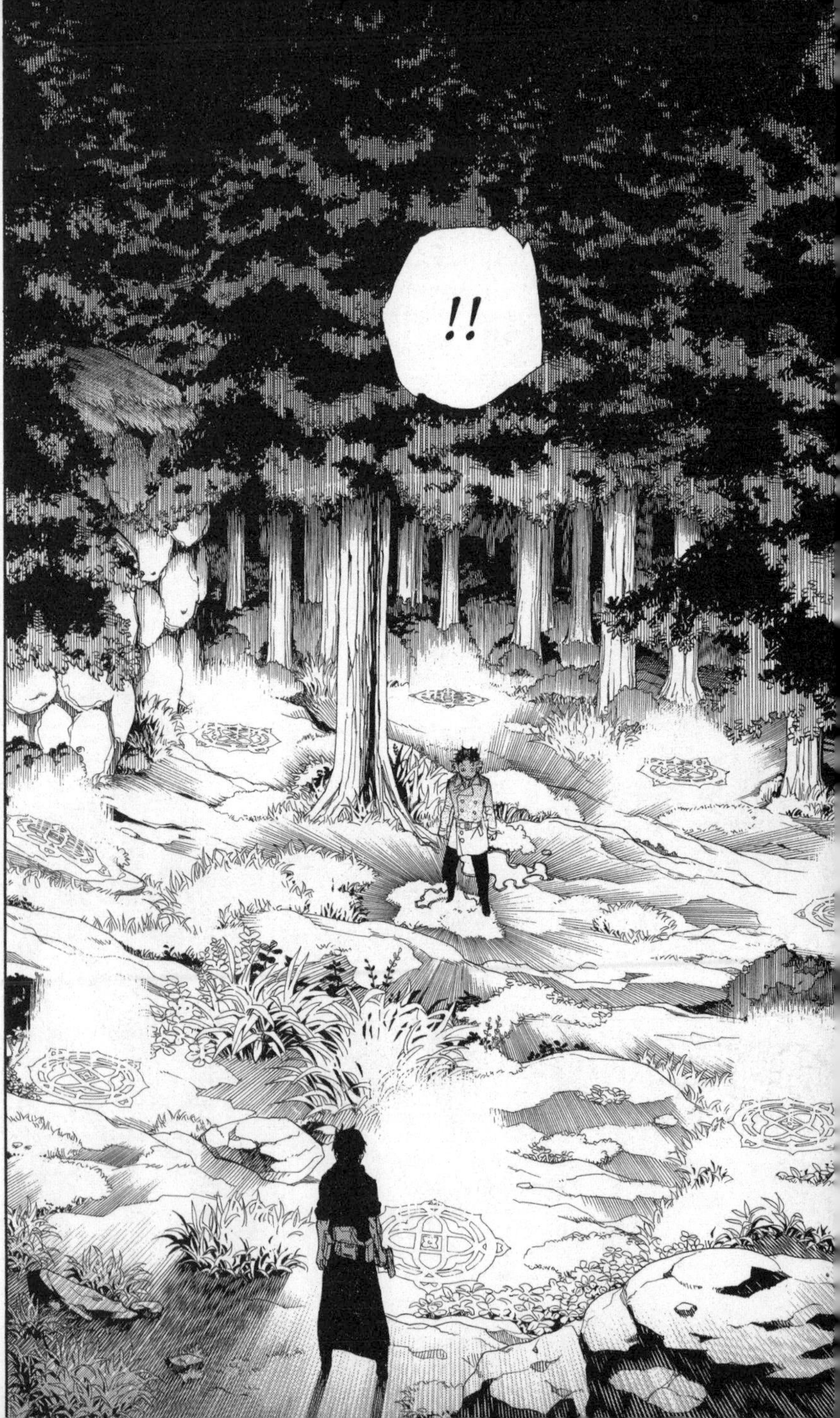
!!

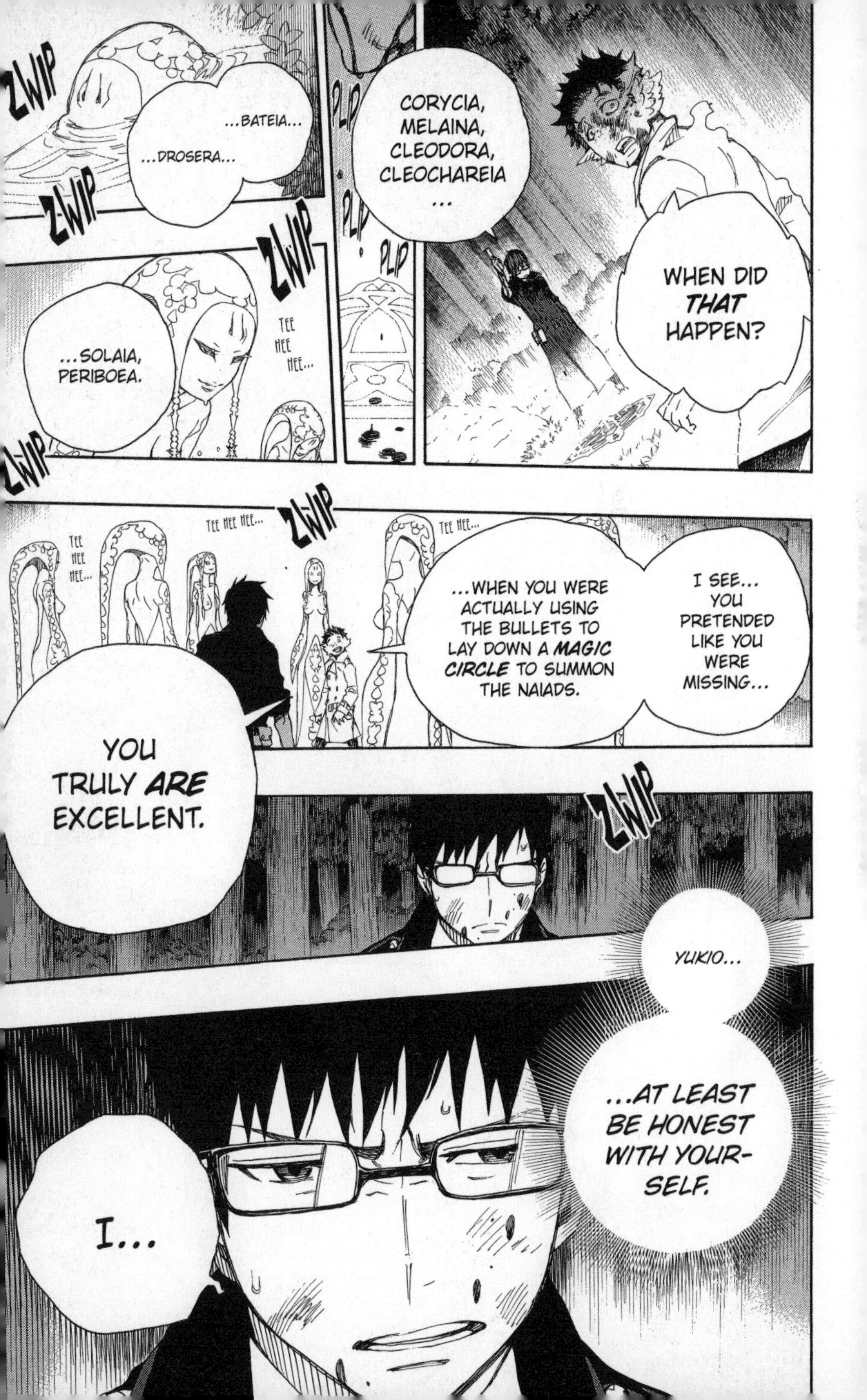
WHEN DID THAT HAPPEN?
PLIP
PLIP
PLIP
CORYCIA, MELAINA, CLEODORA, CLEOCHAREIA ...
ZWIP
...BATEIA...
...DROSERA...
ZWIP
ZWIP
TEE HEE HEE...
...SOLAIA, PERIBOEA.
ZWIP
I SEE... YOU PRETENDED LIKE YOU WERE MISSING...
...WHEN YOU WERE ACTUALLY USING THE BULLETS TO LAY DOWN A MAGIC CIRCLE TO SUMMON THE NAIADS.
TEE HEE...
ZWIP
TEE HEE HEE...
TEE HEE HEE...
YOU TRULY ARE EXCELLENT.
ZWIP
YUKIO...
...AT LEAST BE HONEST WITH YOUR-SELF.
I...

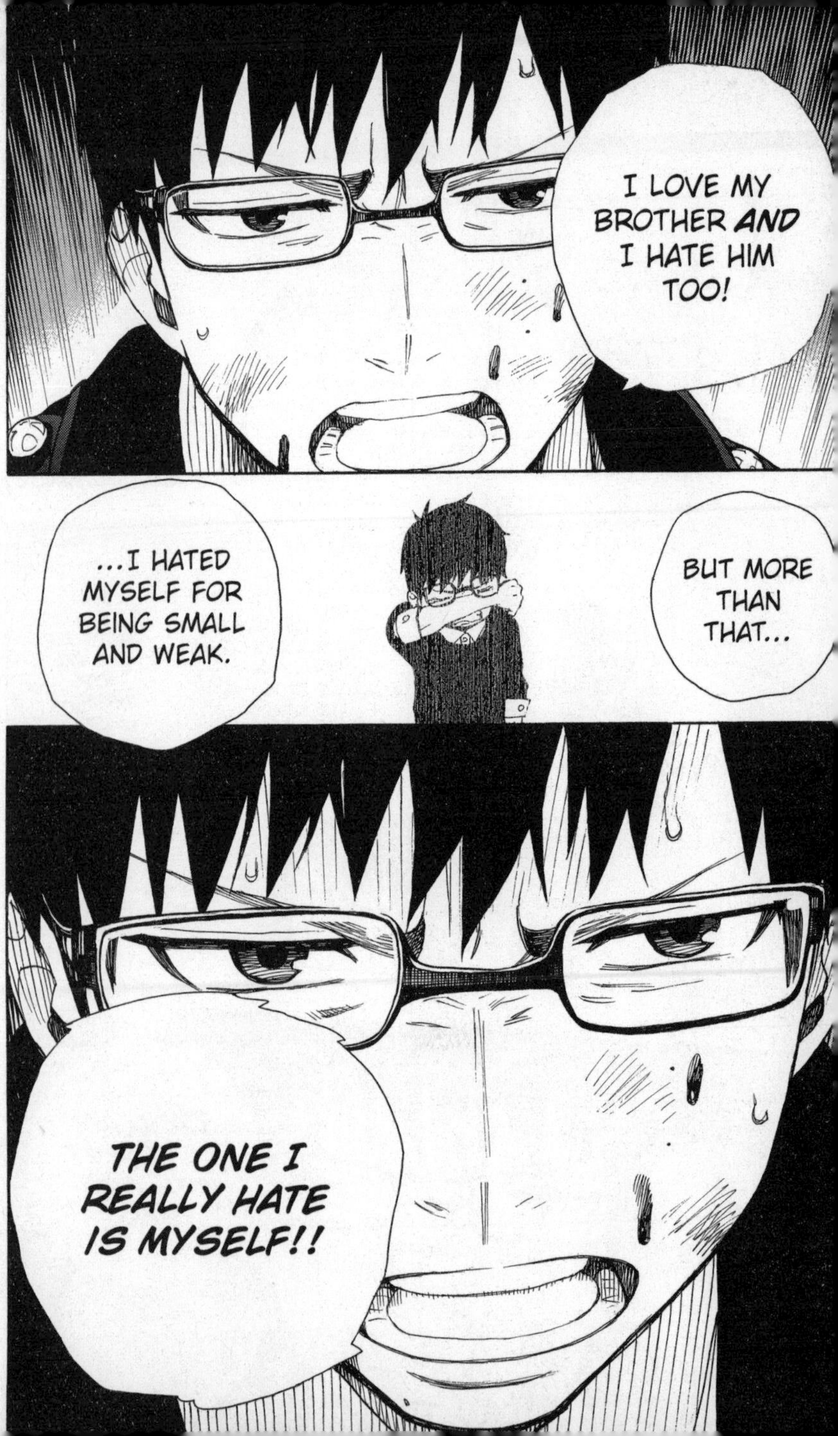
I LOVE MY BROTHER AND I HATE HIM TOO!
...I HATED MYSELF FOR BEING SMALL AND WEAK.
BUT MORE THAN THAT...
THE ONE I REALLY HATE IS MYSELF!!

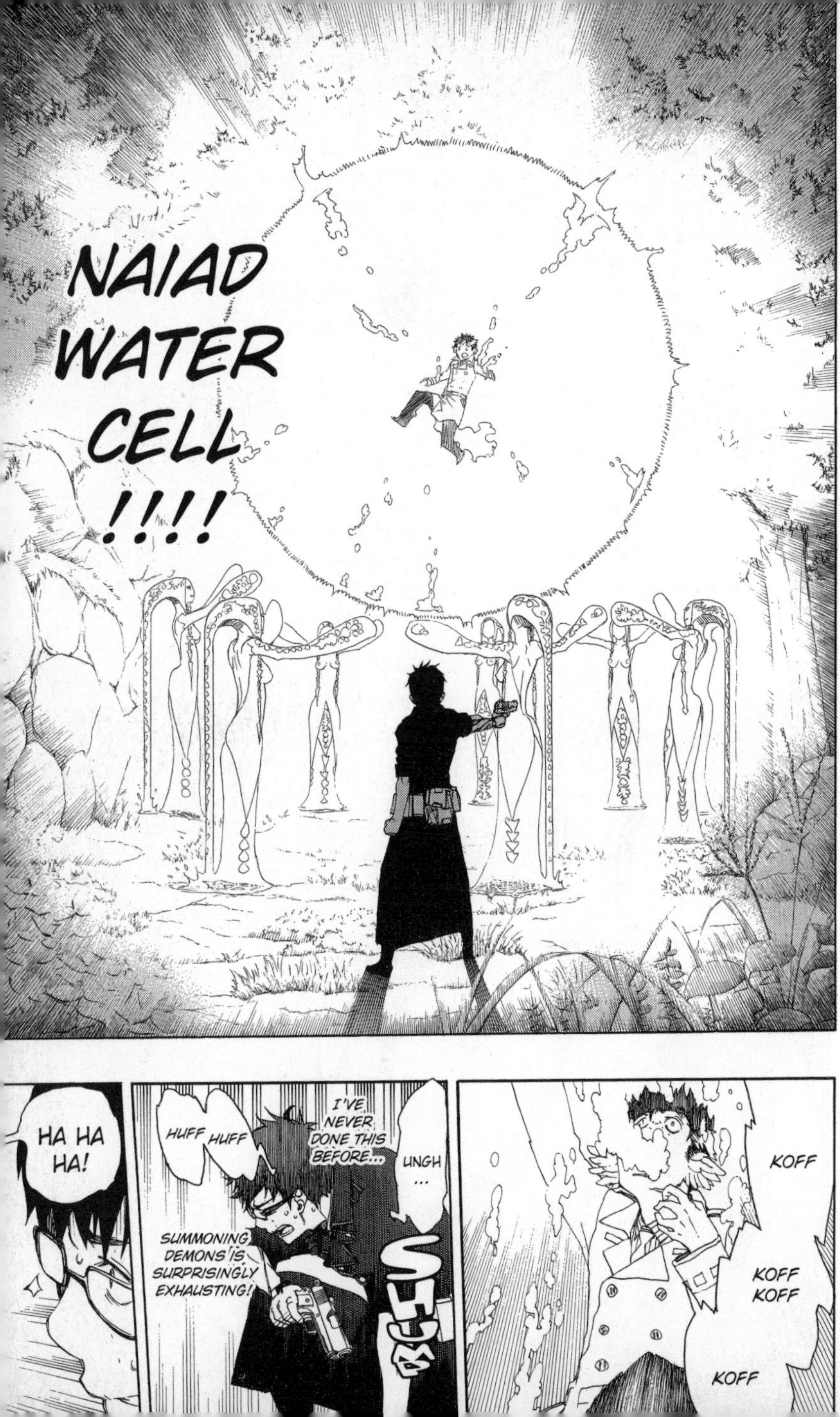
NAIAD WATER CELL!!!!
KOFF
KOFF KOFF
KOFF
UNGH ...
I'VE NEVER DONE THIS BEFORE...
HUFF HUFF
SHUMP
SUMMONING DEMONS IS SURPRISINGLY EXHAUSTING!
HA HA HA!

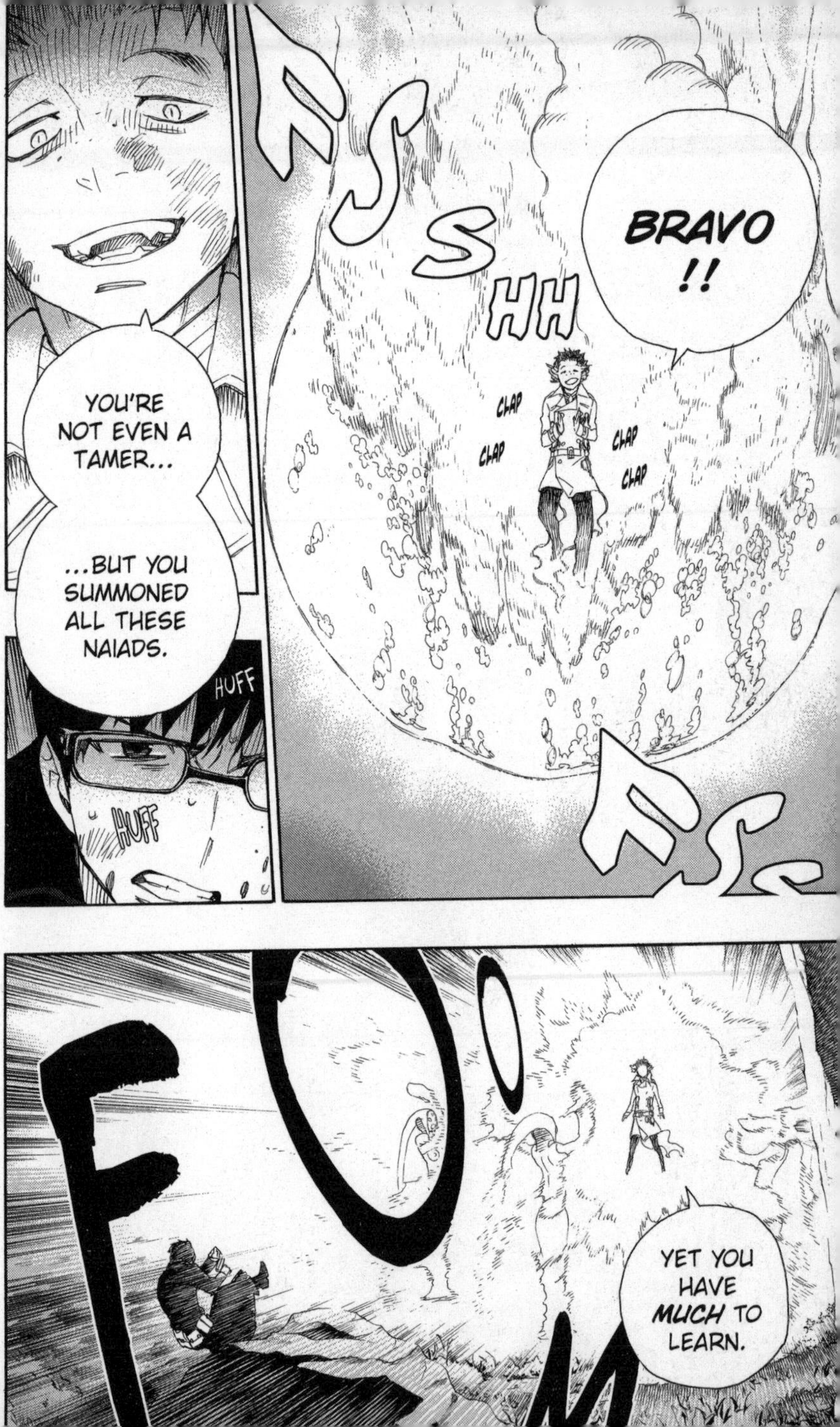
FSSHH
BRAVO!!
CLAP
CLAP
CLAP
CLAP
FSSS
YOU'RE NOT EVEN A TAMER...
...BUT YOU SUMMONED ALL THESE NAIADS.
HUFF
HUFF
FOOM
YET YOU HAVE MUCH TO LEARN.

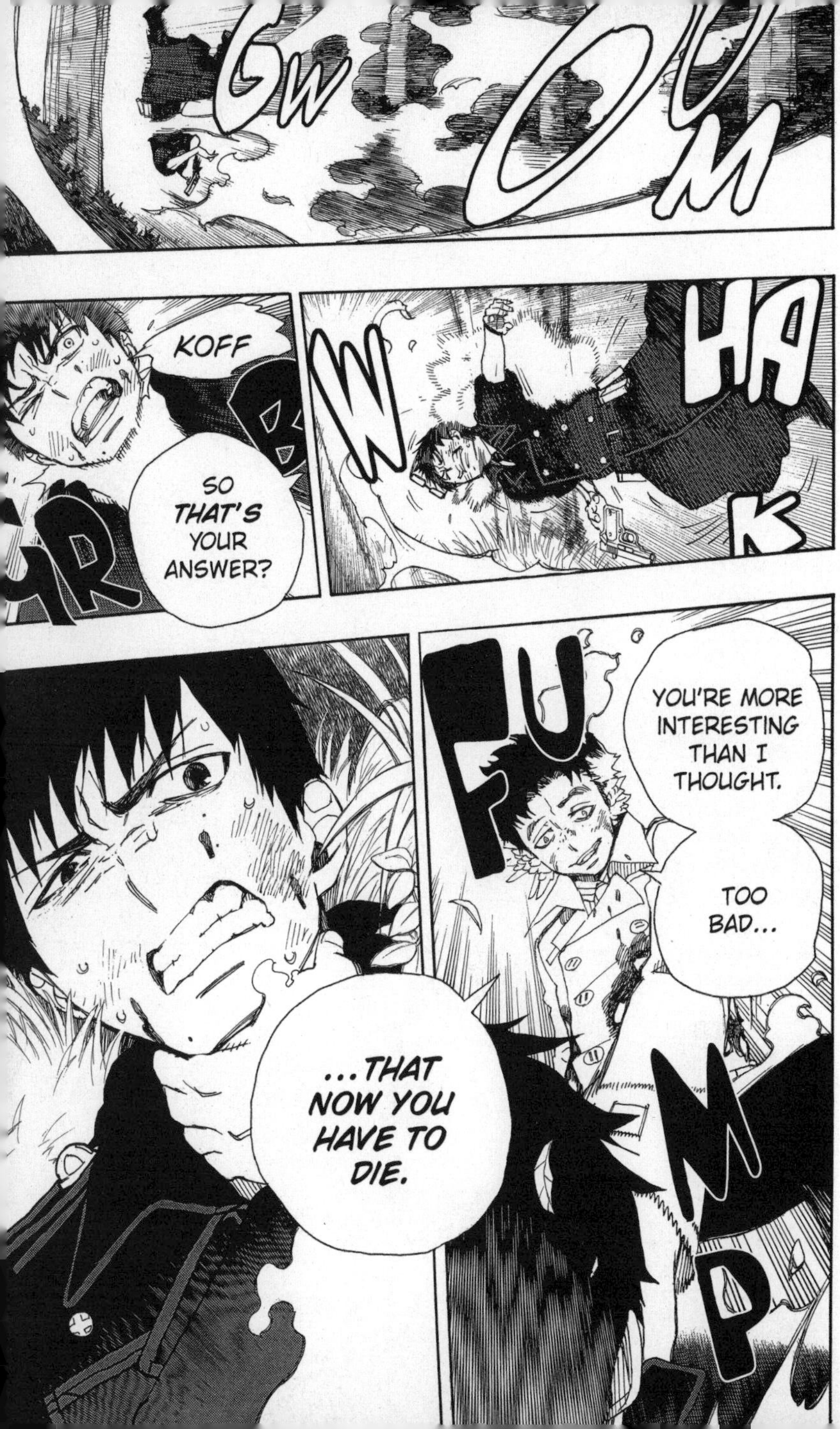
WHAK
KOFF
SO THAT'S YOUR ANSWER?
YOU'RE MORE INTERESTING THAN I THOUGHT.
TOO BAD...
...THAT NOW YOU HAVE TO DIE.

Blue Exorcist Chapter 29 Barrier Spell

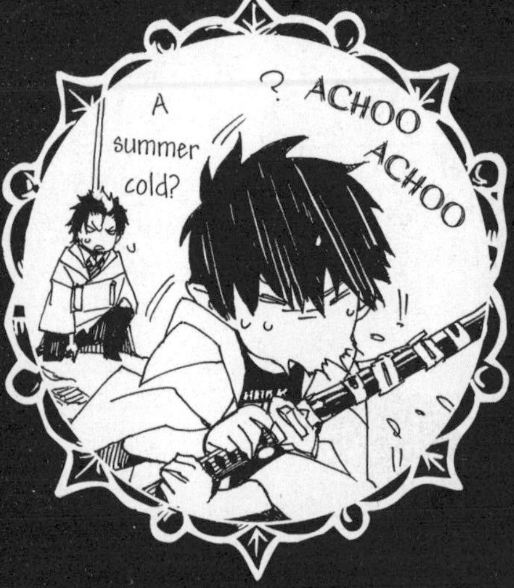
ACHOO ACHOO
A summer cold?

Chapter 30: Fateful Occurrence

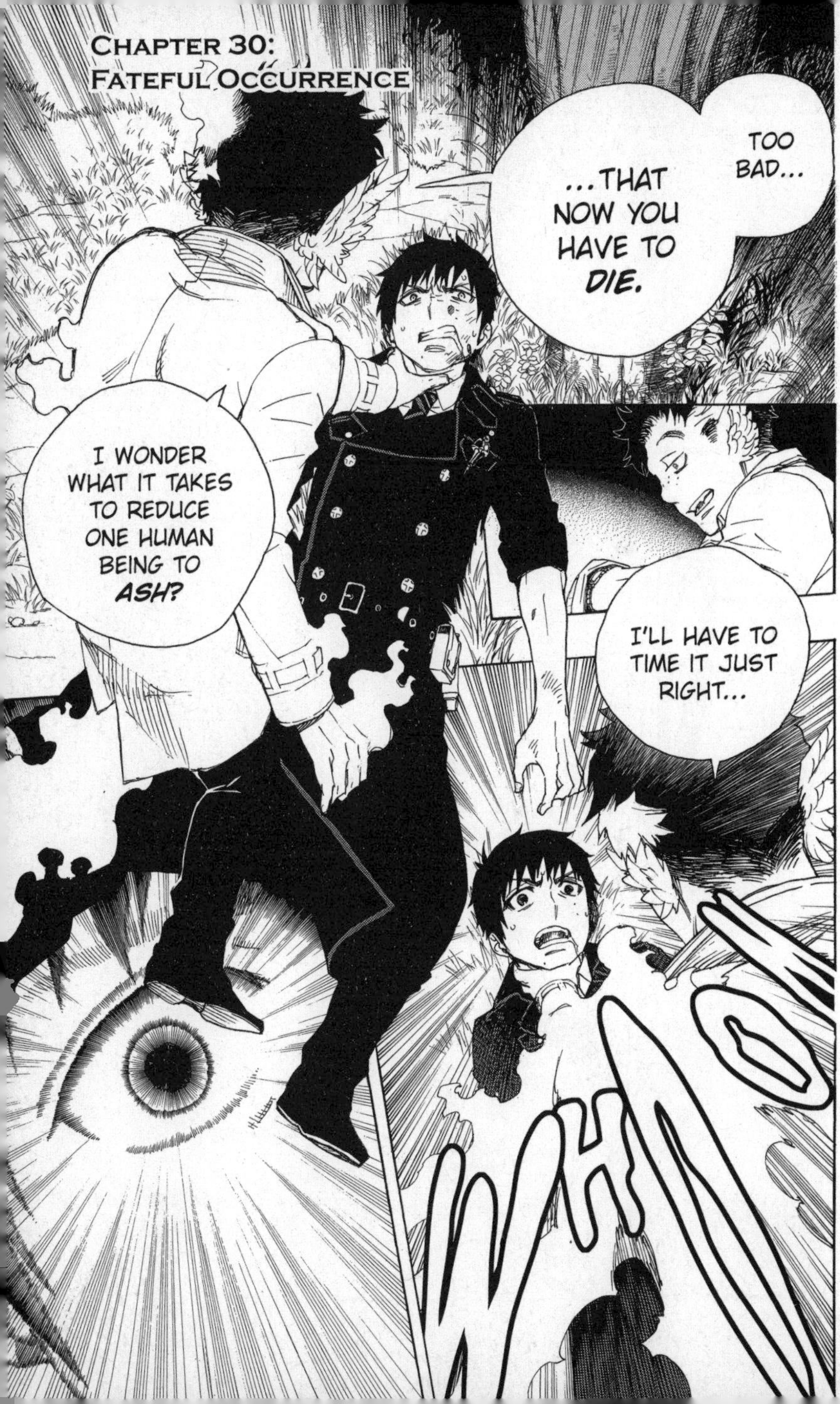
TOO BAD...
...THAT NOW YOU HAVE TO DIE.
I WONDER WHAT IT TAKES TO REDUCE ONE HUMAN BEING TO ASH?
I'LL HAVE TO TIME IT JUST RIGHT...

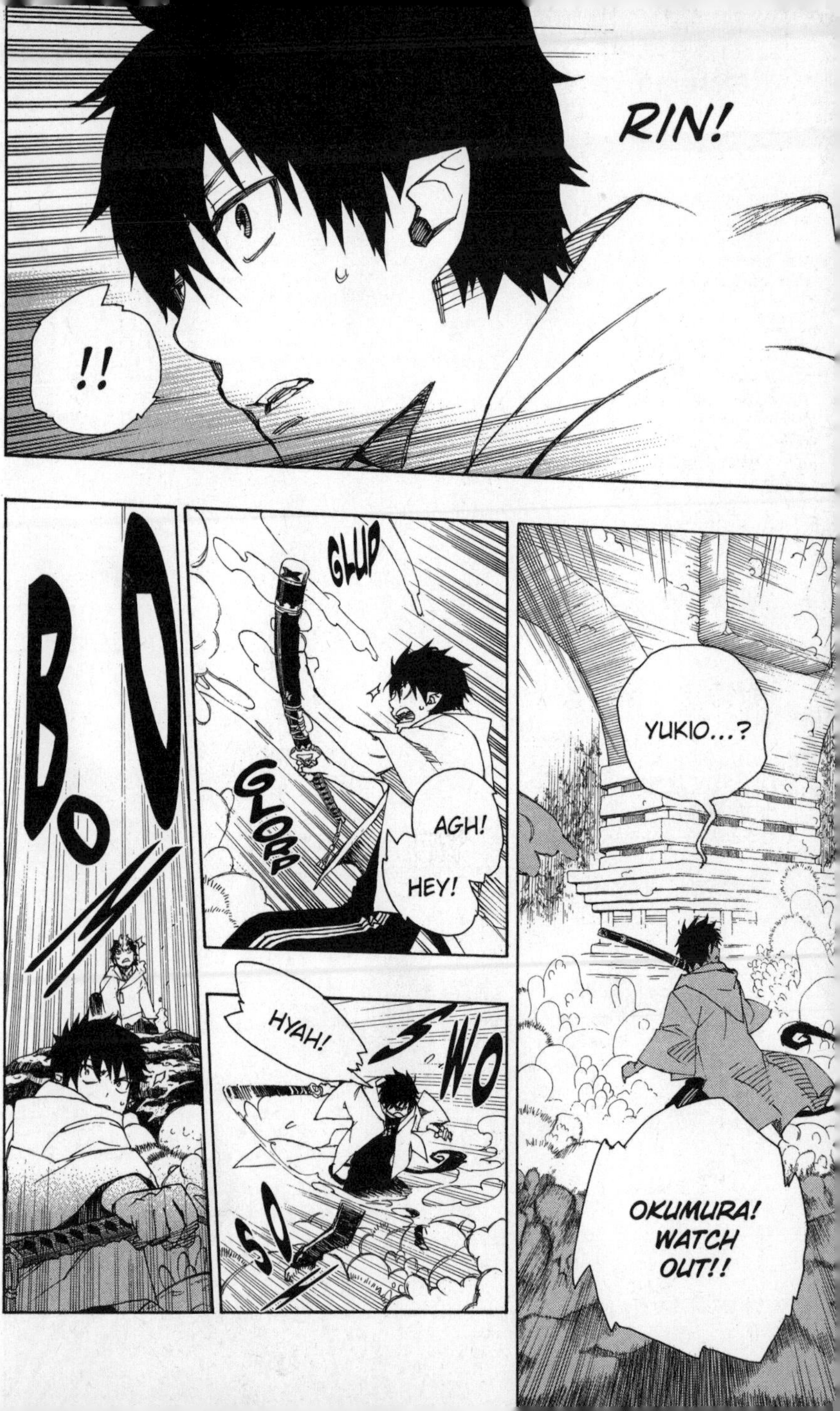
RIN!
!!
YUKIO...?
OKUMURA! WATCH OUT!!
GLUP
GLORP
AGH!
HEY!
HYAH!
BOOM

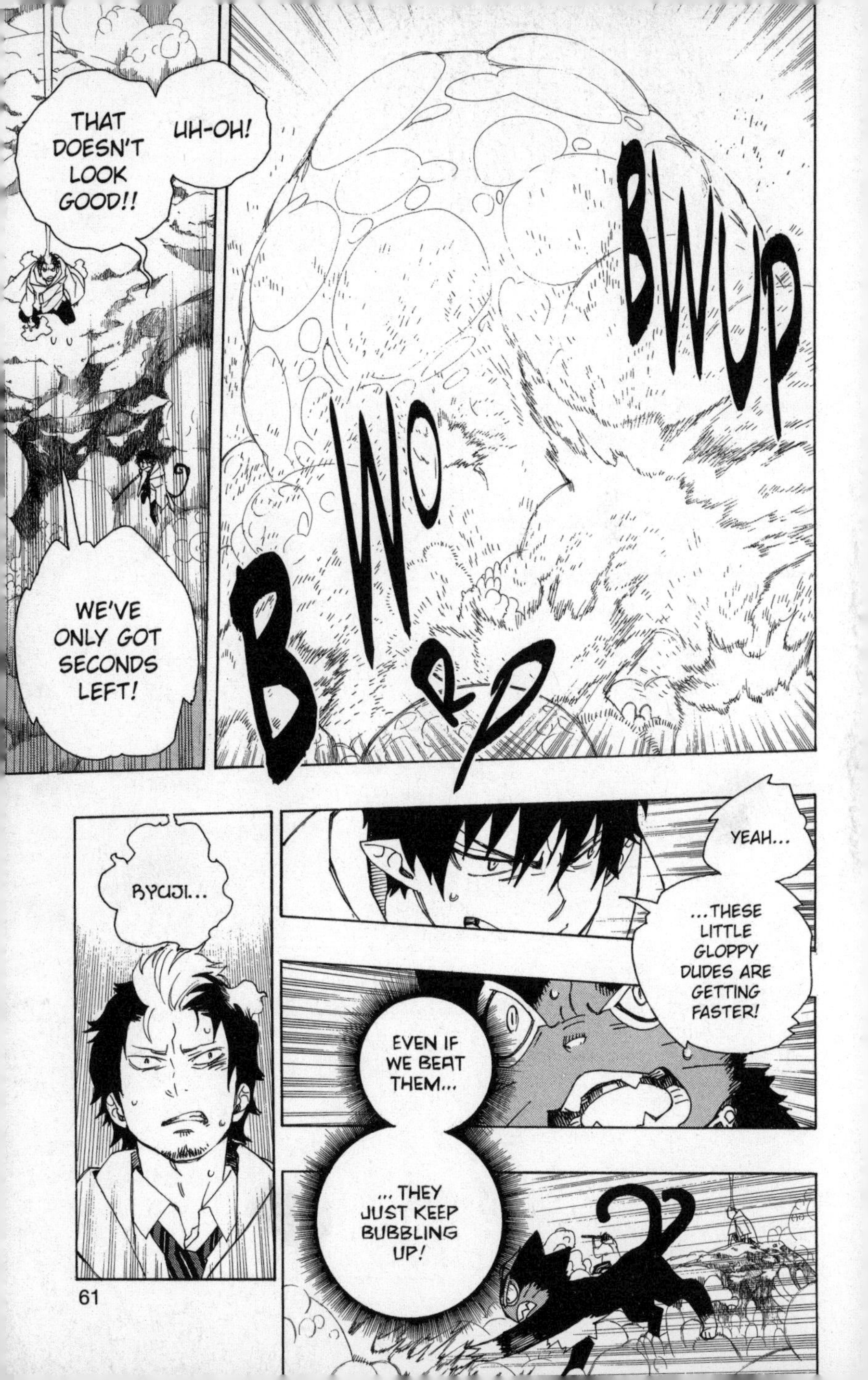
BWUP
BWORP
UH-OH!
THAT DOESN'T LOOK GOOD!!
WE'VE ONLY GOT SECONDS LEFT!
YEAH...
...THESE LITTLE GLOPPY DUDES ARE GETTING FASTER!
EVEN IF WE BEAT THEM...
...THEY JUST KEEP BUBBLING UP!
RYUJI...

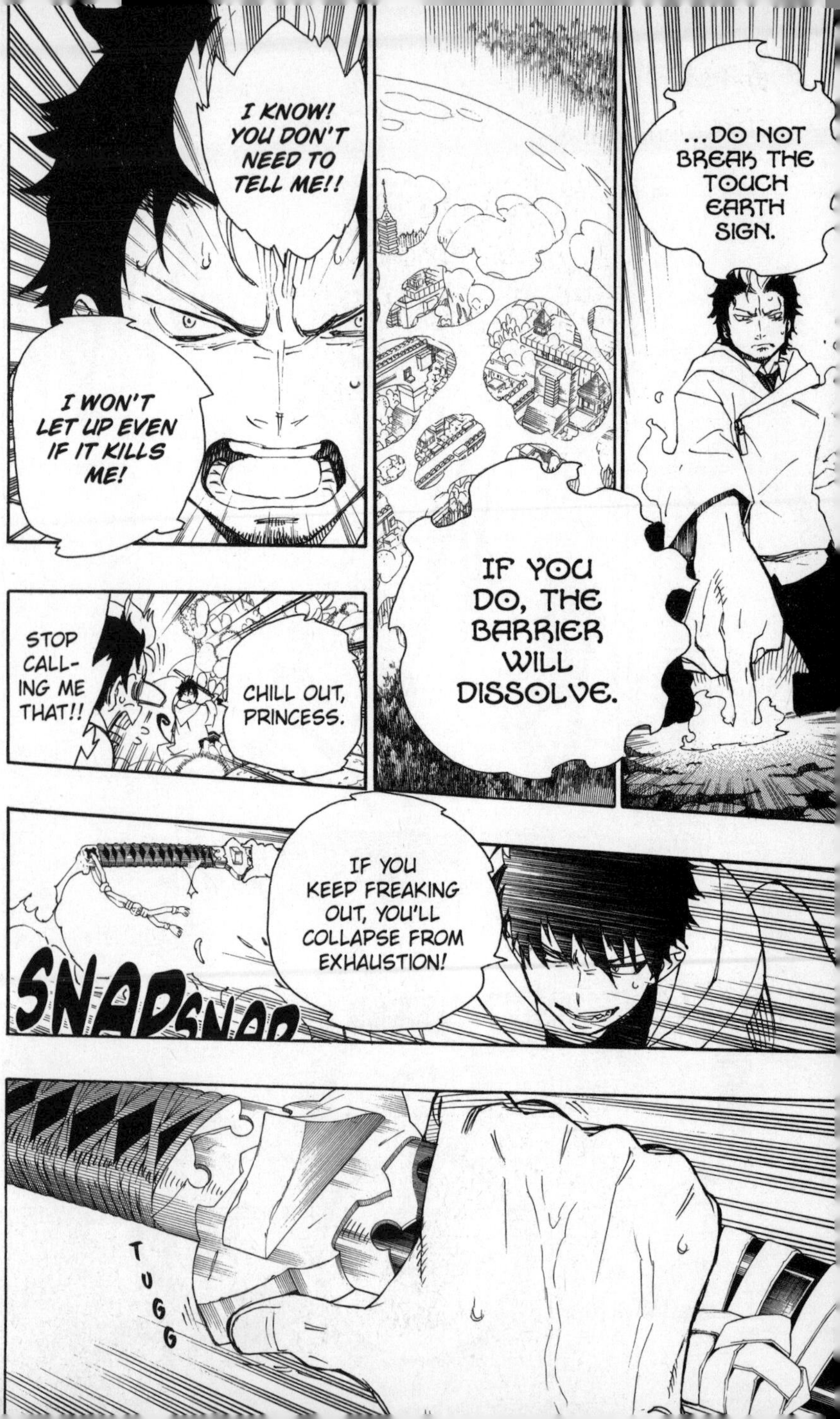
...DO NOT BREAK THE TOUCH EARTH SIGN.
IF YOU DO, THE BARRIER WILL DISSOLVE.
I KNOW! YOU DON'T NEED TO TELL ME!!
I WON'T LET UP EVEN IF IT KILLS ME!
CHILL OUT, PRINCESS.
STOP CALL-ING ME THAT!!
IF YOU KEEP FREAKING OUT, YOU'LL COLLAPSE FROM EXHAUSTION!
SNAPSNAP
TUGG

Chapter 30: Fateful Occurrence

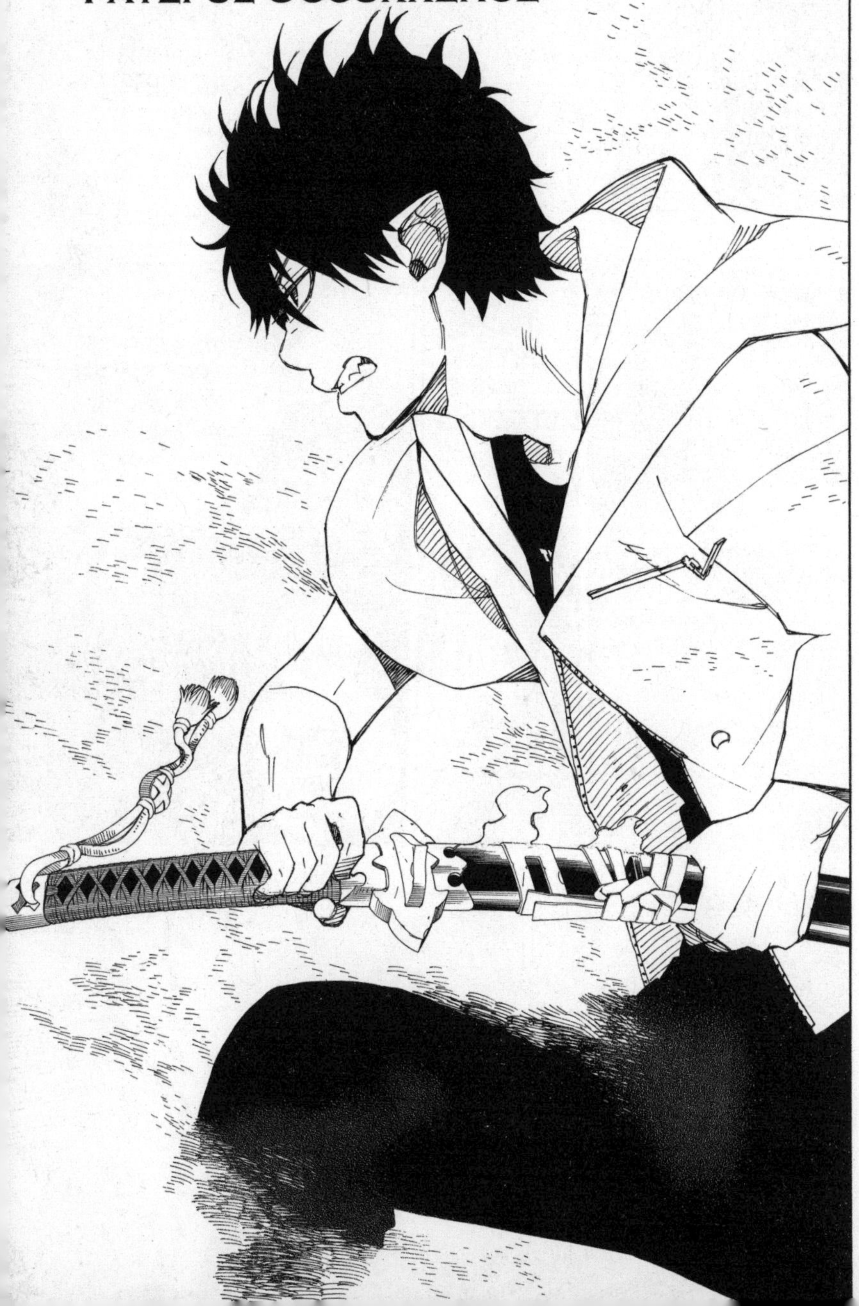

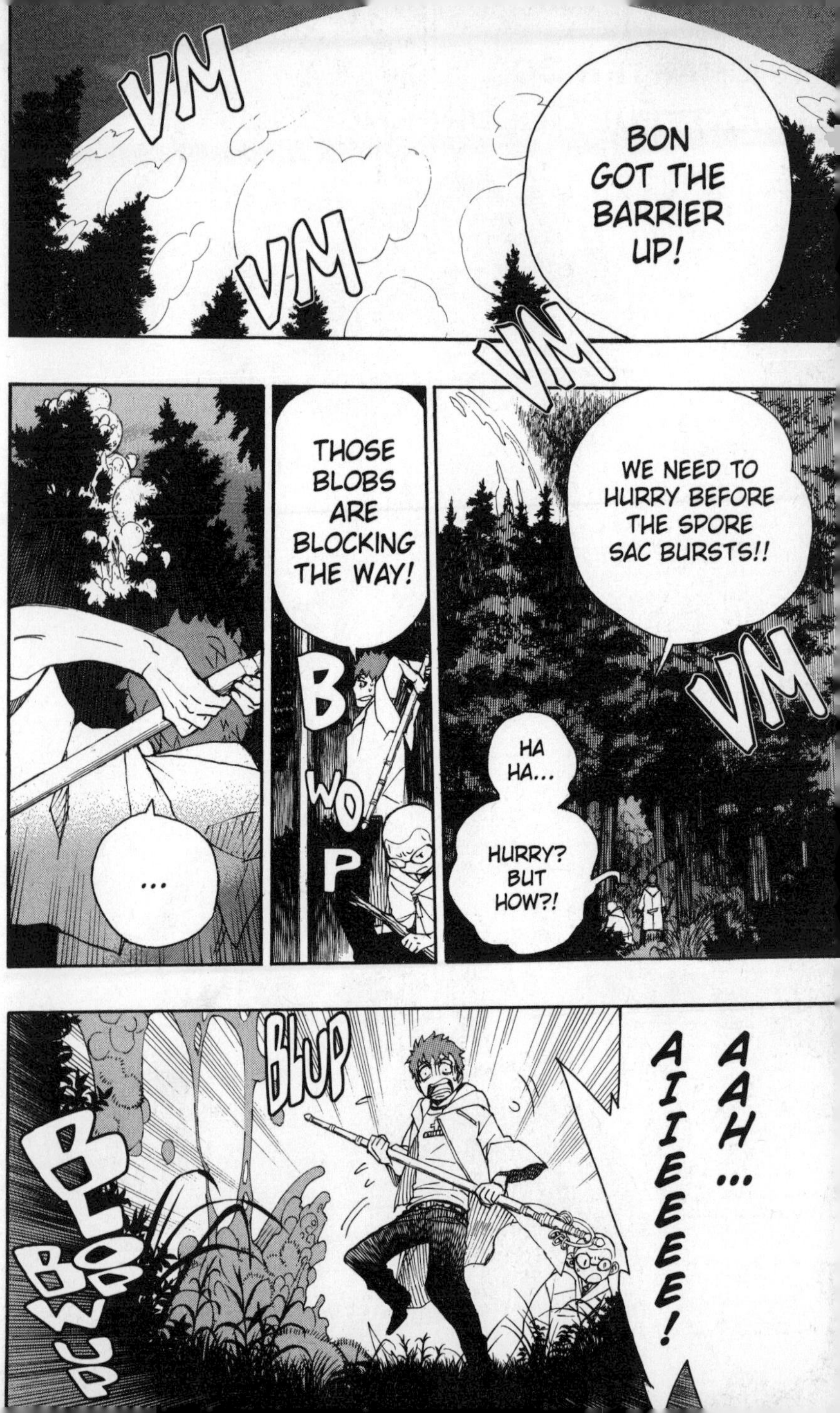
BON GOT THE BARRIER UP!
VM
VM
VM
WE NEED TO HURRY BEFORE THE SPORE SAC BURSTS!!
VM
HA HA...
HURRY? BUT HOW?!
THOSE BLOBS ARE BLOCKING THE WAY!
BWOP
...
AAH...
AIIEEEEE!
BLUP
BLOOP
BWUP

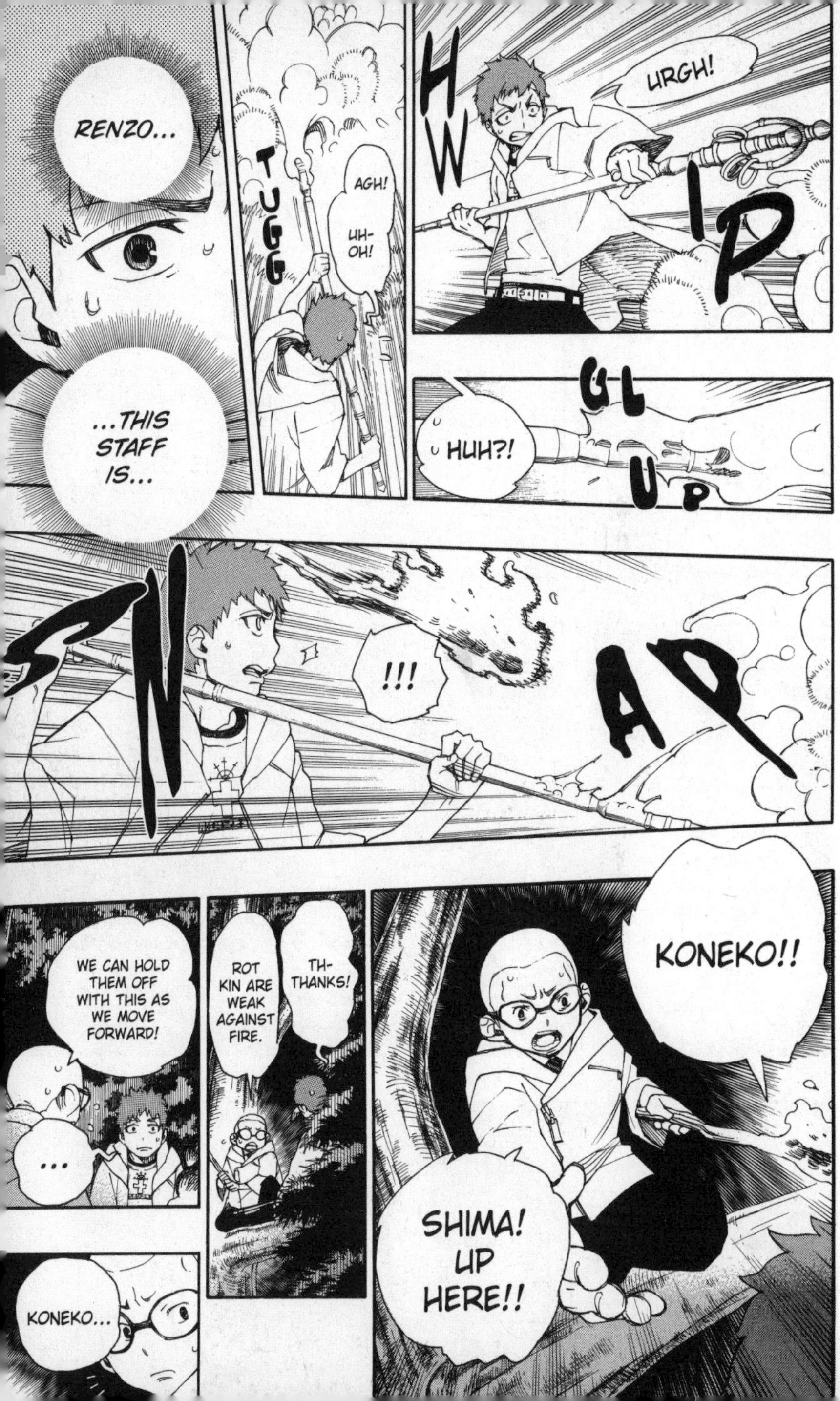
HWIP
URGH!
GLUP
HUH?!
TUGG
AGH!
UH-OH!
RENZO...
...THIS STAFF IS...
SNAP
!!!
KONEKO!!
SHIMA! UP HERE!!
TH-THANKS!
ROT KIN ARE WEAK AGAINST FIRE.
WE CAN HOLD THEM OFF WITH THIS AS WE MOVE FORWARD!
...
KONEKO...

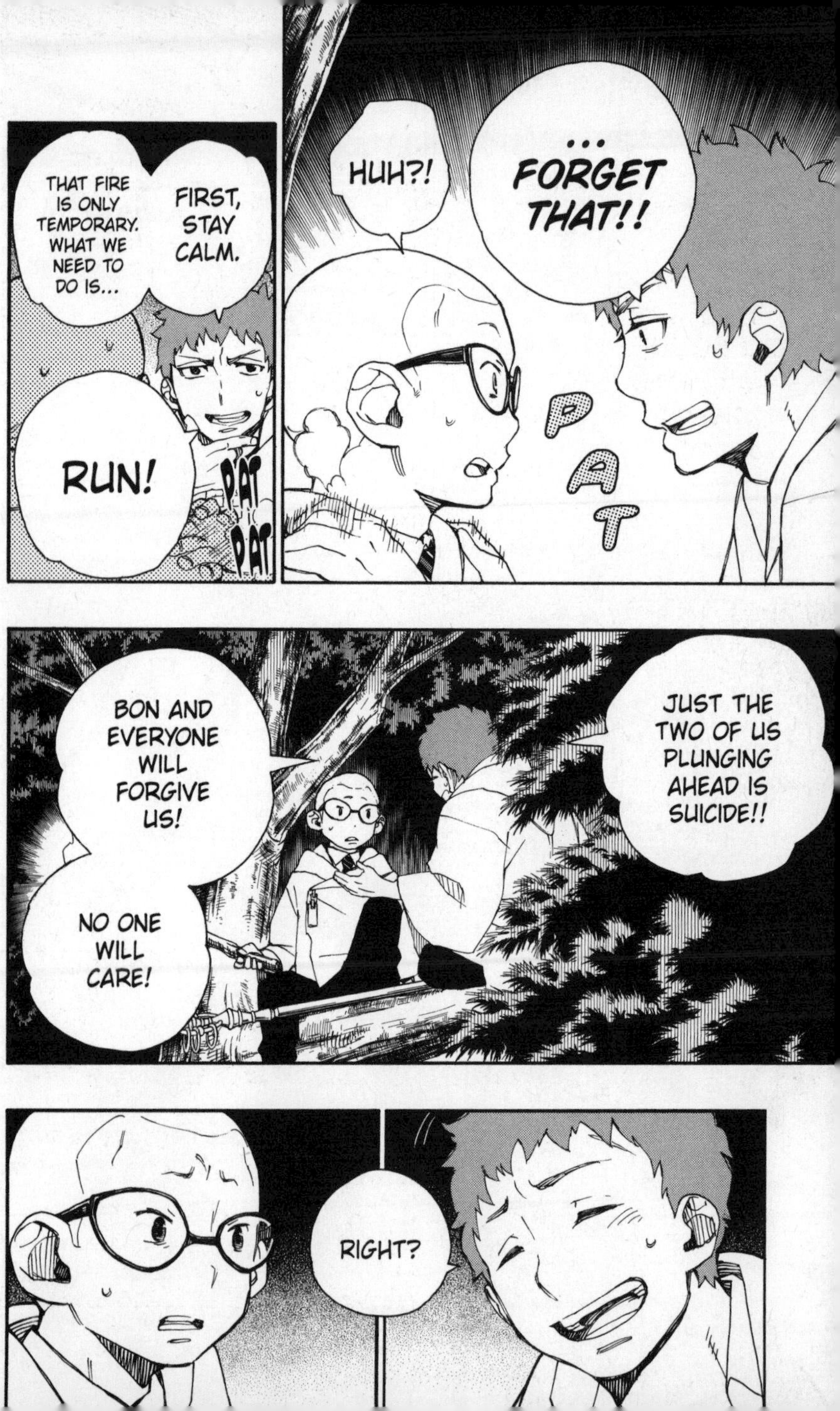
...FORGET THAT!!
HUH?!
PAT
FIRST, STAY CALM.
THAT FIRE IS ONLY TEMPORARY. WHAT WE NEED TO DO IS...
RUN!
PAT PAT
JUST THE TWO OF US PLUNGING AHEAD IS SUICIDE!!
BON AND EVERYONE WILL FORGIVE US!
NO ONE WILL CARE!
RIGHT?

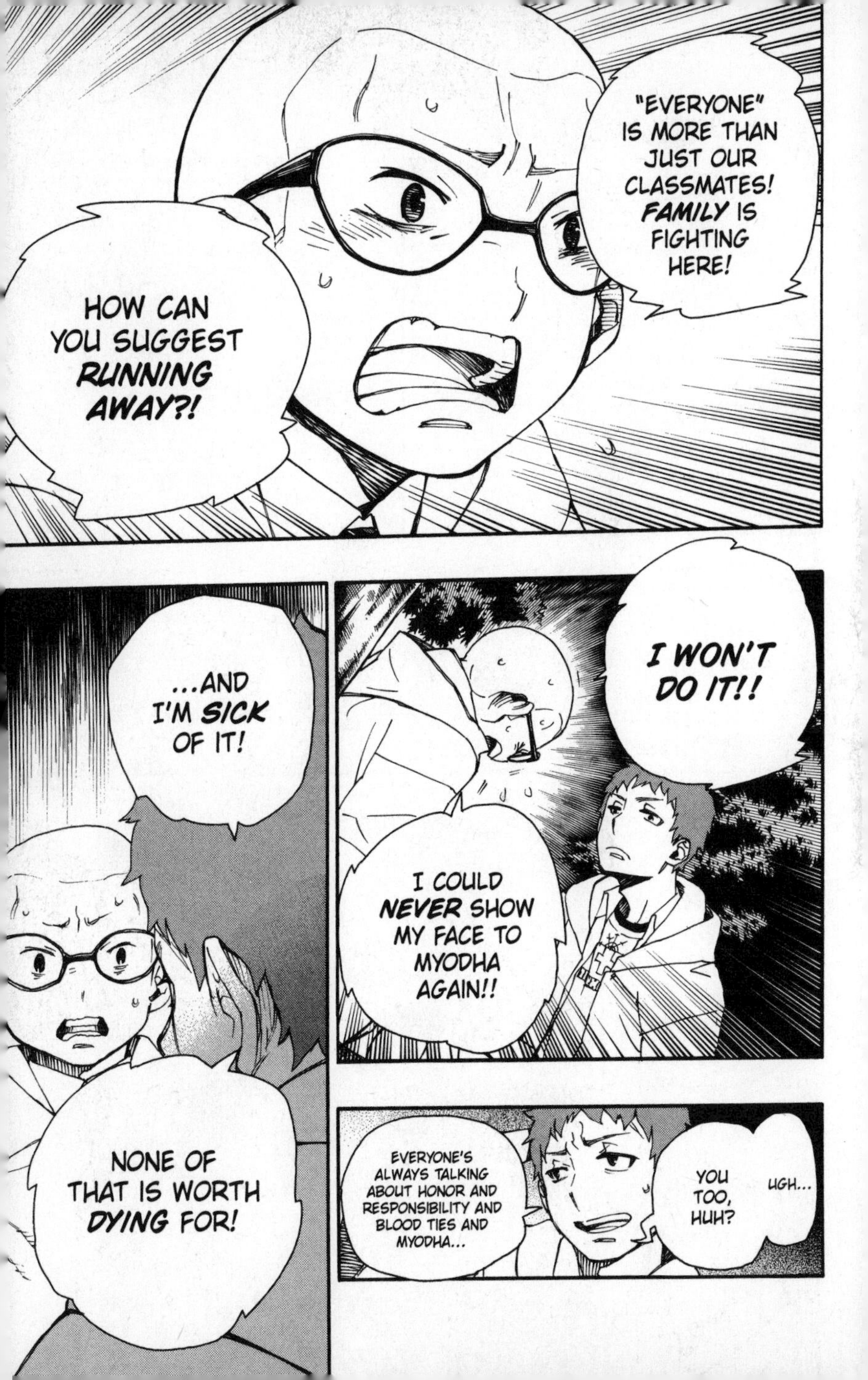
"EVERYONE" IS MORE THAN JUST OUR CLASSMATES! FAMILY IS FIGHTING HERE!
HOW CAN YOU SUGGEST RUNNING AWAY?!
I WON'T DO IT!!
I COULD NEVER SHOW MY FACE TO MYODHA AGAIN!!
UGH...
YOU TOO, HUH?
EVERYONE'S ALWAYS TALKING ABOUT HONOR AND RESPONSIBILITY AND BLOOD TIES AND MYODHA...
...AND I'M SICK OF IT!
NONE OF THAT IS WORTH DYING FOR!

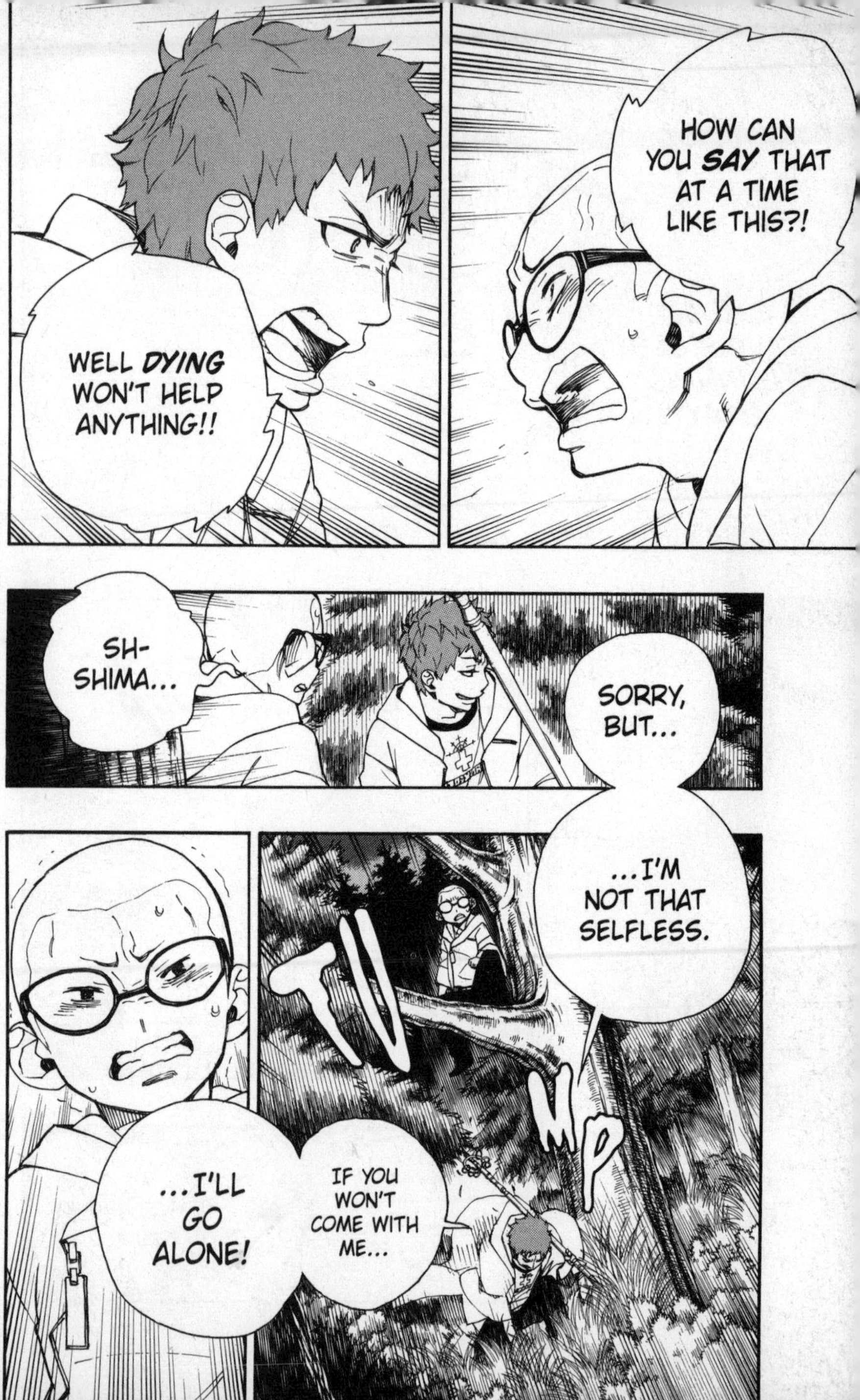
HOW CAN YOU SAY THAT AT A TIME LIKE THIS?!
WELL DYING WON'T HELP ANYTHING!!
SORRY, BUT...
SH-SHIMA...
...I'M NOT THAT SELFLESS.
TMP
IF YOU WON'T COME WITH ME...
...I'LL GO ALONE!

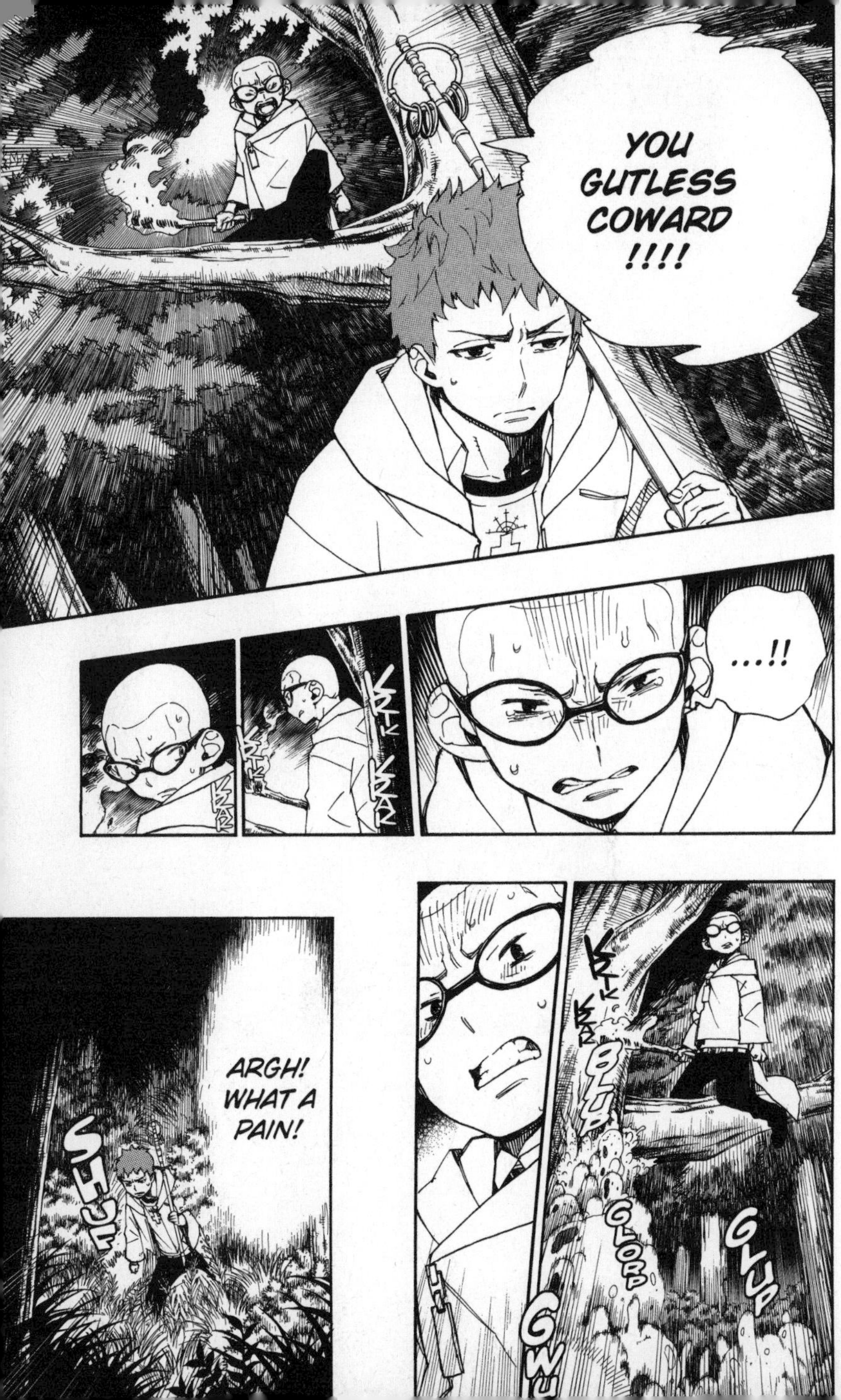
YOU GUTLESS COWARD !!!!
...!!
KRTK
KRAK
KRTK
KRAK
KRTK
KRAK
BLUP
GLUP
GLORP
GWU
ARGH! WHAT A PAIN!
SHUF

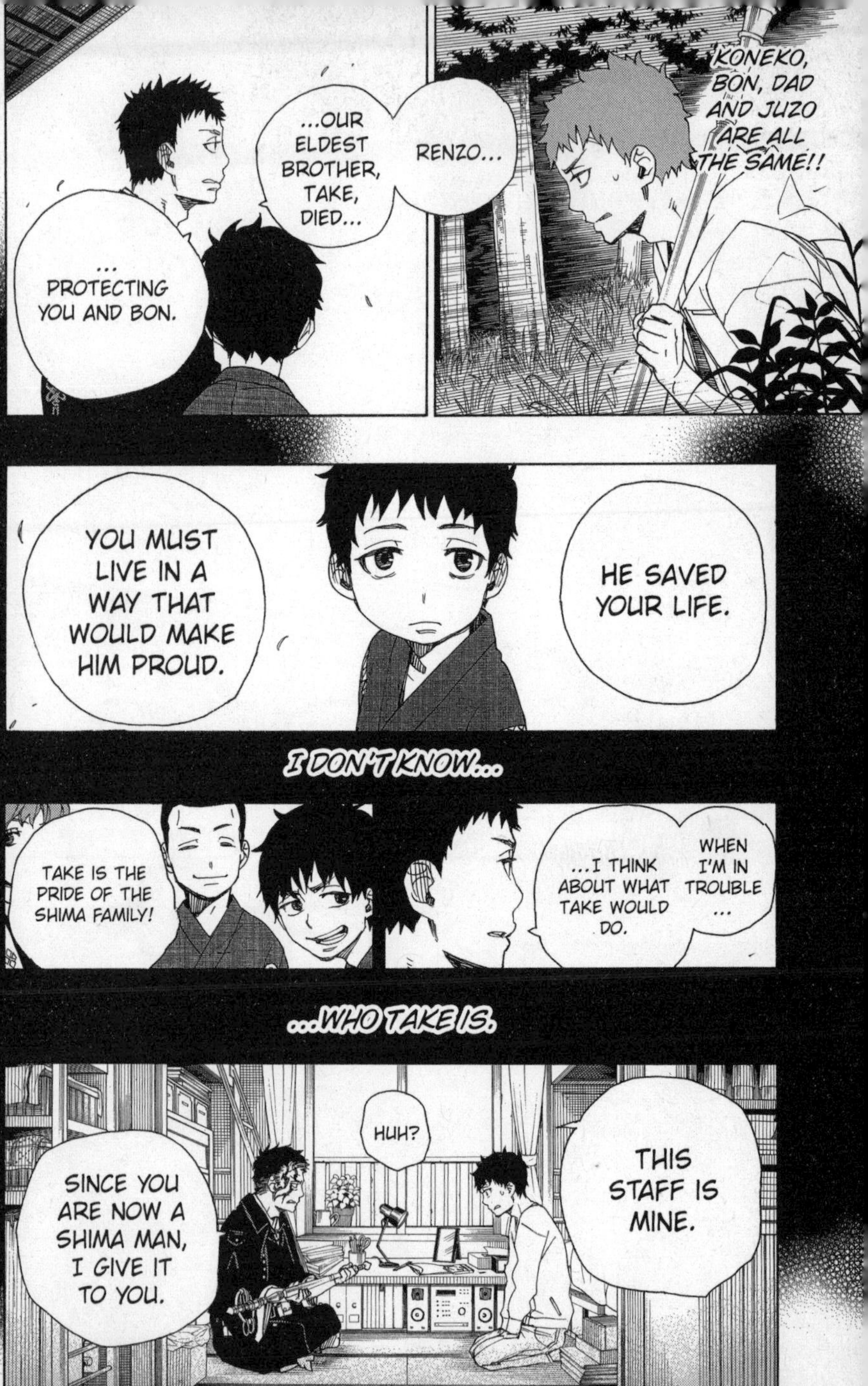
KONEKO, BON, DAD AND JUZO ARE ALL THE SAME!!
RENZO...
...OUR ELDEST BROTHER, TAKE, DIED...
... PROTECTING YOU AND BON.
HE SAVED YOUR LIFE.
YOU MUST LIVE IN A WAY THAT WOULD MAKE HIM PROUD.
I DON'T KNOW...
WHEN I'M IN TROUBLE ...
...I THINK ABOUT WHAT TAKE WOULD DO.
TAKE IS THE PRIDE OF THE SHIMA FAMILY!
...WHO TAKE IS.
THIS STAFF IS MINE.
HUH?
SINCE YOU ARE NOW A SHIMA MAN, I GIVE IT TO YOU.

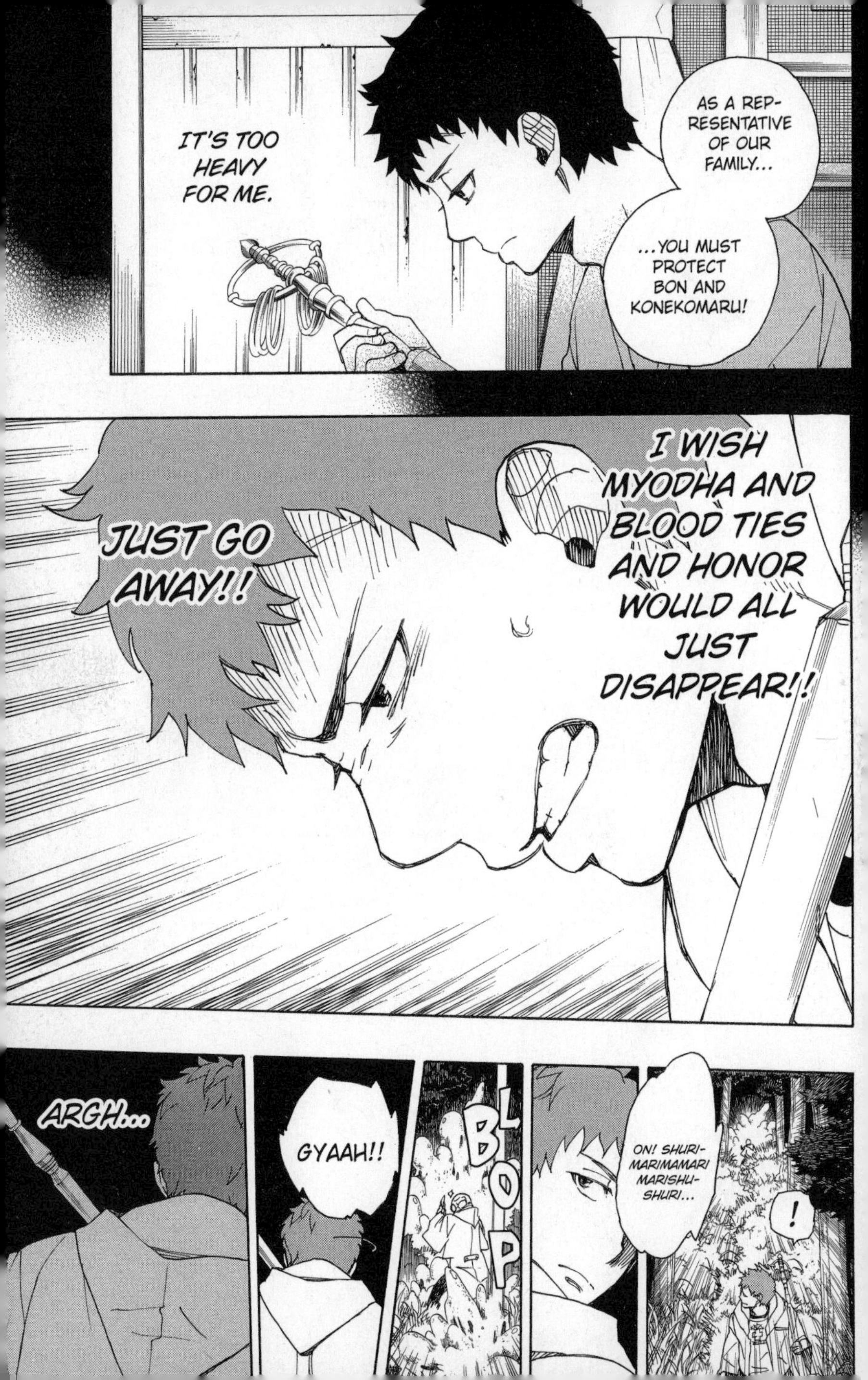
AS A REPRESENTATIVE OF OUR FAMILY...
...YOU MUST PROTECT BON AND KONEKOMARU!
IT'S TOO HEAVY FOR ME.
I WISH MYODHA AND BLOOD TIES AND HONOR WOULD ALL JUST DISAPPEAR!!
JUST GO AWAY!!
ON! SHURIMARIMAMARI MARISHUSHURI...
!
BLOOP
GYAAH!!
ARGH...

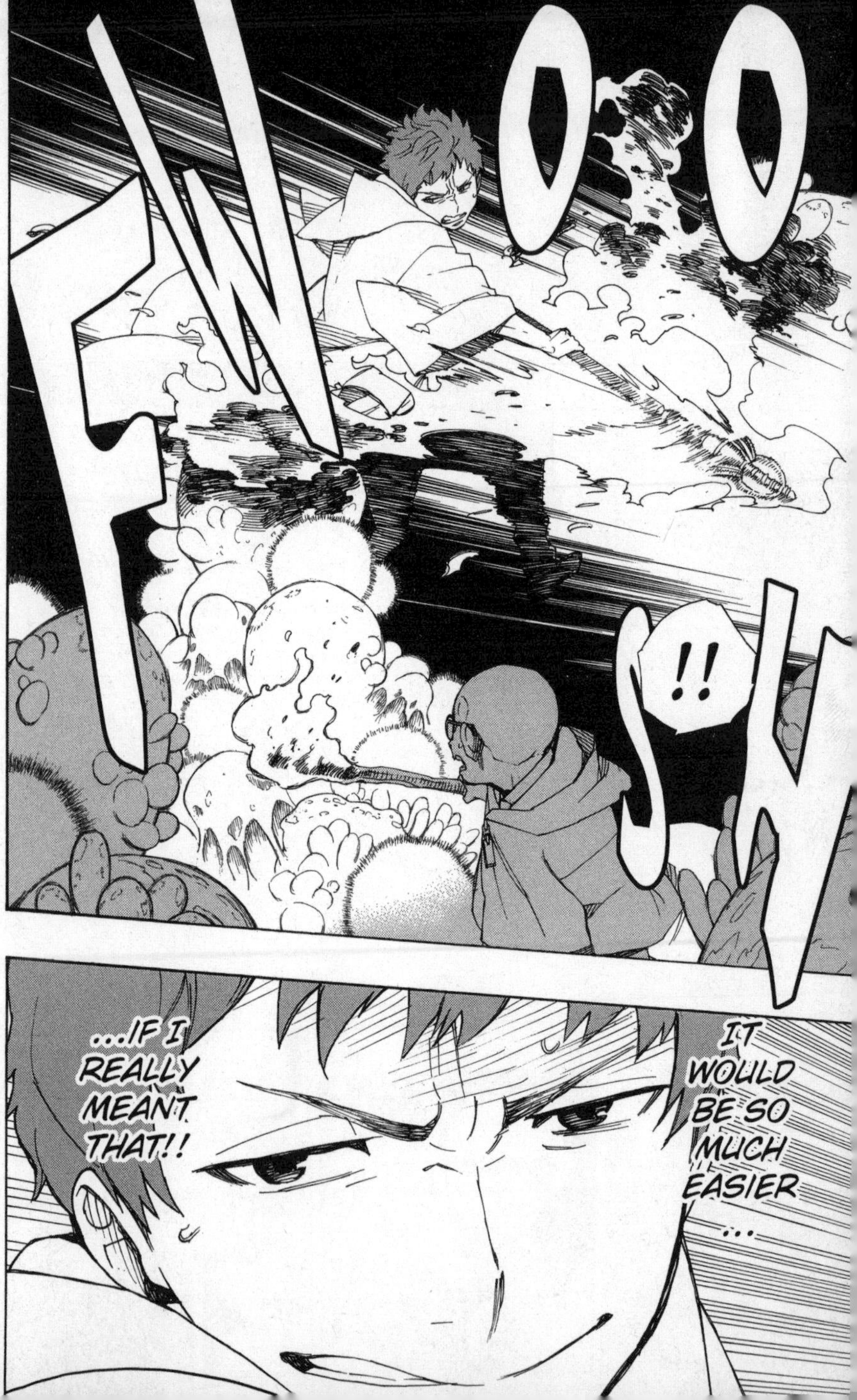
FWOO
!!
IT WOULD BE SO MUCH EASIER ...
...IF I REALLY MEANT THAT!!

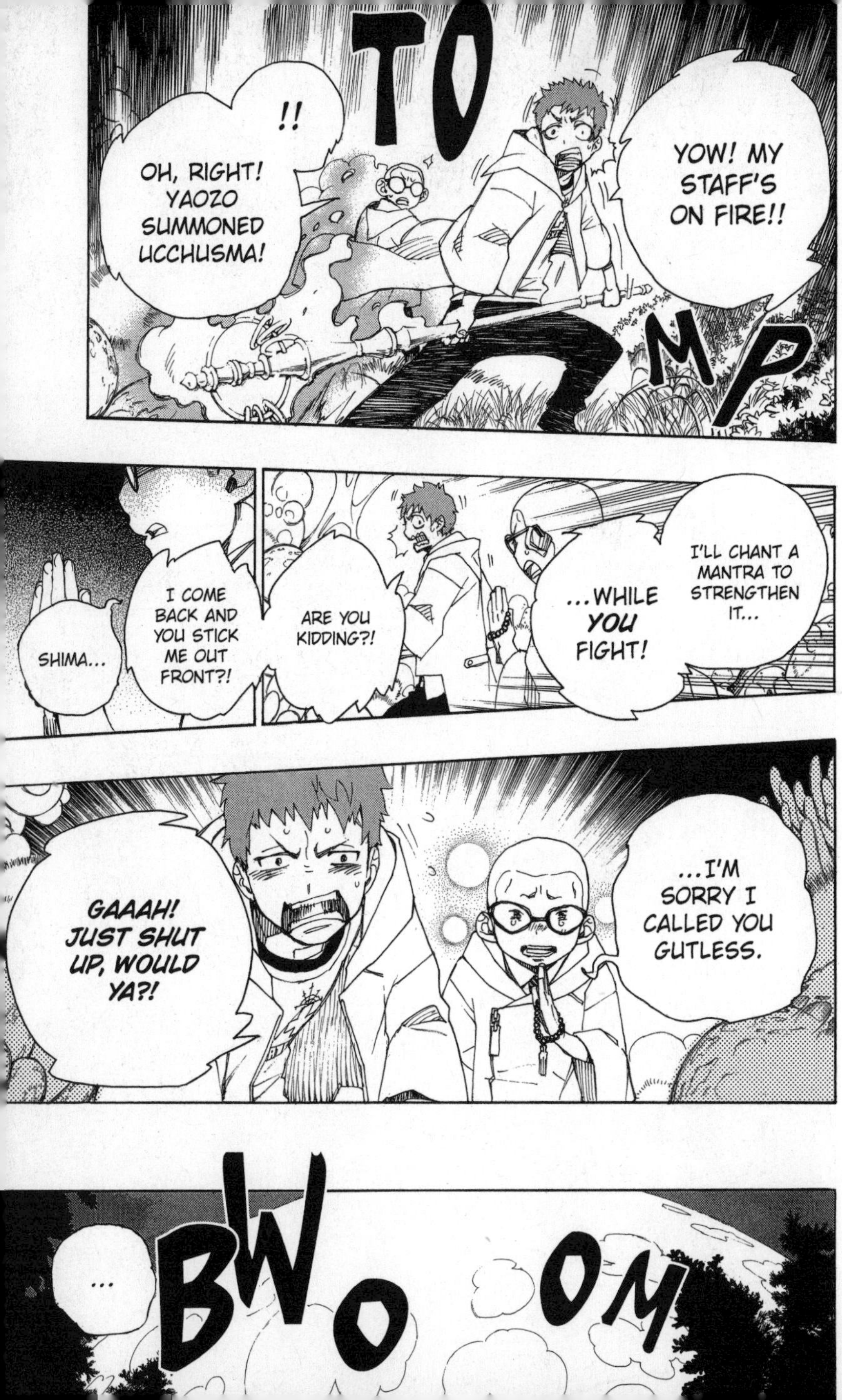
YOW! MY STAFF'S ON FIRE!!
TOMP
!!
OH, RIGHT! YAOZO SUMMONED UCCHUSMA!
I'LL CHANT A MANTRA TO STRENGTHEN IT...
...WHILE *YOU* FIGHT!
ARE YOU KIDDING?!
I COME BACK AND YOU STICK ME OUT FRONT?!
SHIMA...
...I'M SORRY I CALLED YOU GUTLESS.
GAAAH! JUST SHUT UP, WOULD YA?!
BWOOM
...

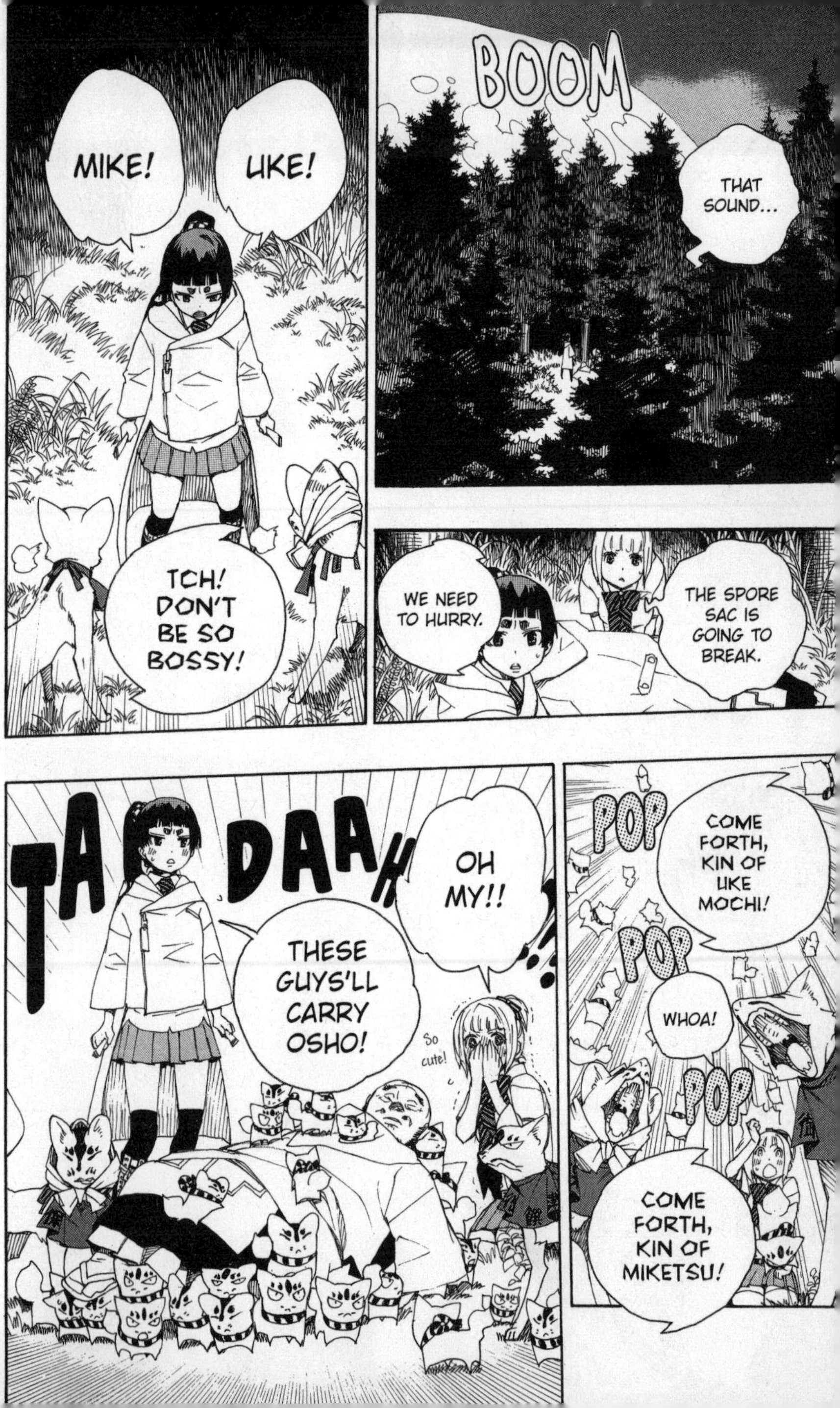

BOOM
THAT SOUND...
THE SPORE SAC IS GOING TO BREAK.
WE NEED TO HURRY.
UKE!
MIKE!
TCH! DON'T BE SO BOSSY!
COME FORTH, KIN OF UKE MOCHI!
POP
POP
WHOA!
POP
COME FORTH, KIN OF MIKETSU!
OH MY!!
TA DAAH
THESE GUYS'LL CARRY OSHO!
So cute!

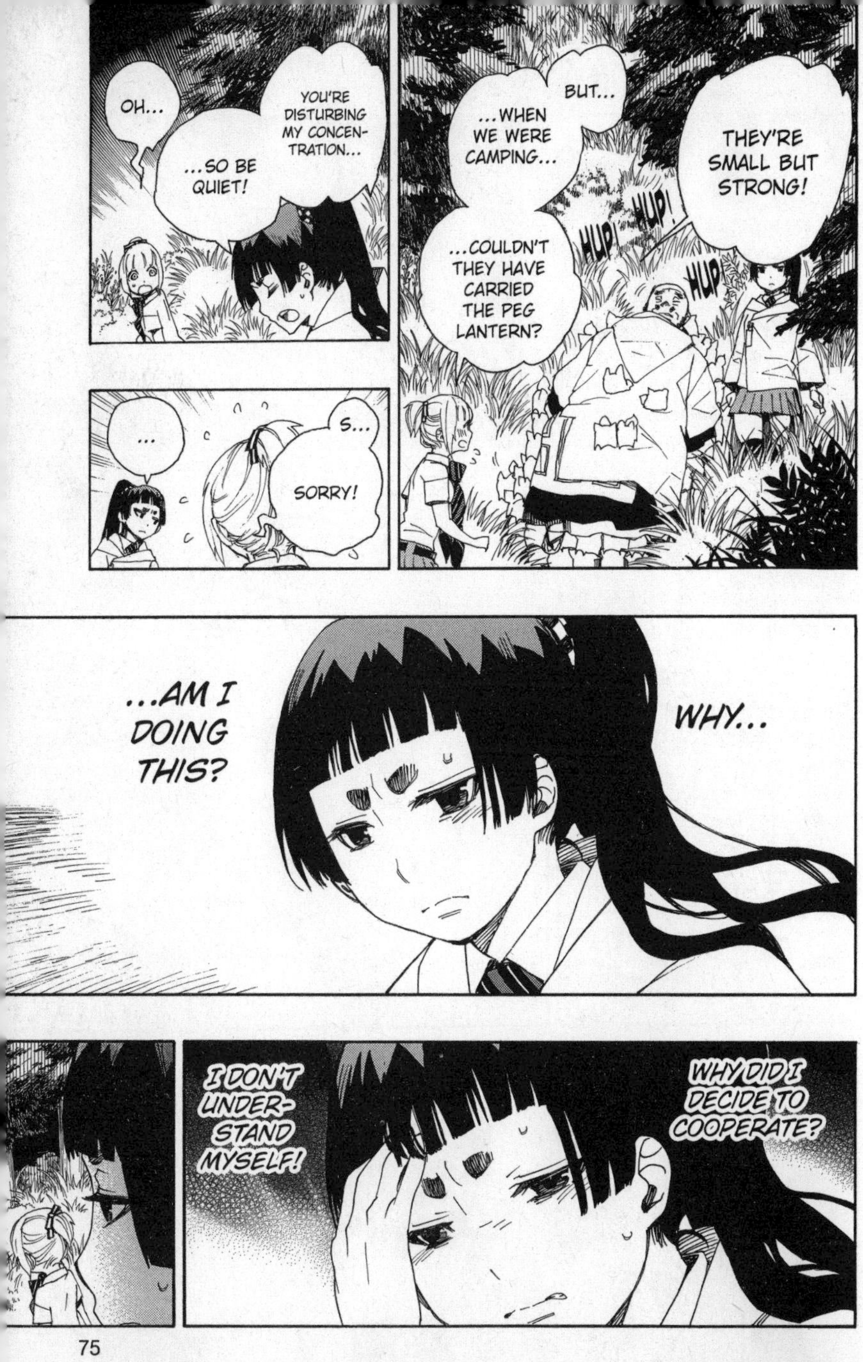
THEY'RE SMALL BUT STRONG!
HUP HUP! HUP! HUP
BUT...
...WHEN WE WERE CAMPING...
...COULDN'T THEY HAVE CARRIED THE PEG LANTERN?
YOU'RE DISTURBING MY CONCEN- TRATION...
...SO BE QUIET!
OH...
S...
SORRY!
...
WHY...
...AM I DOING THIS?
WHY DID I DECIDE TO COOPERATE?
I DON'T UNDER- STAND MYSELF!

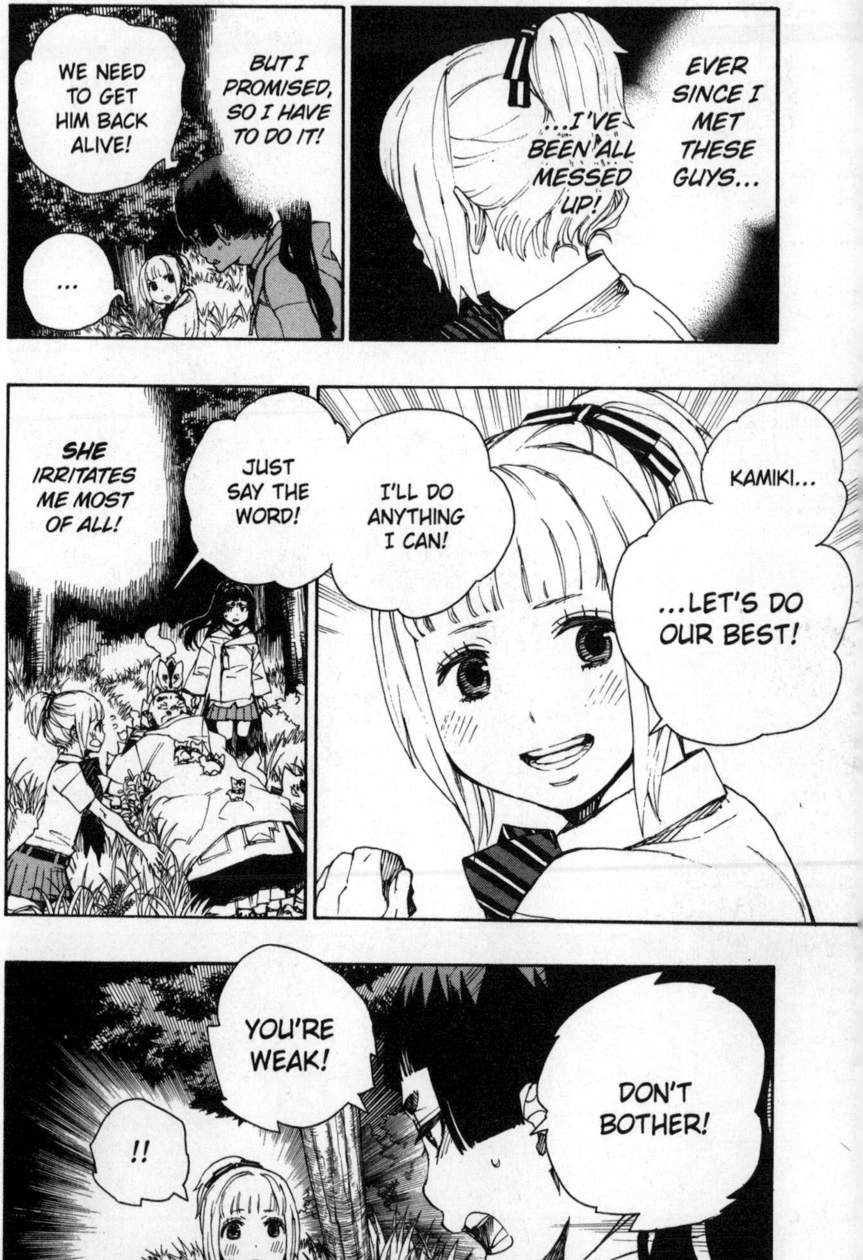
EVER SINCE I MET THESE GUYS...
...I'VE BEEN ALL MESSED UP!
BUT I PROMISED, SO I HAVE TO DO IT!
WE NEED TO GET HIM BACK ALIVE!
...
KAMIKI...
...LET'S DO OUR BEST!
I'LL DO ANYTHING I CAN!
JUST SAY THE WORD!
SHE IRRITATES ME MOST OF ALL!
DON'T BOTHER!
YOU'RE WEAK!
!!

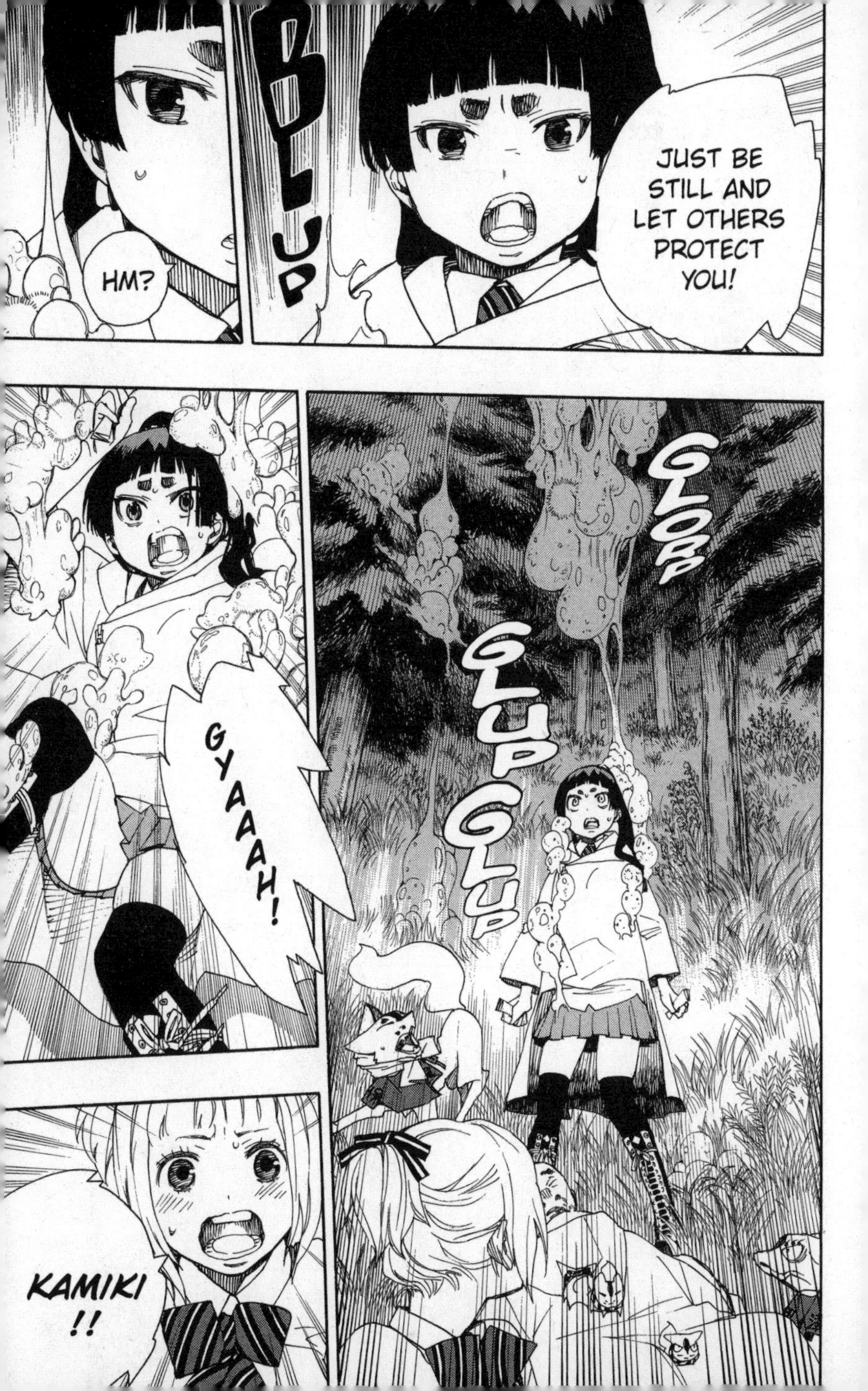
JUST BE STILL AND LET OTHERS PROTECT YOU!
BLUP
HM?
GLOPP
GLUP GLUP
GYAAAH!
KAMIKI !!

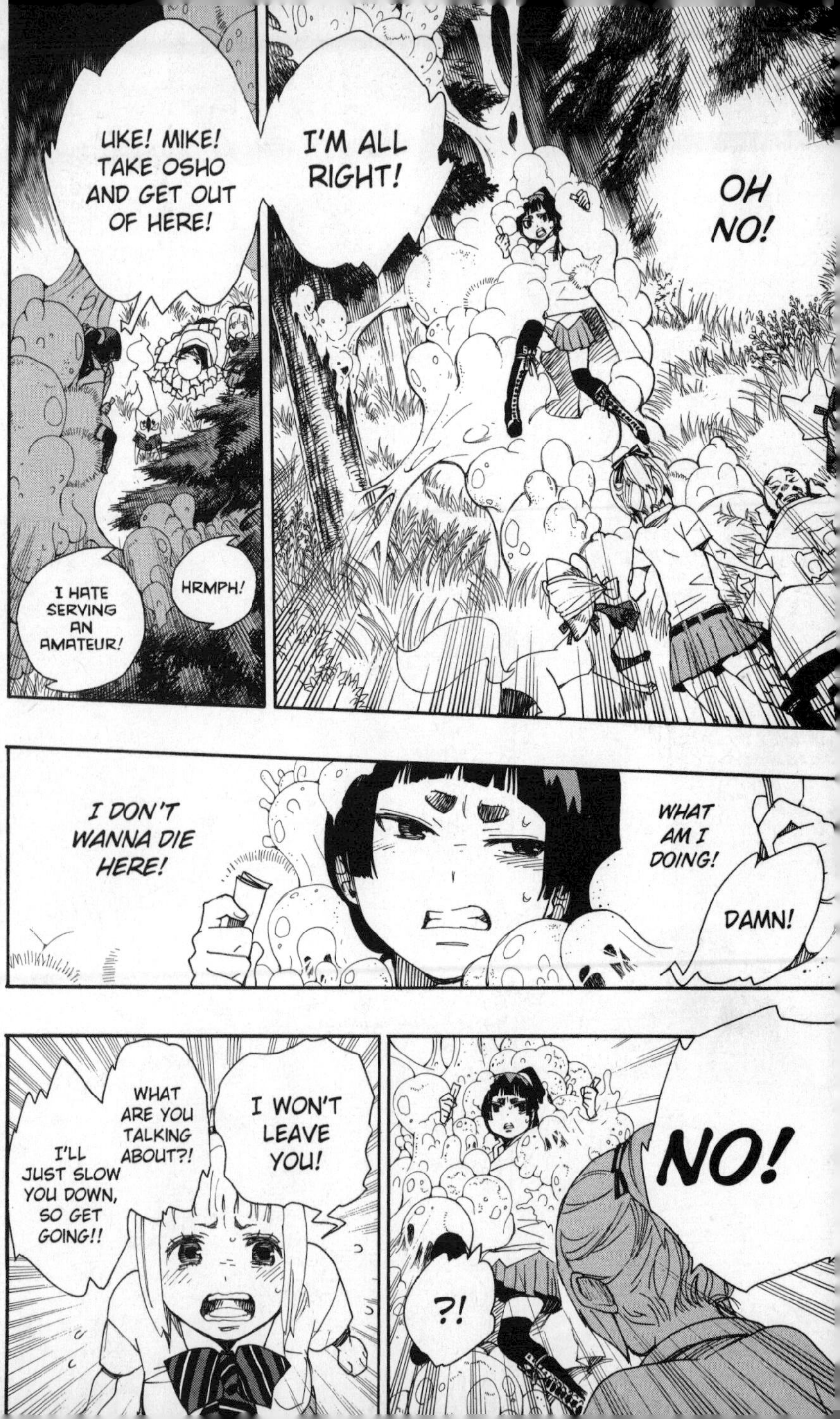
OH NO!
I'M ALL RIGHT!
UKE! MIKE! TAKE OSHO AND GET OUT OF HERE!
HRMPH!
I HATE SERVING AN AMATEUR!
WHAT AM I DOING!
DAMN!
I DON'T WANNA DIE HERE!
NO!
?!
I WON'T LEAVE YOU!
WHAT ARE YOU TALKING ABOUT?!
I'LL JUST SLOW YOU DOWN, SO GET GOING!!

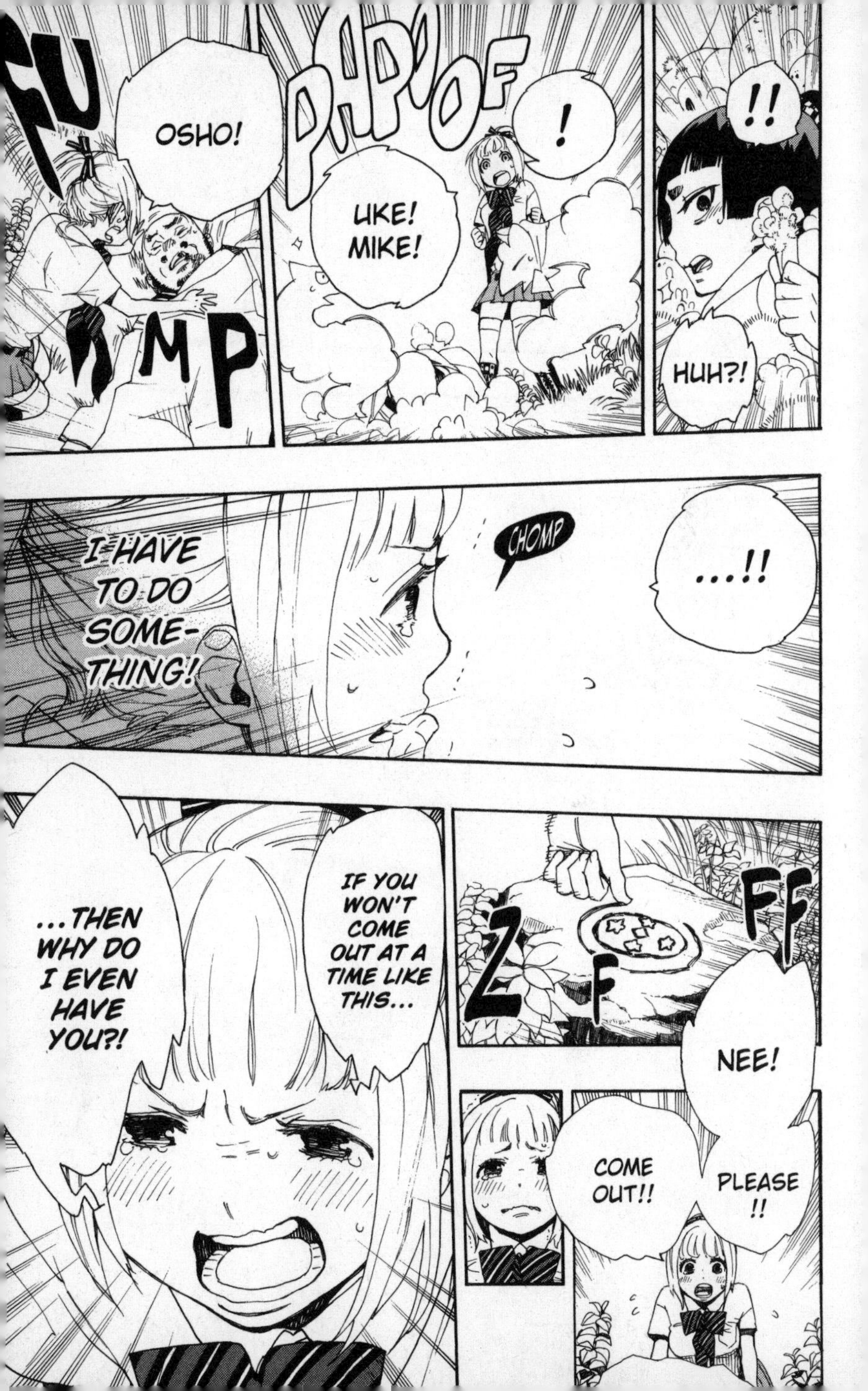
!!
HUH?!
PHPOOF
!
UKE! MIKE!
FU
MP
OSHO!
...!!
CHOMP
I HAVE TO DO SOME-THING!
FF
Z
F
NEE!
PLEASE !!
COME OUT!!
IF YOU WON'T COME OUT AT A TIME LIKE THIS...
...THEN WHY DO I EVEN HAVE YOU?!

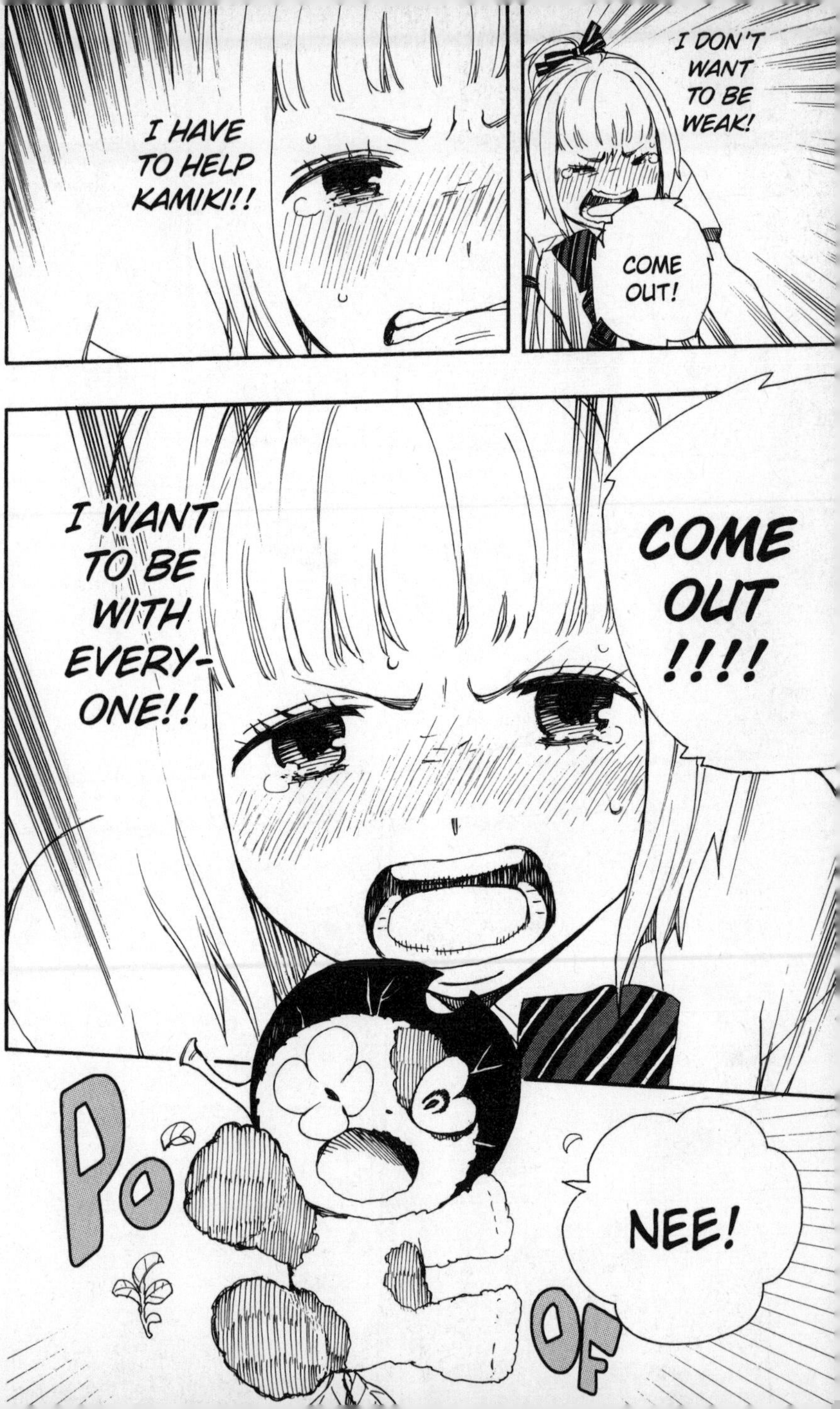
I DON'T WANT TO BE WEAK!
COME OUT!
I HAVE TO HELP KAMIKI!!
COME OUT!!!!
I WANT TO BE WITH EVERY-ONE!!
NEE!
POOF

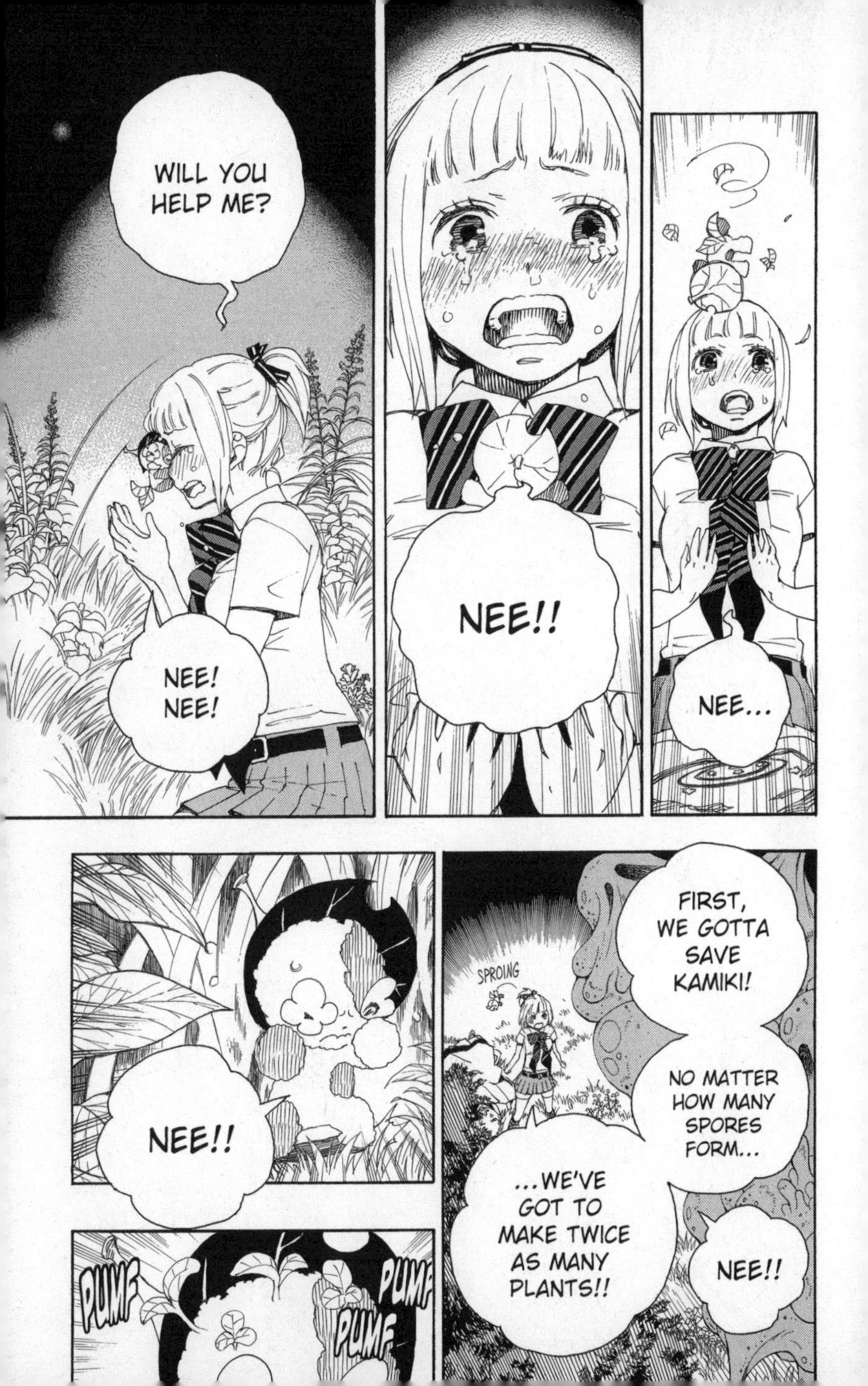
NEE...
NEE!!
WILL YOU HELP ME?
NEE! NEE!
FIRST, WE GOTTA SAVE KAMIKI!
SPROING
NO MATTER HOW MANY SPORES FORM...
...WE'VE GOT TO MAKE TWICE AS MANY PLANTS!!
NEE!!
NEE!!
PUMF
PUMF
PUMF

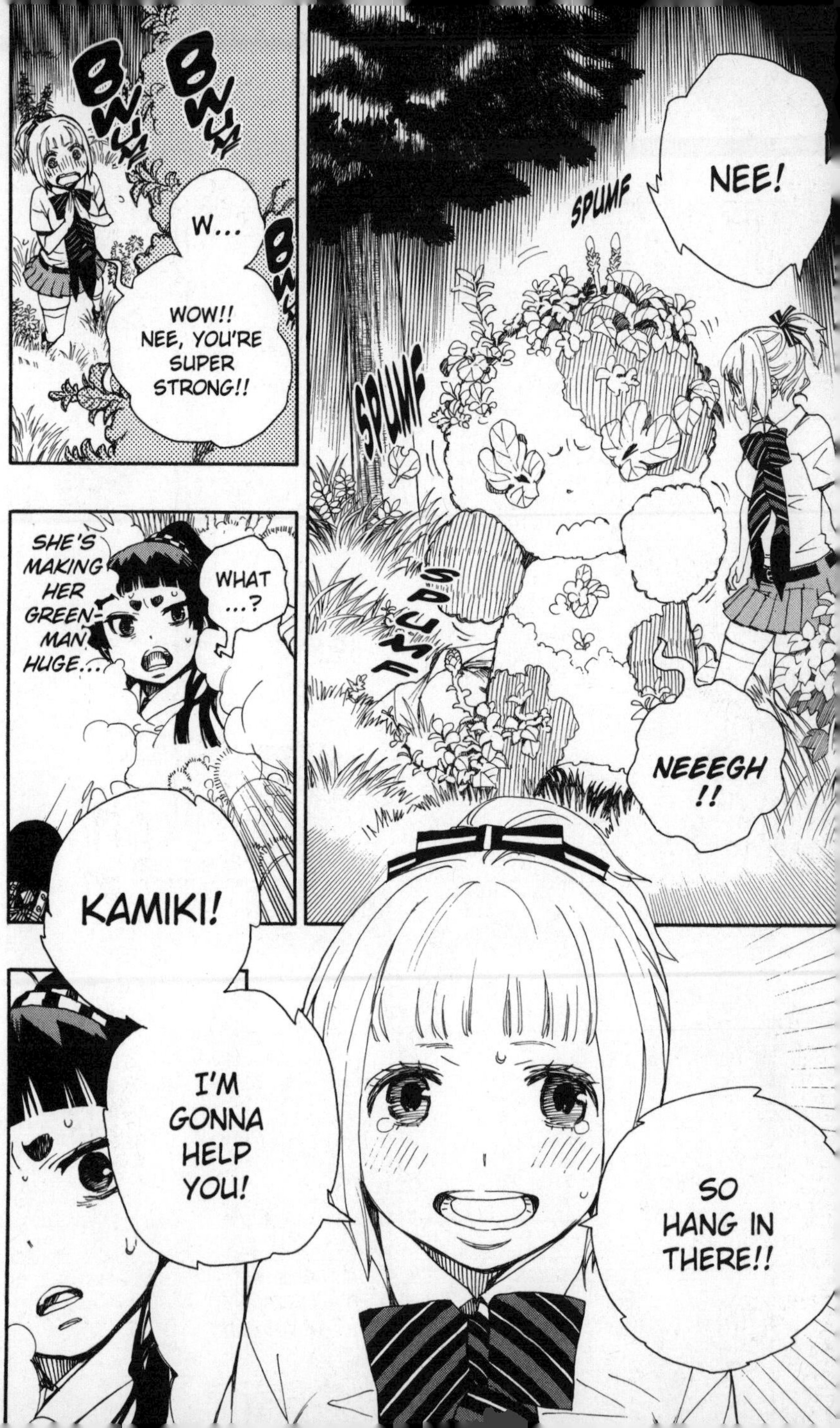
NEE!
SPUMF
SPUMF
SPUMF
NEEEGH!!
BWAH
BWAH
W...
WOW!! NEE, YOU'RE SUPER STRONG!!
BWAH
WHAT...?
SHE'S MAKING HER GREEN-MAN HUGE...
KAMIKI!
I'M GONNA HELP YOU!
SO HANG IN THERE!!

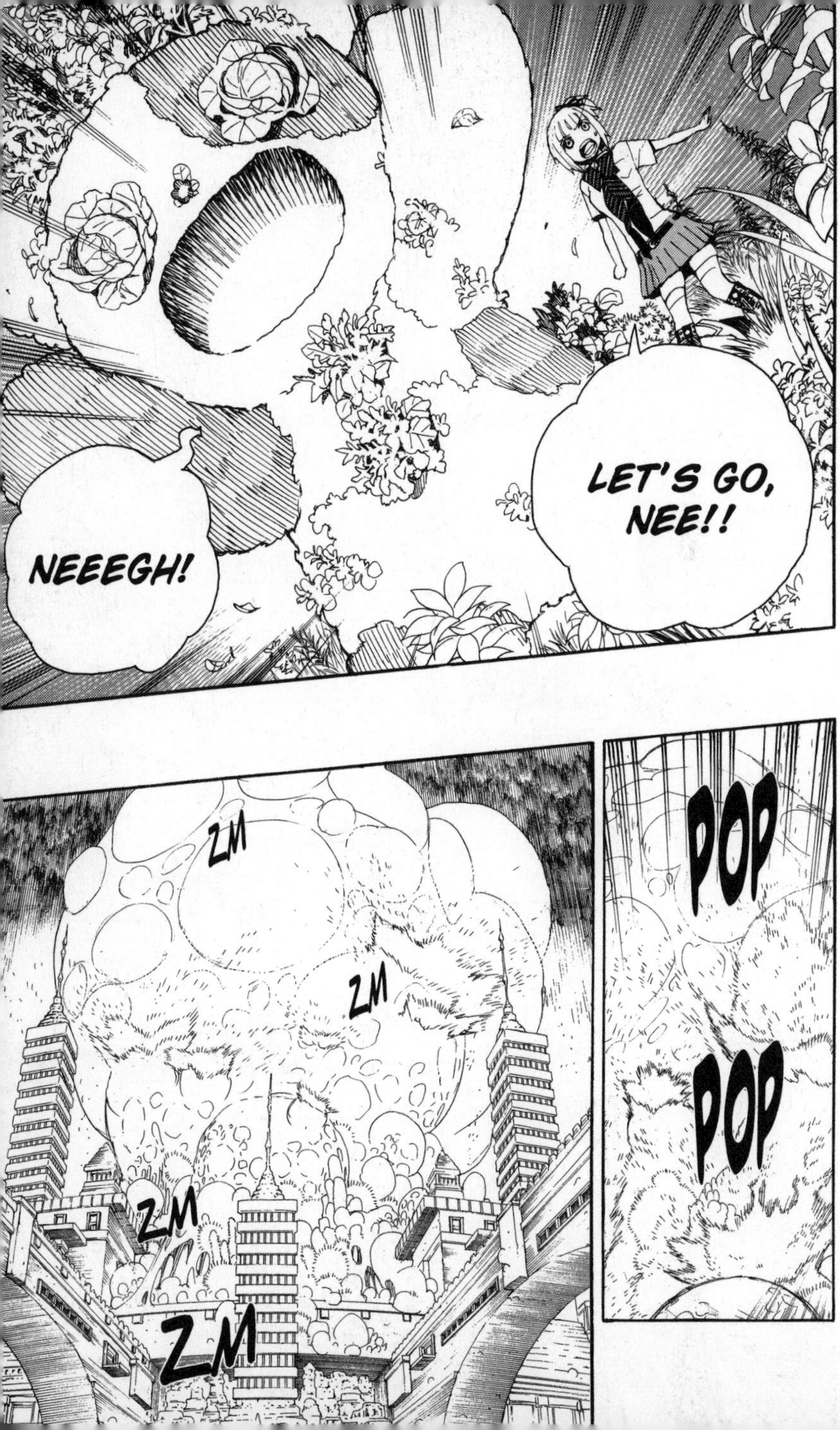
LET'S GO, NEE!!
NEEEGH!
POP
POP
ZM
ZM
ZM
ZM

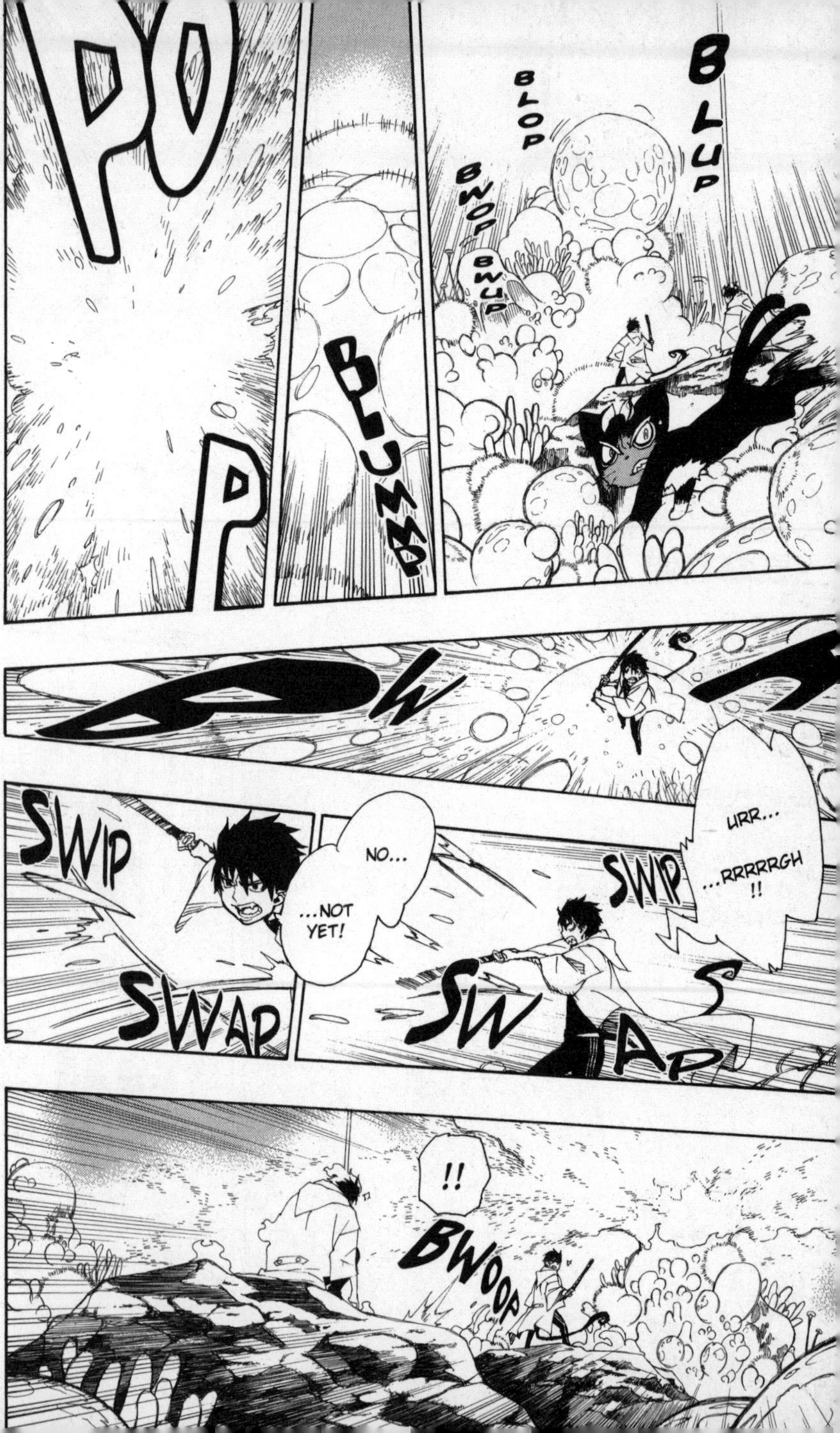
BLUP
BLOP
BWOP
BWUP
BLUMMP
POP
POW
URR...
...RRRRGH!!
SWIP
SWAP
NO...
...NOT YET!
SWIP
SWAP
!!
BWOOP

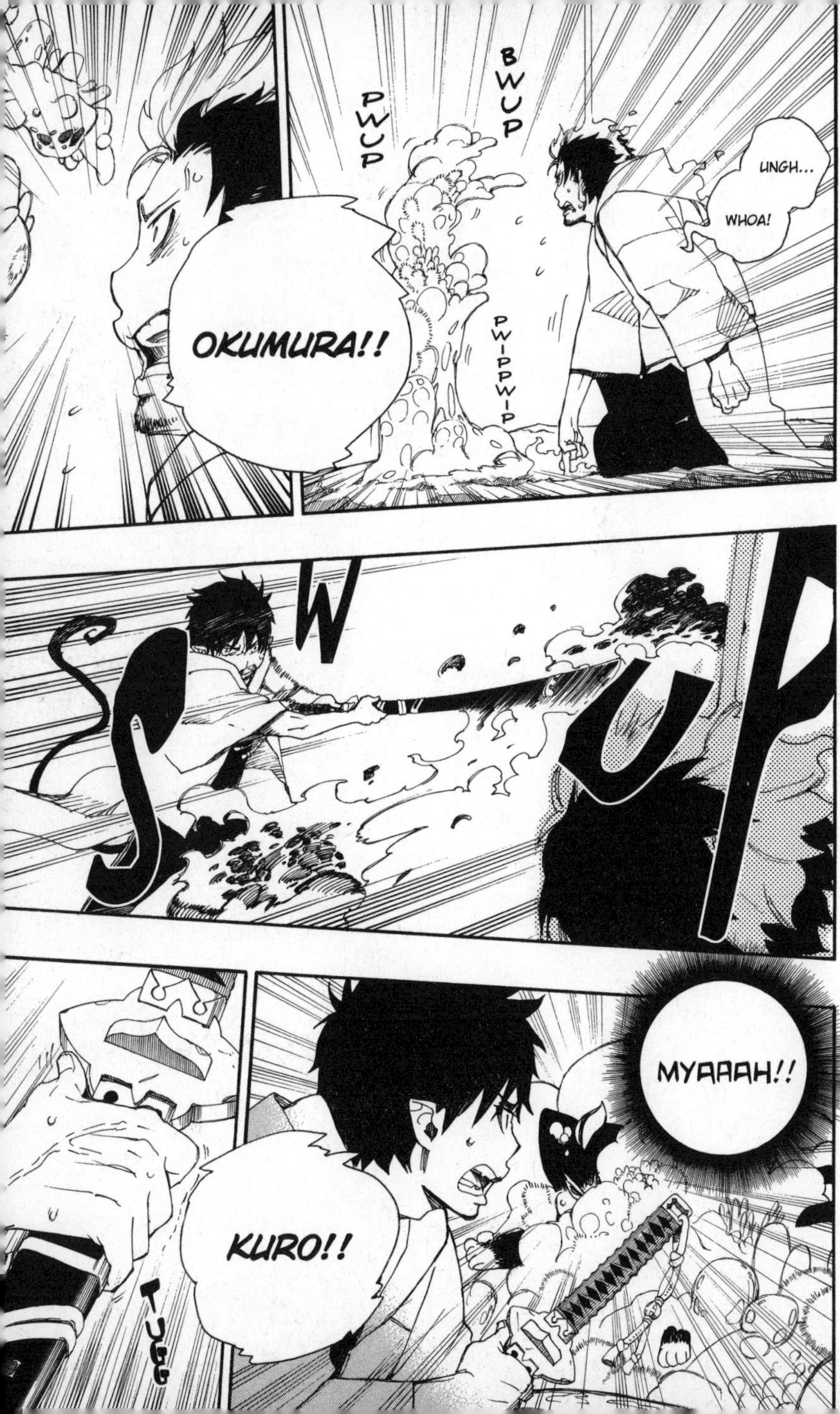
UNGH...
WHOA!
BWUP
PWUP
PWIPPWIP
OKUMURA!!
SWUP
MYAAAH!!
KURO!!
TUG

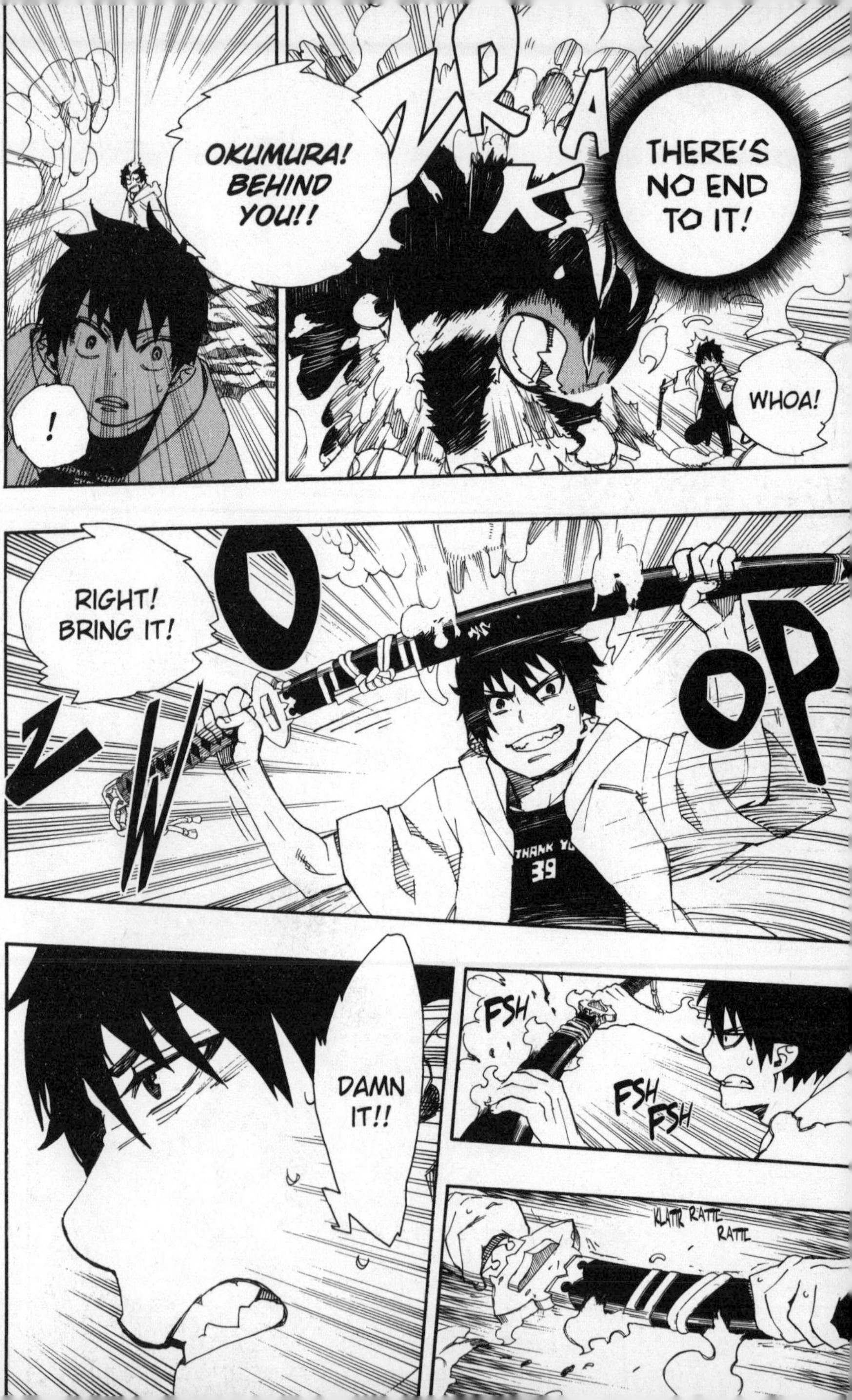
ZRAK
THERE'S NO END TO IT!
WHOA!
OKUMURA! BEHIND YOU!!
!
RIGHT! BRING IT!
ZWOOP
FSH
FSH FSH
KLATR RATTL RATTL
DAMN IT!!

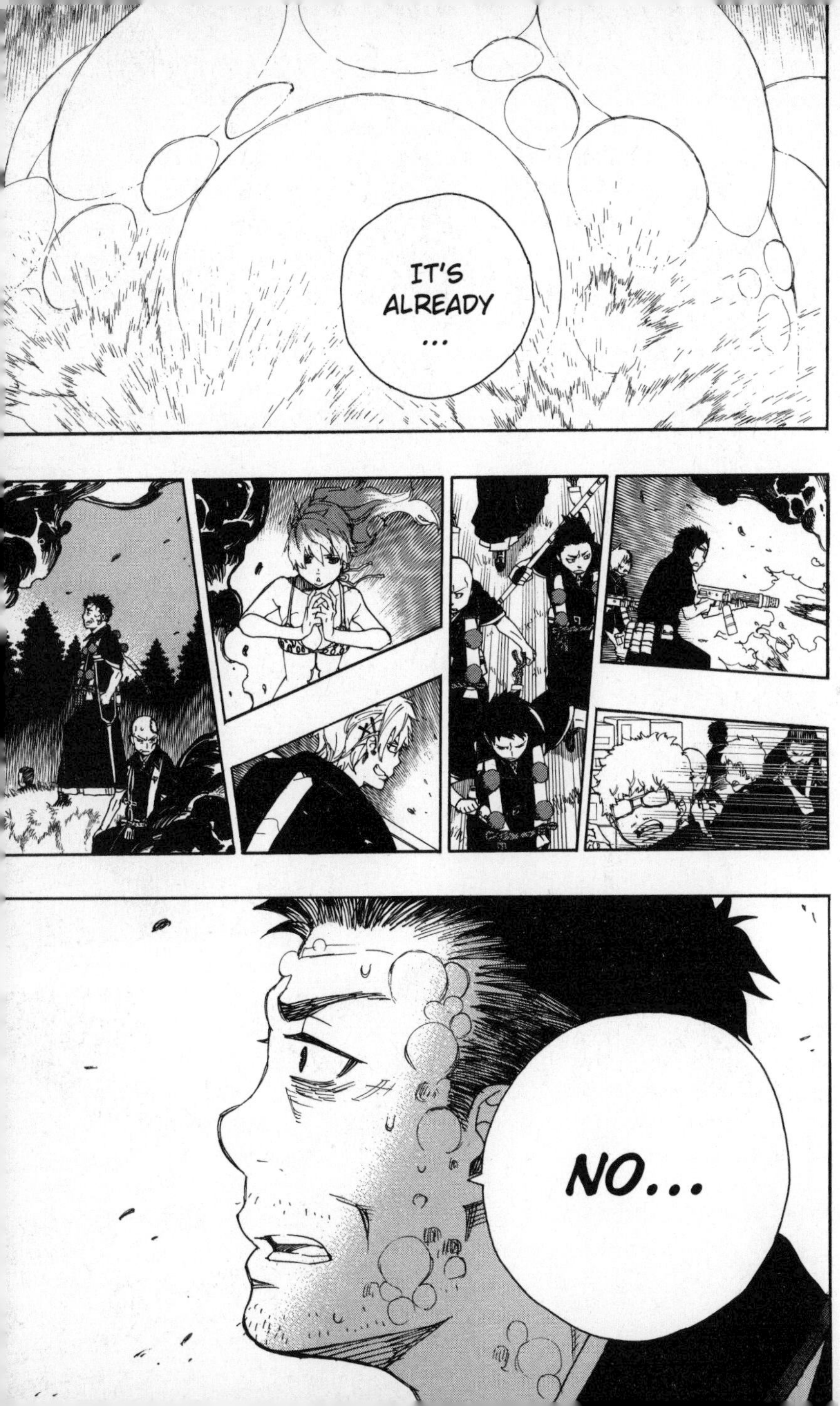
IT'S ALREADY ...
NO...

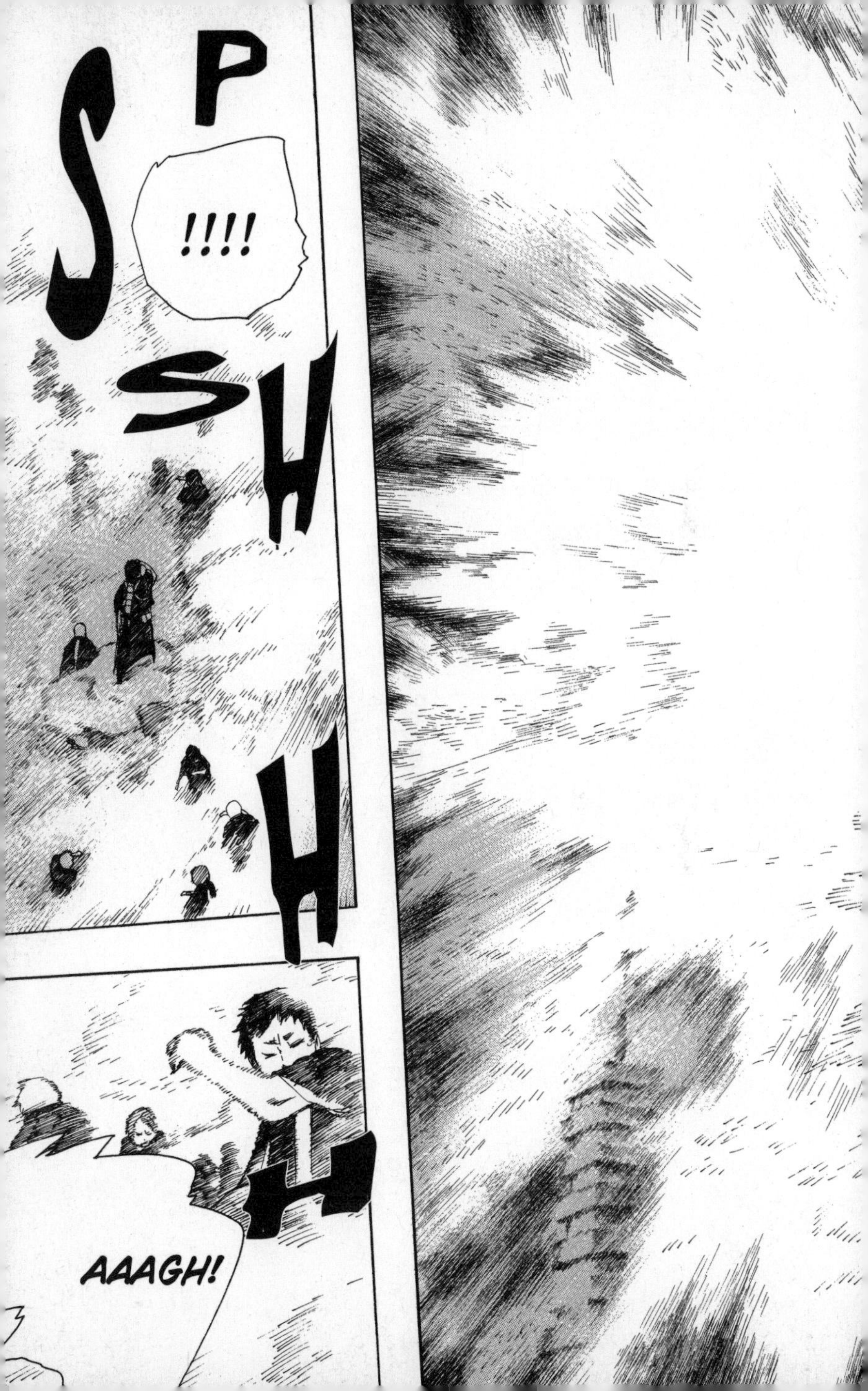
!!!!
SPSSHHH
AAAGH!

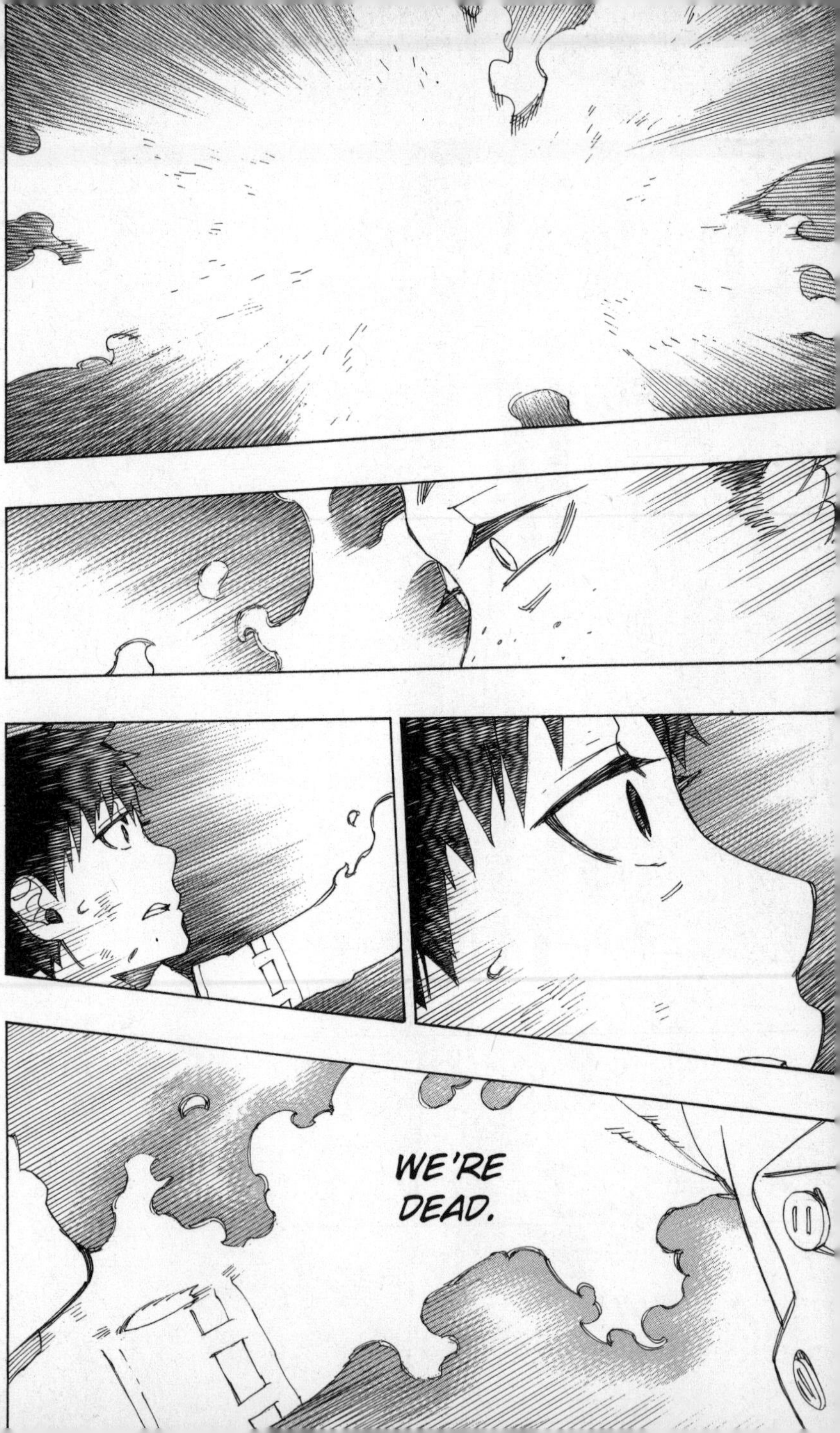
WE'RE DEAD.

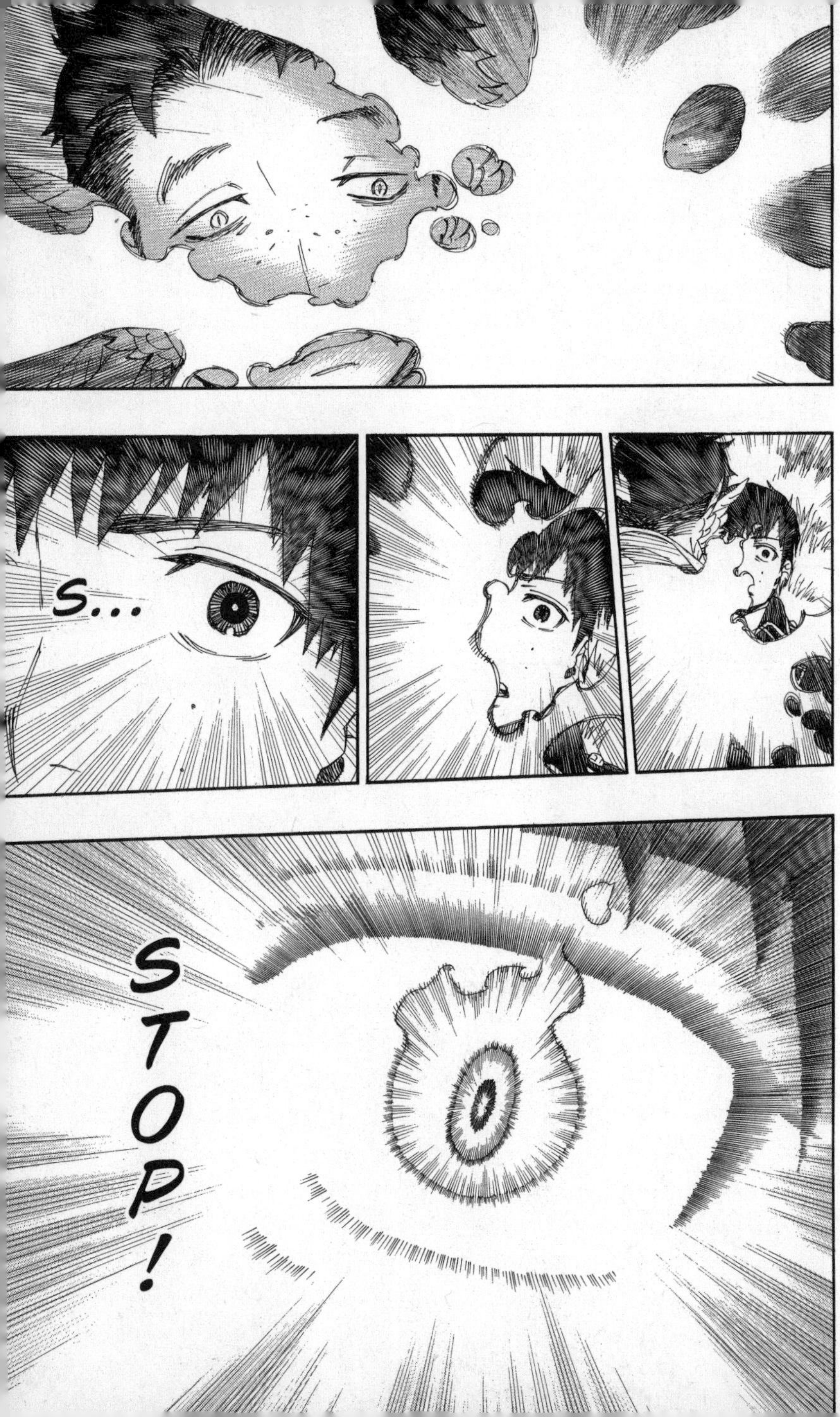
S...
STOP!

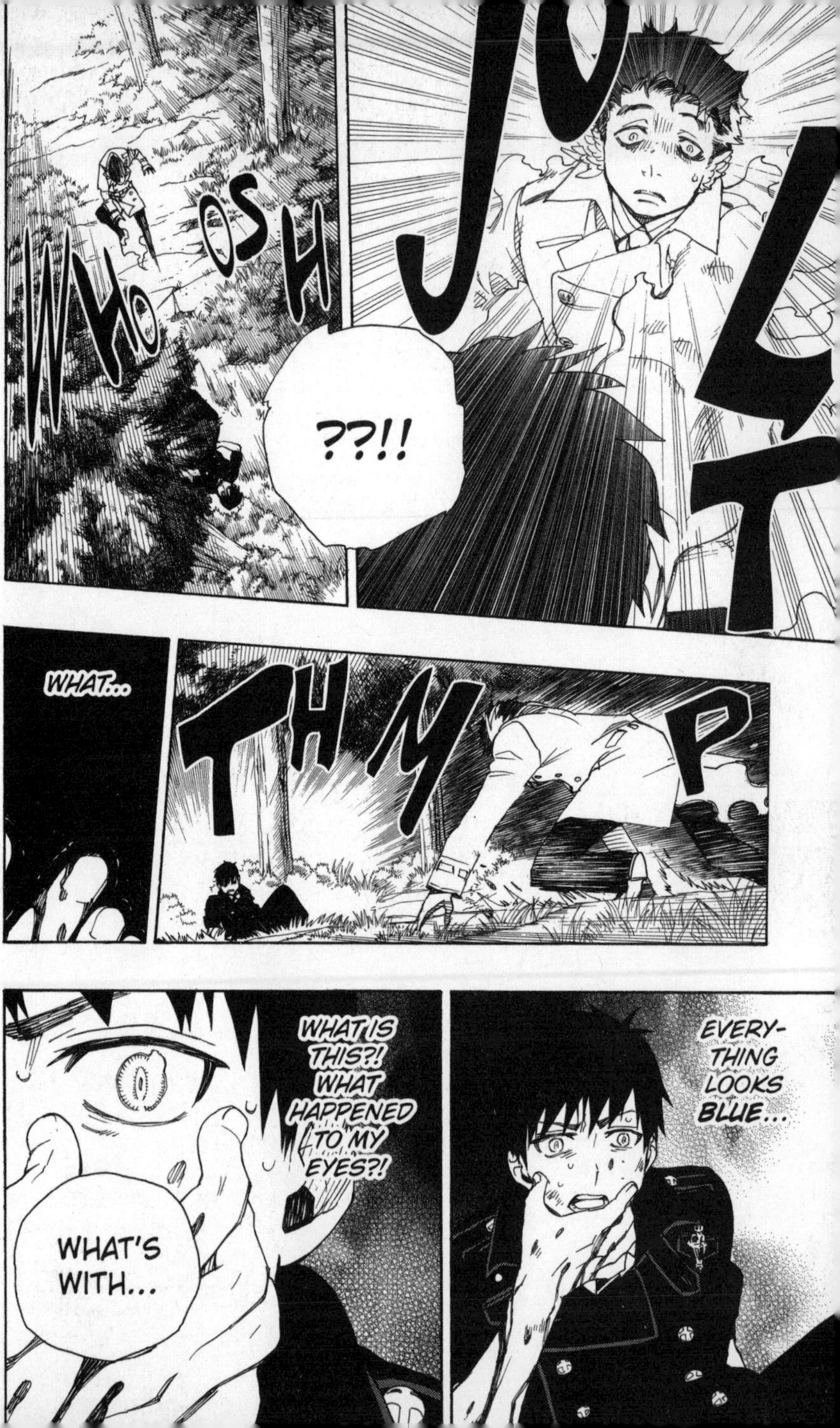
JOLT
??!!
WHOOSH
THUMP
WHAT...
EVERY-THING LOOKS BLUE...
WHAT IS THIS?! WHAT HAPPENED TO MY EYES?!
WHAT'S WITH...

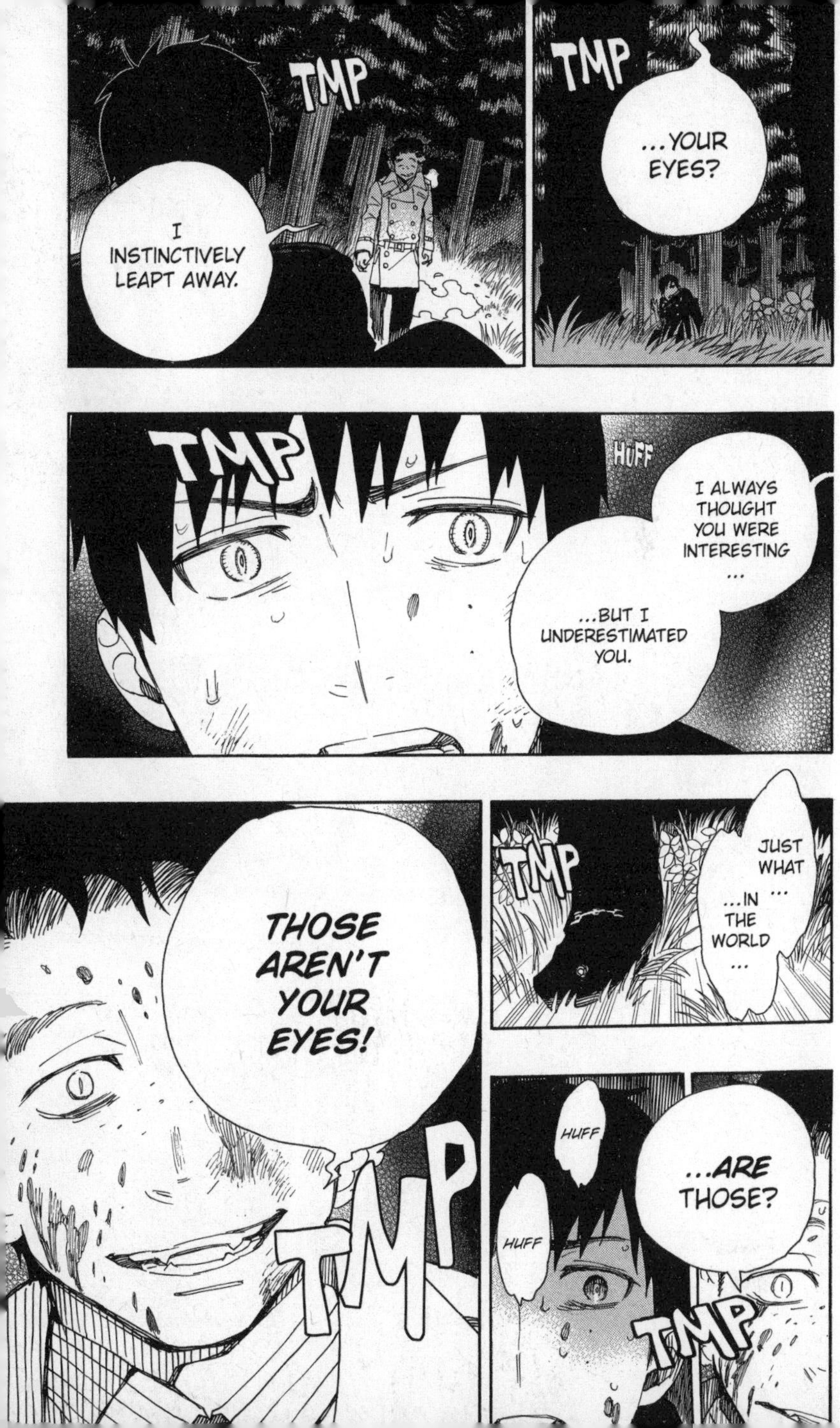
TMP
...YOUR EYES?
TMP
I INSTINCTIVELY LEAPT AWAY.
HUFF
I ALWAYS THOUGHT YOU WERE INTERESTING...
TMP
...BUT I UNDERESTIMATED YOU.
JUST WHAT...
...IN THE WORLD...
TMP
HUFF
...ARE THOSE?
HUFF
TMP
THOSE AREN'T YOUR EYES!
TMP

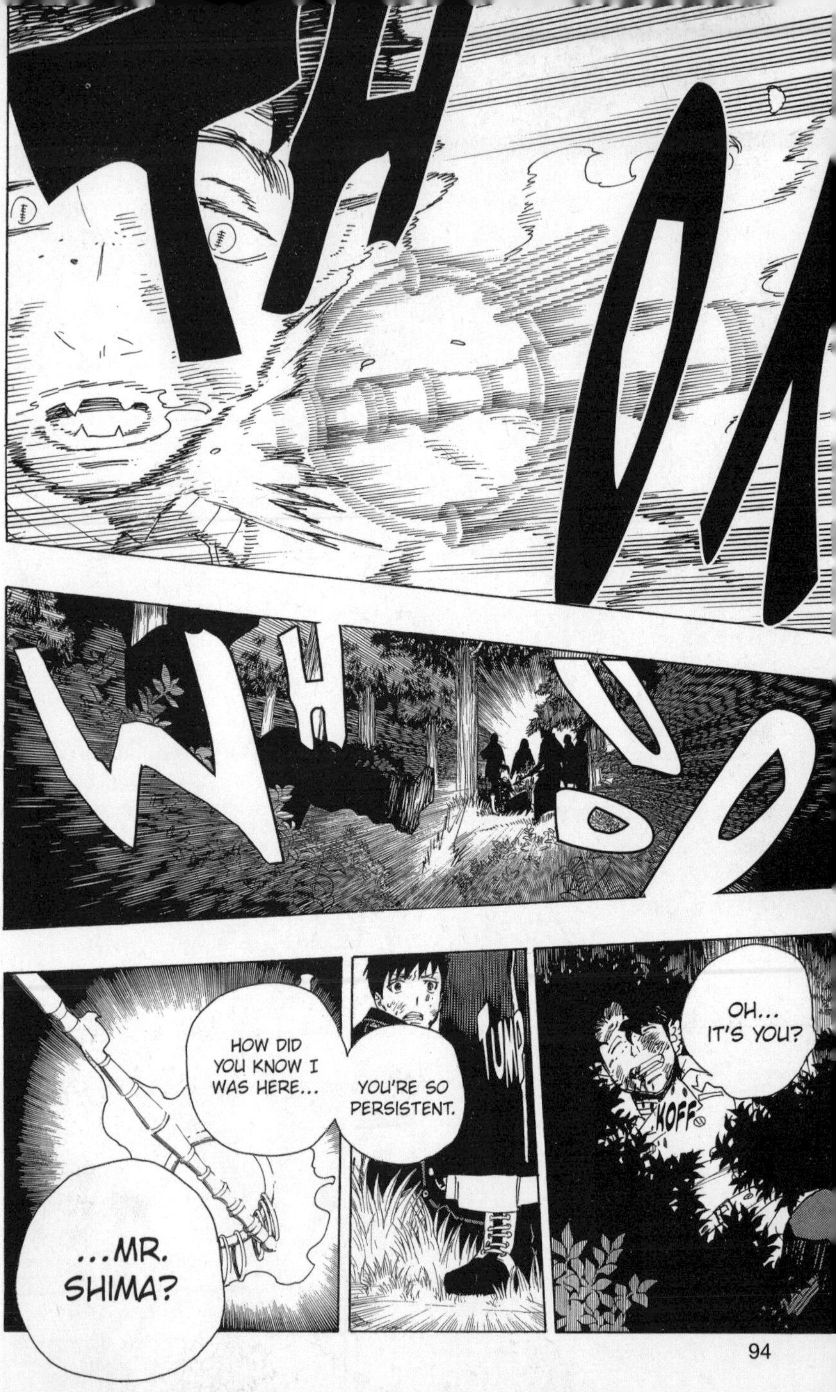
OH...
IT'S YOU?
KOFF
TUMP
HOW DID YOU KNOW I WAS HERE...
YOU'RE SO PERSISTENT.
...MR. SHIMA?

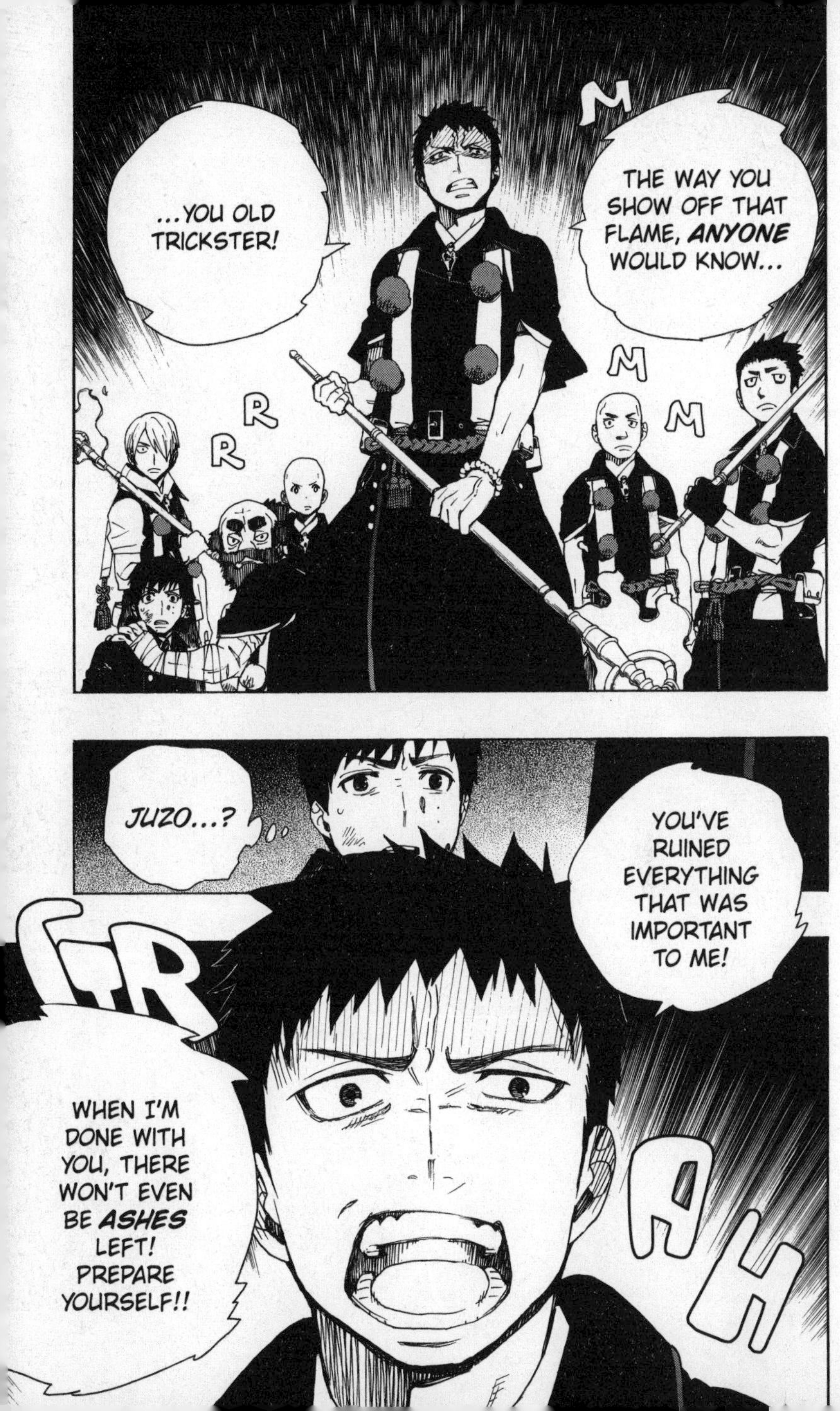

M
THE WAY YOU SHOW OFF THAT FLAME, ANYONE WOULD KNOW...
...YOU OLD TRICKSTER!
M
M
R
R
JUZO...?
YOU'VE RUINED EVERYTHING THAT WAS IMPORTANT TO ME!
AH
GR
WHEN I'M DONE WITH YOU, THERE WON'T EVEN BE ASHES LEFT! PREPARE YOURSELF!!

Blue Exorcist Chapter 30: Fateful Occurrence

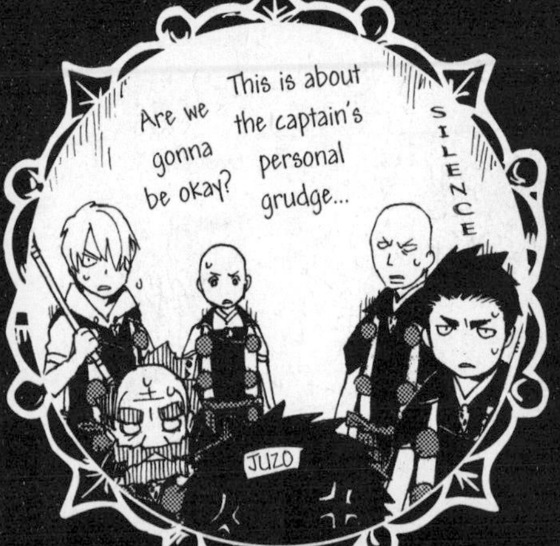
SILENCE
This is about the captain's personal grudge...
Are we gonna be okay?
JUZO

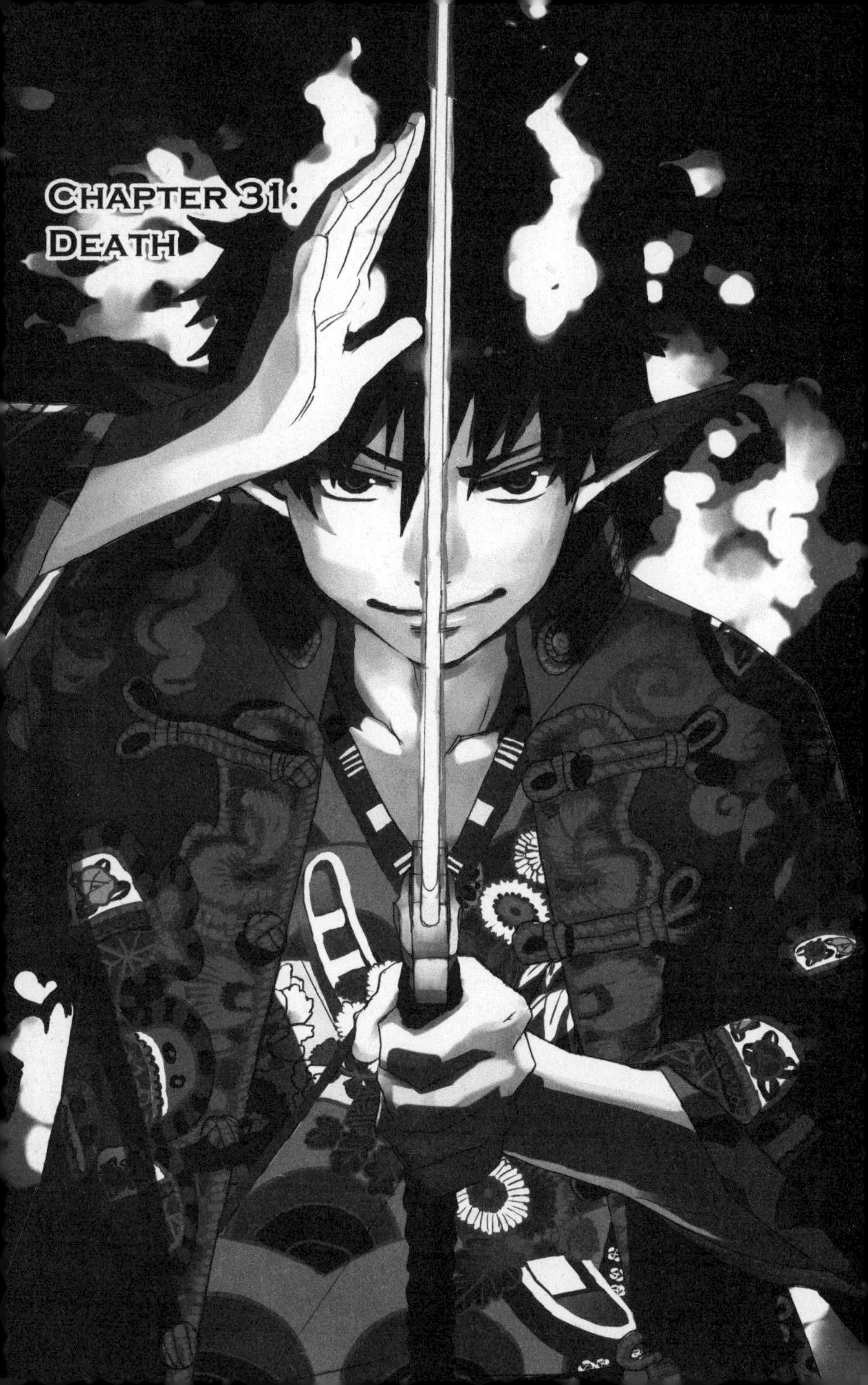
Chapter 31:
Death

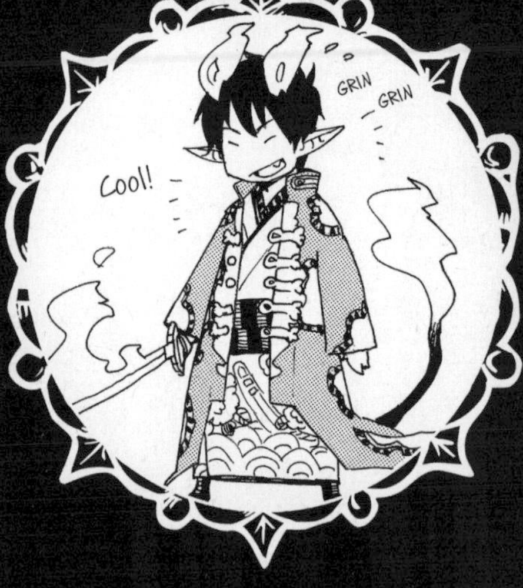
Cool!
GRIN
GRIN

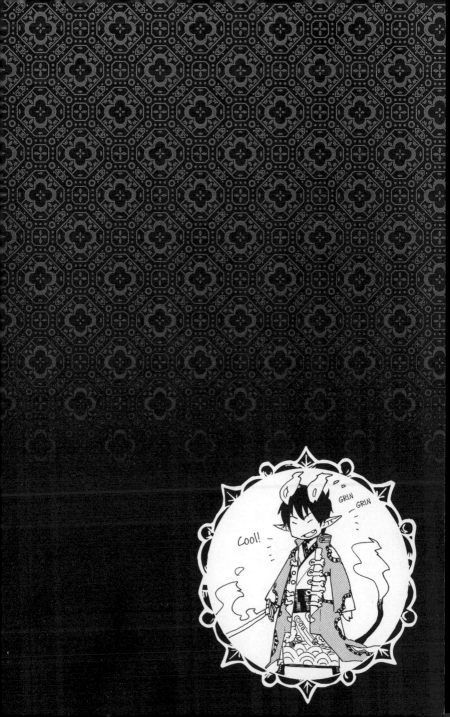

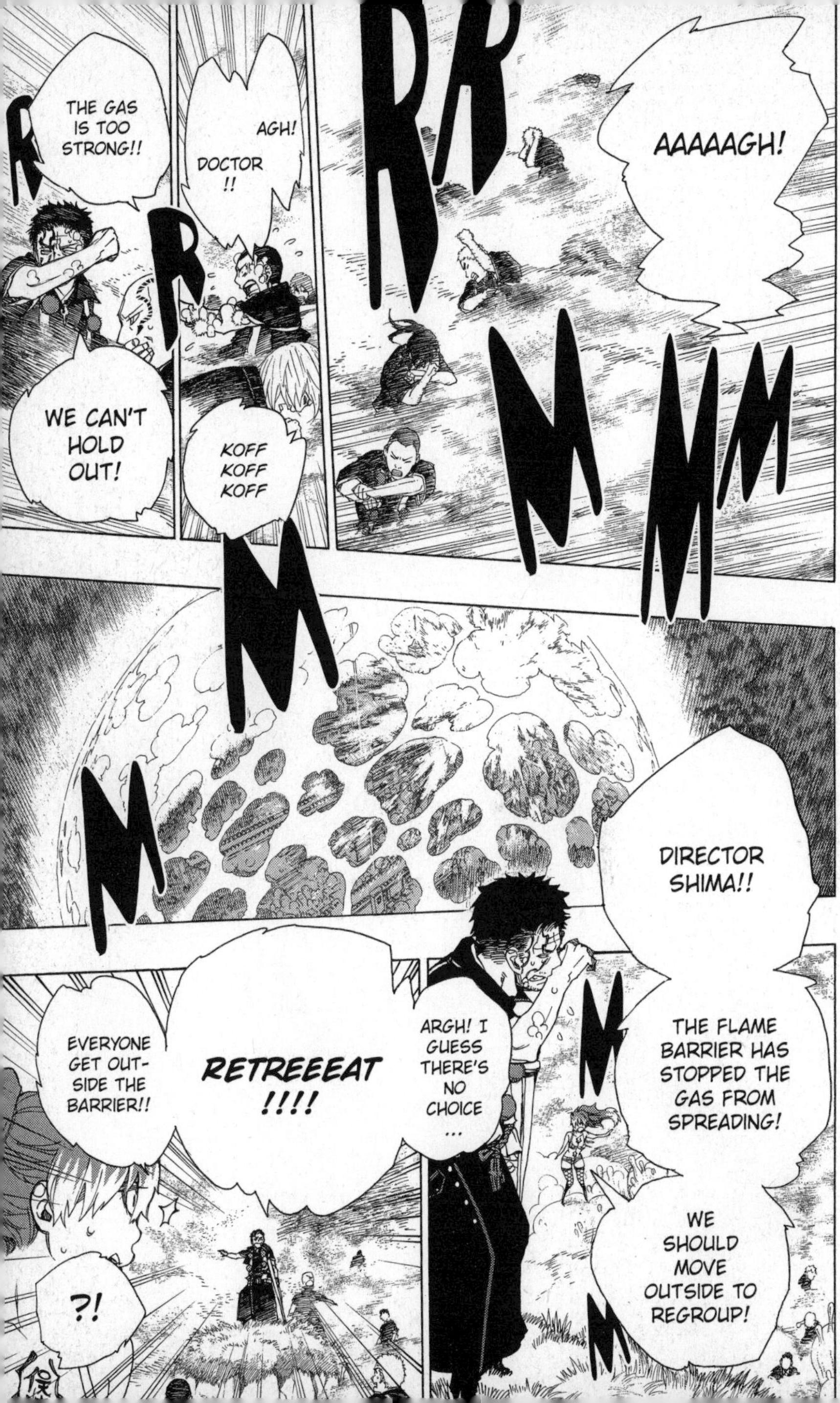
AAAAAGH!
RRRRMMMMMM
AGH!
DOCTOR!!
KOFF KOFF KOFF
THE GAS IS TOO STRONG!!
WE CAN'T HOLD OUT!
MMM
DIRECTOR SHIMA!!
THE FLAME BARRIER HAS STOPPED THE GAS FROM SPREADING!
WE SHOULD MOVE OUTSIDE TO REGROUP!
MM
ARGH! I GUESS THERE'S NO CHOICE...
RETREEEAT!!!!
EVERYONE GET OUTSIDE THE BARRIER!!
?!

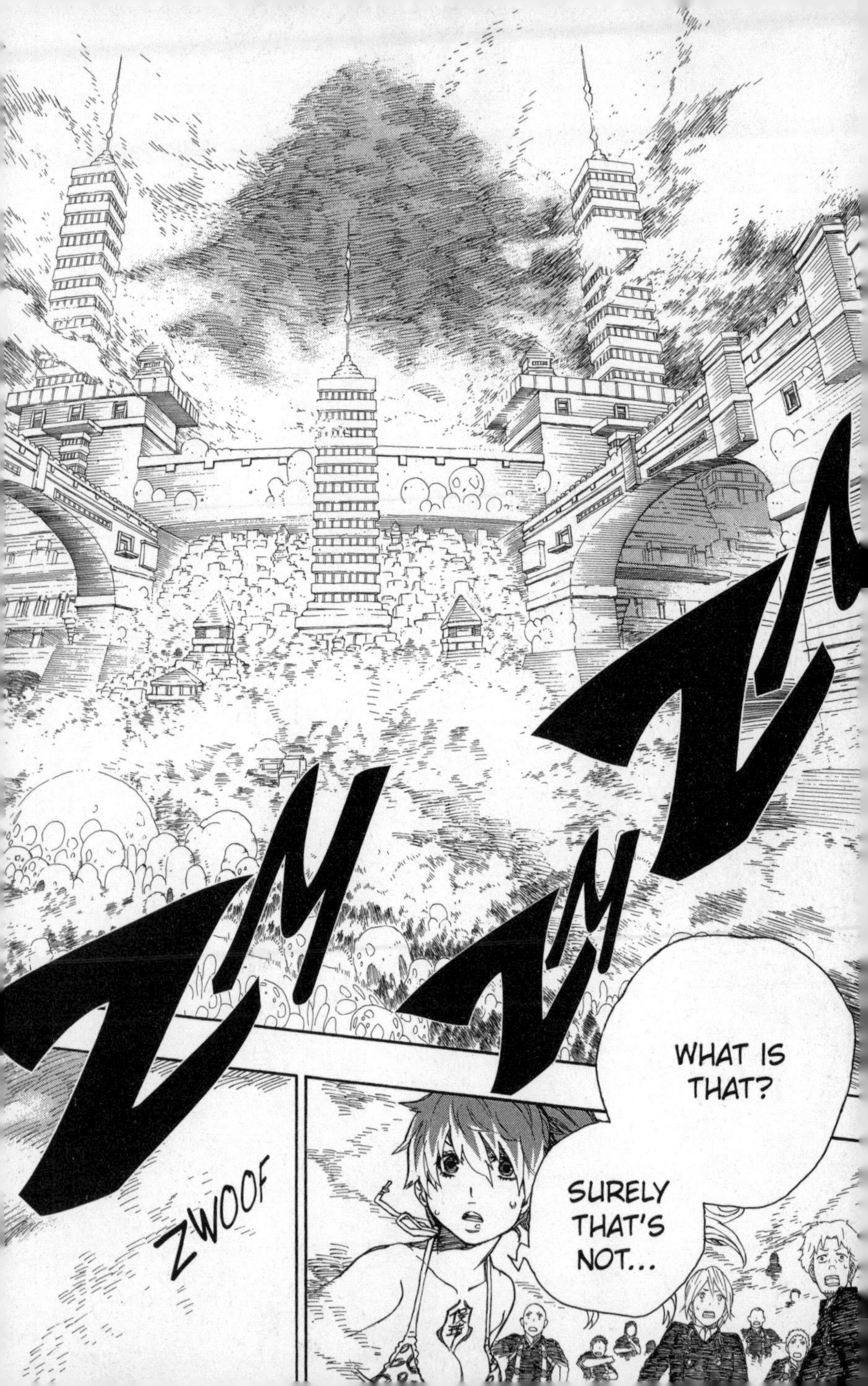
ZWOOF
WHAT IS THAT?
SURELY THAT'S NOT...

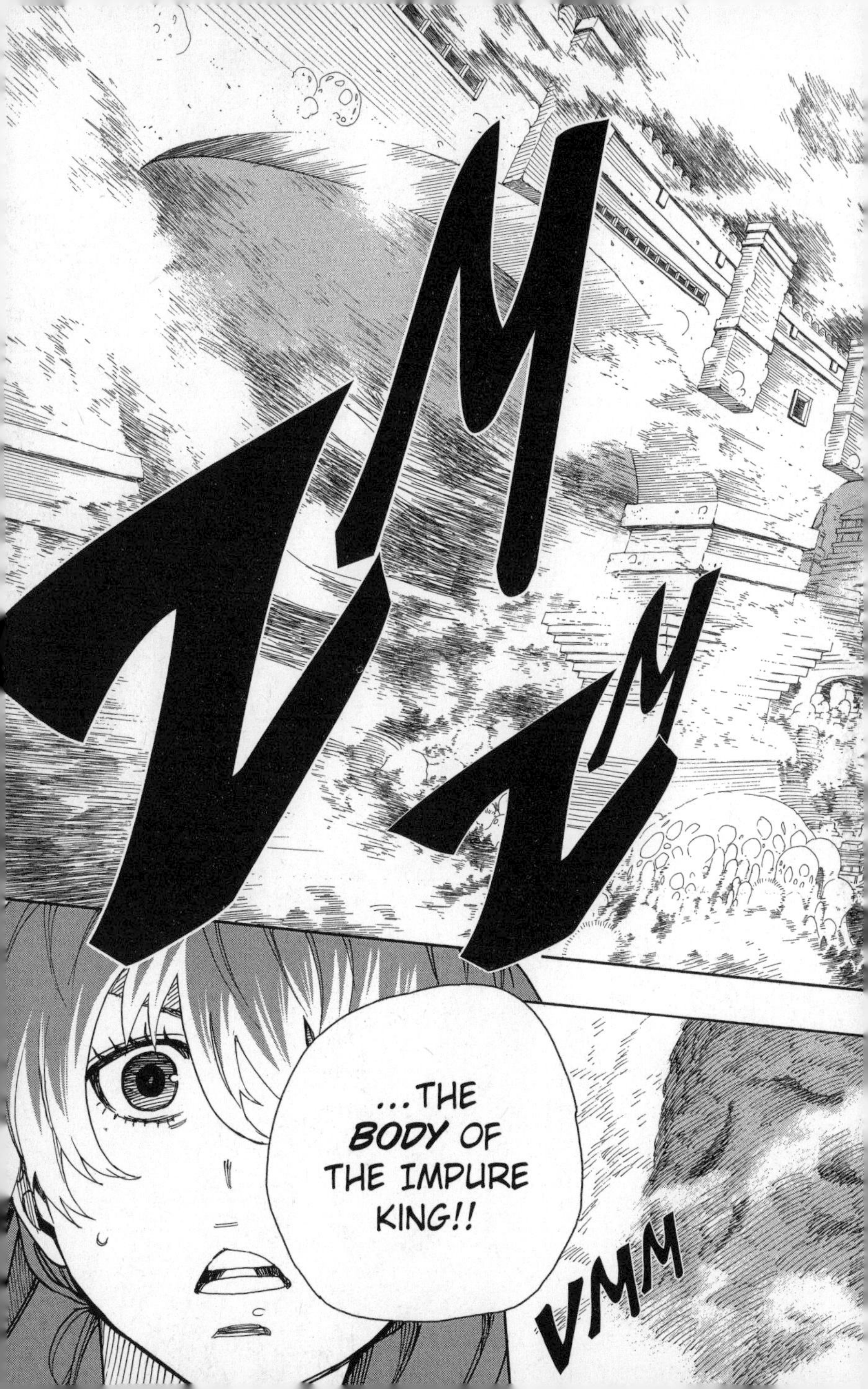
...THE *BODY* OF THE IMPURE KING!!
VMM

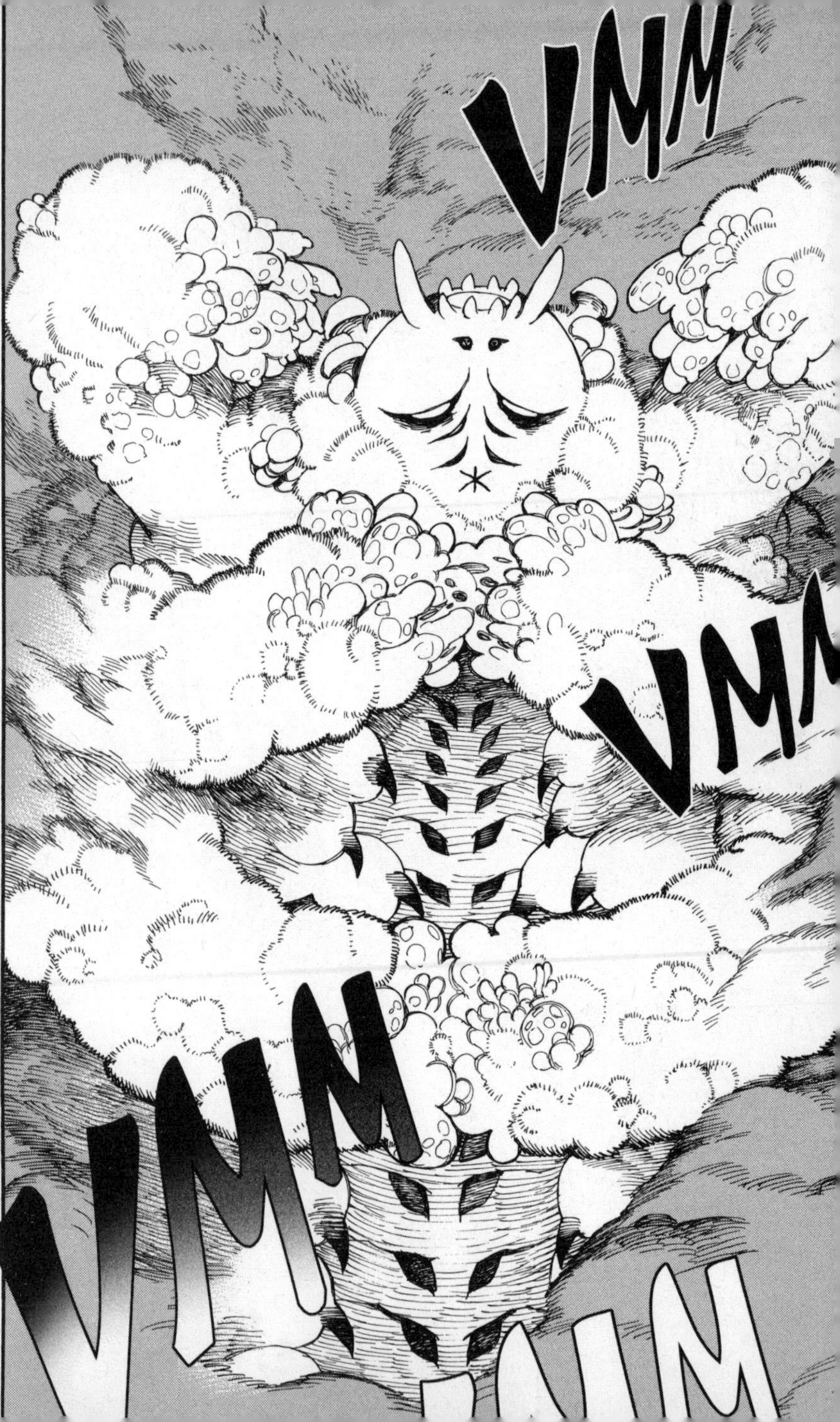
VMM
VMM
VMM

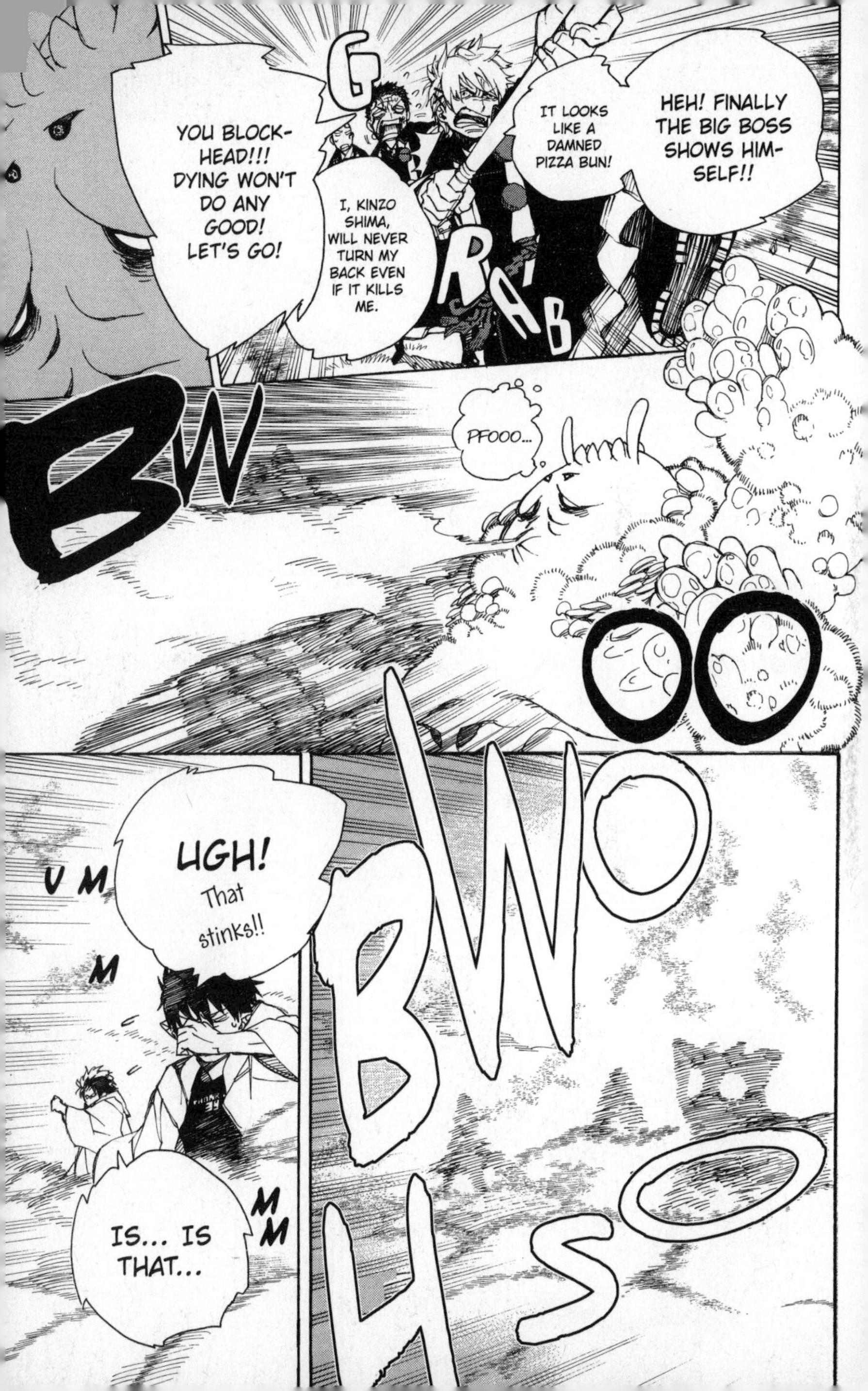
HEH! FINALLY THE BIG BOSS SHOWS HIMSELF!!
IT LOOKS LIKE A DAMNED PIZZA BUN!
GRAB
I, KINZO SHIMA, WILL NEVER TURN MY BACK EVEN IF IT KILLS ME.
YOU BLOCKHEAD!!! DYING WON'T DO ANY GOOD! LET'S GO!
PFOOO...
BWOO
BWOOSH
UGH! That stinks!!
UMMMM
IS... IS THAT...

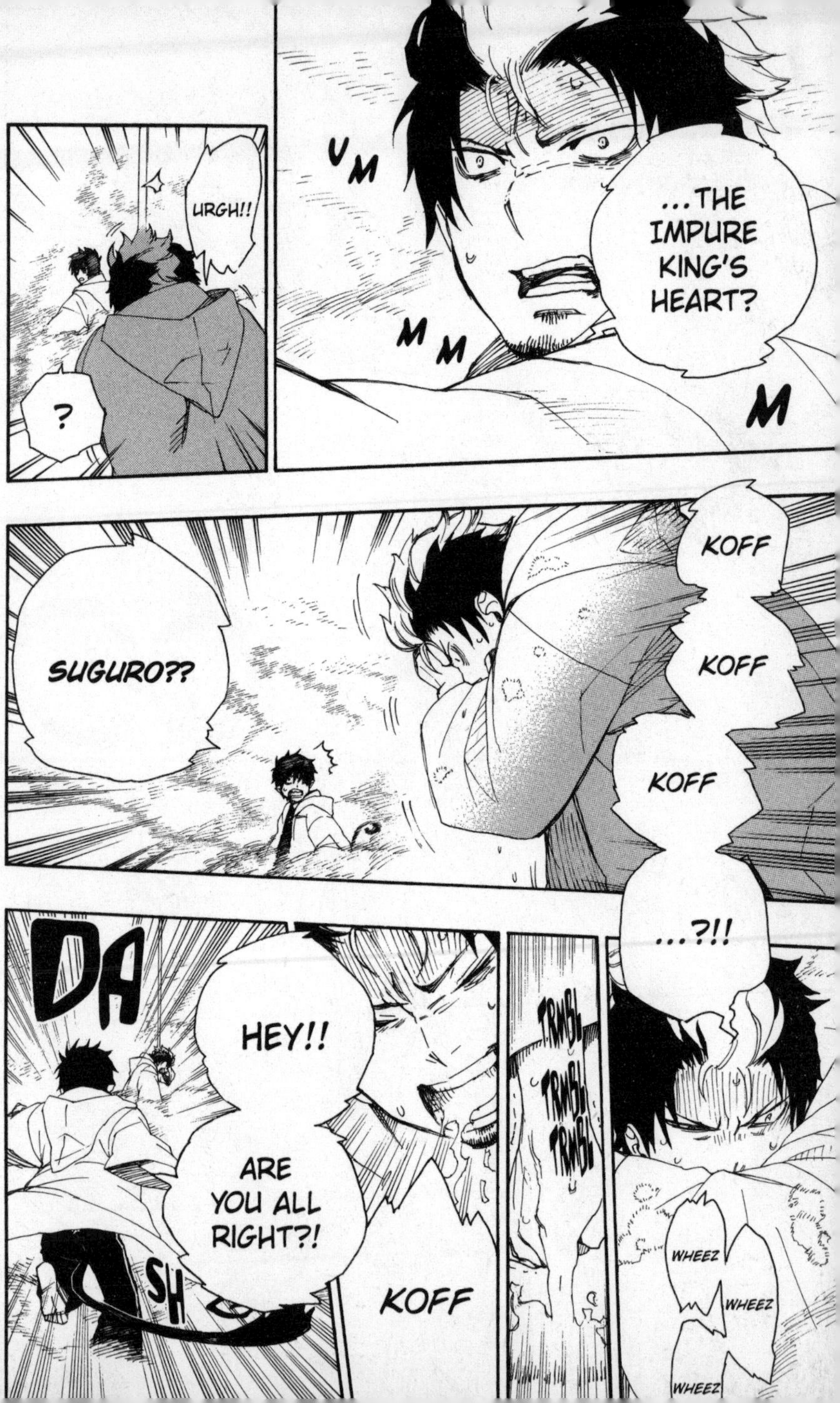
UM
MM
M
...THE IMPURE KING'S HEART?
URGH!!
?
KOFF
KOFF
KOFF
...?!!
SUGURO??
WHEEZ
WHEEZ
WHEEZ
TRMBL
TRMBL
TRMBL
DA
HEY!!
ARE YOU ALL RIGHT?!
KOFF
SH

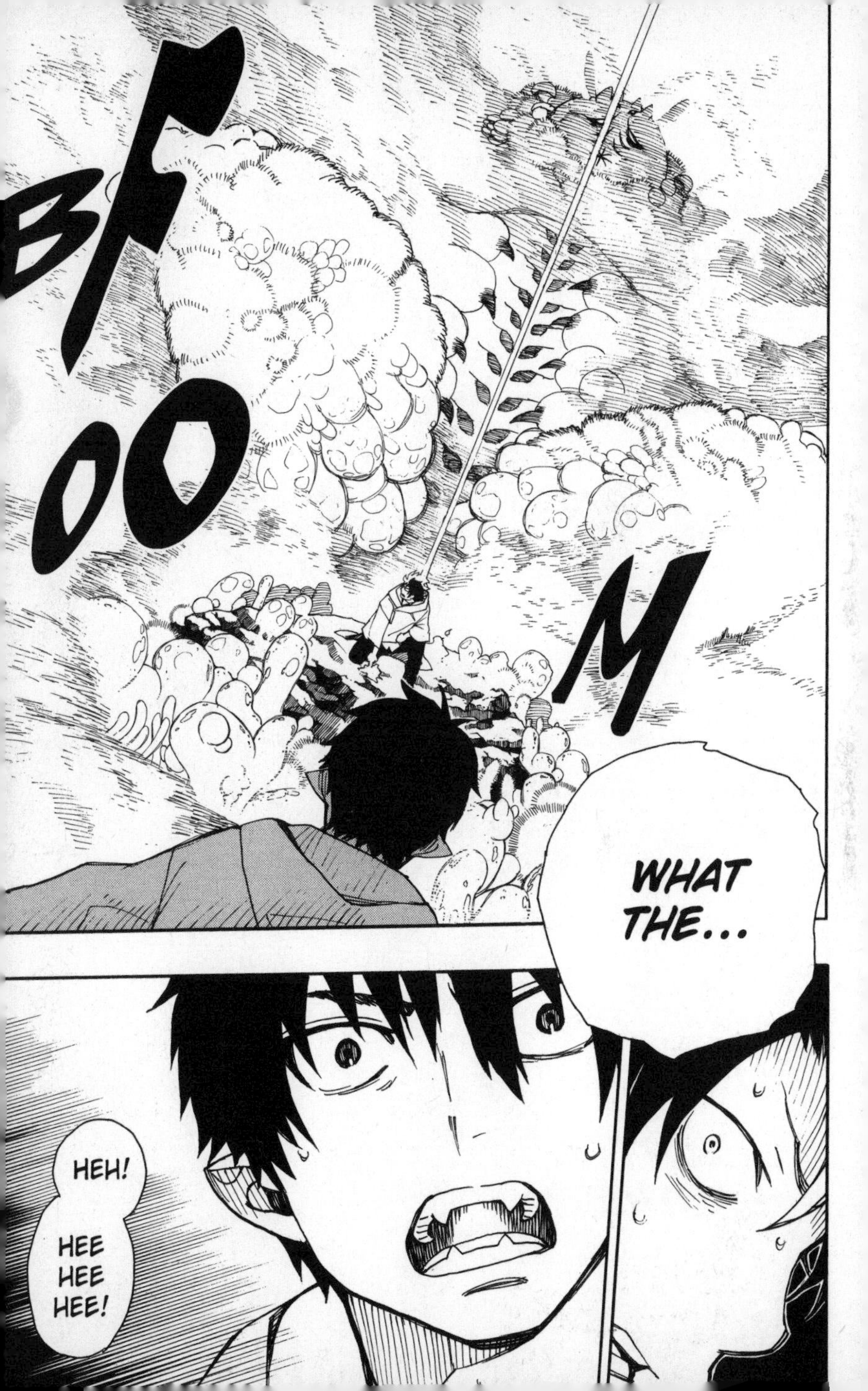
BFOOM
WHAT THE...
HEH!
HEE HEE HEE!

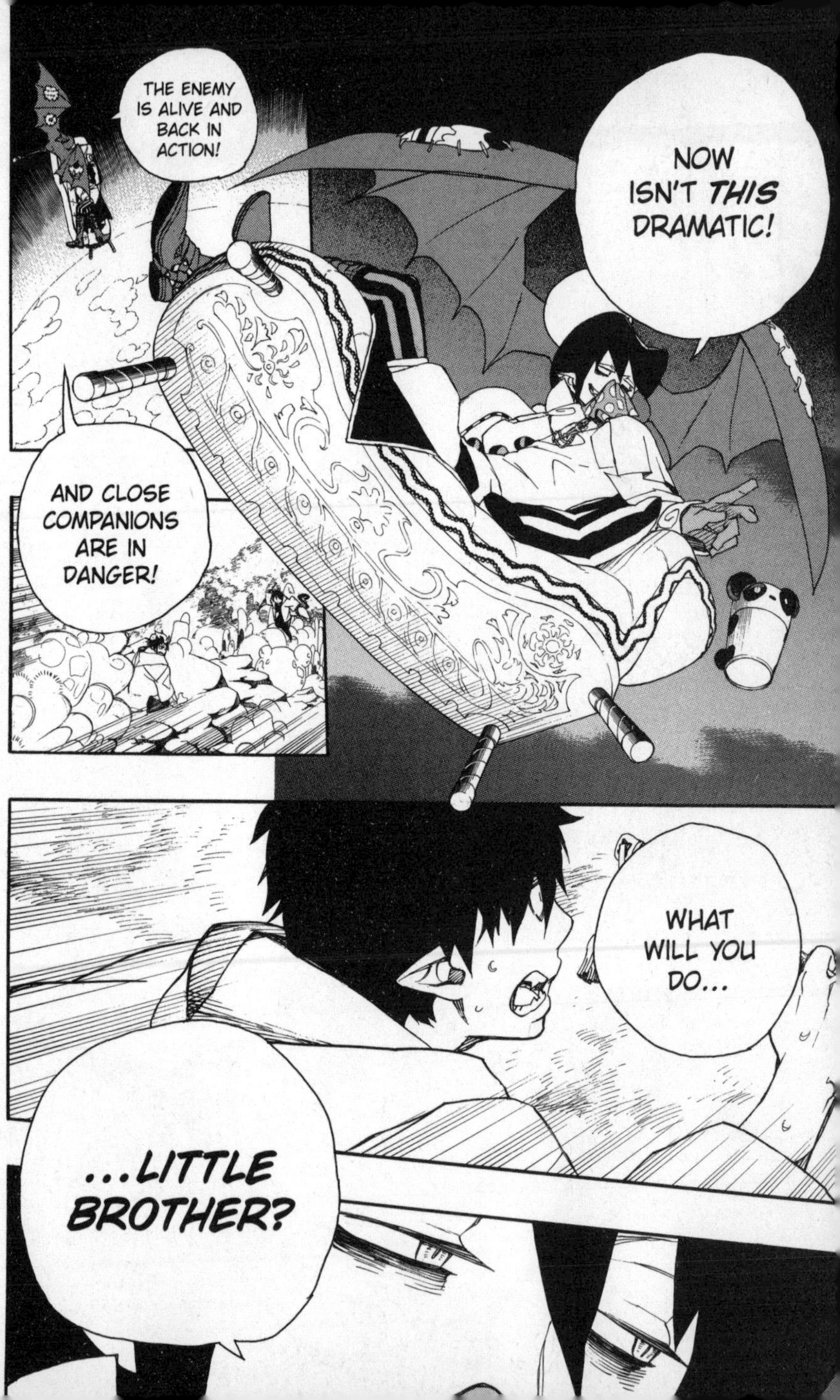
NOW ISN'T *THIS* DRAMATIC!
THE ENEMY IS ALIVE AND BACK IN ACTION!
AND CLOSE COMPANIONS ARE IN DANGER!
WHAT WILL YOU DO...
...LITTLE BROTHER?

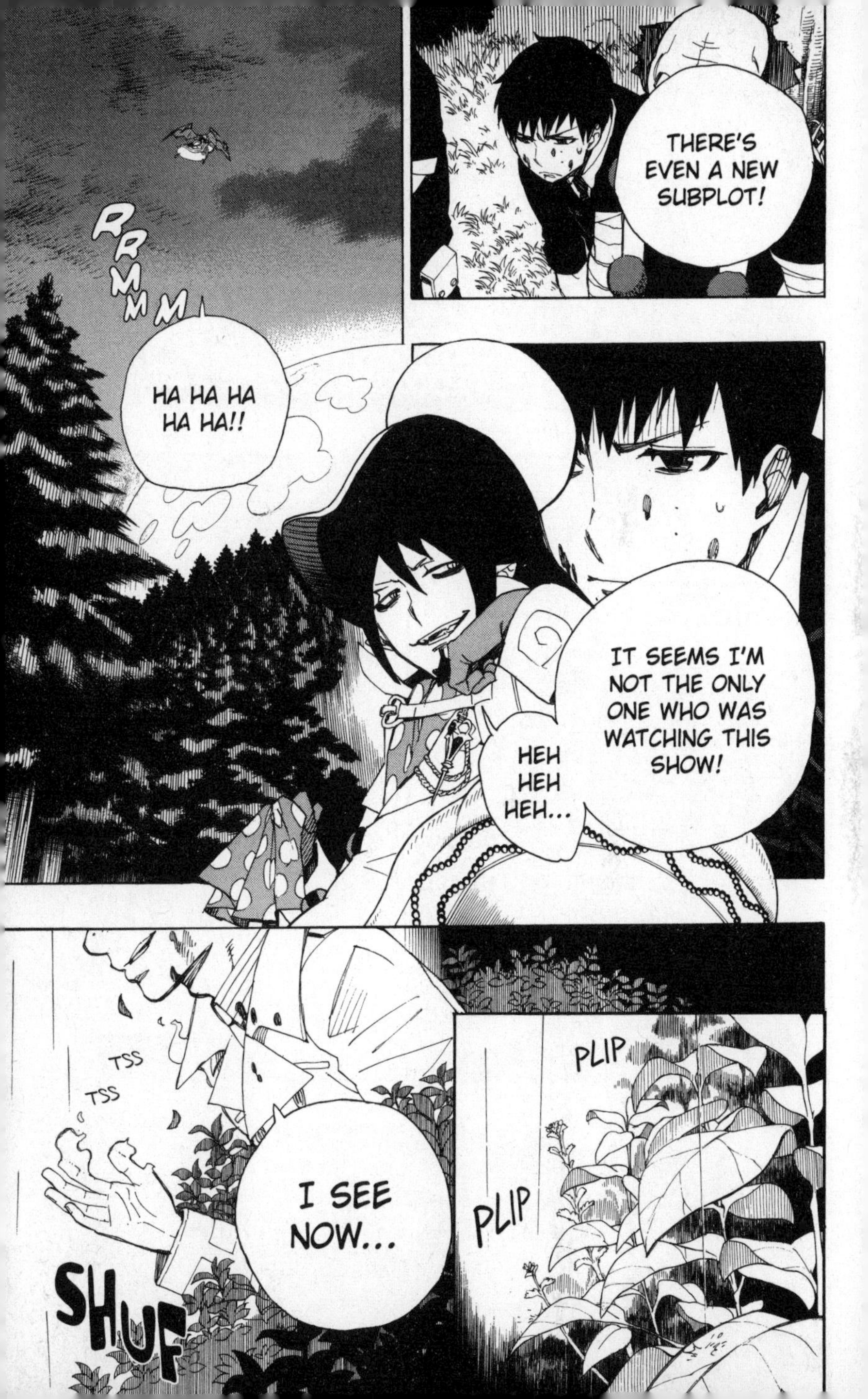
THERE'S EVEN A NEW SUBPLOT!
IT SEEMS I'M NOT THE ONLY ONE WHO WAS WATCHING THIS SHOW!
HEH HEH HEH...
RRMMMM
HA HA HA HA HA!!
PLIP
PLIP
TSS
TSS
I SEE NOW...
SHUF

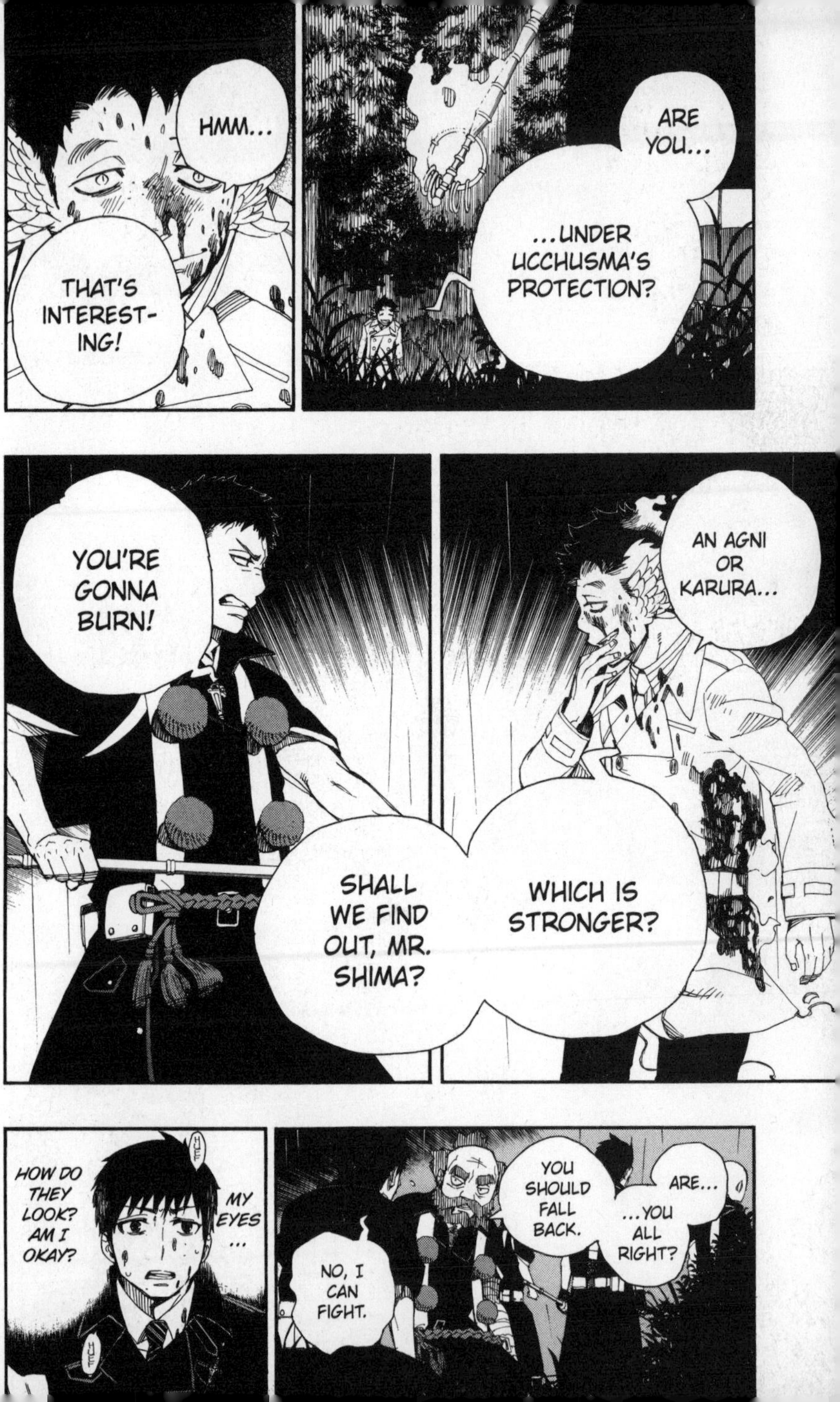
ARE YOU...
...UNDER UCCHUSMA'S PROTECTION?
HMM...
THAT'S INTEREST-ING!
AN AGNI OR KARURA...
WHICH IS STRONGER?
SHALL WE FIND OUT, MR. SHIMA?
YOU'RE GONNA BURN!
ARE...
...YOU ALL RIGHT?
YOU SHOULD FALL BACK.
NO, I CAN FIGHT.
MY EYES...
HOW DO THEY LOOK? AM I OKAY?

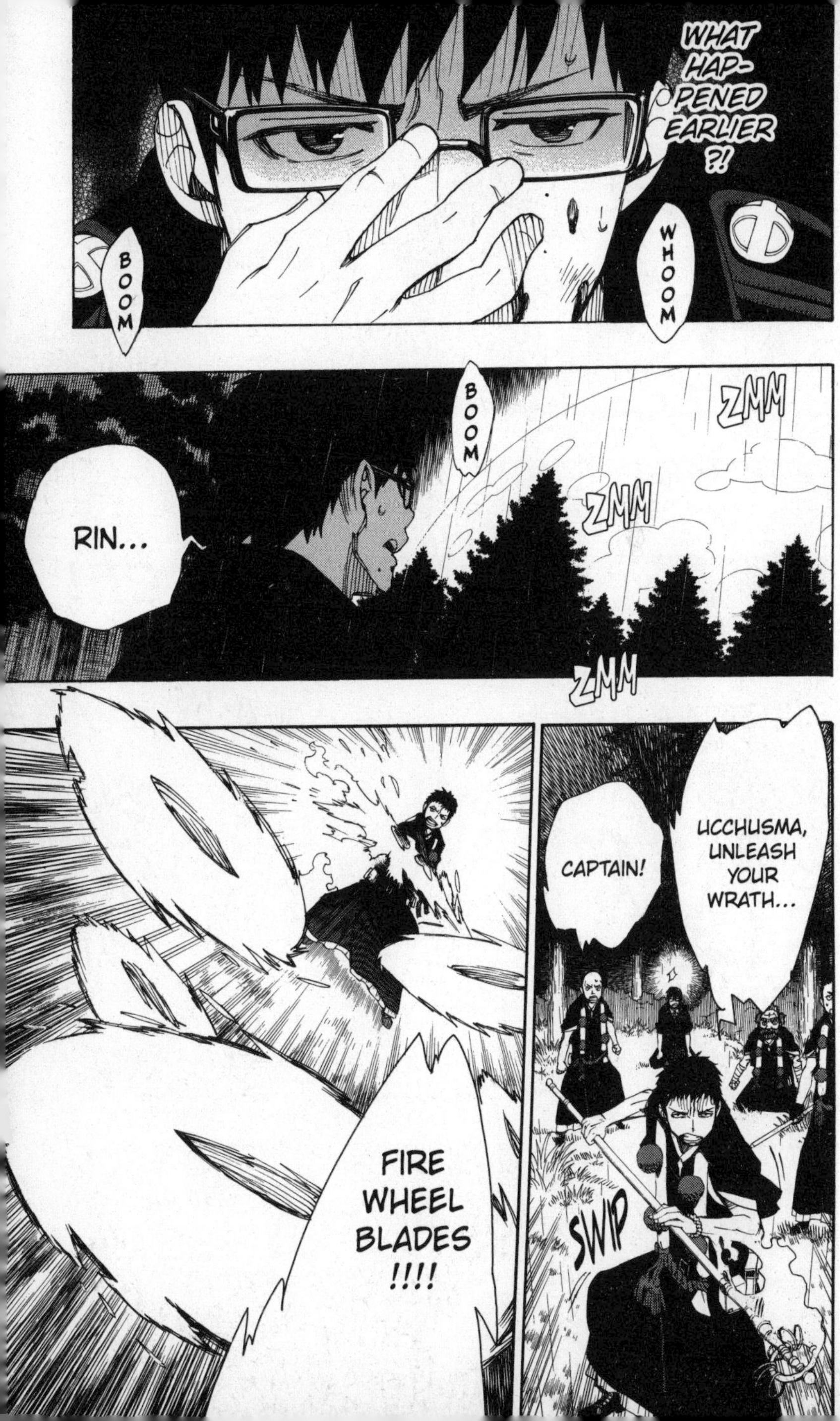
WHAT HAP-PENED EARLIER ?!
WHOOM
BOOM
ZMM
BOOM
ZMM
RIN...
ZMM
UCCHUSMA, UNLEASH YOUR WRATH...
CAPTAIN!
SWIP
FIRE WHEEL BLADES !!!!

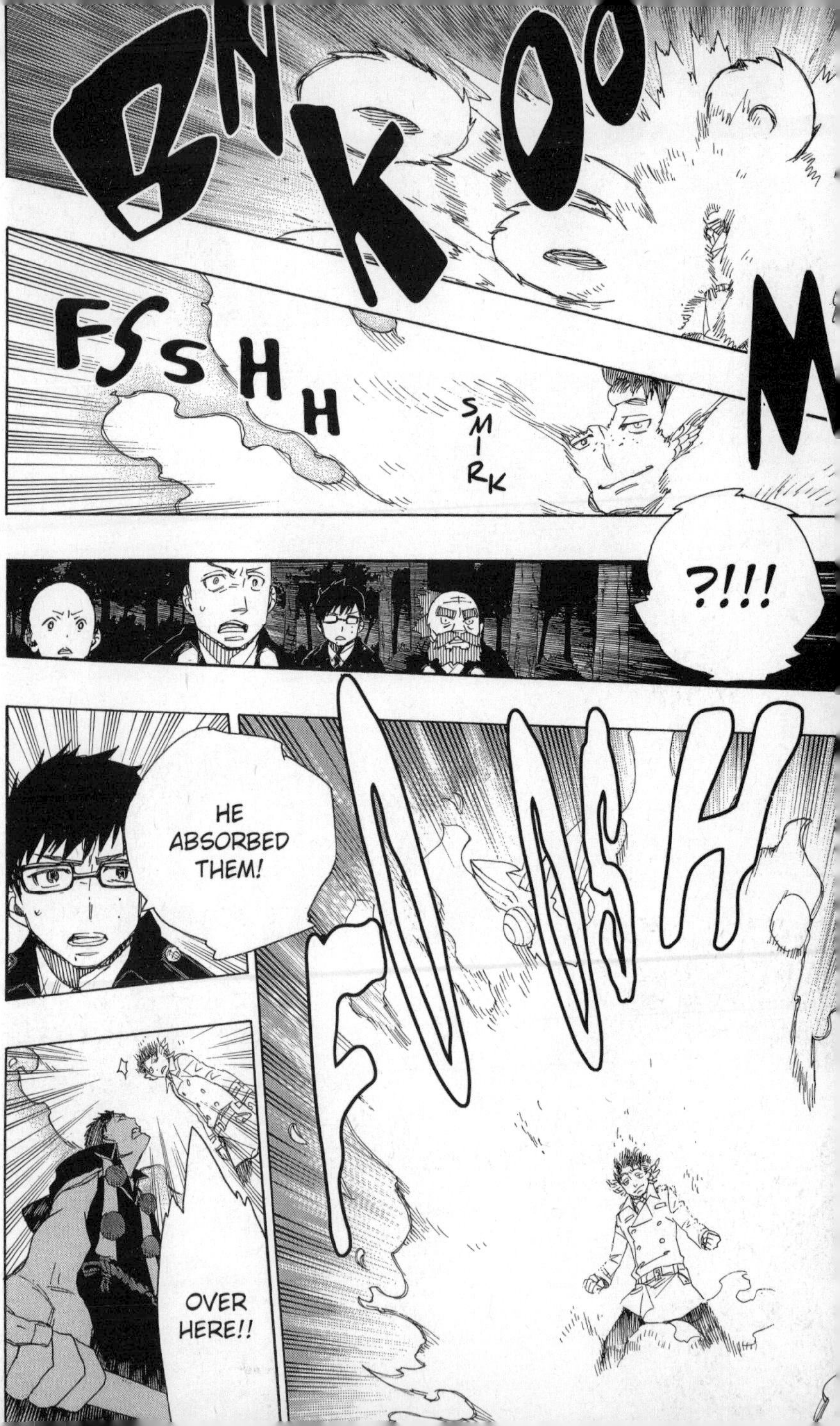
BAKOOOM
FSSHH
SMIRK
?!!!
FWOSH
HE ABSORBED THEM!
OVER HERE!!

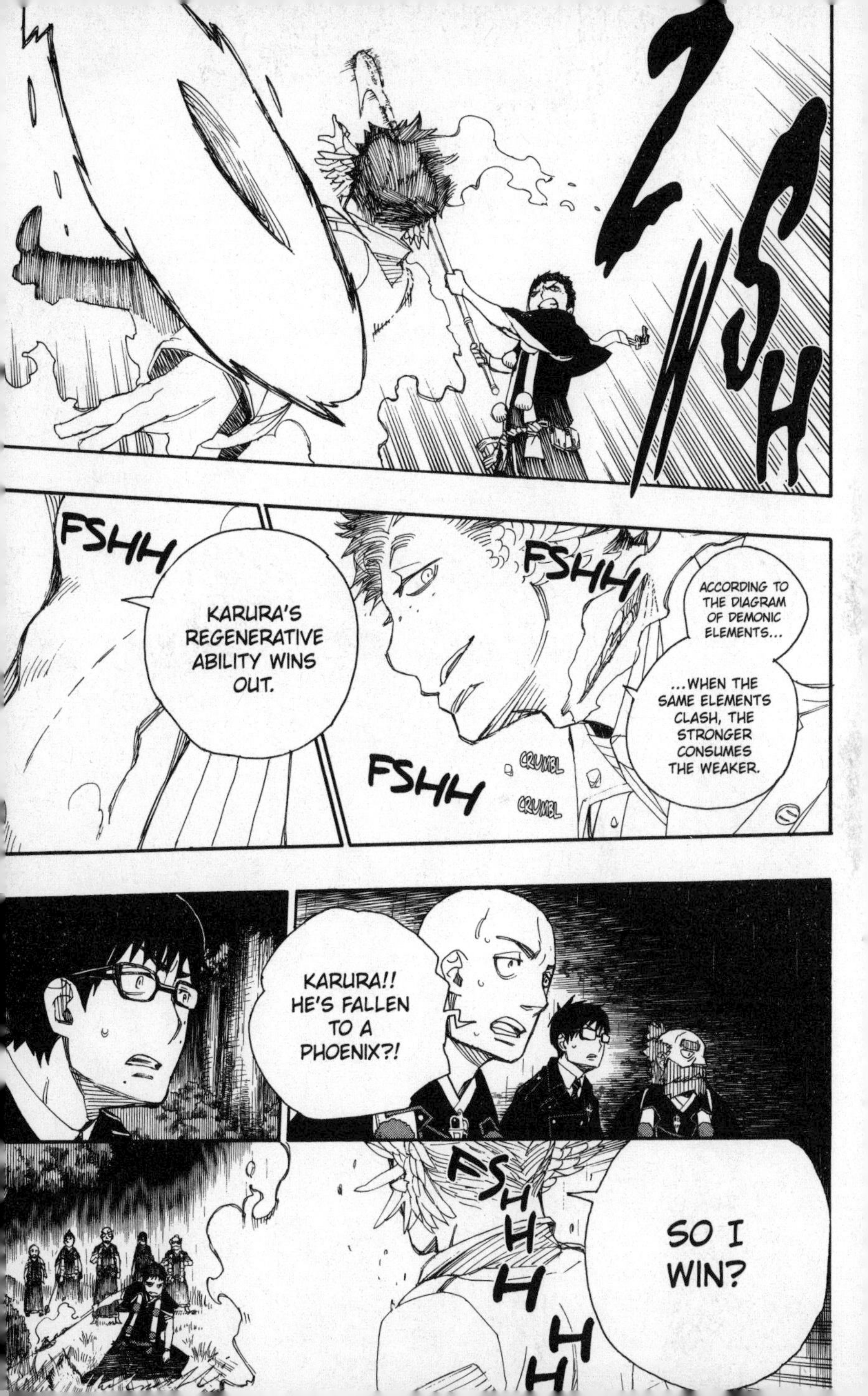
ZWSH
FSHH
ACCORDING TO THE DIAGRAM OF DEMONIC ELEMENTS...
...WHEN THE SAME ELEMENTS CLASH, THE STRONGER CONSUMES THE WEAKER.
CRUMBL
CRUMBL
FSHH
FSHH
KARURA'S REGENERATIVE ABILITY WINS OUT.
KARURA!! HE'S FALLEN TO A PHOENIX?!
FSHHHHHHH
SO I WIN?

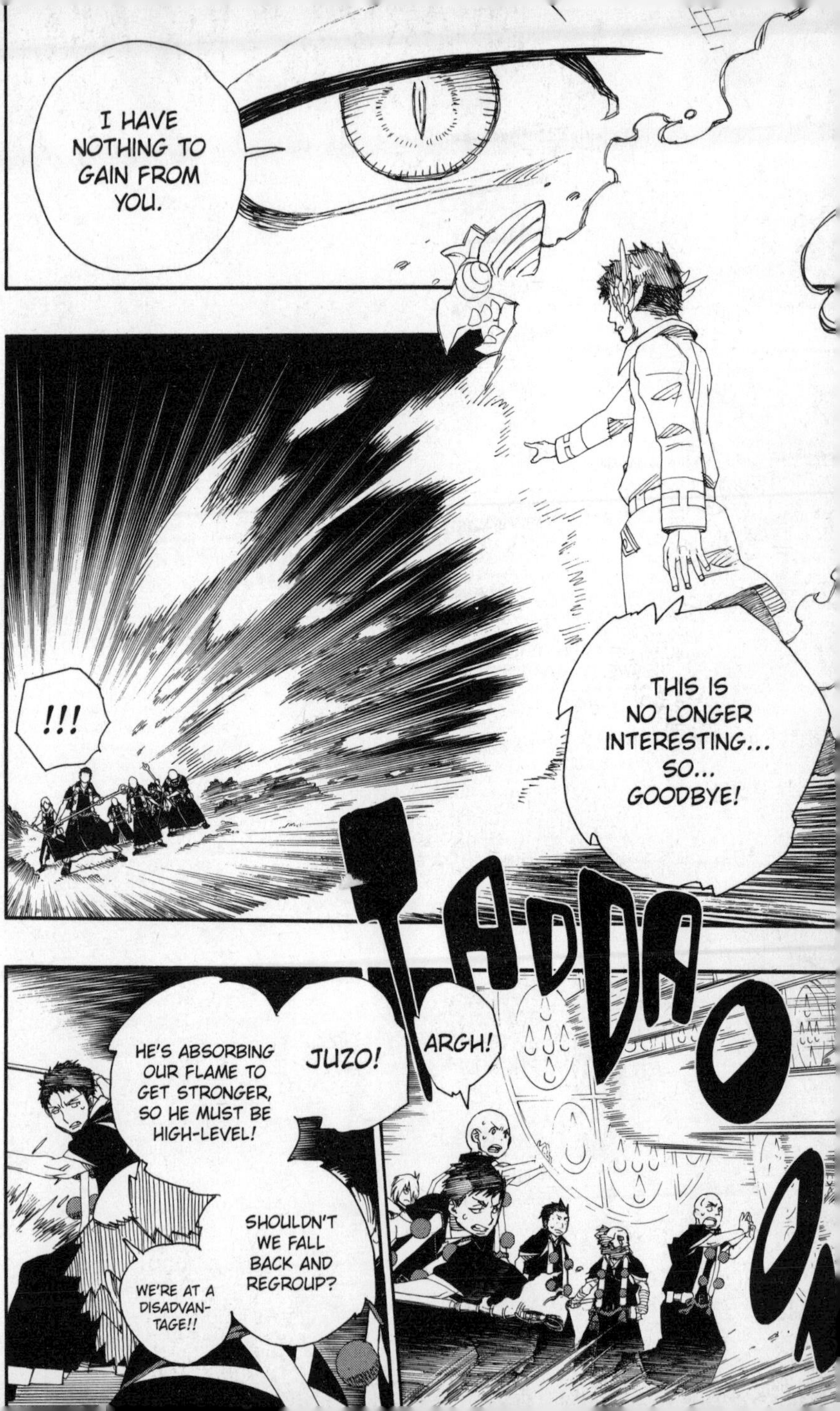
I HAVE NOTHING TO GAIN FROM YOU.
THIS IS NO LONGER INTERESTING... SO... GOODBYE!
!!!
ARGH!
JUZO!
HE'S ABSORBING OUR FLAME TO GET STRONGER, SO HE MUST BE HIGH-LEVEL!
SHOULDN'T WE FALL BACK AND REGROUP?
WE'RE AT A DISADVAN-TAGE!!

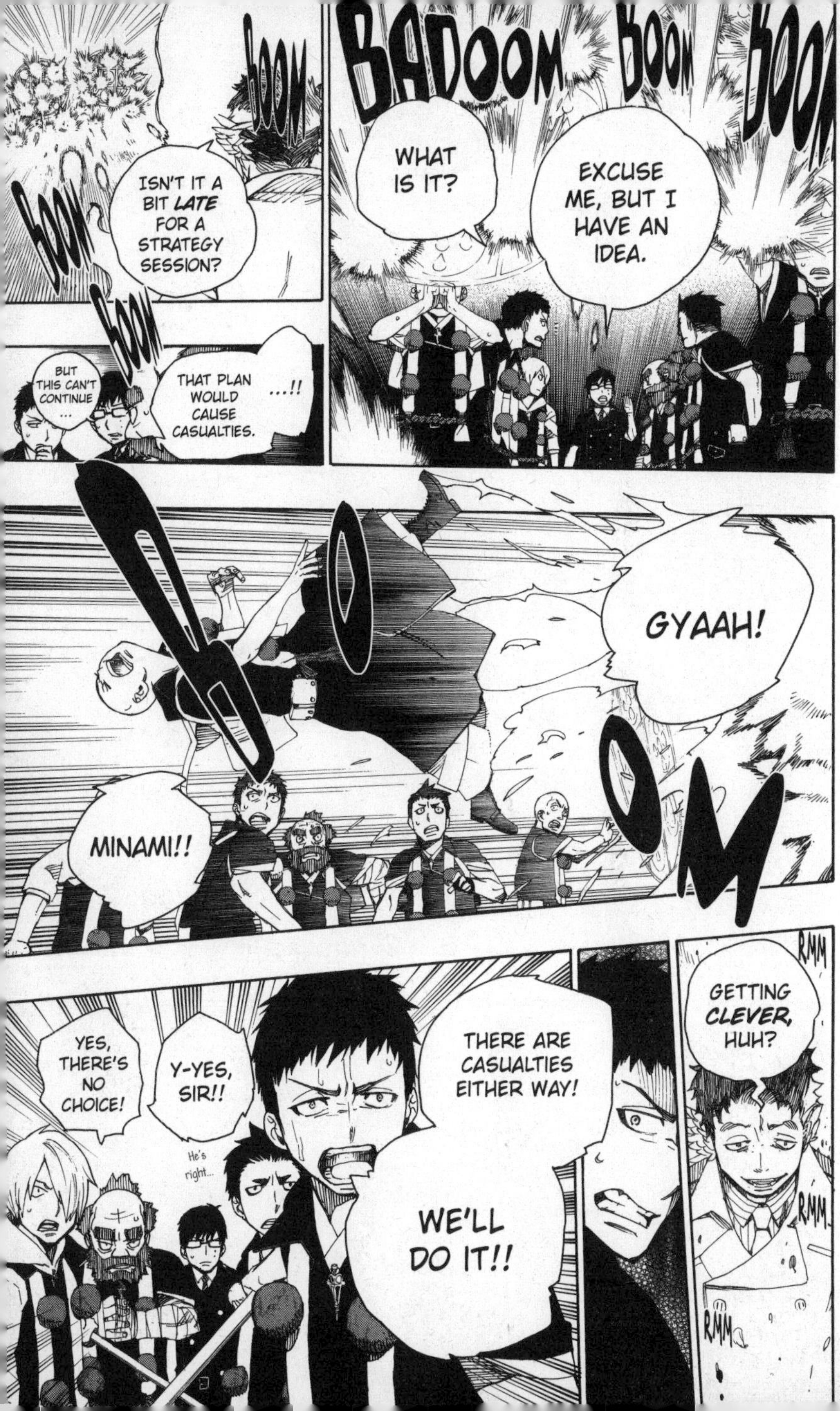
BOOM
BOOM
EXCUSE ME, BUT I HAVE AN IDEA.
BADOOM
WHAT IS IT?
BOOM
ISN'T IT A BIT *LATE* FOR A STRATEGY SESSION?
BOOM
BOOM
...!!
THAT PLAN WOULD CAUSE CASUALTIES.
BUT THIS CAN'T CONTINUE...
GYAAH!
BOOM
MINAMI!!
RMM
GETTING *CLEVER,* HUH?
RMM
RMM
THERE ARE CASUALTIES EITHER WAY!
WE'LL DO IT!!
Y-YES, SIR!!
He's right...
YES, THERE'S NO CHOICE!

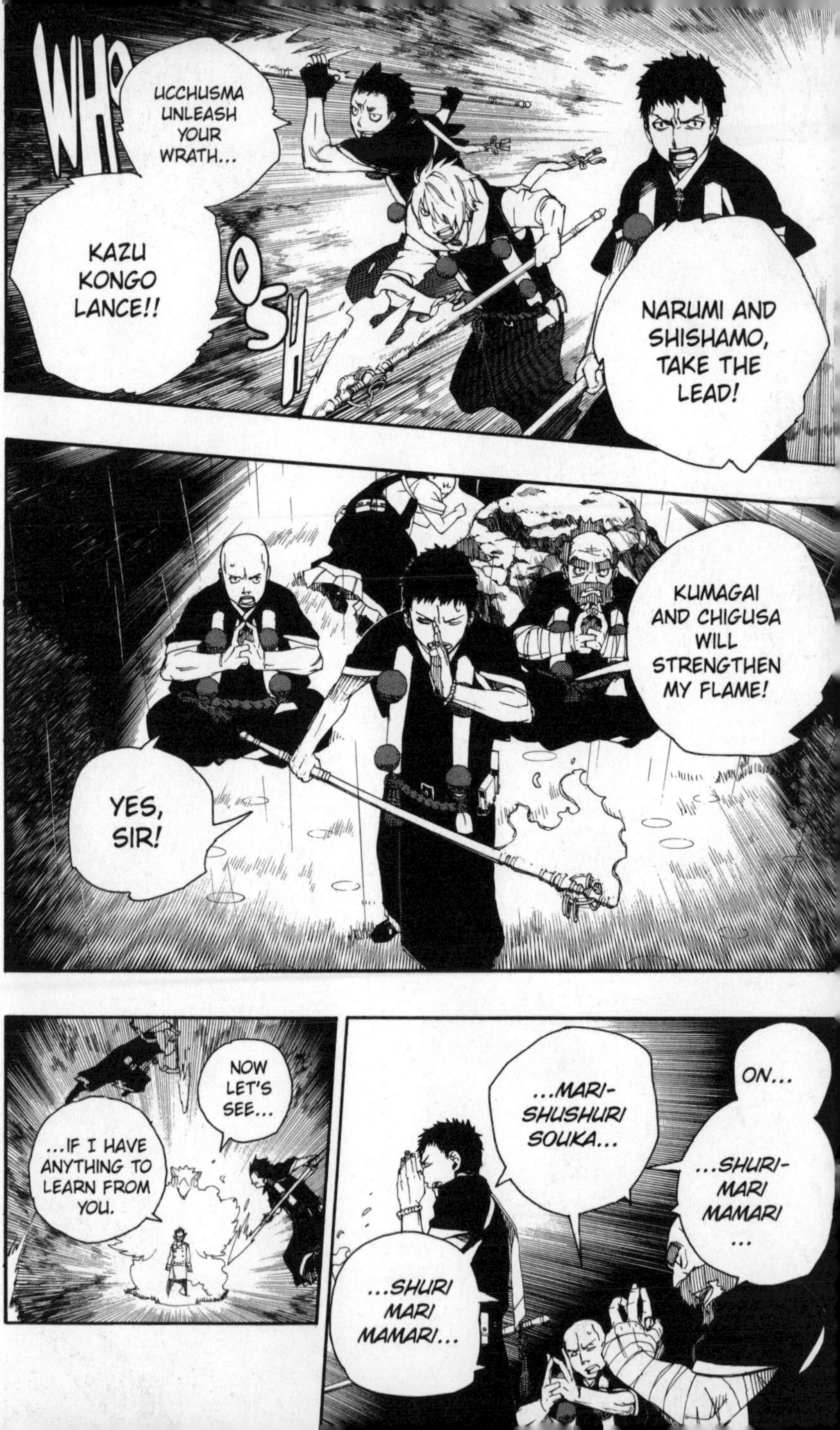
NARUMI AND SHISHAMO, TAKE THE LEAD!
UCCHUSMA UNLEASH YOUR WRATH...
KAZU KONGO LANCE!!
WHOOSH
KUMAGAI AND CHIGUSA WILL STRENGTHEN MY FLAME!
YES, SIR!
ON...
...MARI-SHUSHURI SOUKA...
...SHURI-MARI MAMARI ...
...SHURI MARI MAMARI...
NOW LET'S SEE...
...IF I HAVE ANYTHING TO LEARN FROM YOU.

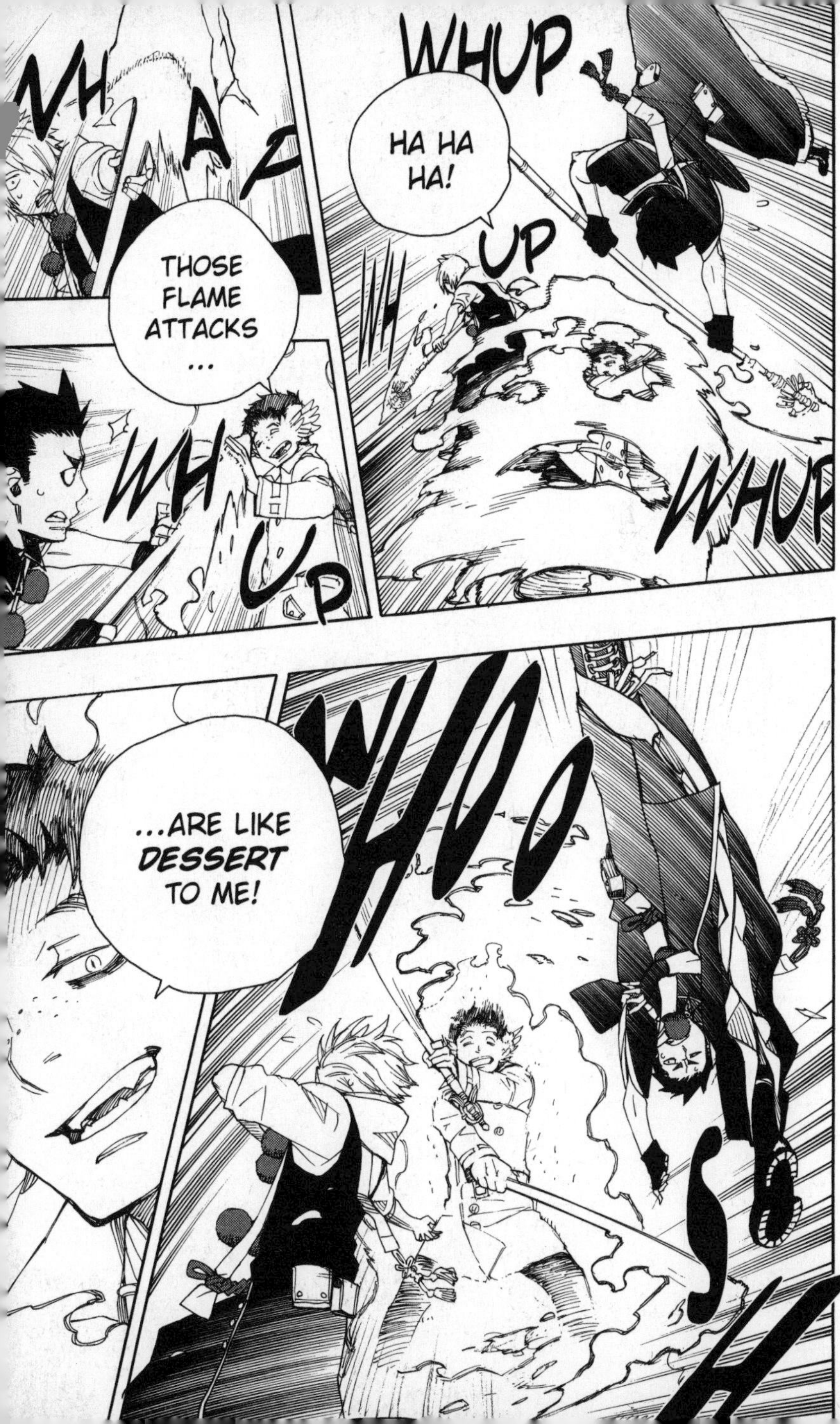
WHUP
HA HA HA!
WH UP
WHUP
THOSE FLAME ATTACKS ...
WH UP
WHOOSH
...ARE LIKE DESSERT TO ME!

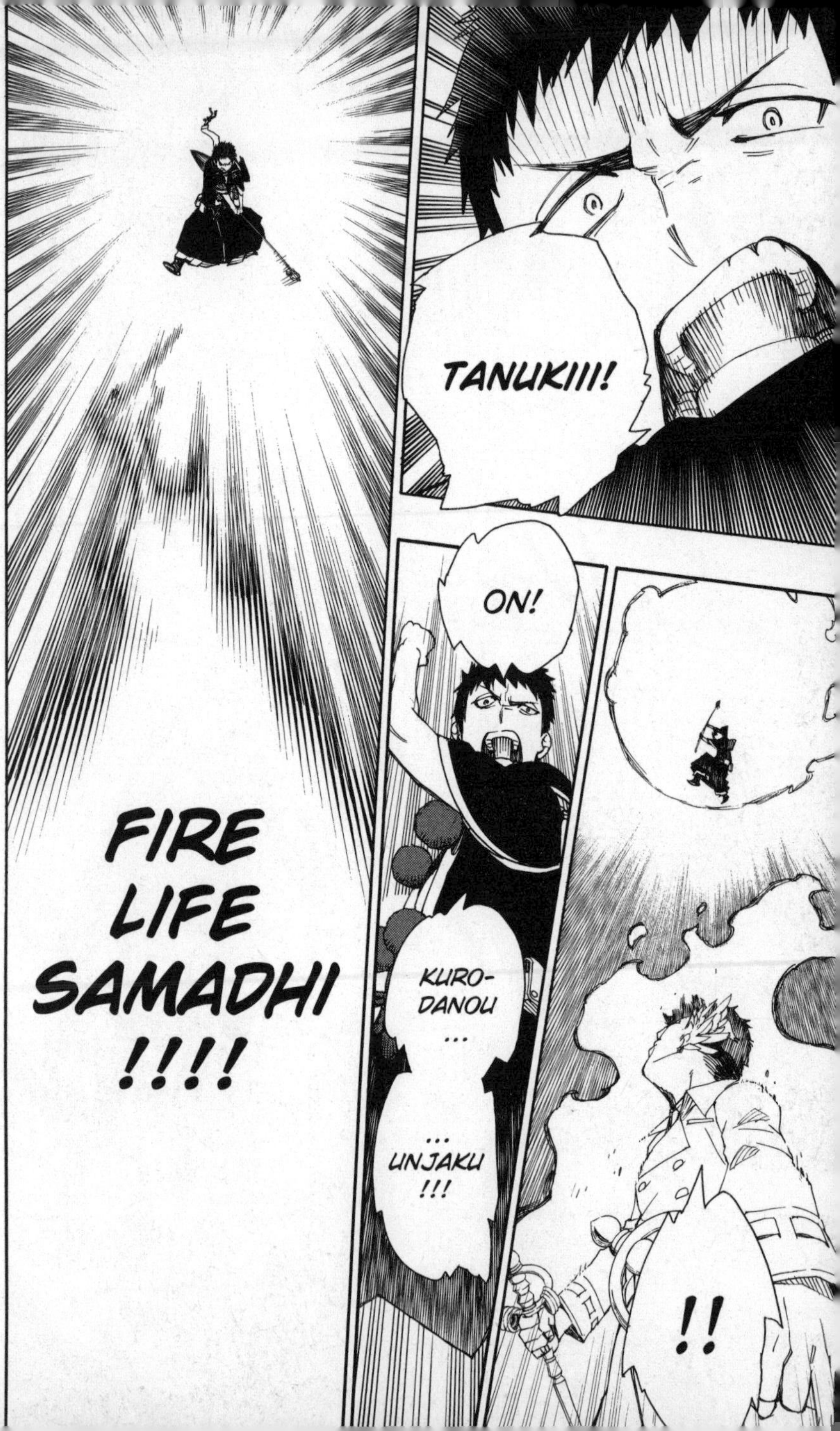
TANUKIII!
!!
ON!
KURO-DANOU...
...UNJAKU!!!
FIRE LIFE SAMADHI!!!!

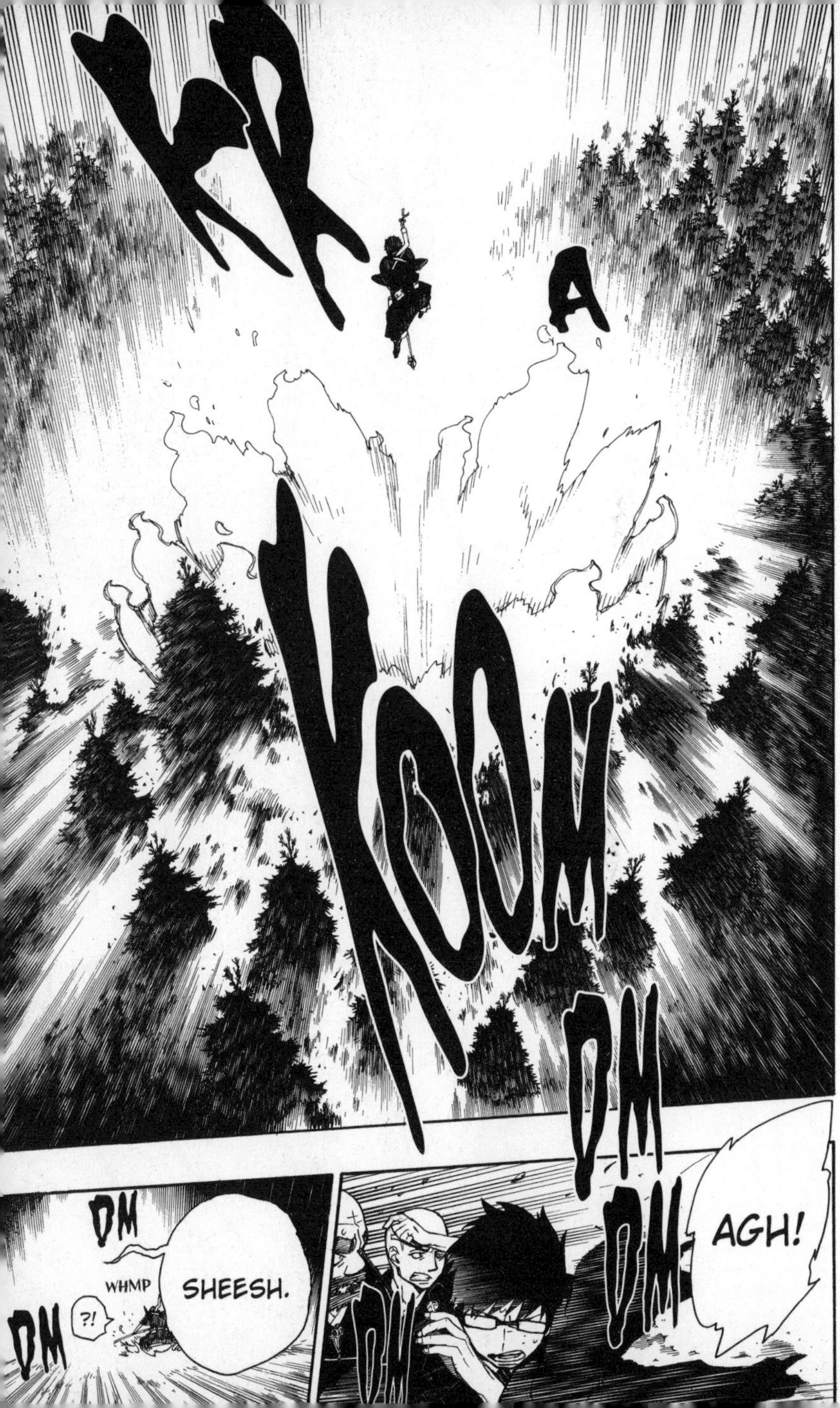
KRAKOOM
DM DM
AGH!
DM DM
DM
SHEESH.
WHMP
?!
DM

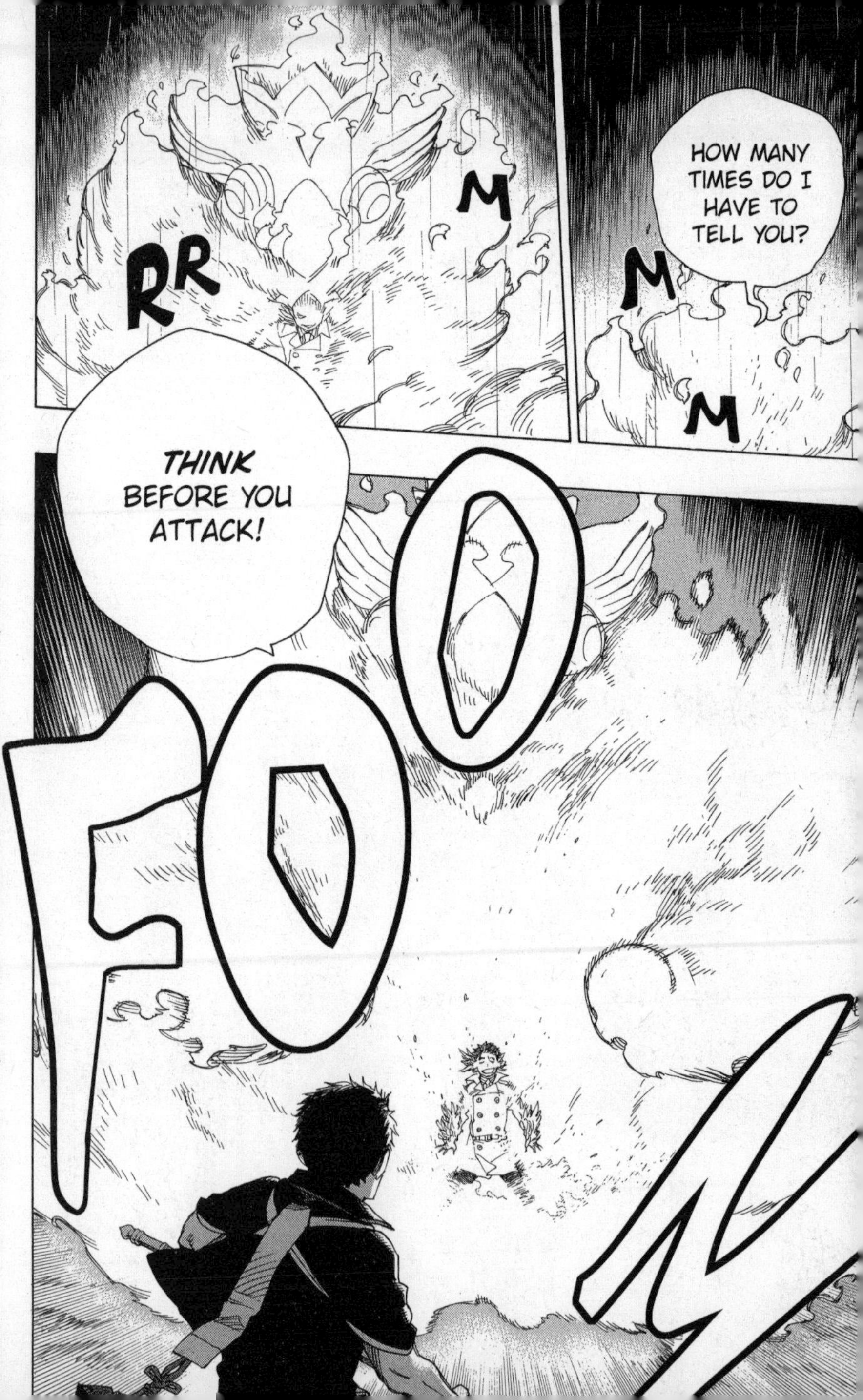
HOW MANY TIMES DO I HAVE TO TELL YOU?
M
M
M
RR
M
THINK BEFORE YOU ATTACK!
FOOM

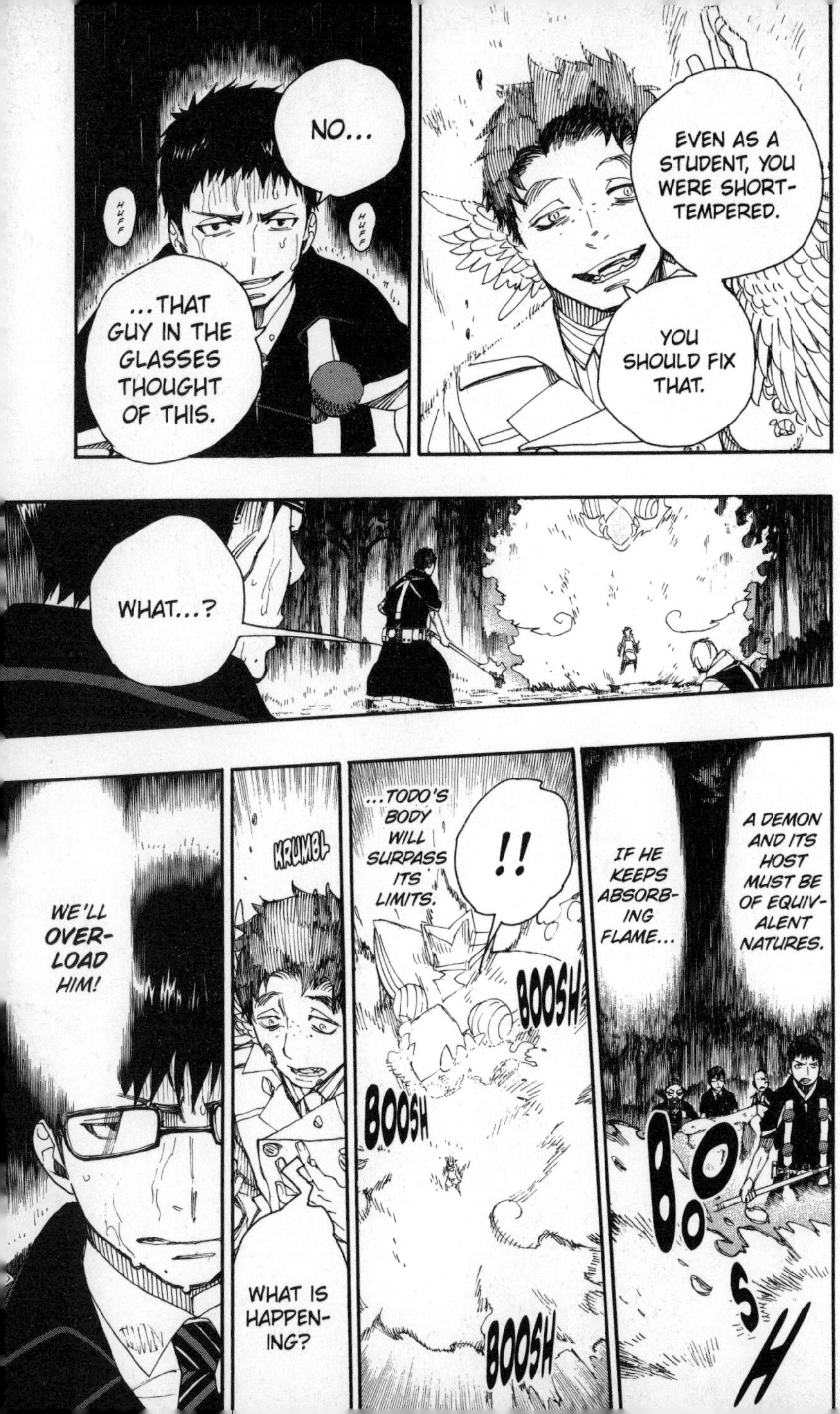
EVEN AS A STUDENT, YOU WERE SHORT-TEMPERED.
YOU SHOULD FIX THAT.
HUFF
HUFF
NO...
...THAT GUY IN THE GLASSES THOUGHT OF THIS.
WHAT...?
A DEMON AND ITS HOST MUST BE OF EQUIVALENT NATURES.
IF HE KEEPS ABSORBING FLAME...
BOOSH
...TODO'S BODY WILL SURPASS ITS LIMITS.
!!
BOOSH
BOOSH
KRUMBL
WHAT IS HAPPENING?
WE'LL OVERLOAD HIM!

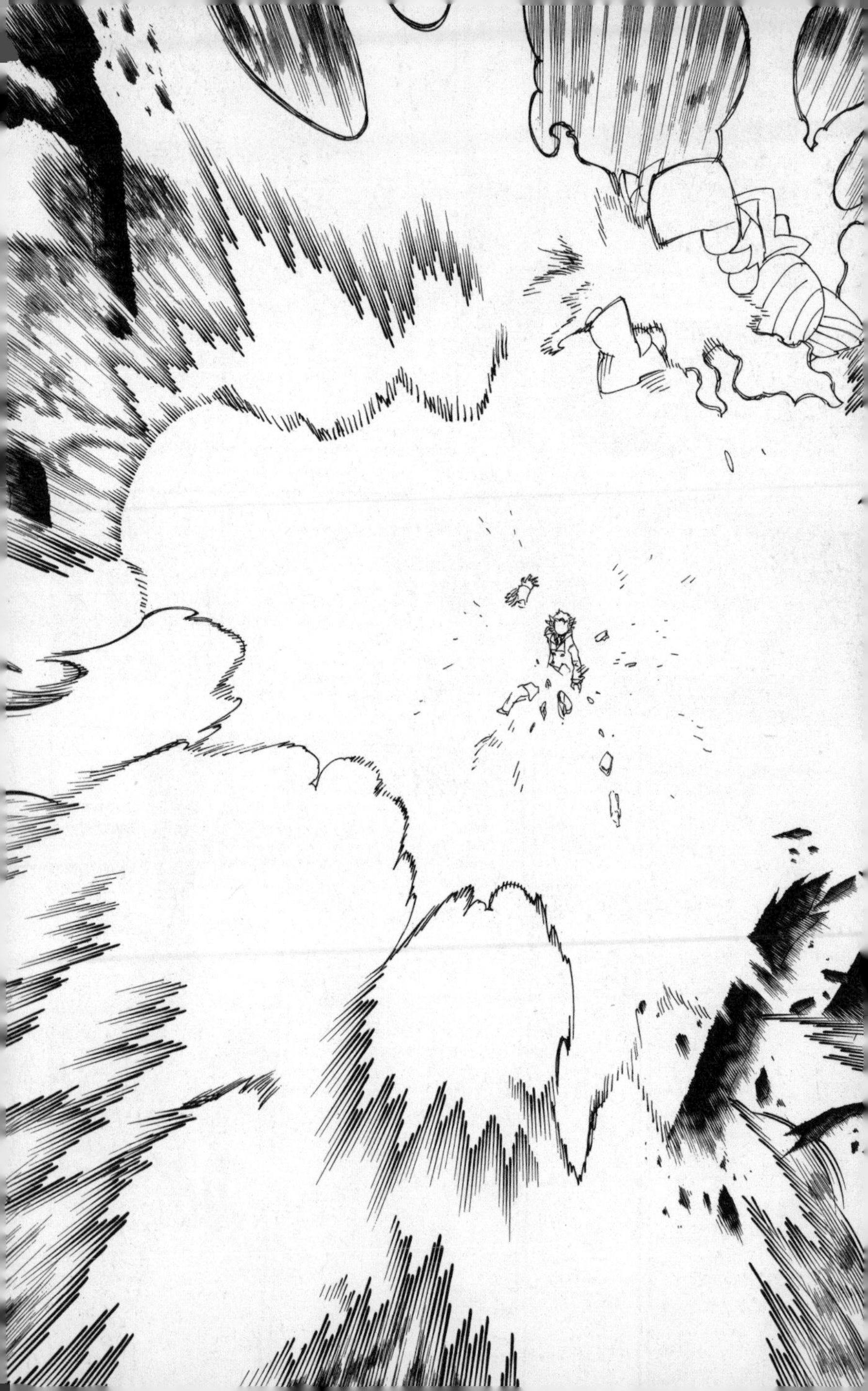

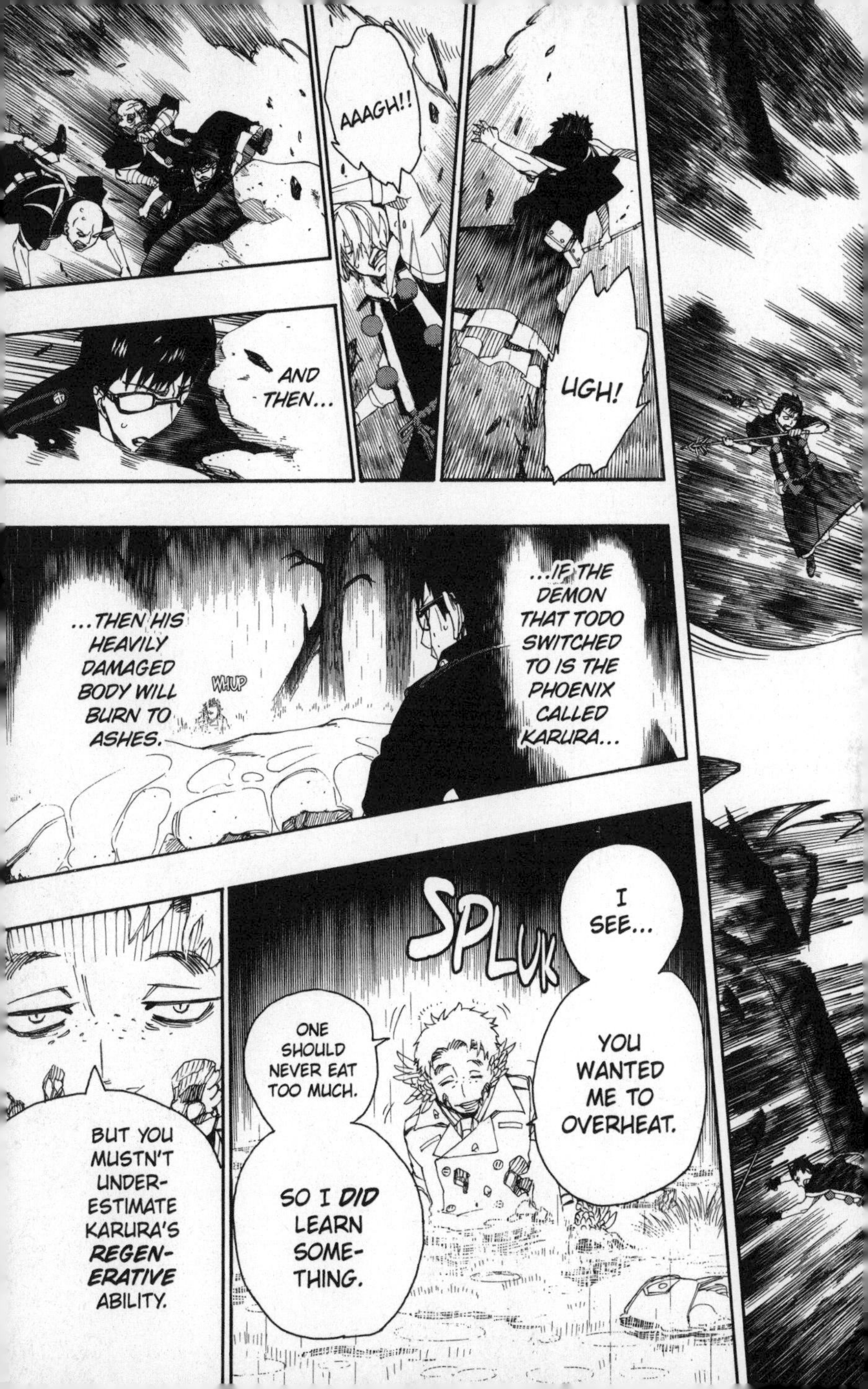
UGH!
AAAGH!!
AND THEN...
...IF THE DEMON THAT TODO SWITCHED TO IS THE PHOENIX CALLED KARURA...
WHUP
...THEN HIS HEAVILY DAMAGED BODY WILL BURN TO ASHES.
SPLUK
I SEE...
YOU WANTED ME TO OVERHEAT.
ONE SHOULD NEVER EAT TOO MUCH.
SO I *DID* LEARN SOMETHING.
BUT YOU MUSTN'T UNDER-ESTIMATE KARURA'S ***REGEN-ERATIVE*** ABILITY.

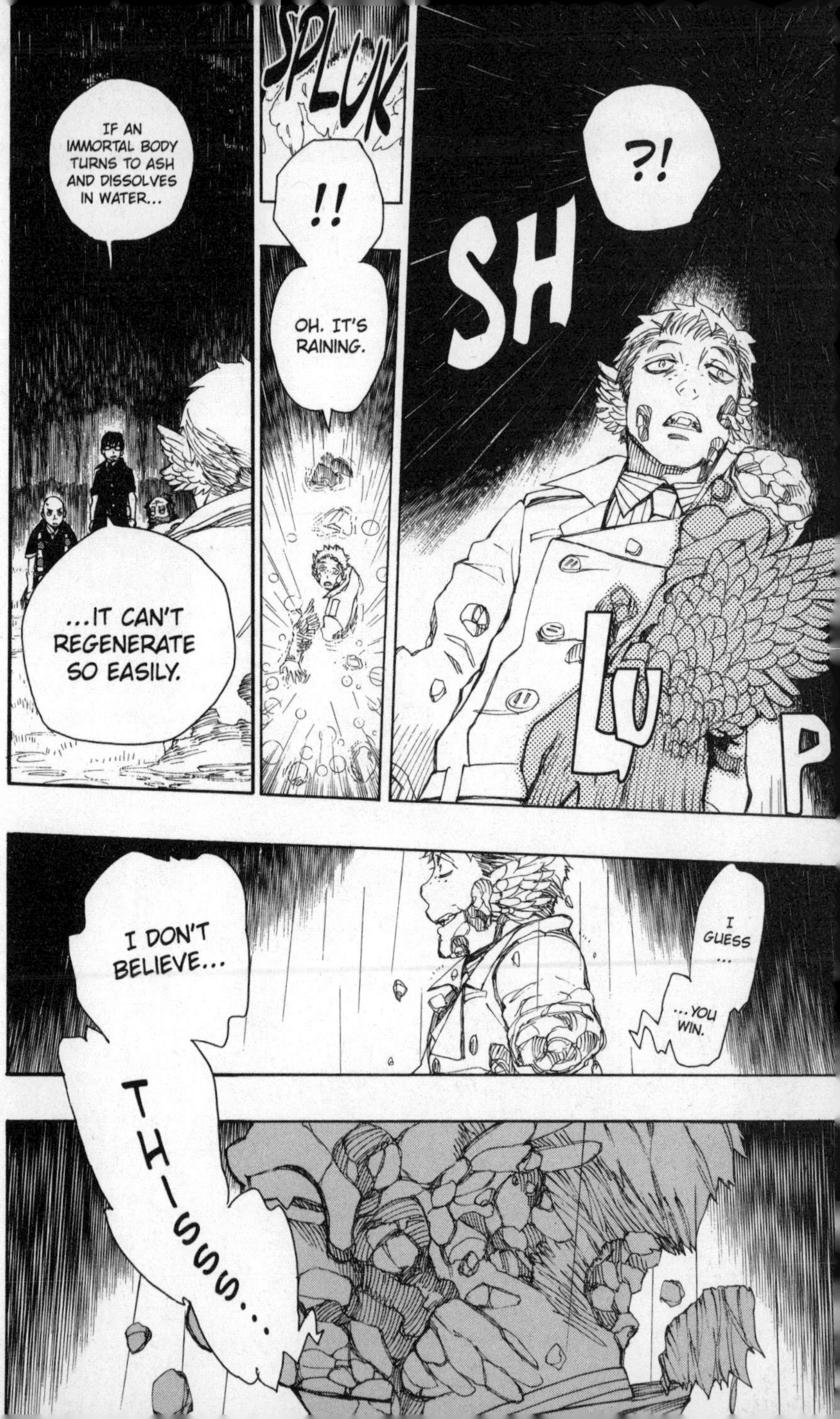
?!
SH
LUP
SPLUK
!!
OH. IT'S RAINING.
IF AN IMMORTAL BODY TURNS TO ASH AND DISSOLVES IN WATER...
...IT CAN'T REGENERATE SO EASILY.
I GUESS...
...YOU WIN.
I DON'T BELIEVE...
THISSS...

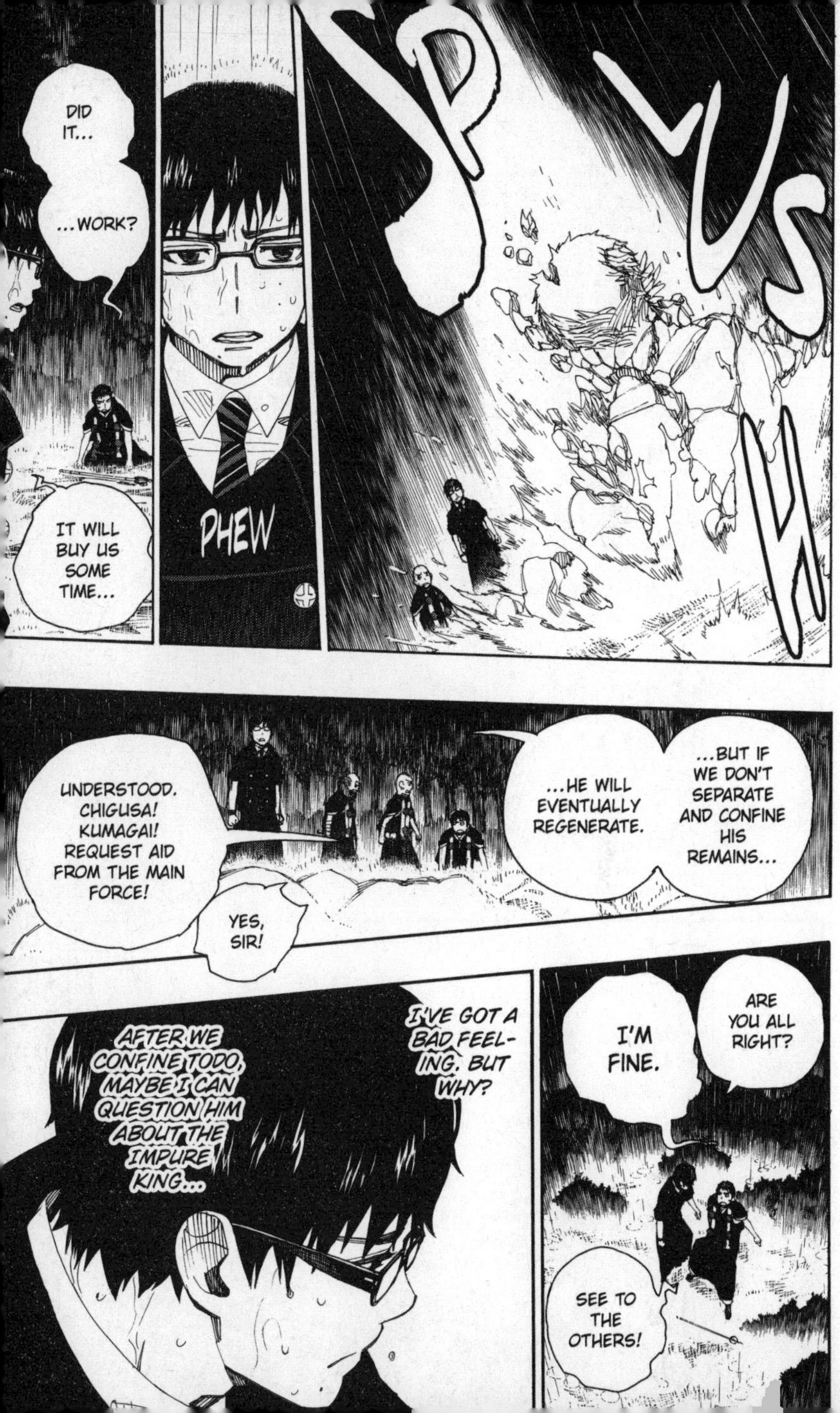
SPLUSH
PHEW
DID IT...
...WORK?
IT WILL BUY US SOME TIME...
...BUT IF WE DON'T SEPARATE AND CONFINE HIS REMAINS...
...HE WILL EVENTUALLY REGENERATE.
UNDERSTOOD. CHIGUSA! KUMAGAI! REQUEST AID FROM THE MAIN FORCE!
YES, SIR!
ARE YOU ALL RIGHT?
I'M FINE.
SEE TO THE OTHERS!
I'VE GOT A BAD FEEL-ING. BUT WHY?
AFTER WE CONFINE TODO, MAYBE I CAN QUESTION HIM ABOUT THE IMPURE KING...

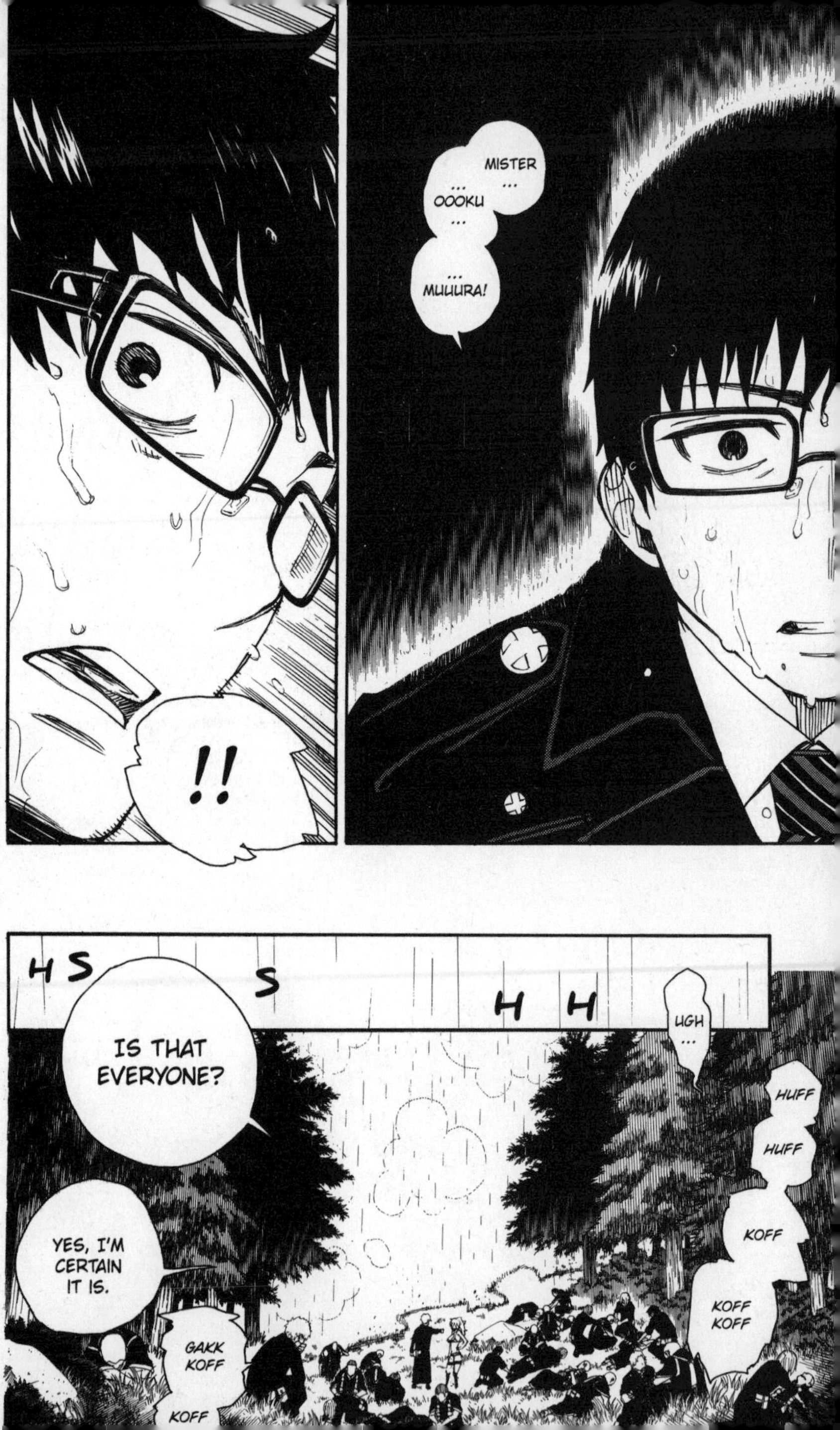
MISTER ... OOOKU ... MUURA!
!!
HS S H H
UGH ...
HUFF
HUFF
KOFF
KOFF KOFF
IS THAT EVERYONE?
YES, I'M CERTAIN IT IS.
GAKK KOFF
KOFF

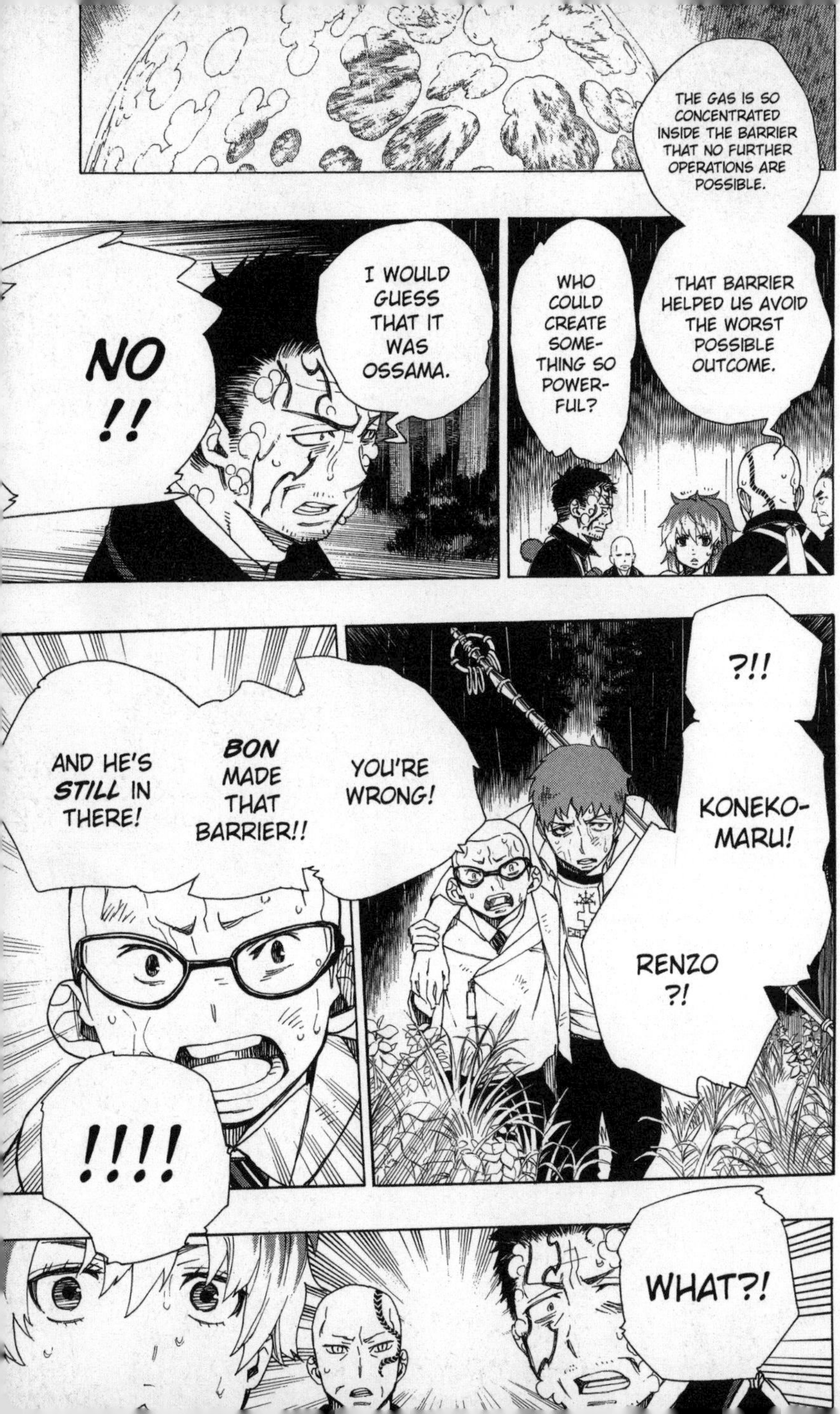
THE GAS IS SO CONCENTRATED INSIDE THE BARRIER THAT NO FURTHER OPERATIONS ARE POSSIBLE.
THAT BARRIER HELPED US AVOID THE WORST POSSIBLE OUTCOME.
WHO COULD CREATE SOME-THING SO POWER-FUL?
I WOULD GUESS THAT IT WAS OSSAMA.
NO !!
?!!
KONEKO-MARU!
RENZO ?!
YOU'RE WRONG!
BON MADE THAT BARRIER!!
AND HE'S *STILL* IN THERE!
!!!!
WHAT?!

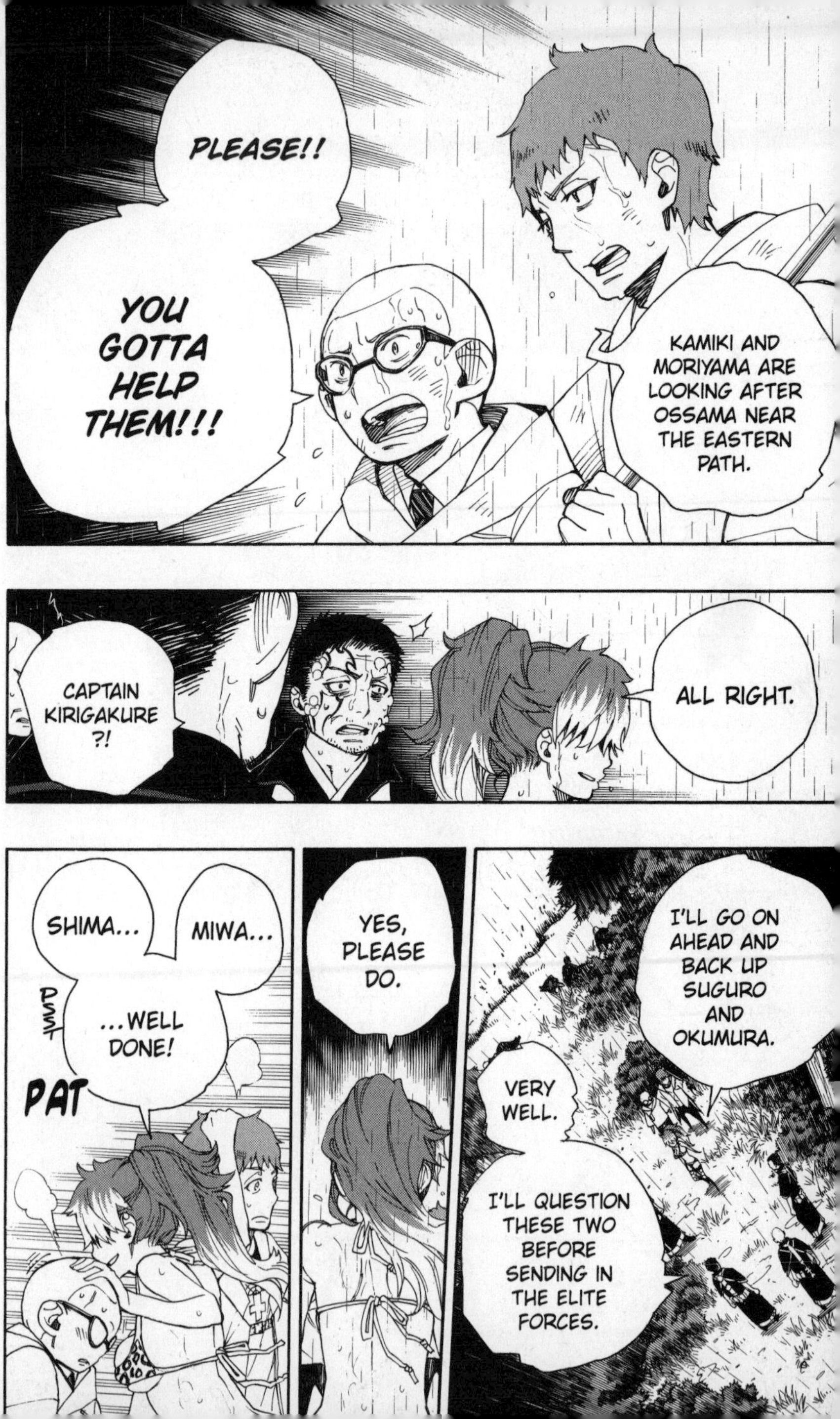

KAMIKI AND MORIYAMA ARE LOOKING AFTER OSSAMA NEAR THE EASTERN PATH.
PLEASE!!
YOU GOTTA HELP THEM!!!
ALL RIGHT.
CAPTAIN KIRIGAKURE?!
I'LL GO ON AHEAD AND BACK UP SUGURO AND OKUMURA.
VERY WELL.
I'LL QUESTION THESE TWO BEFORE SENDING IN THE ELITE FORCES.
YES, PLEASE DO.
SHIMA...
MIWA...
PSST
...WELL DONE!
PAT

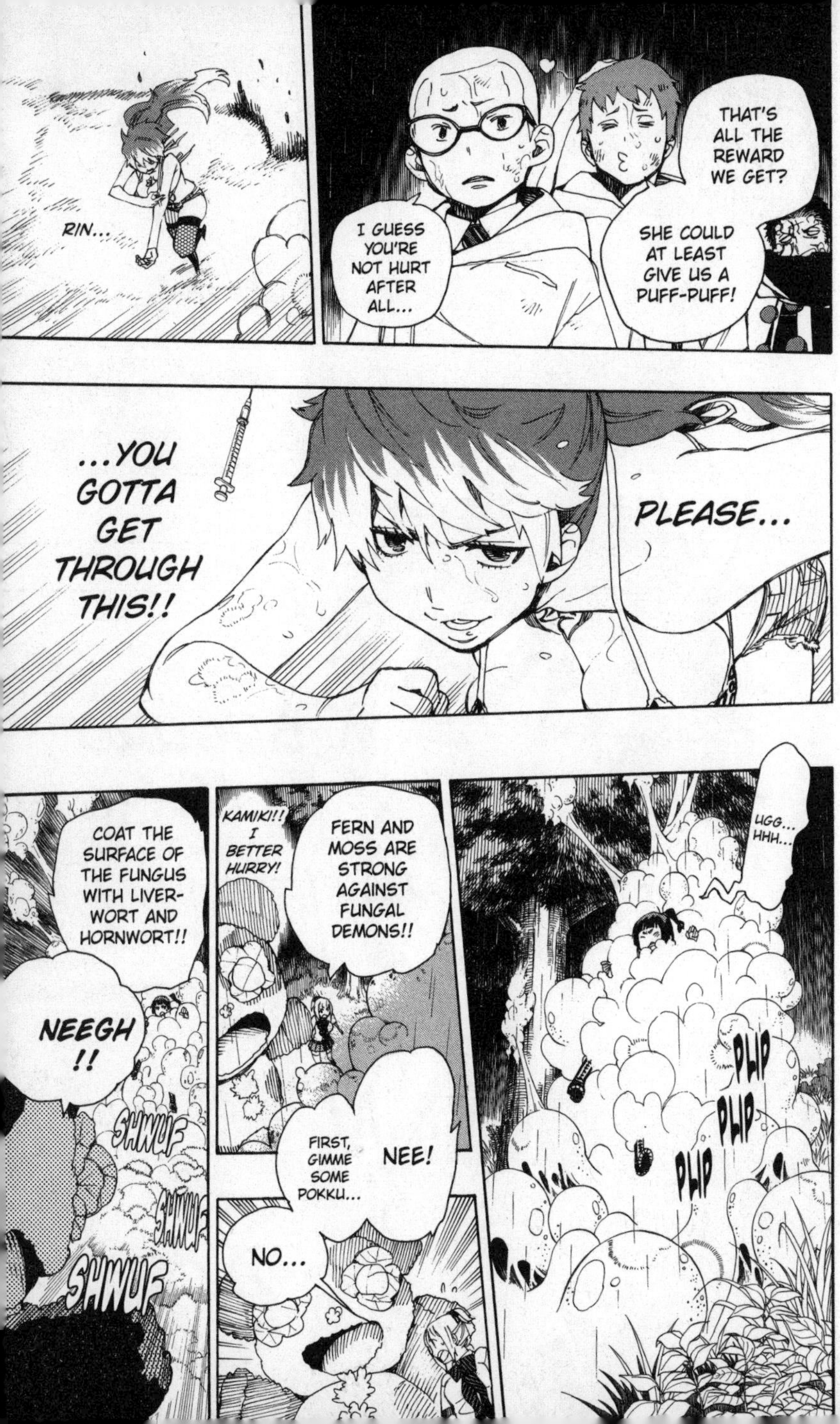
THAT'S ALL THE REWARD WE GET?
SHE COULD AT LEAST GIVE US A PUFF-PUFF!
I GUESS YOU'RE NOT HURT AFTER ALL...
RIN...
PLEASE...
...YOU GOTTA GET THROUGH THIS!!
UGG... HHH...
PLIP
PLIP
PLIP
FERN AND MOSS ARE STRONG AGAINST FUNGAL DEMONS!!
KAMIKI!! I BETTER HURRY!
NEE!
FIRST, GIMME SOME POKKU...
NO...
COAT THE SURFACE OF THE FUNGUS WITH LIVER-WORT AND HORNWORT!!
NEEGH !!
SHNUF
SHNUF
SHNUF

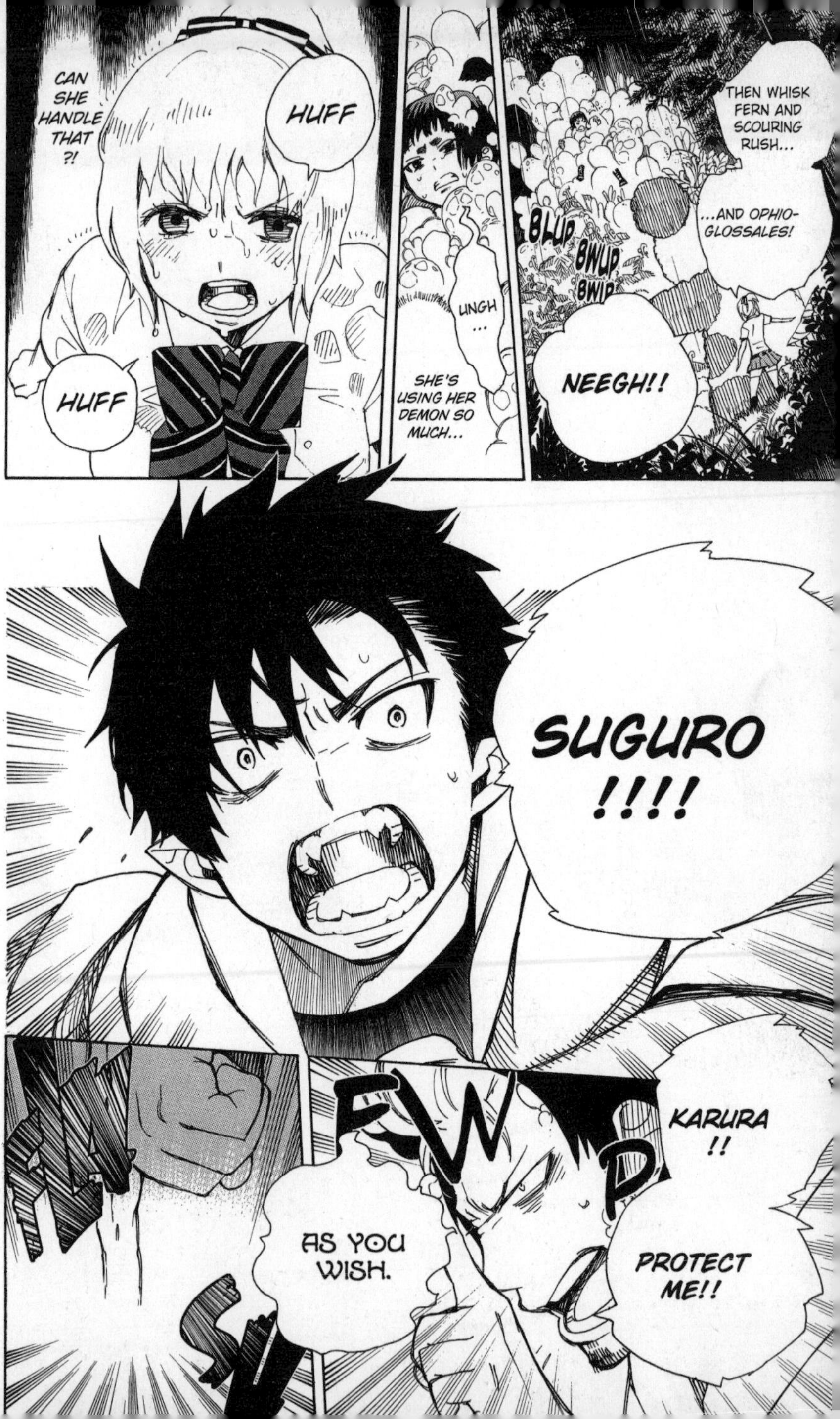
THEN WHISK FERN AND SCOURING RUSH...
...AND OPHIO-GLOSSALES!
BLUP
BWUP
BWIP
NEEGH!!
UNGH...
SHE'S USING HER DEMON SO MUCH...
HUFF
CAN SHE HANDLE THAT?!
HUFF
SUGURO!!!!
KARURA!!
PROTECT ME!!
FWD
AS YOU WISH.

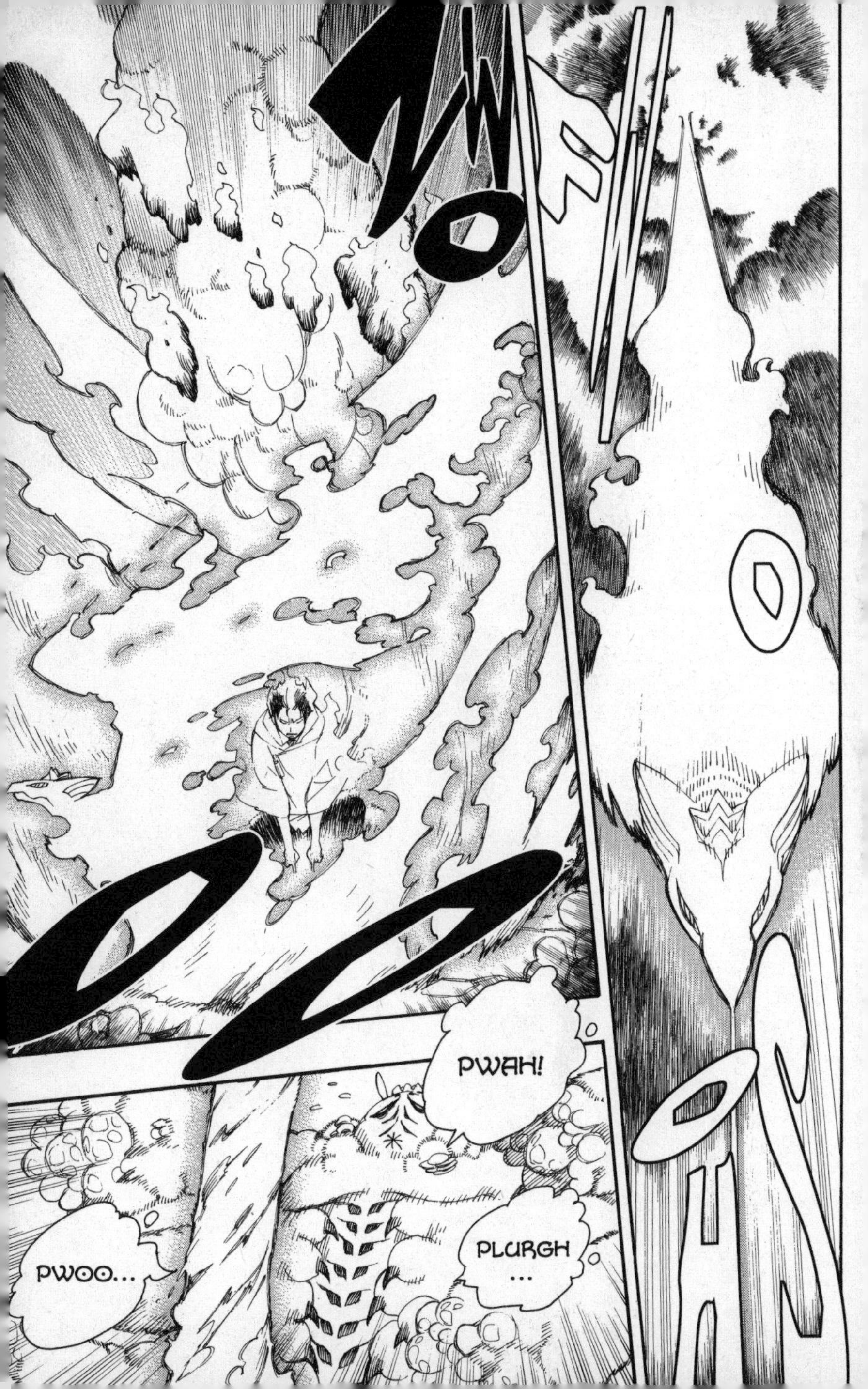
PWAH!
PLURGH ...
PWOO...

Blue Exorcist Chapter 31: Death

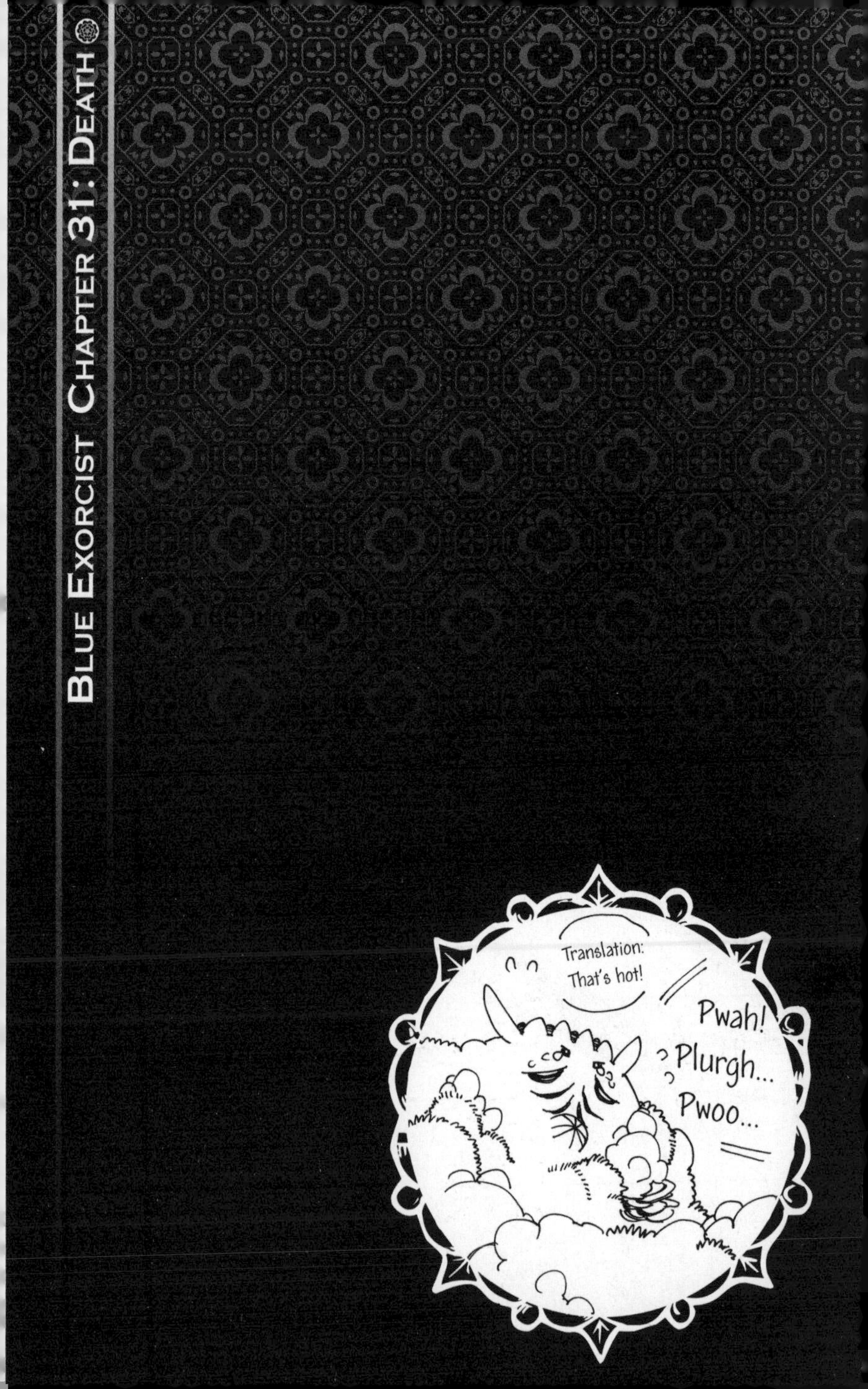
Pwah! Plurgh... Pwoo...
Translation: That's hot!

Chapter 32: Abyss

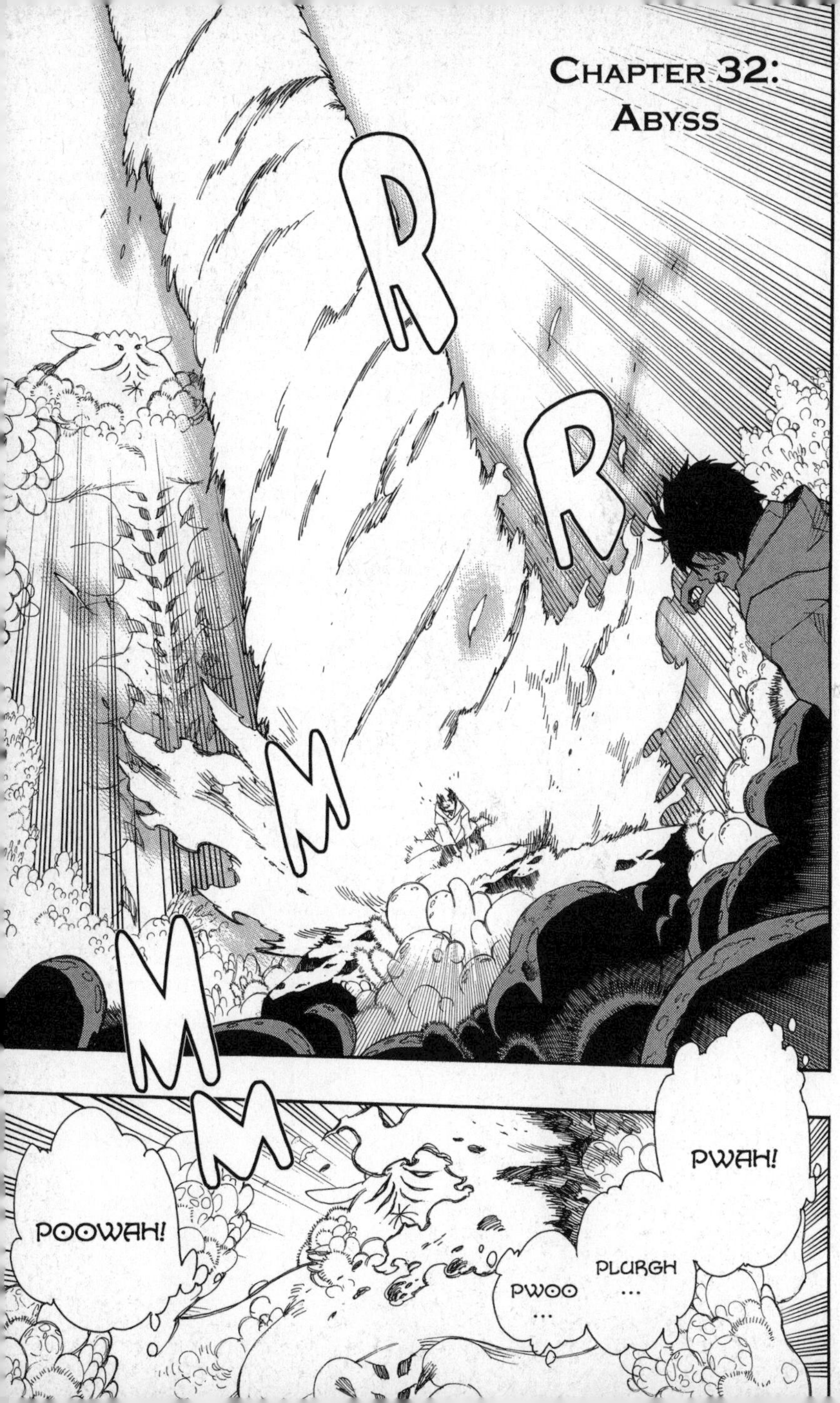
RRRMMMM
PWAH!
PLURGH ...
PWOO ...
POOWAH!

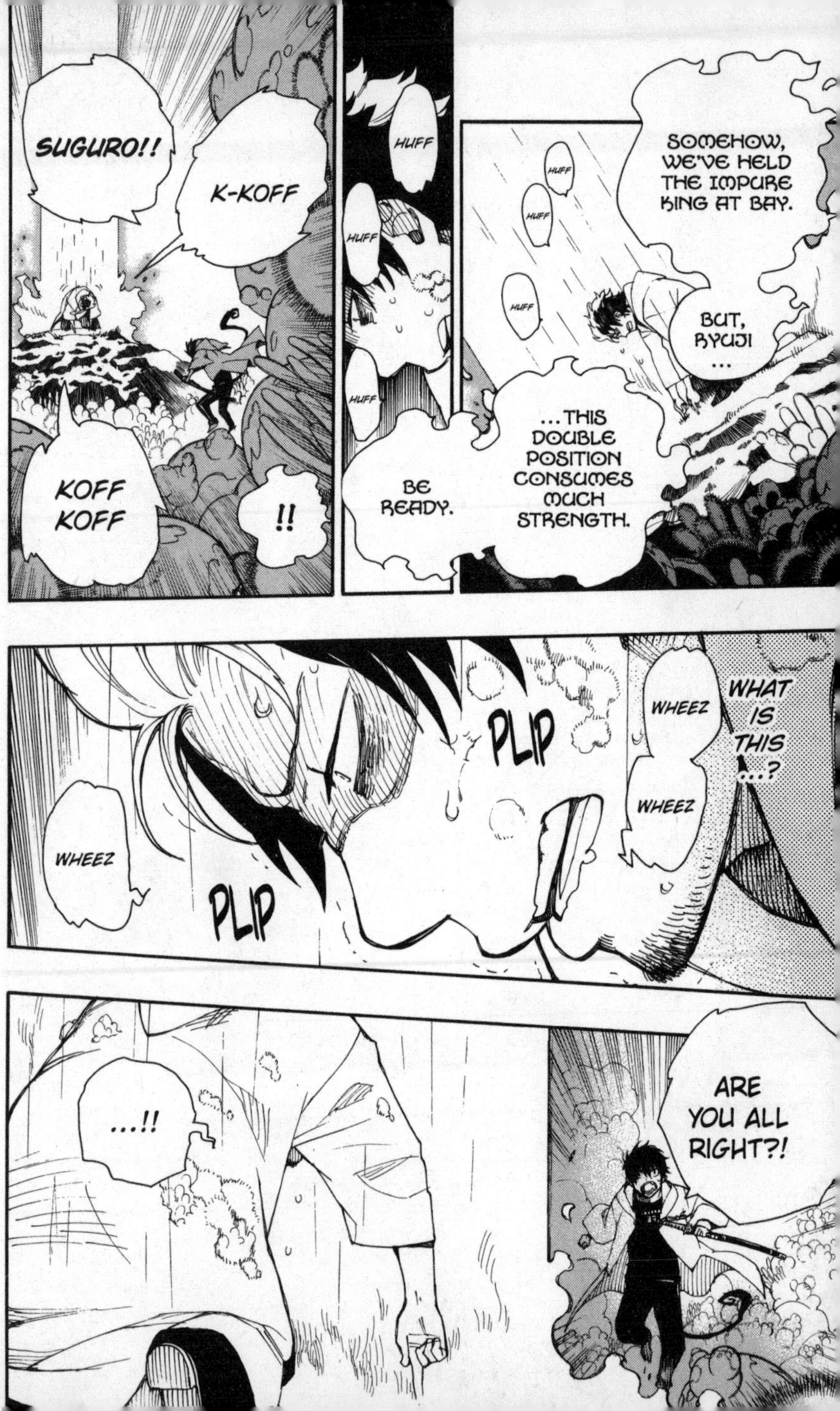
SOMEHOW, WE'VE HELD THE IMPURE KING AT BAY.
HUFF
HUFF
HUFF
BUT, RYUJI ...
...THIS DOUBLE POSITION CONSUMES MUCH STRENGTH.
HUFF
HUFF
HUFF
BE READY.
SUGURO!!
K-KOFF
KOFF KOFF
!!
WHAT IS THIS ...?
WHEEZ
WHEEZ
PLIP
PLIP
WHEEZ
ARE YOU ALL RIGHT?!
...!!

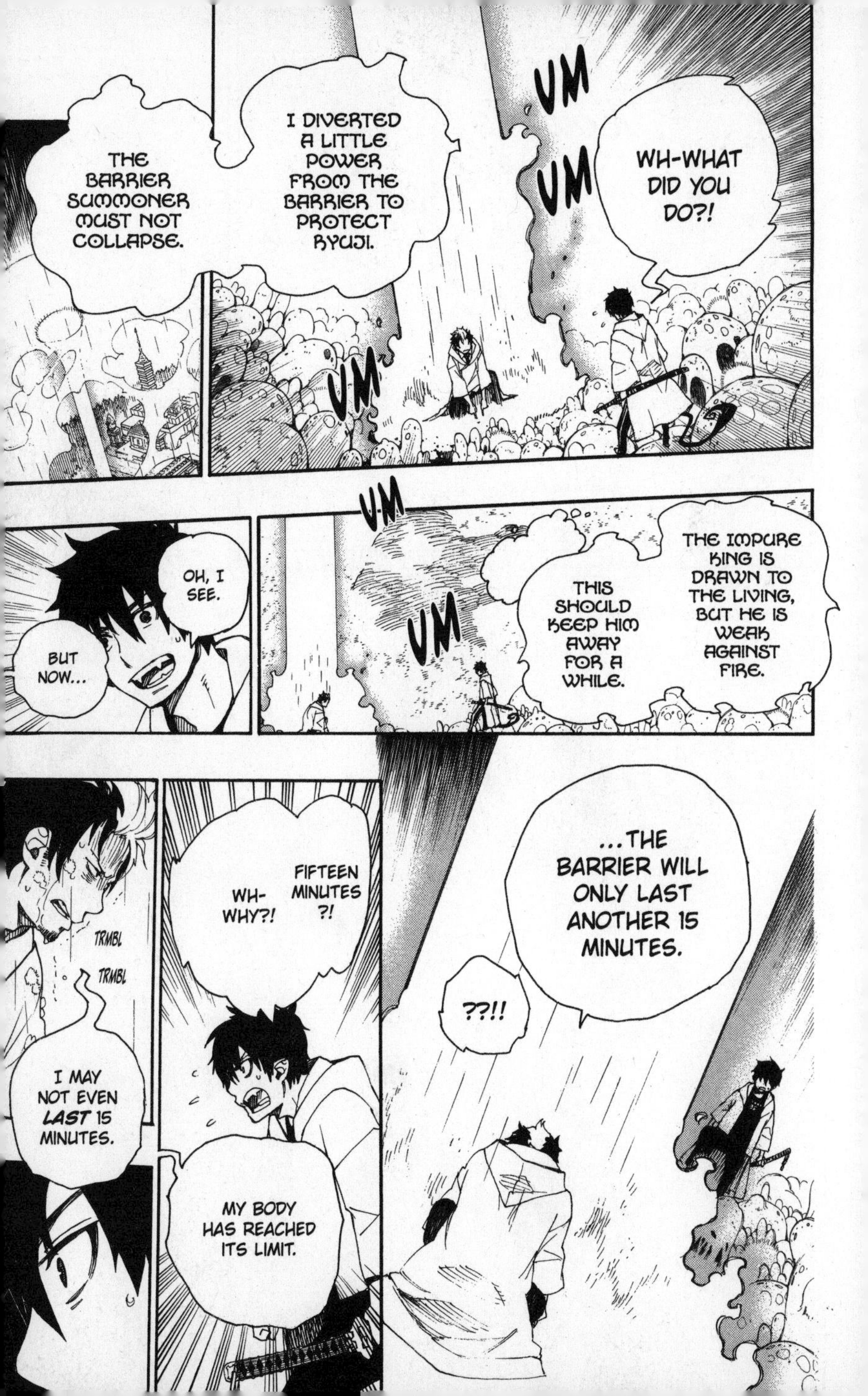
VM
VM
WH-WHAT DID YOU DO?!
VM
I DIVERTED A LITTLE POWER FROM THE BARRIER TO PROTECT RYUJI.
THE BARRIER SUMMONER MUST NOT COLLAPSE.
VM
THE IMPURE KING IS DRAWN TO THE LIVING, BUT HE IS WEAK AGAINST FIRE.
THIS SHOULD KEEP HIM AWAY FOR A WHILE.
VM
OH, I SEE.
BUT NOW...
...THE BARRIER WILL ONLY LAST ANOTHER 15 MINUTES.
??!!
FIFTEEN MINUTES ?!
WH- WHY?!
TRMBL
TRMBL
I MAY NOT EVEN *LAST* 15 MINUTES.
MY BODY HAS REACHED ITS LIMIT.

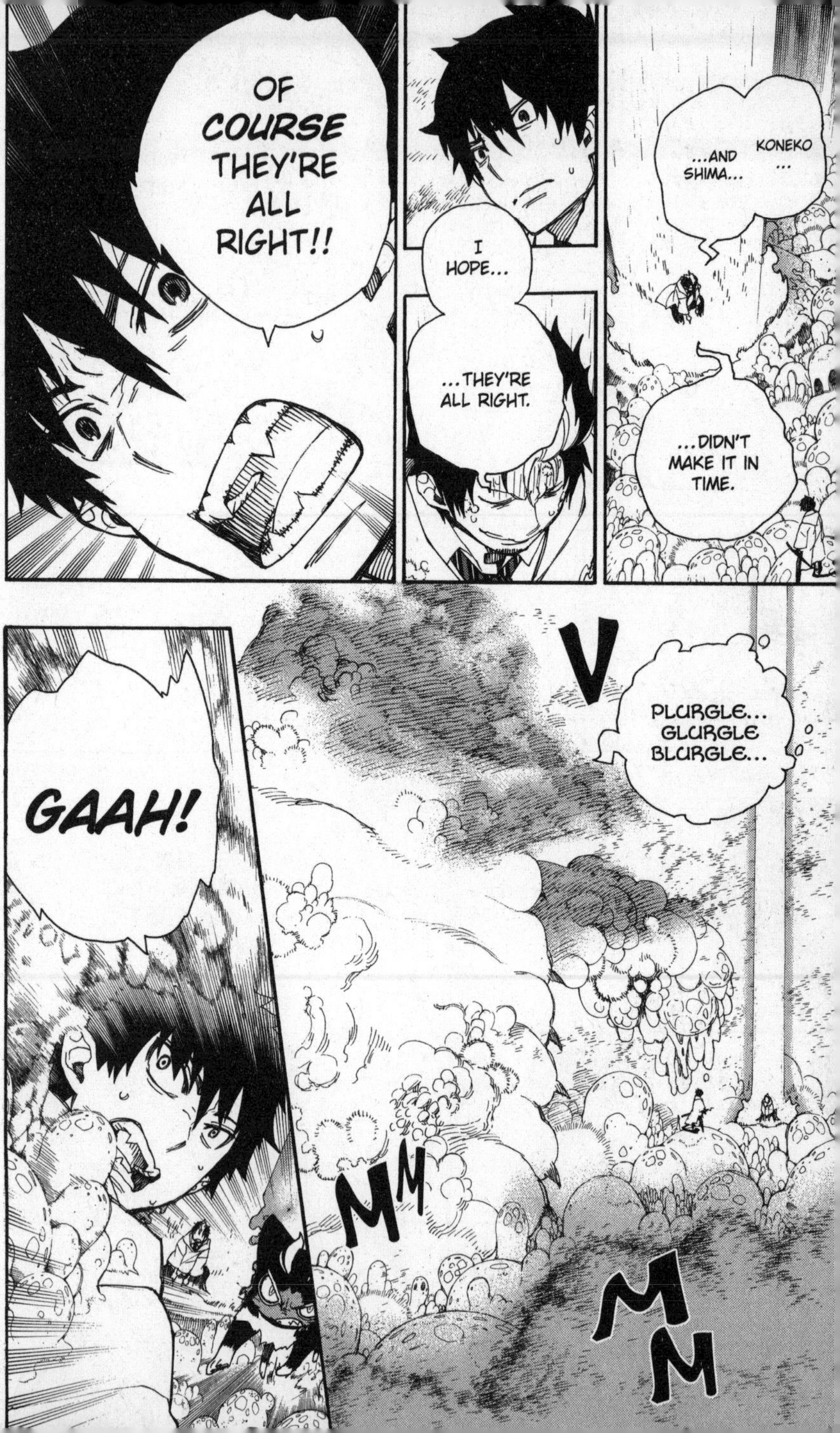
KONEKO...
...AND SHIMA...
...DIDN'T MAKE IT IN TIME.
I HOPE...
...THEY'RE ALL RIGHT.
OF COURSE THEY'RE ALL RIGHT!!
V
PLURGLE... GLURGLE BLURGLE...
MM
MM
GAAH!

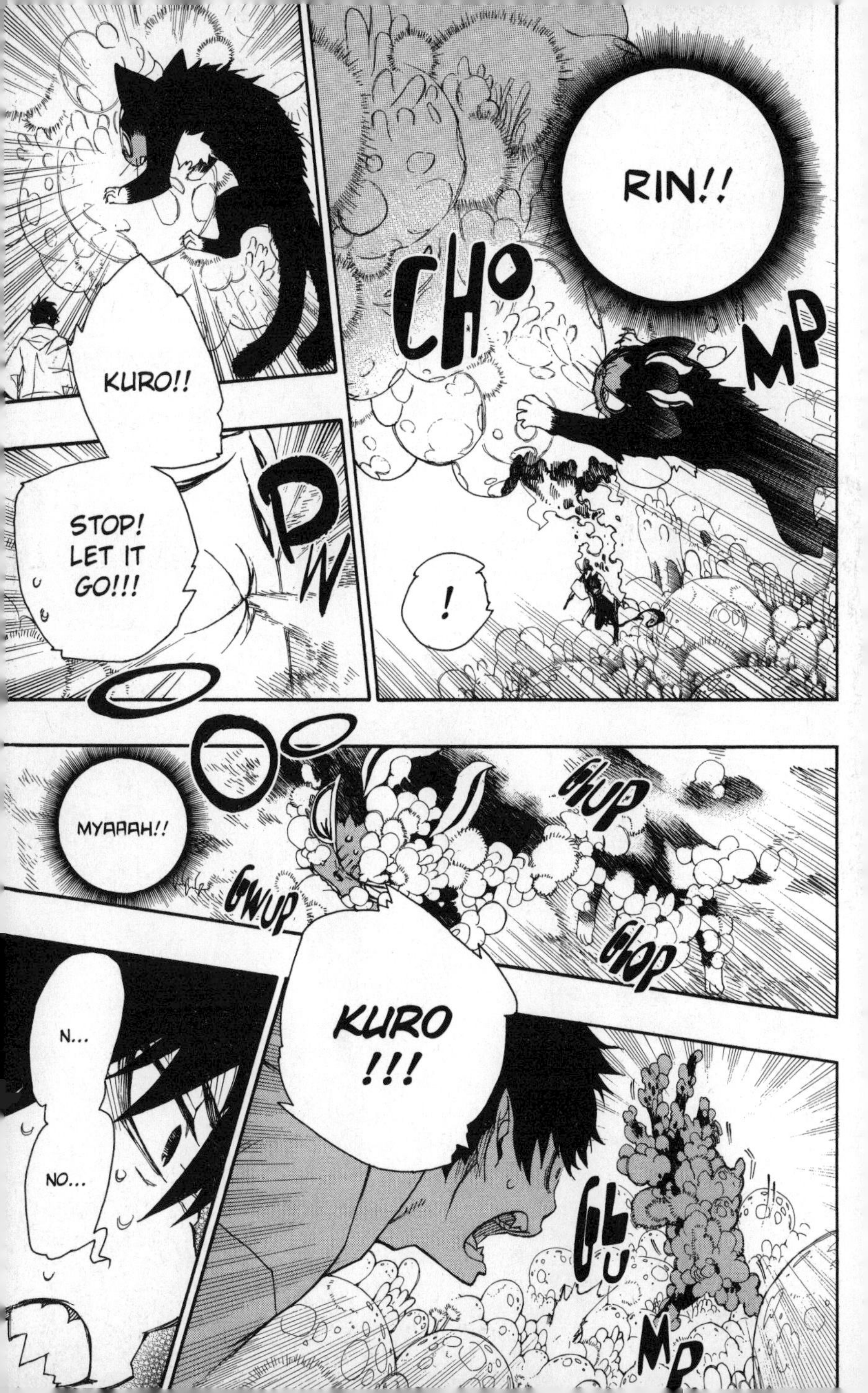
RIN!!
CHOMP
!
KURO!!
STOP! LET IT GO!!!
PW
OOOO
GLUP
MYAAAH!!
GWUP
GLOP
KURO!!!
N...
NO...
GLUMP

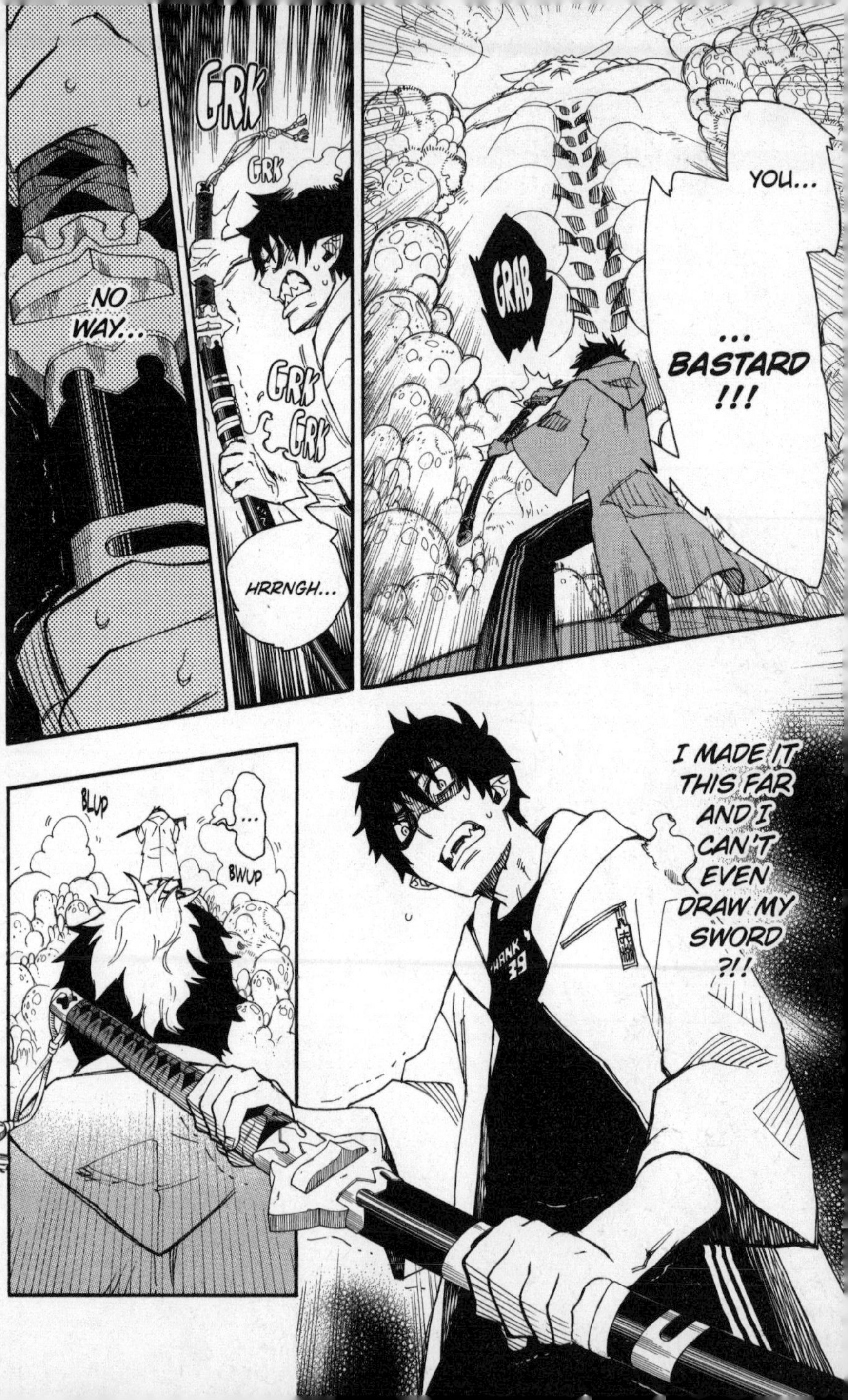
YOU...
...BASTARD!!!
GRAB
GRK
GRK
GRK GRK
HRRNGH...
NO WAY...
I MADE IT THIS FAR AND I CAN'T EVEN DRAW MY SWORD?!!
BLUP
...
BWUP

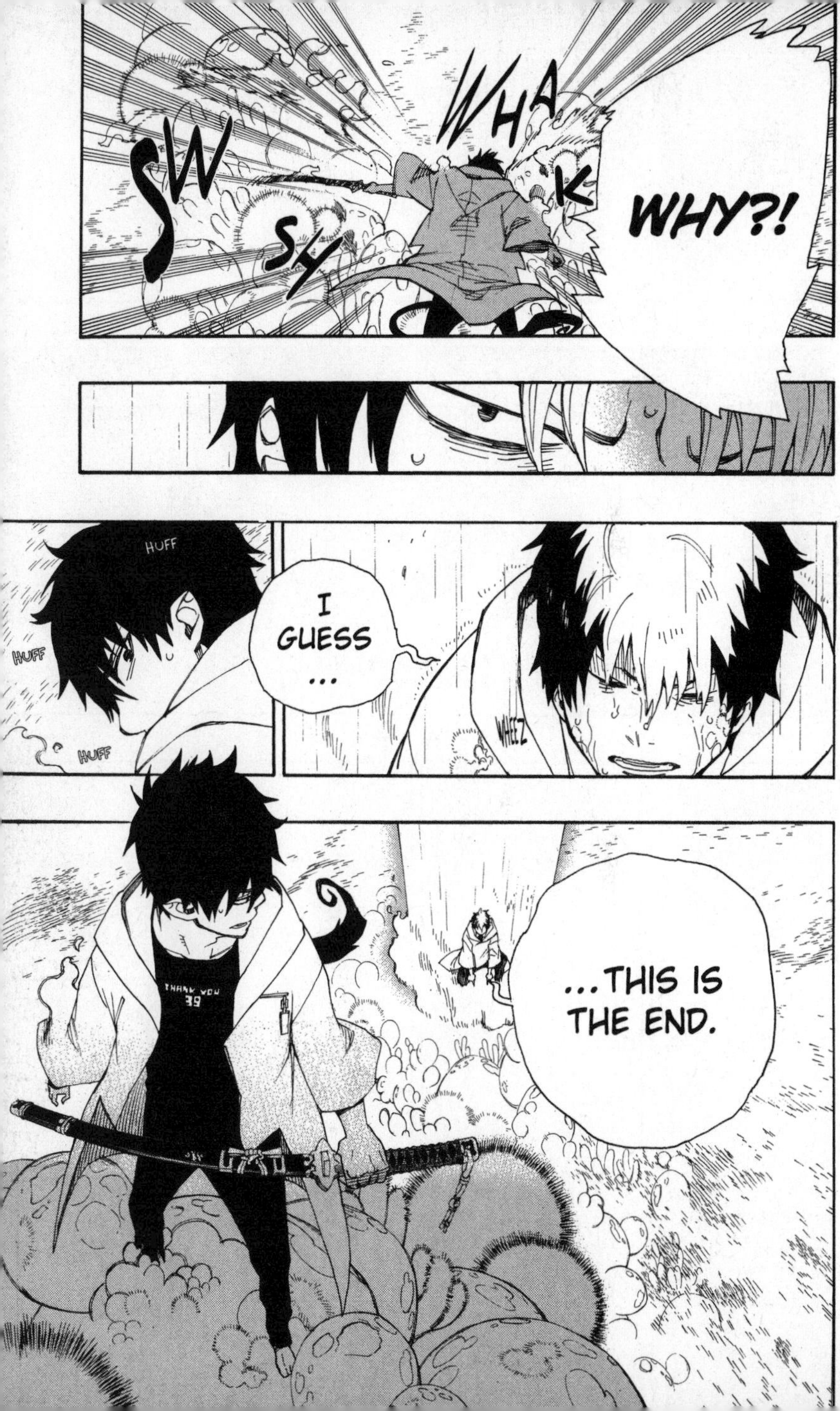
WHY?!
WHAK
SWSH
WHEEZ
I GUESS ...
HUFF
HUFF
HUFF
...THIS IS THE END.
THANK YOU 39

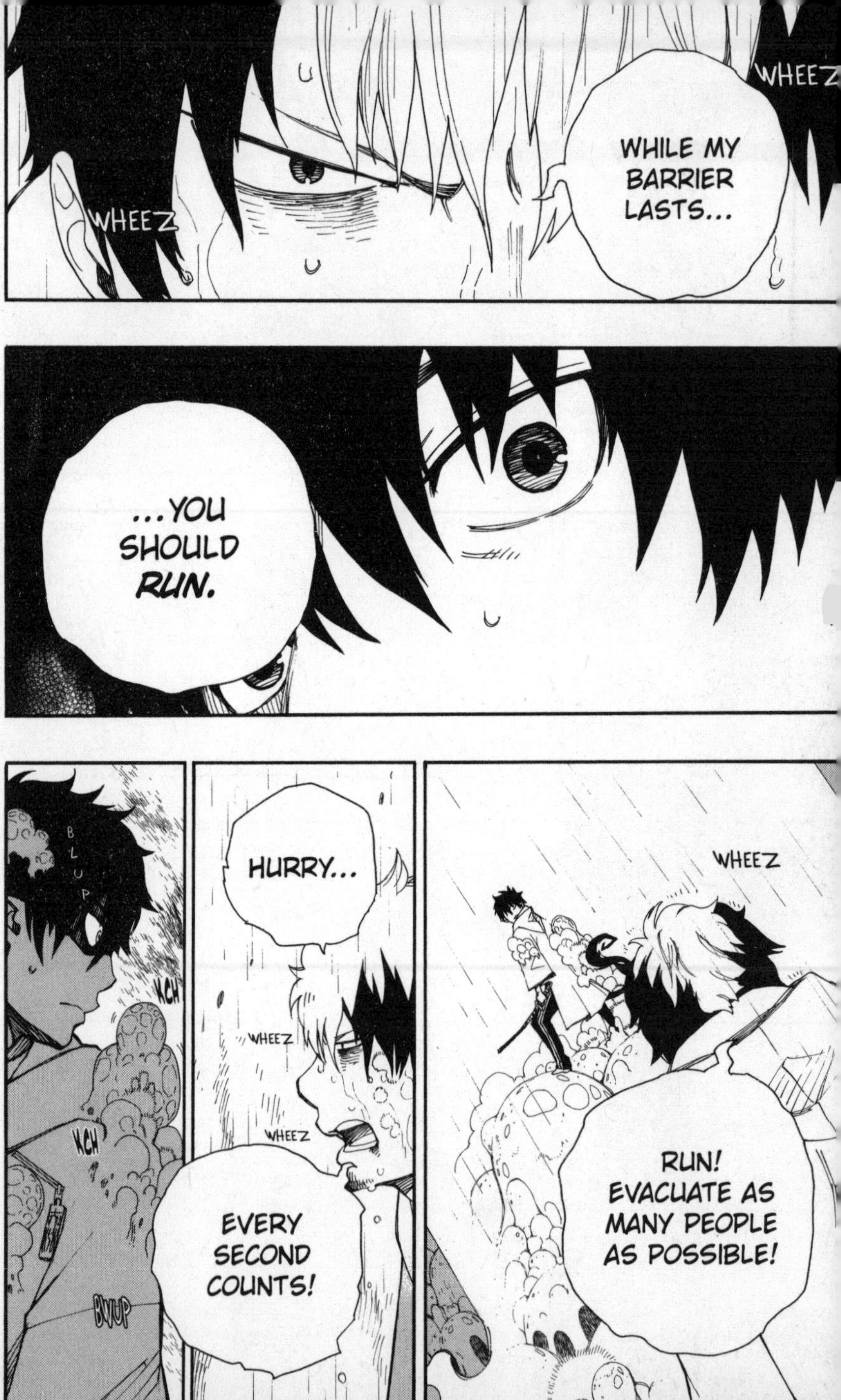
WHEEZ
WHILE MY BARRIER LASTS...
WHEEZ
...YOU SHOULD RUN.
WHEEZ
RUN! EVACUATE AS MANY PEOPLE AS POSSIBLE!
HURRY...
WHEEZ
WHEEZ
EVERY SECOND COUNTS!
BLUP
KCH
KCH
BWUP

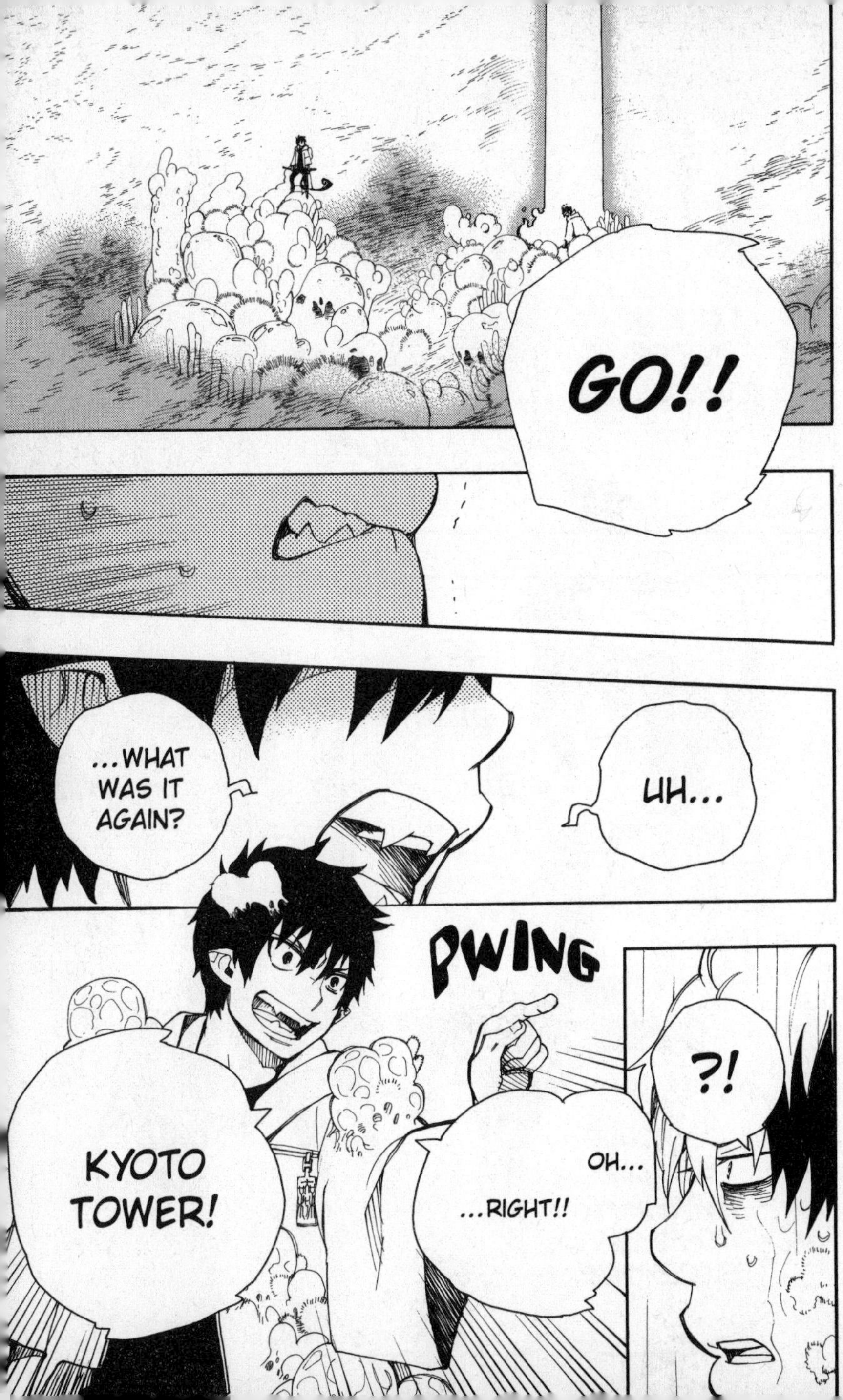
GO!!
UH...
...WHAT WAS IT AGAIN?
PWING
KYOTO TOWER!
?!
OH... ...RIGHT!!

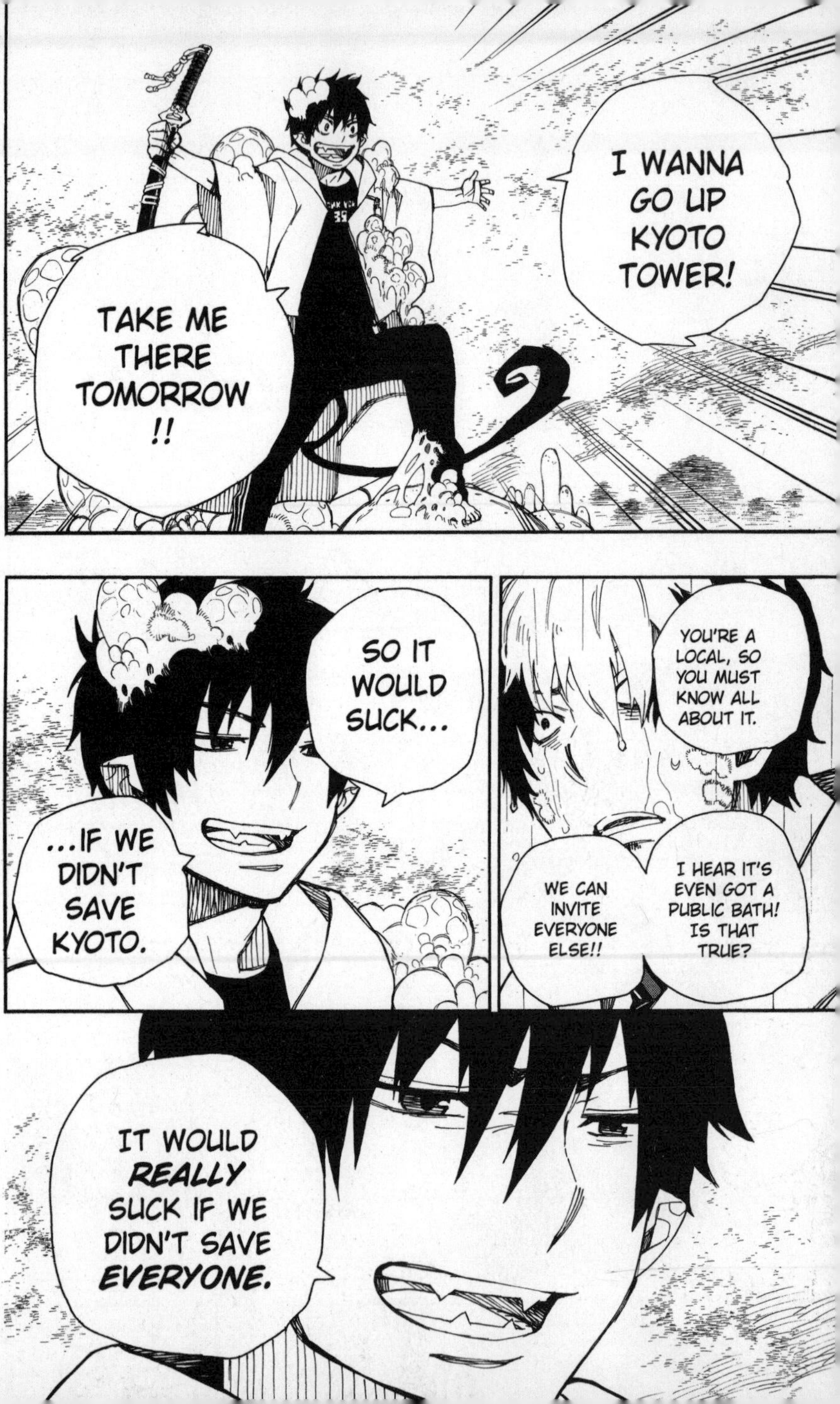
I WANNA GO UP KYOTO TOWER!
TAKE ME THERE TOMORROW!!
YOU'RE A LOCAL, SO YOU MUST KNOW ALL ABOUT IT.
I HEAR IT'S EVEN GOT A PUBLIC BATH! IS THAT TRUE?
WE CAN INVITE EVERYONE ELSE!!
SO IT WOULD SUCK...
...IF WE DIDN'T SAVE KYOTO.
IT WOULD *REALLY* SUCK IF WE DIDN'T SAVE *EVERYONE.*

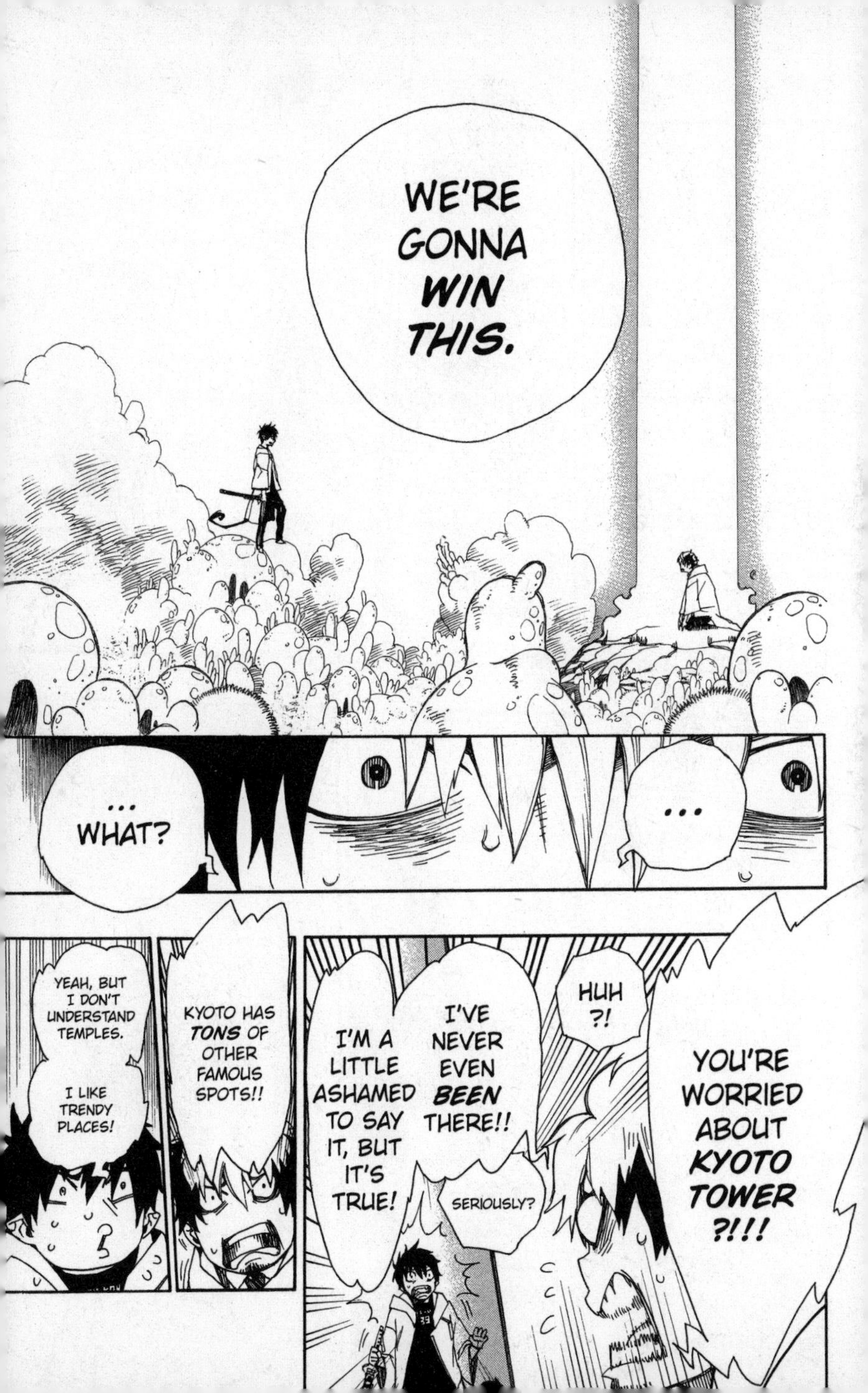
WE'RE GONNA *WIN THIS.*
...
... WHAT?
HUH ?!
YOU'RE WORRIED ABOUT *KYOTO TOWER* ?!!!
I'VE NEVER EVEN *BEEN* THERE!!
I'M A LITTLE ASHAMED TO SAY IT, BUT IT'S TRUE!
SERIOUSLY?
KYOTO HAS *TONS* OF OTHER FAMOUS SPOTS!!
YEAH, BUT I DON'T UNDERSTAND TEMPLES.
I LIKE TRENDY PLACES!

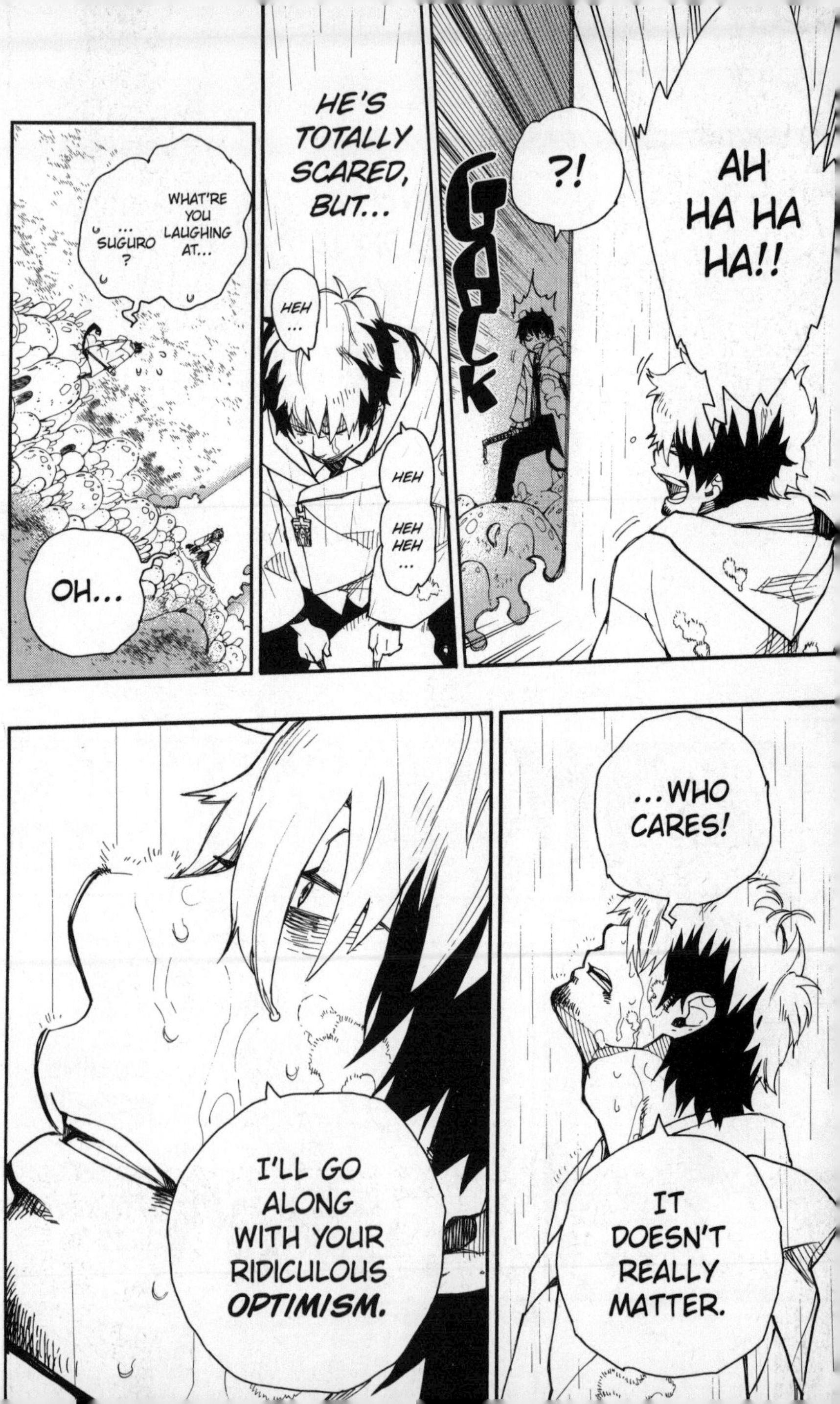
AH HA HA HA!!
?!
GACK
HE'S TOTALLY SCARED, BUT...
HEH...
HEH HEH HEH...
... SUGURO ?
WHAT'RE YOU LAUGHING AT...
OH...
...WHO CARES!
IT DOESN'T REALLY MATTER.
I'LL GO ALONG WITH YOUR RIDICULOUS OPTIMISM.

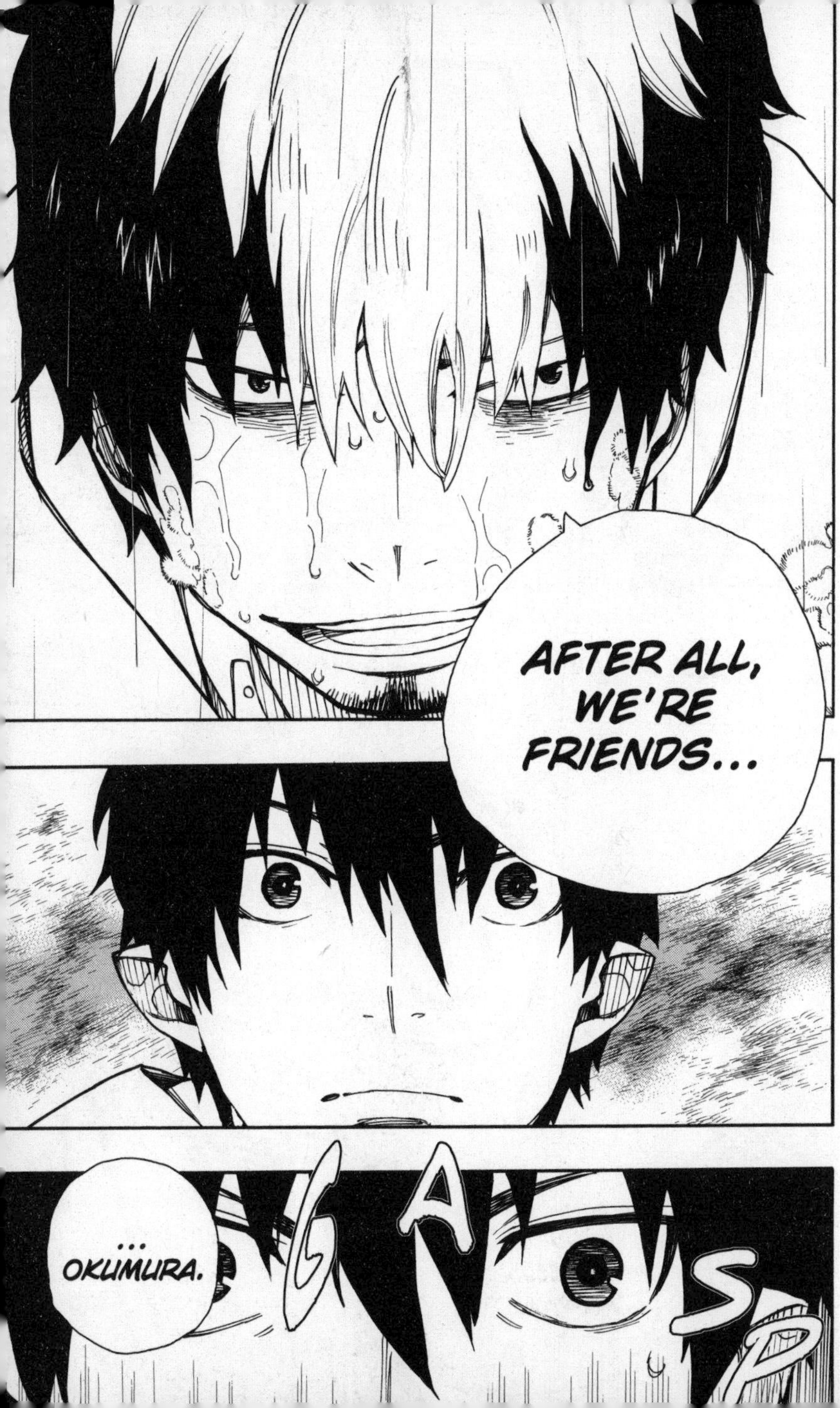
AFTER ALL, WE'RE FRIENDS...
GASP
... OKUMURA.

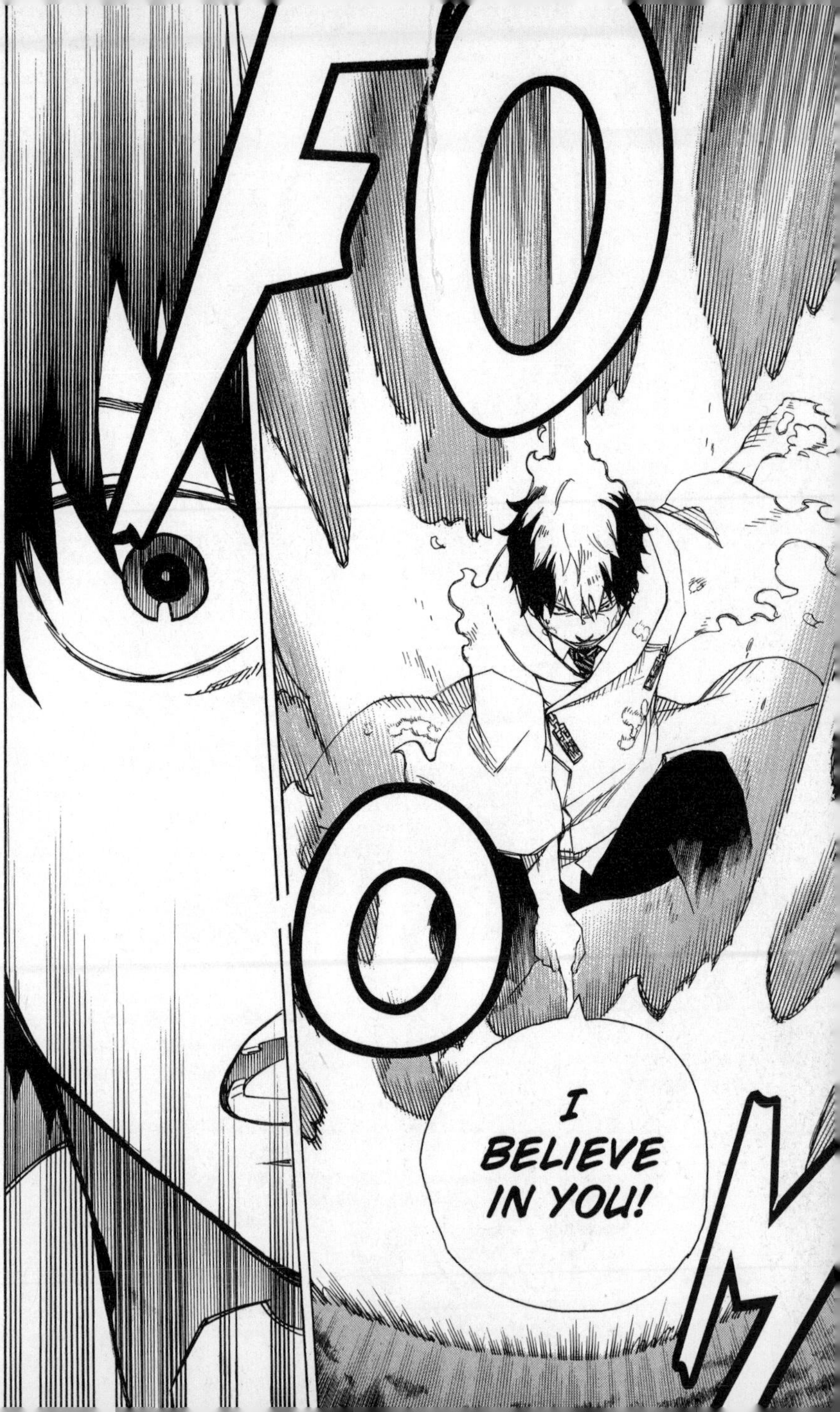
FOOM
I BELIEVE IN YOU!

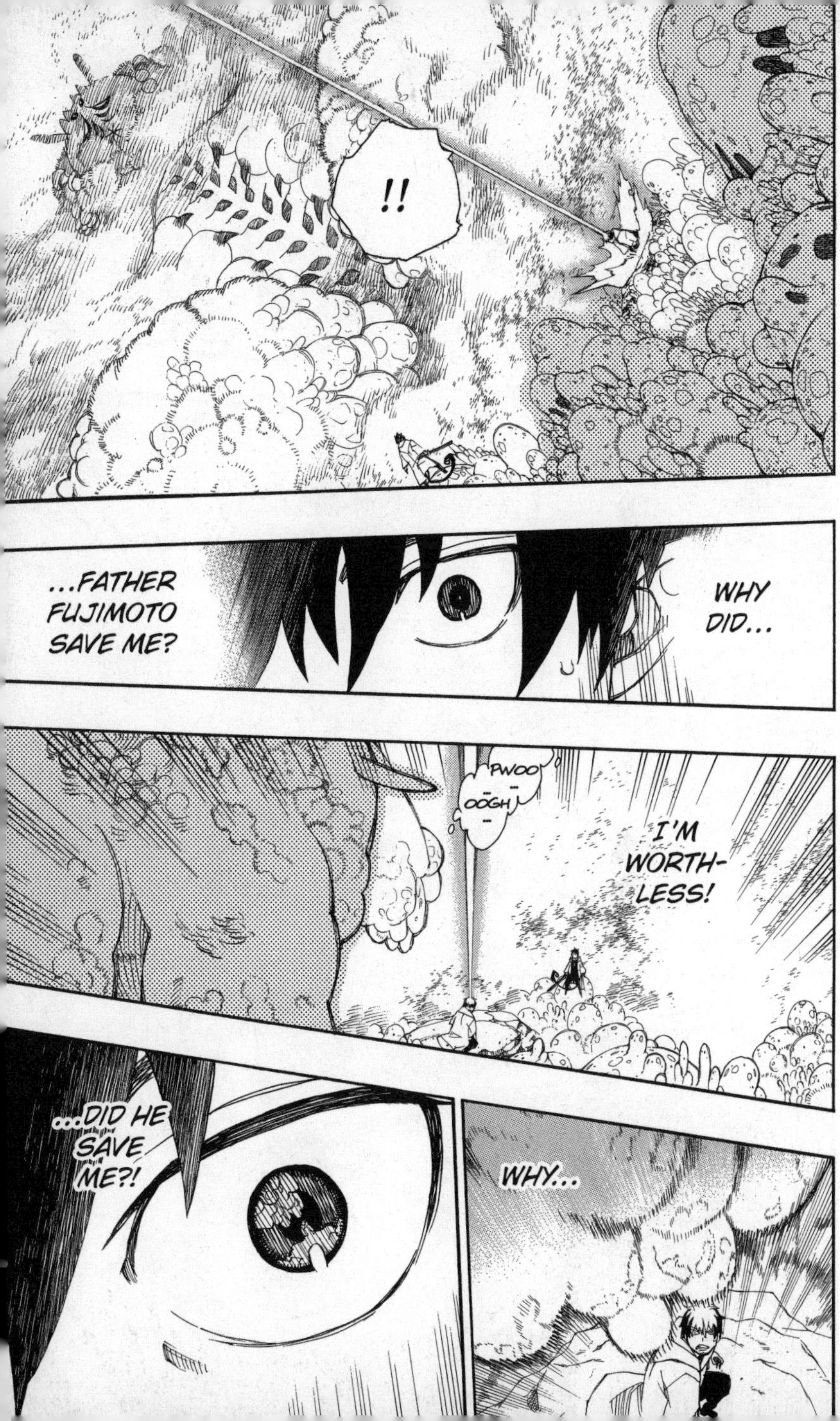
!!
WHY DID...
...FATHER FUJIMOTO SAVE ME?
I'M WORTH-LESS!
PWOO--OOGH--
WHY...
...DID HE SAVE ME?!

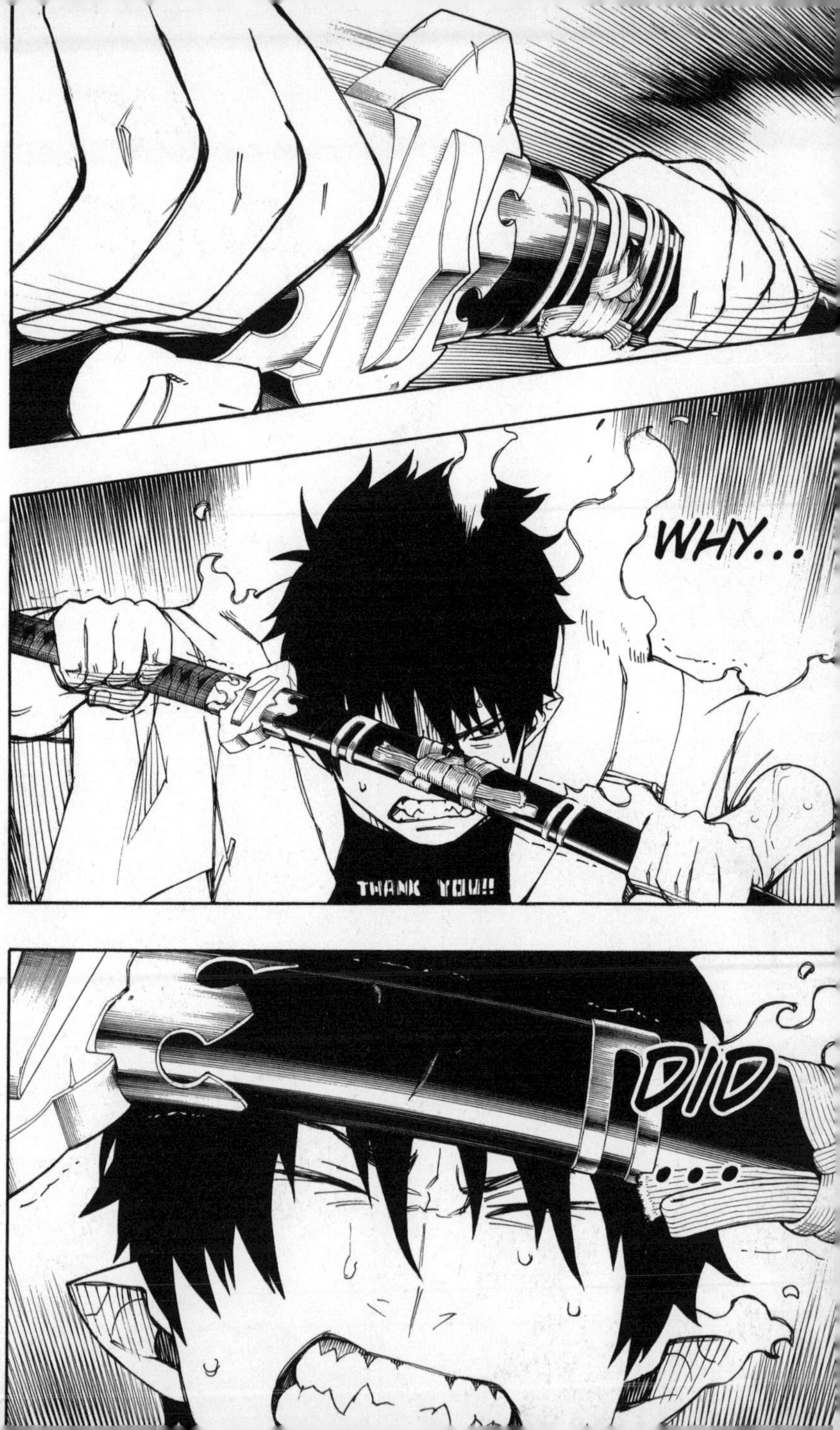
WHY...
THANK YOU!!
DID
....

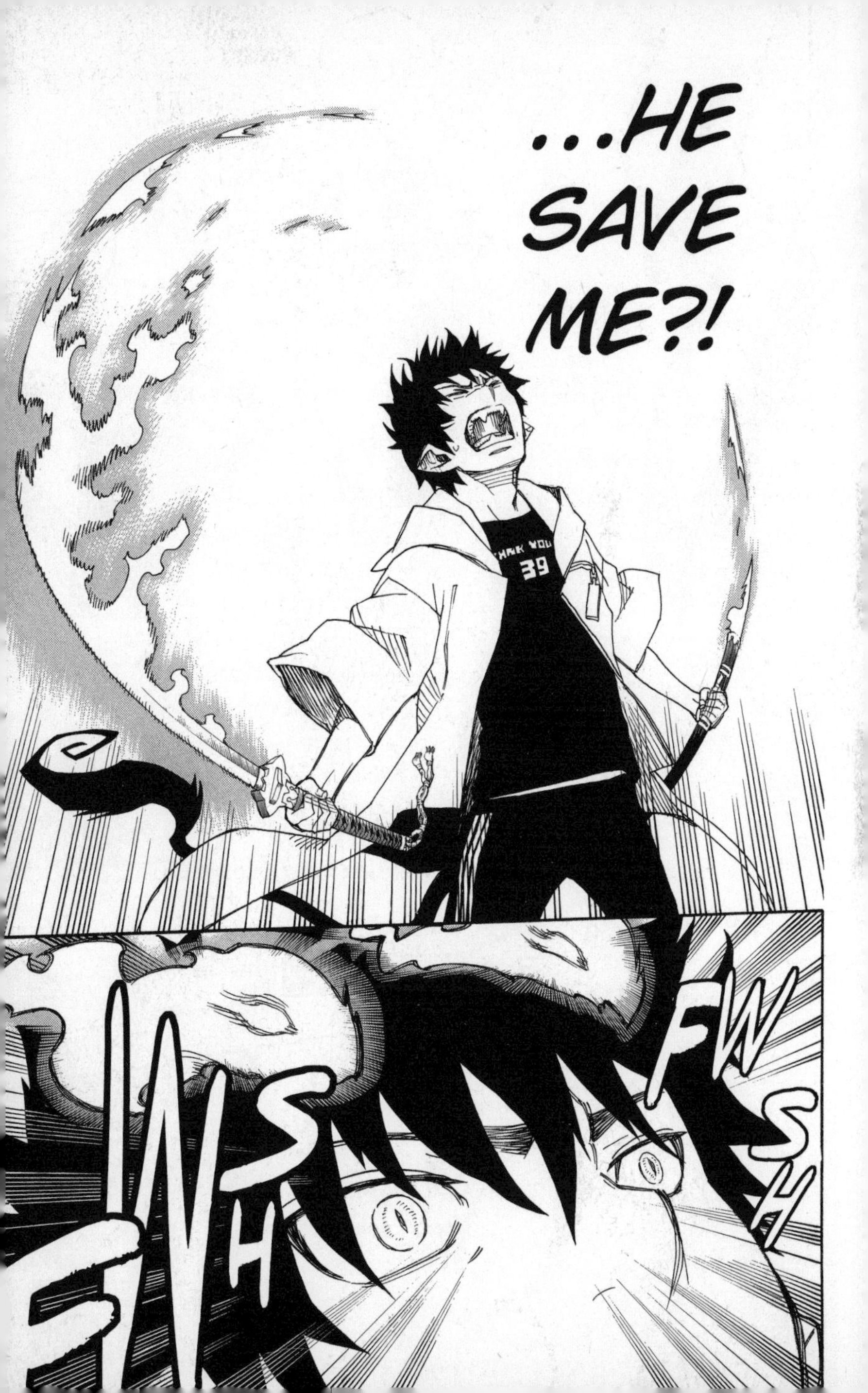
...HE SAVE ME?!
THANK YOU
39
FWSH
WSH

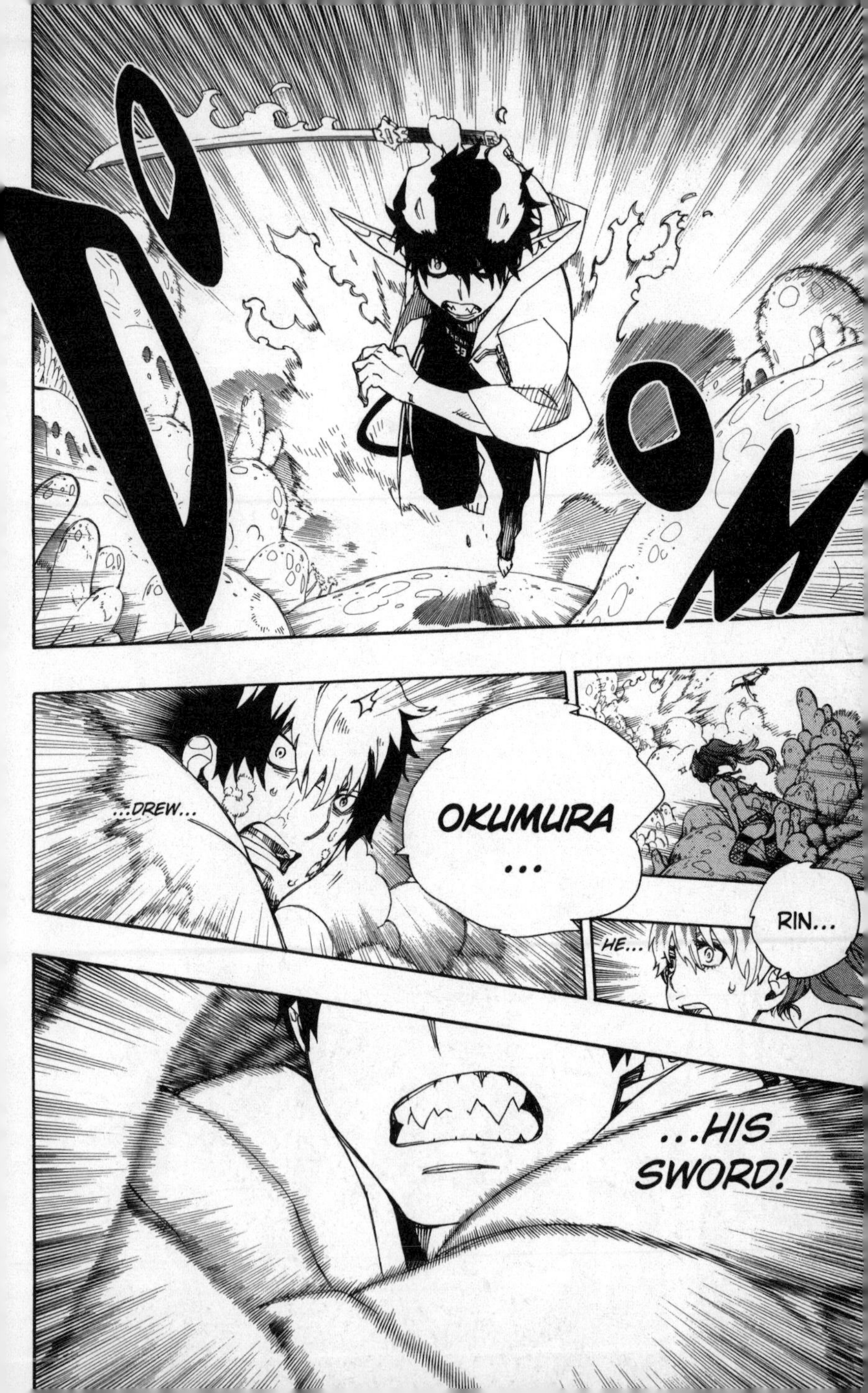
DOOM
RIN...
HE...
OKUMURA ...
...DREW...
...HIS SWORD!

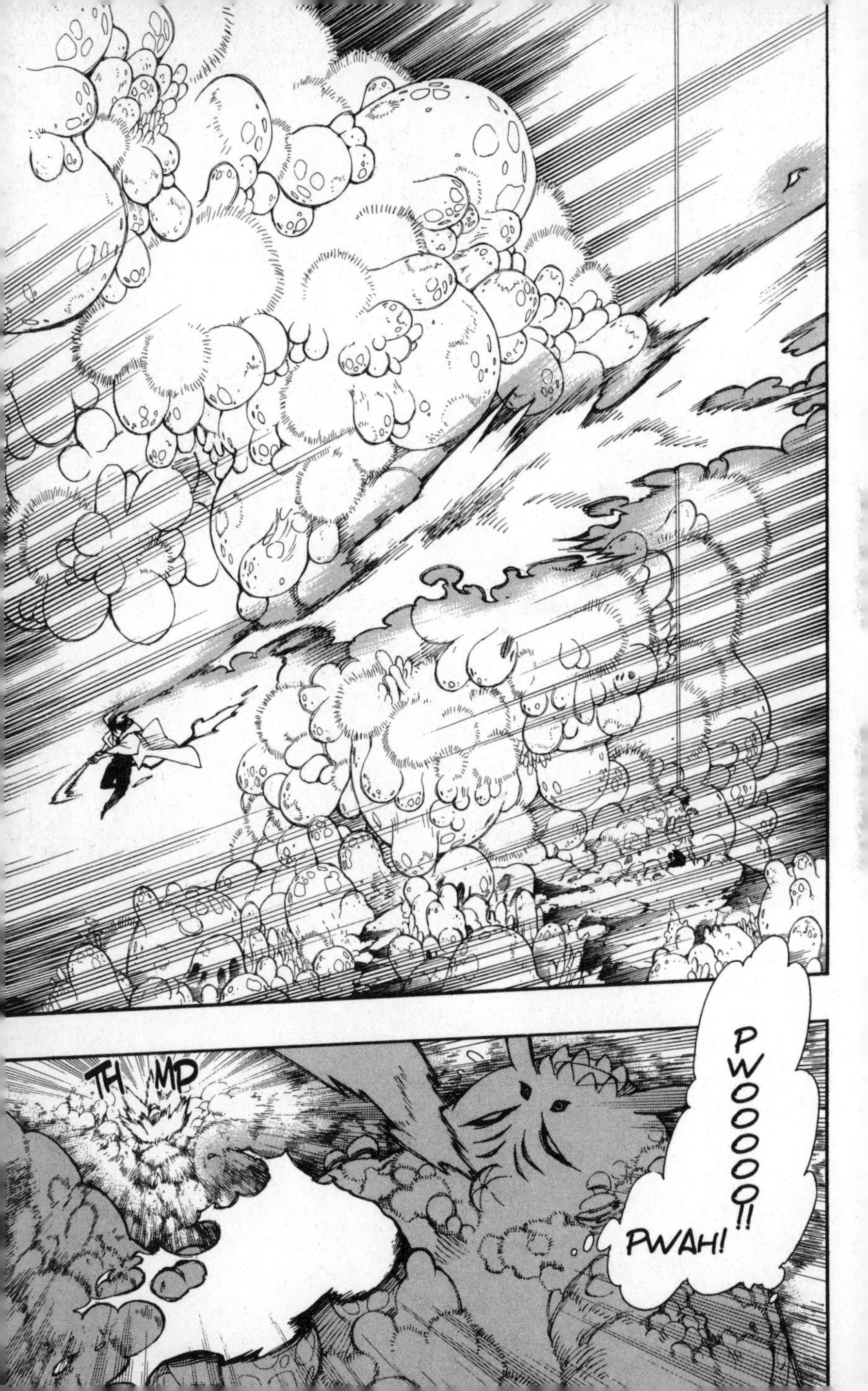
PWOOOOOO!!
PWAH!
TH MP

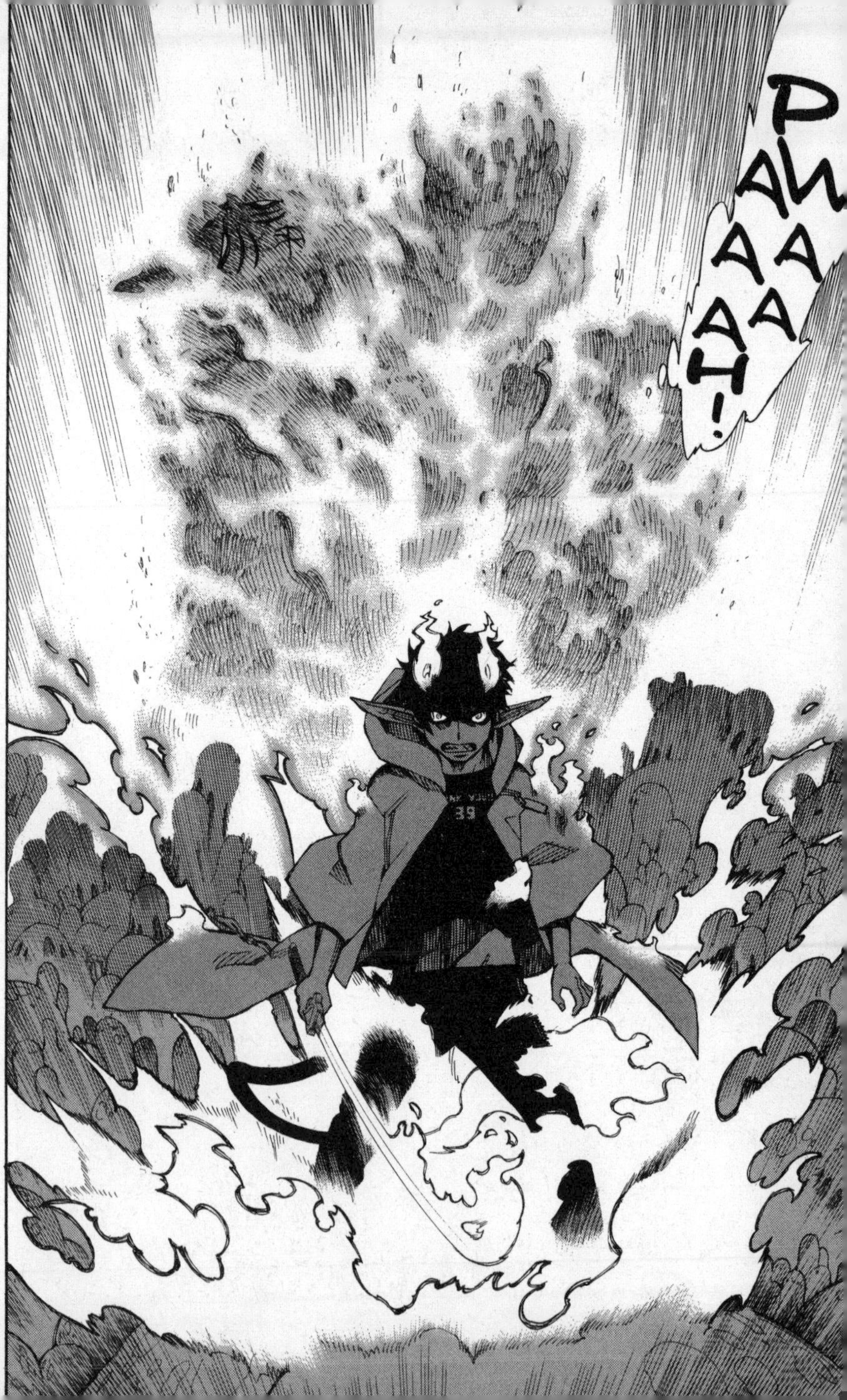
PAAAAAAH!

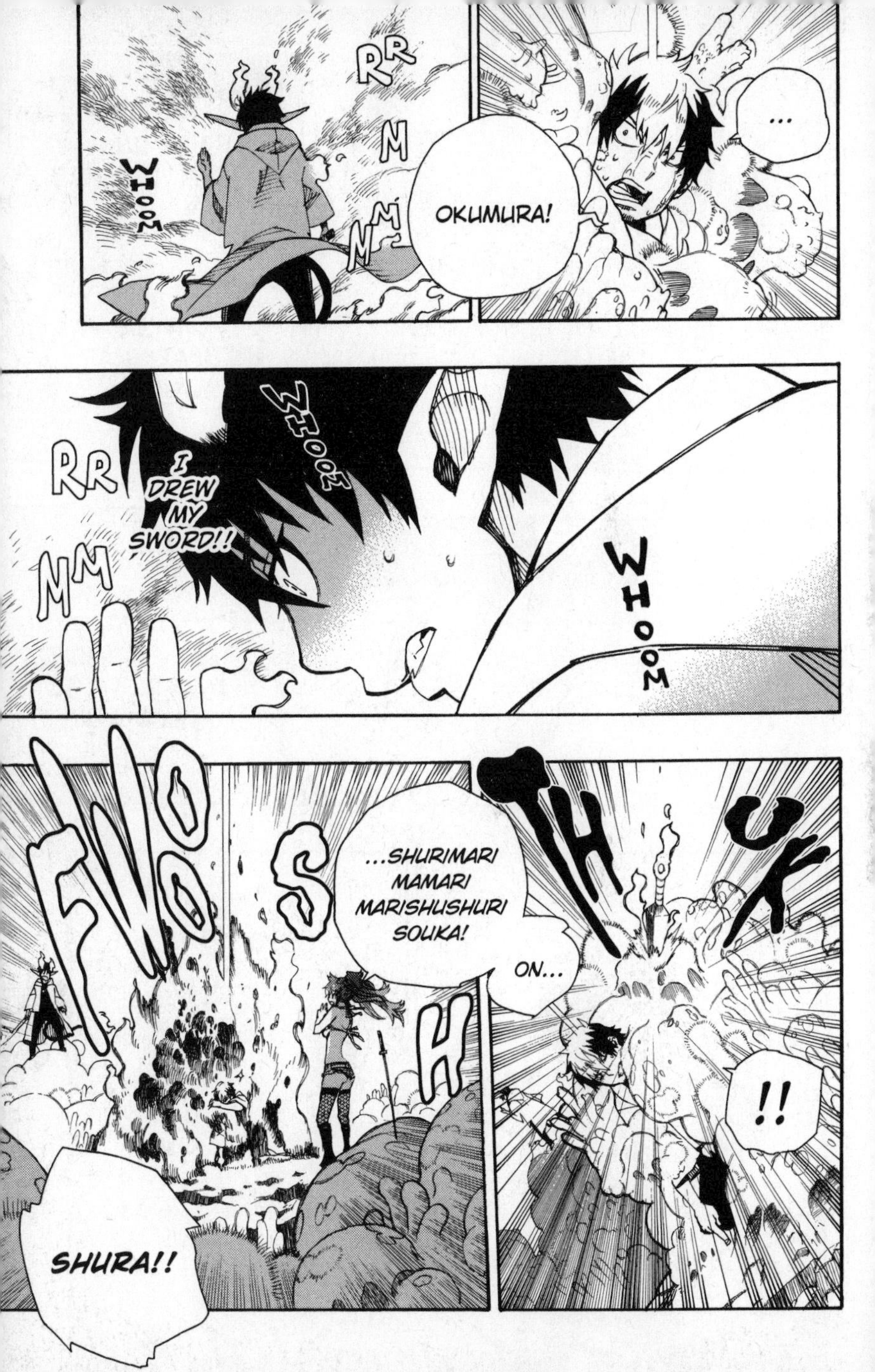
...
OKUMURA!
RRMMMM
WHOOM
WHOOM
WHOOM
I DREW MY SWORD!!
RRMM
THUK
ON...
...SHURIMARI MAMARI MARISHUSHURI SOUKA!
!!
FWOOSH
SHURA!!

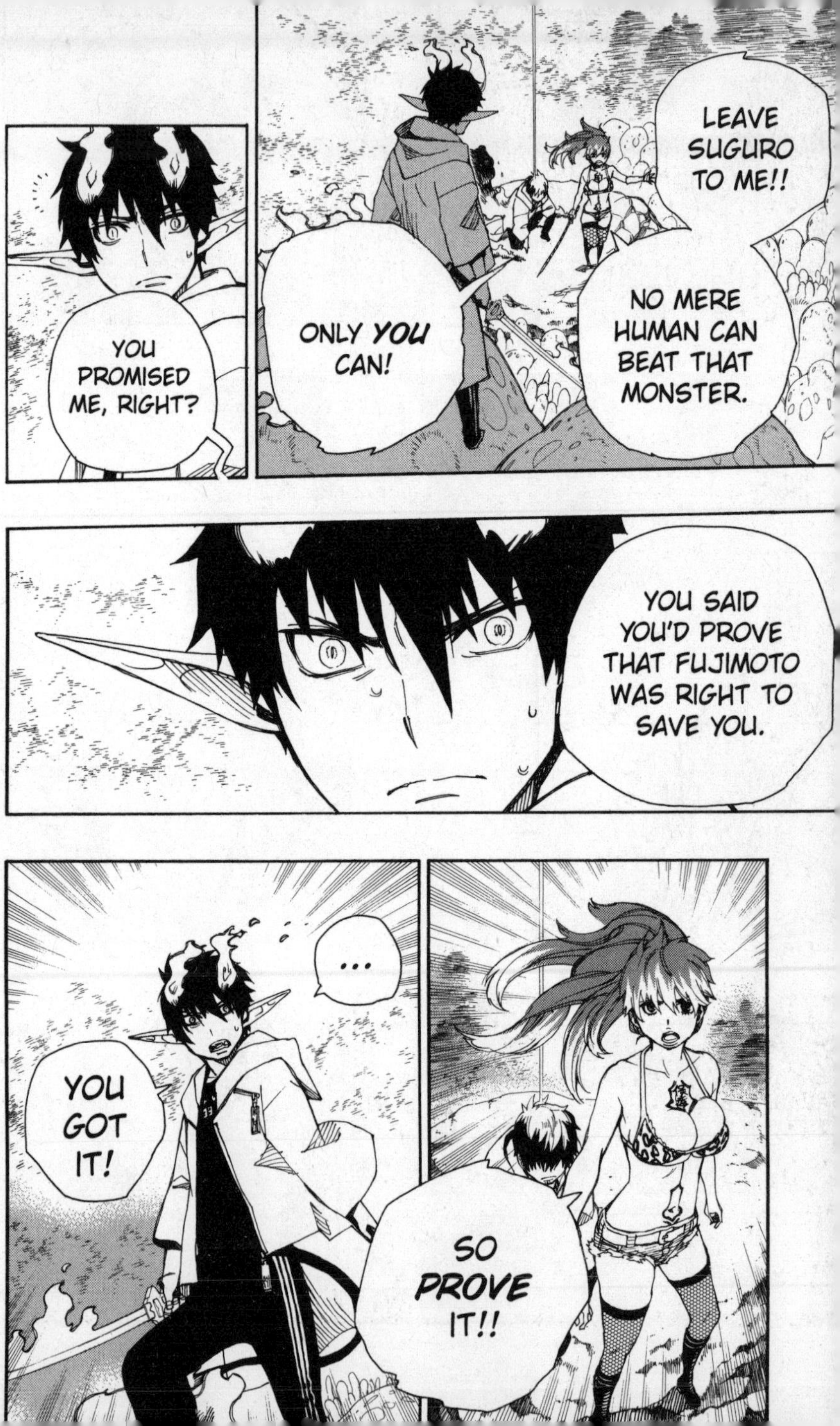
LEAVE SUGURO TO ME!!
NO MERE HUMAN CAN BEAT THAT MONSTER.
ONLY *YOU* CAN!
YOU PROMISED ME, RIGHT?
YOU SAID YOU'D PROVE THAT FUJIMOTO WAS RIGHT TO SAVE YOU.
SO *PROVE* IT!!
...
YOU GOT IT!

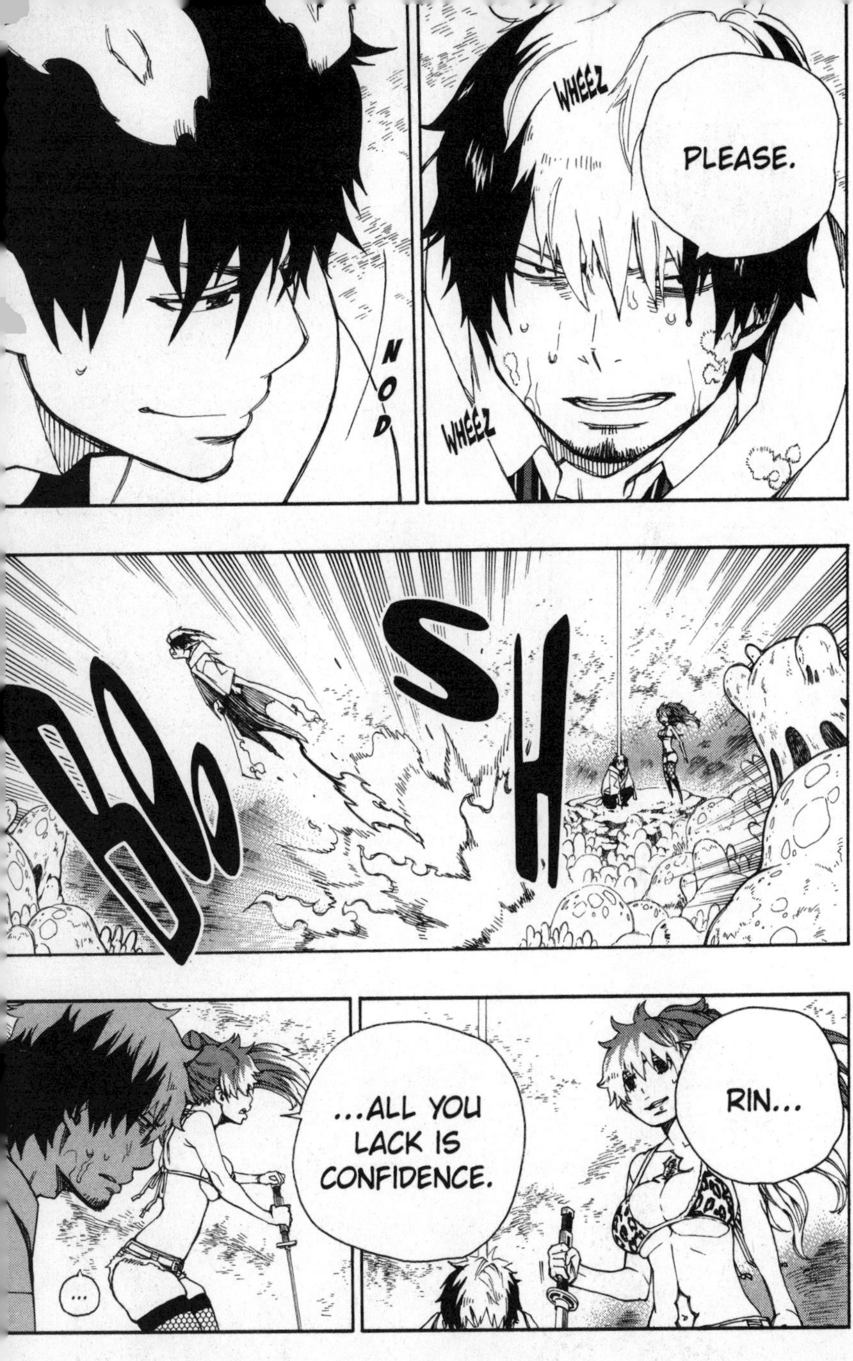
WHEEZ
PLEASE.
WHEEZ
NOD
BOOSH
RIN...
...ALL YOU LACK IS CONFIDENCE.
...

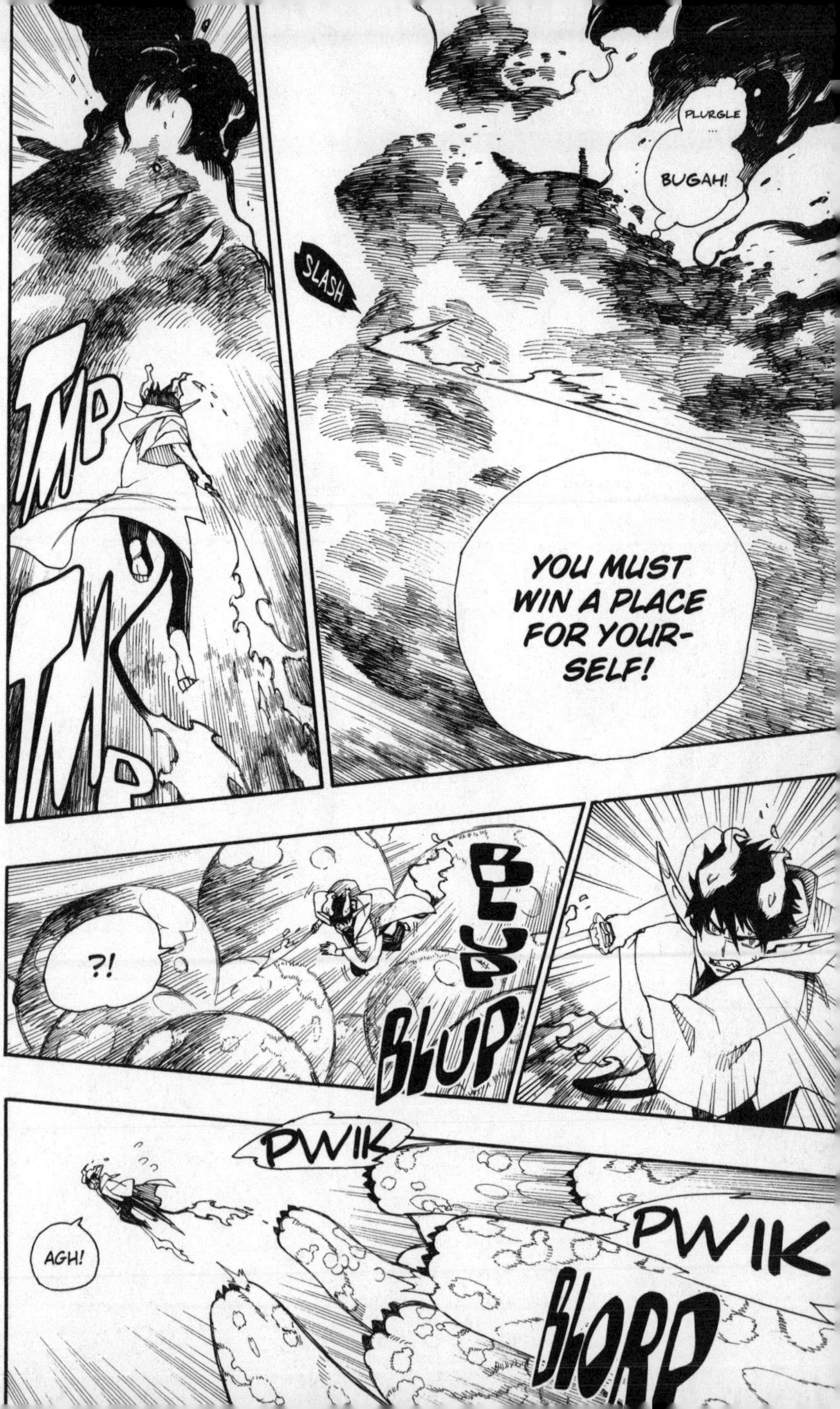
PLURGLE ... BUGAH!
SLASH
YOU MUST WIN A PLACE FOR YOUR-SELF!
TMP
TMP
BLUP
BLUP
?!
PWIK
PWIK
BLORP
AGH!

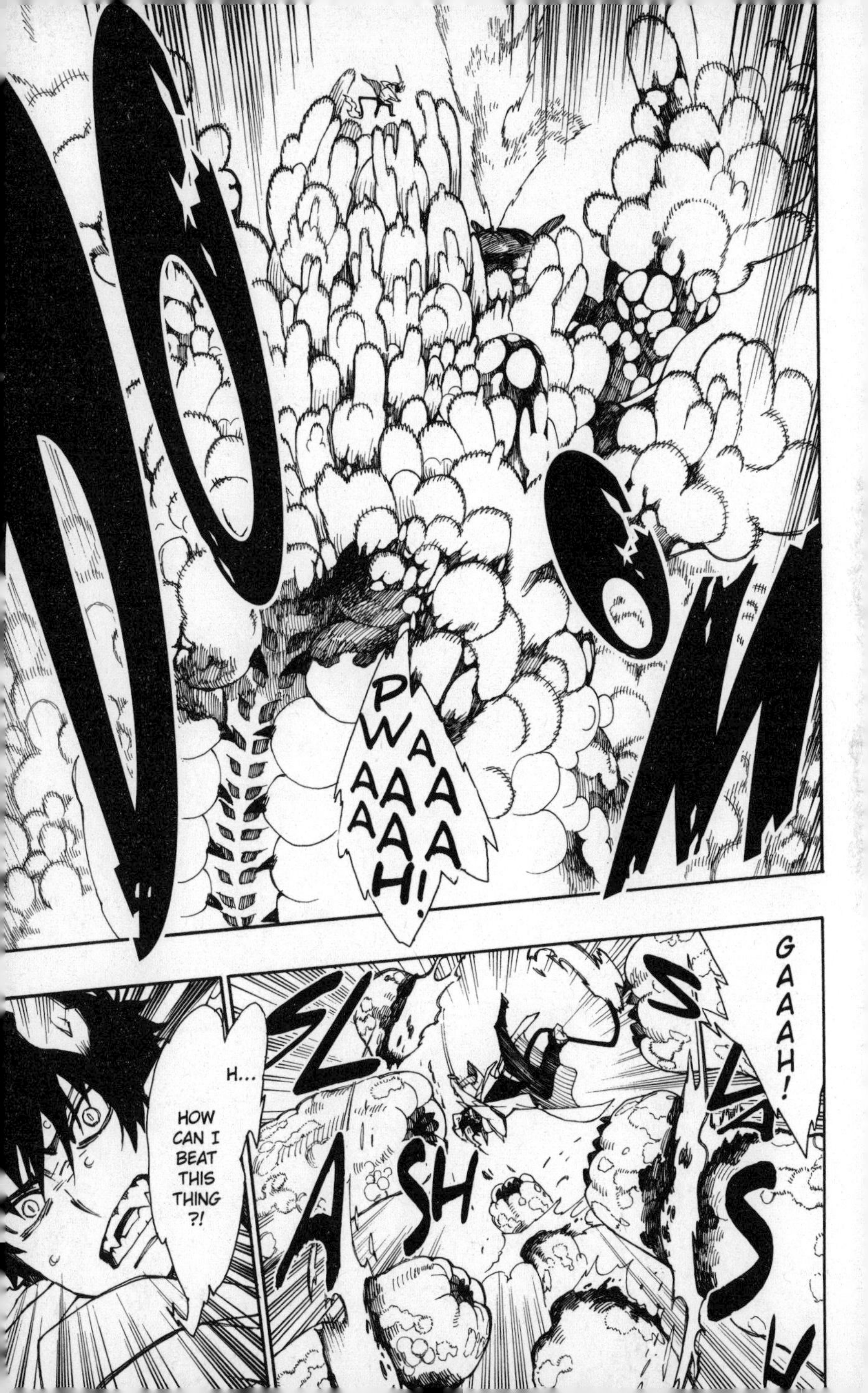
PWAAAAAAAAAH!
GAAAH!
SLASH
SLASH
H...
HOW CAN I BEAT THIS THING?!

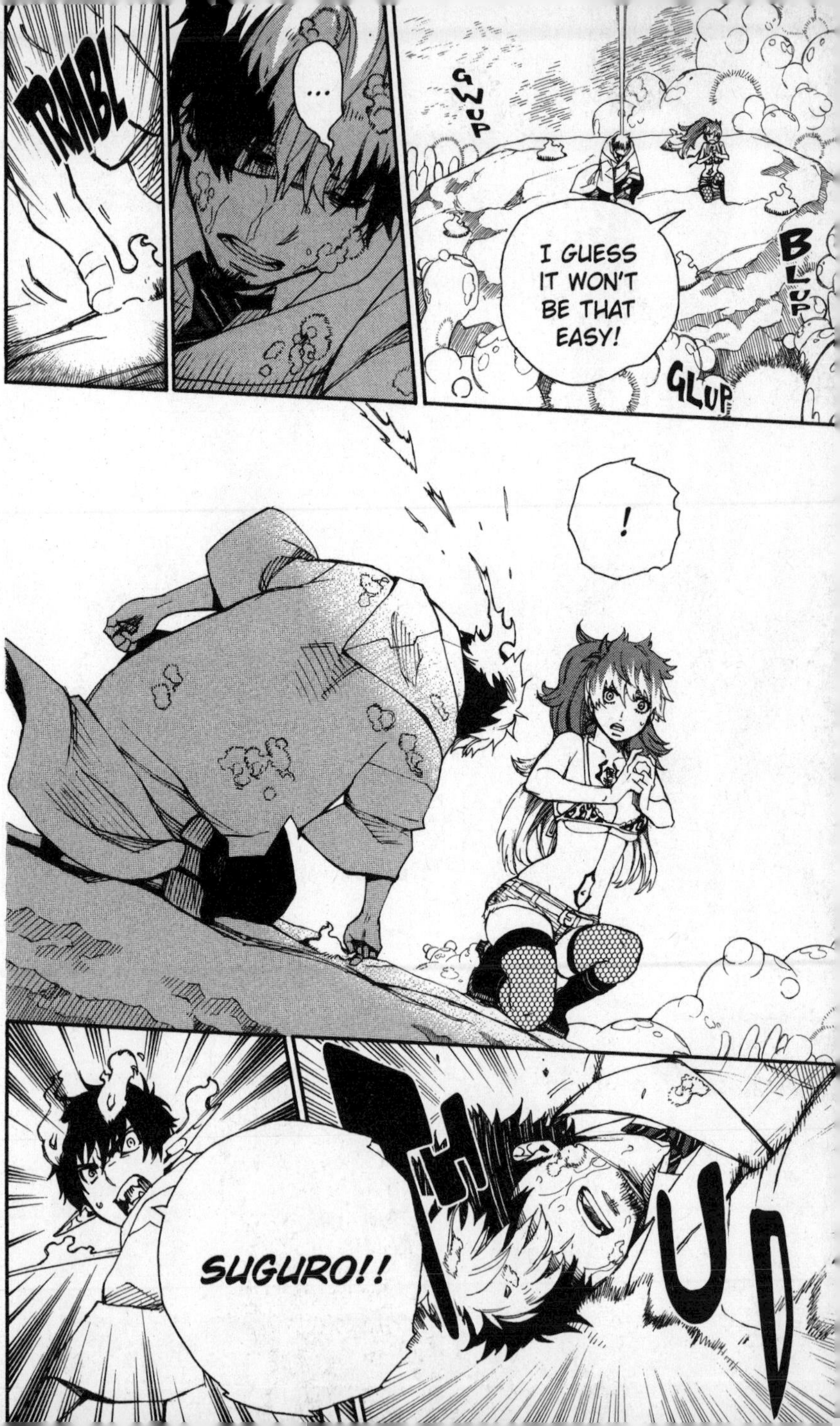
GWUP
I GUESS IT WON'T BE THAT EASY!
BLUP
GLUP
...
TRMBL
!
THUD
SUGURO!!

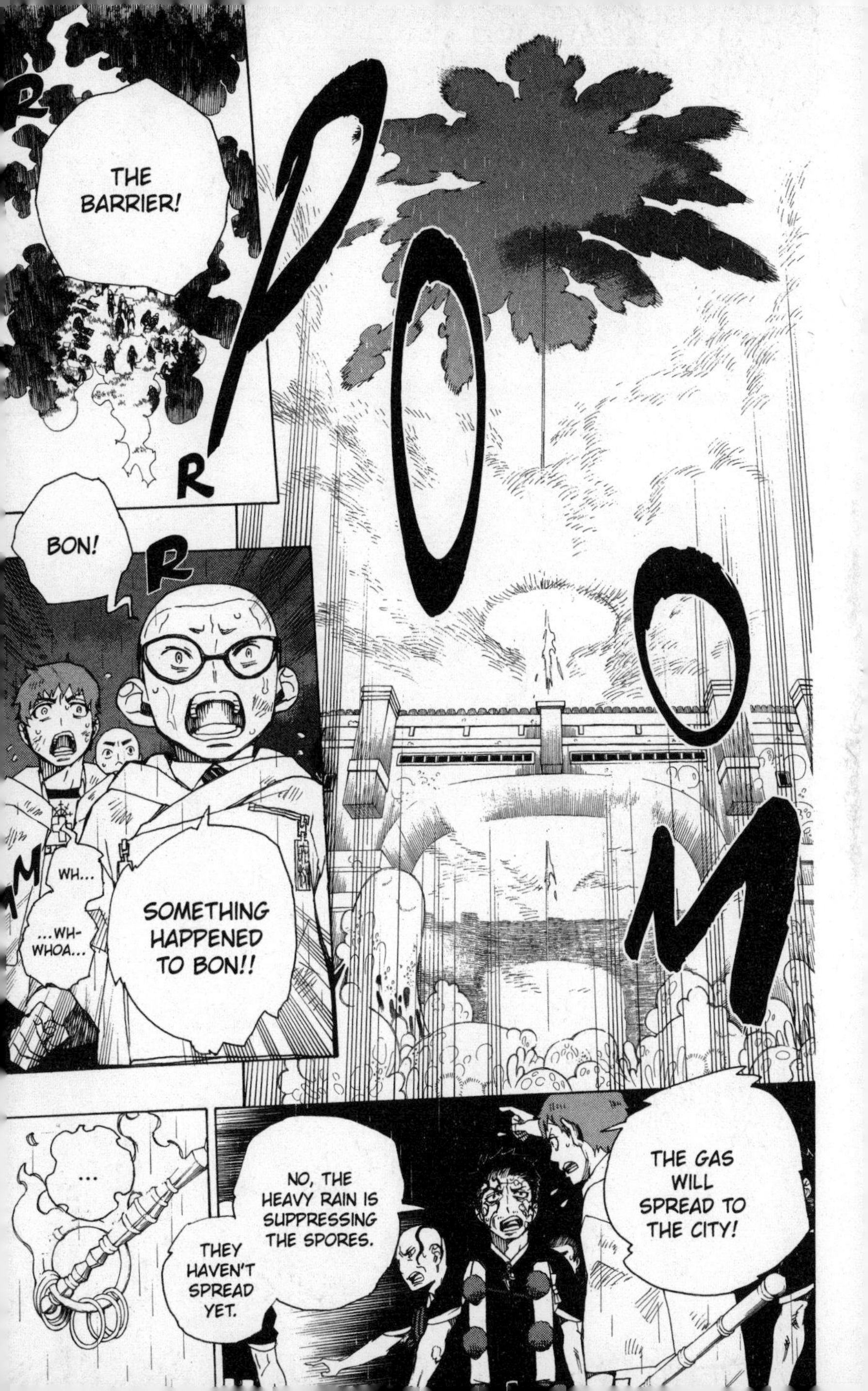
RRROOM
THE BARRIER!
BON!
SOMETHING HAPPENED TO BON!!
WH...
...WH- WHOA...
THE GAS WILL SPREAD TO THE CITY!
NO, THE HEAVY RAIN IS SUPPRESSING THE SPORES.
THEY HAVEN'T SPREAD YET.
...

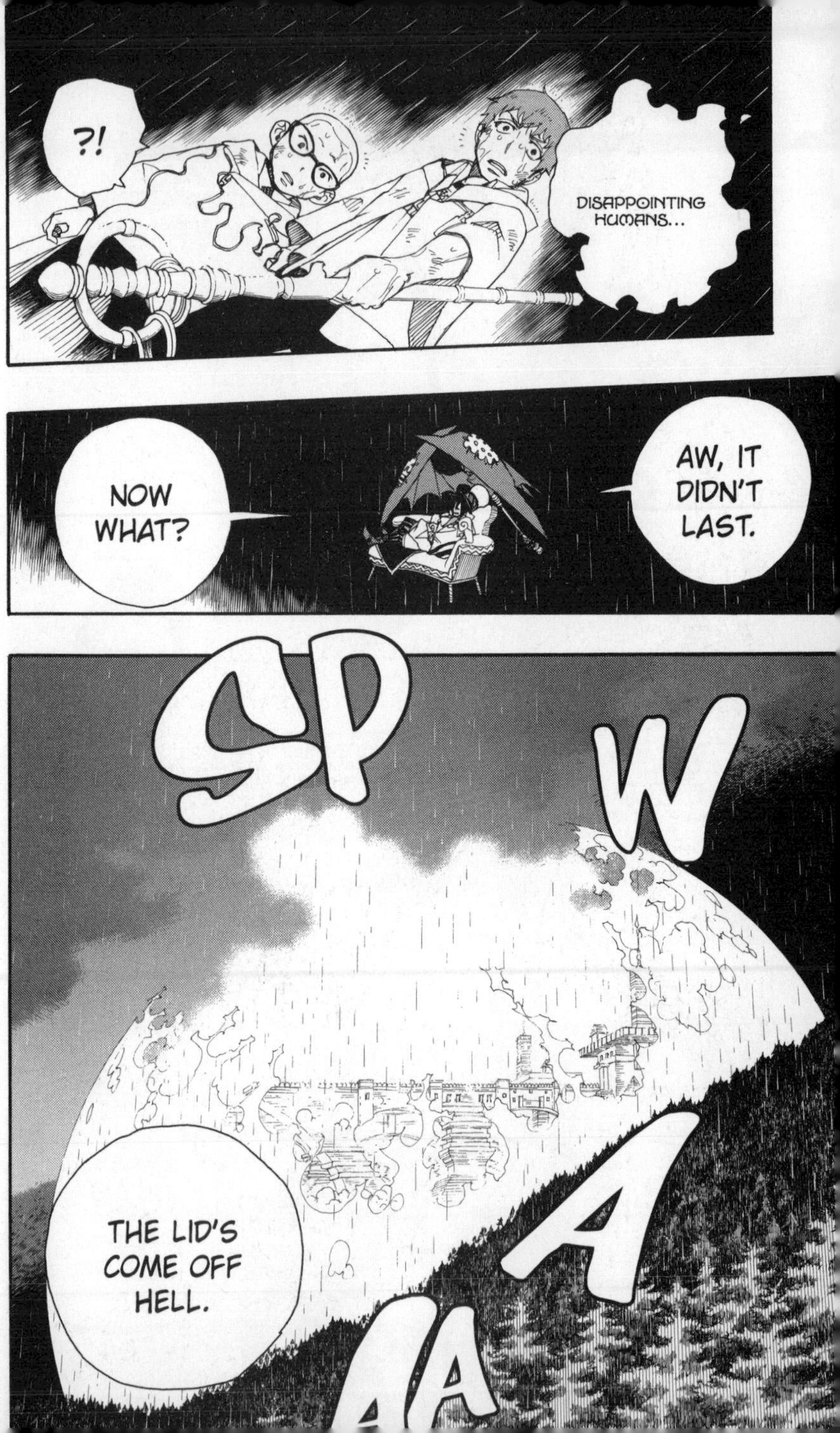
DISAPPOINTING HUMANS...
?!
AW, IT DIDN'T LAST.
NOW WHAT?
SPWAAA
THE LID'S COME OFF HELL.

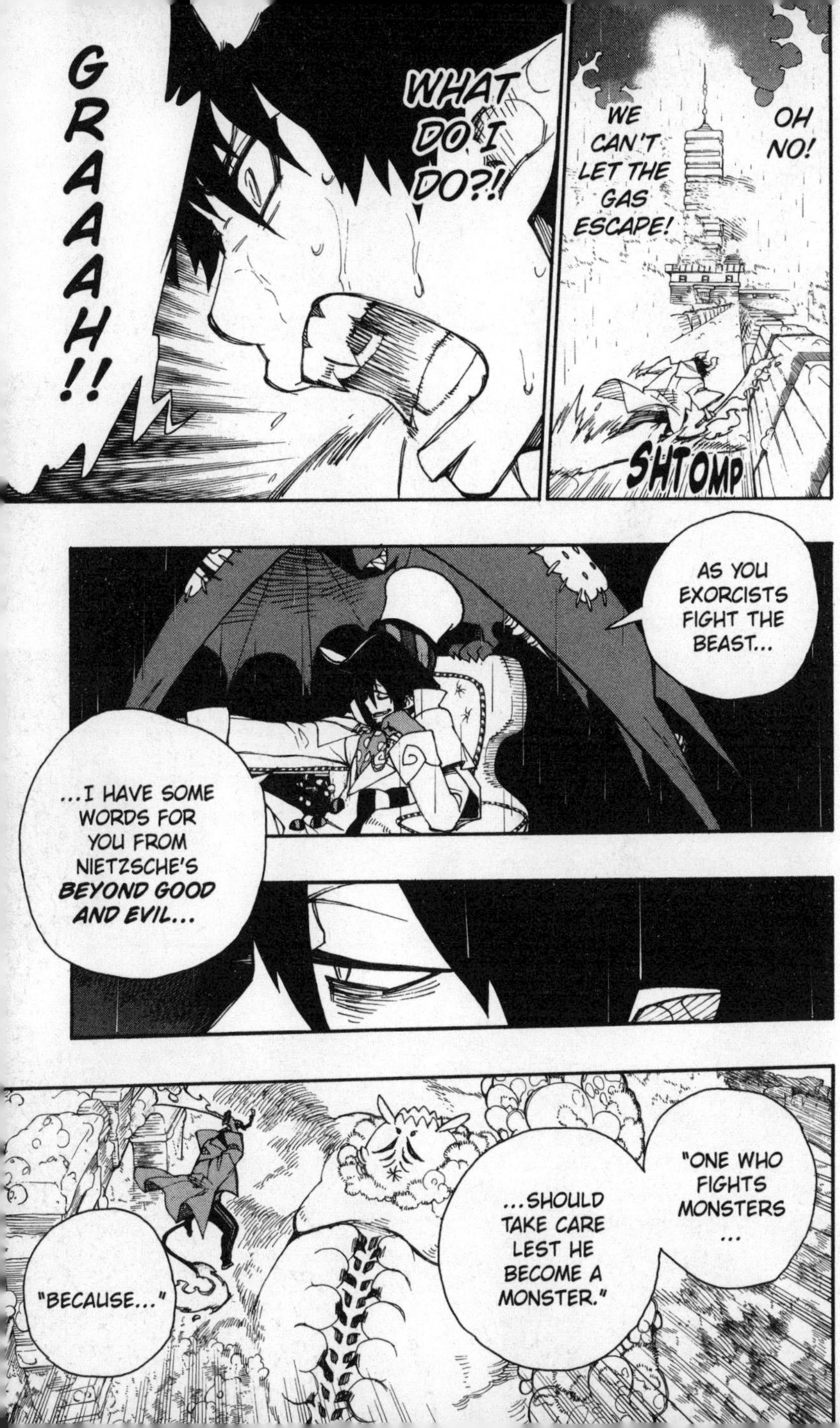
OH NO!
WE CAN'T LET THE GAS ESCAPE!
SHTOMP
WHAT DO I DO?!
GRAAAAH!!
AS YOU EXORCISTS FIGHT THE BEAST...
...I HAVE SOME WORDS FOR YOU FROM NIETZSCHE'S BEYOND GOOD AND EVIL...
"ONE WHO FIGHTS MONSTERS ...
...SHOULD TAKE CARE LEST HE BECOME A MONSTER."
"BECAUSE..."

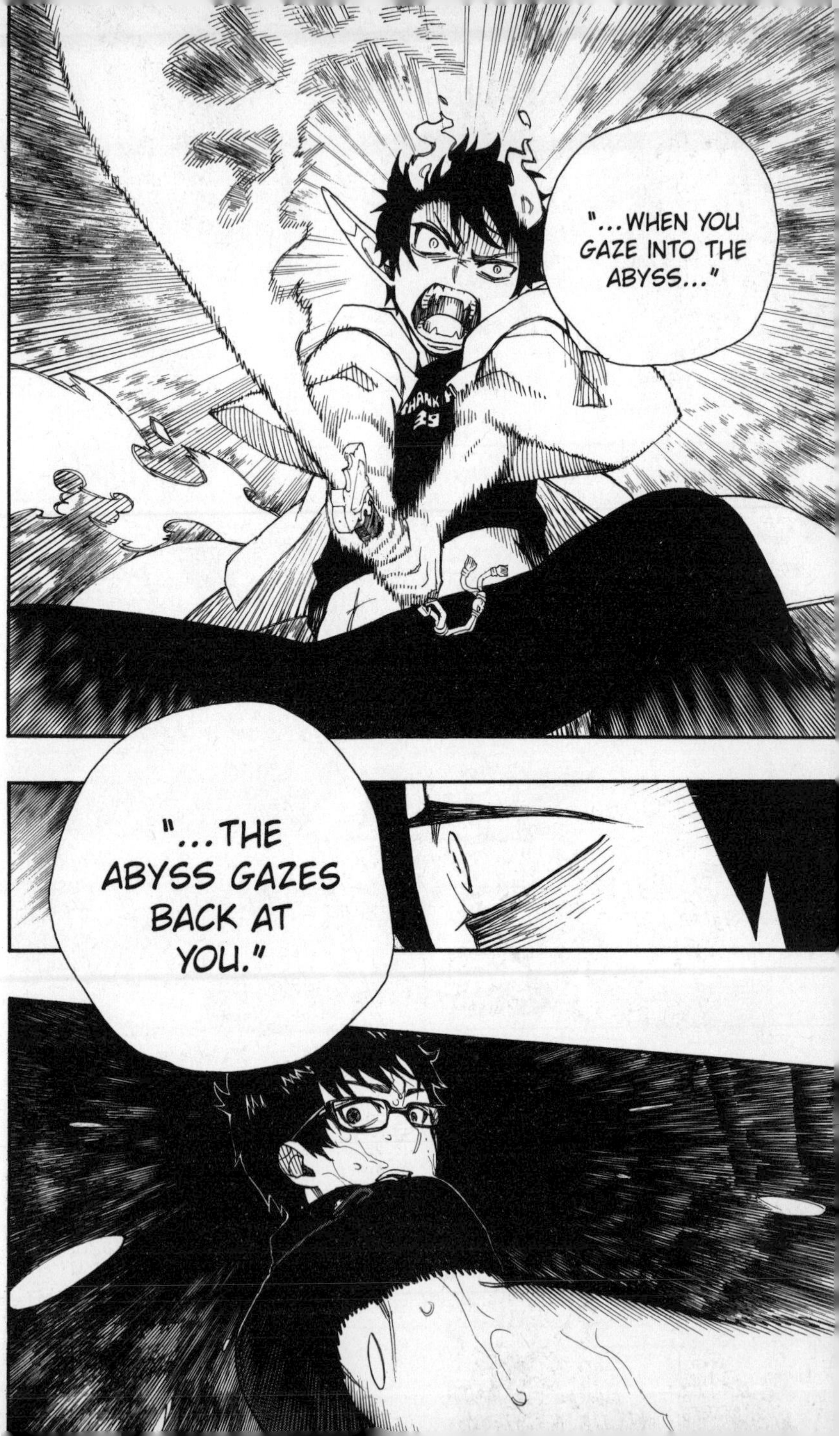
"...WHEN YOU GAZE INTO THE ABYSS..."
"...THE ABYSS GAZES BACK AT YOU."

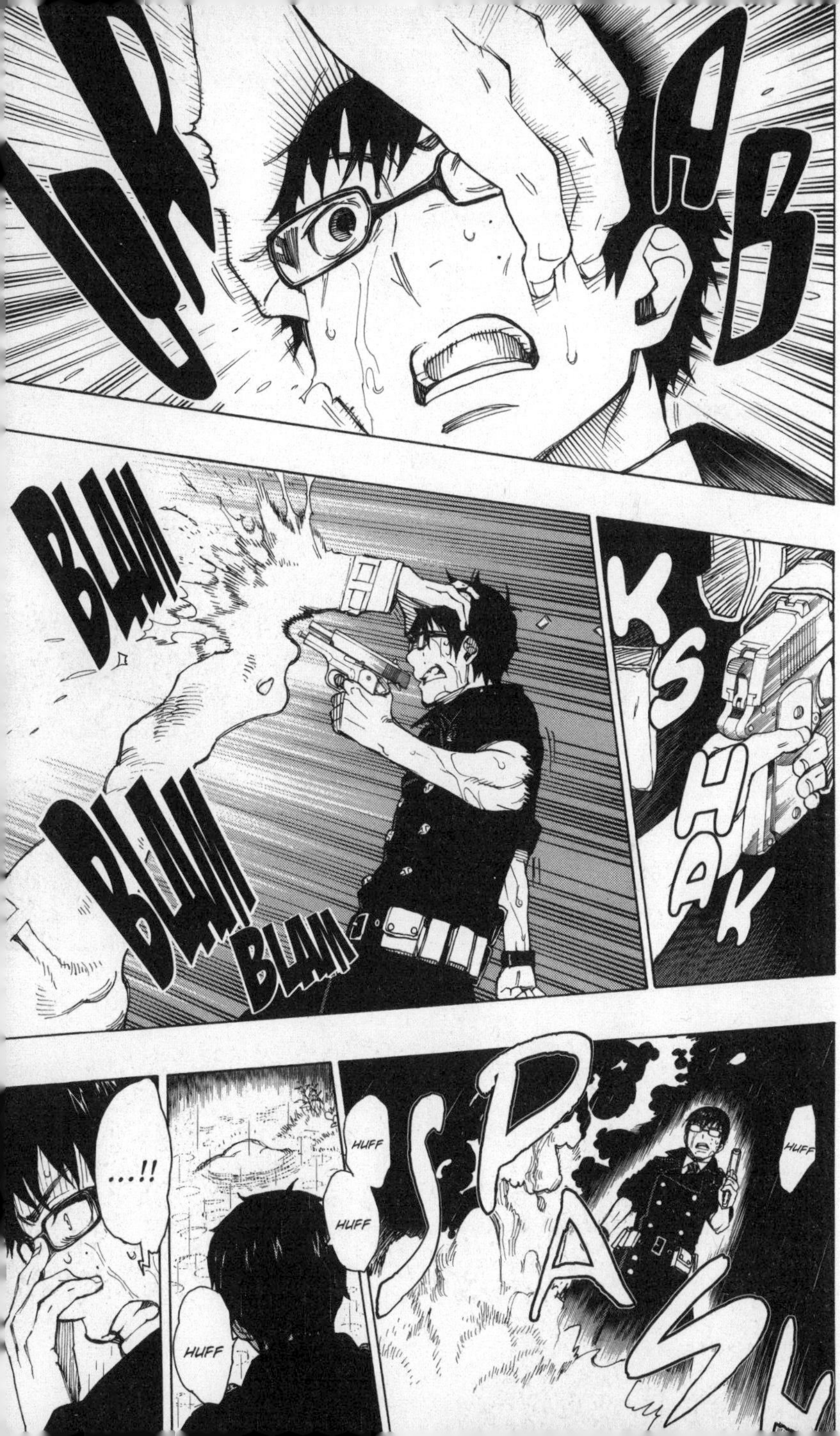
KSHAK
BLAM
BLAM
BLAM
HUFF
HUFF
HUFF
HUFF
...!!

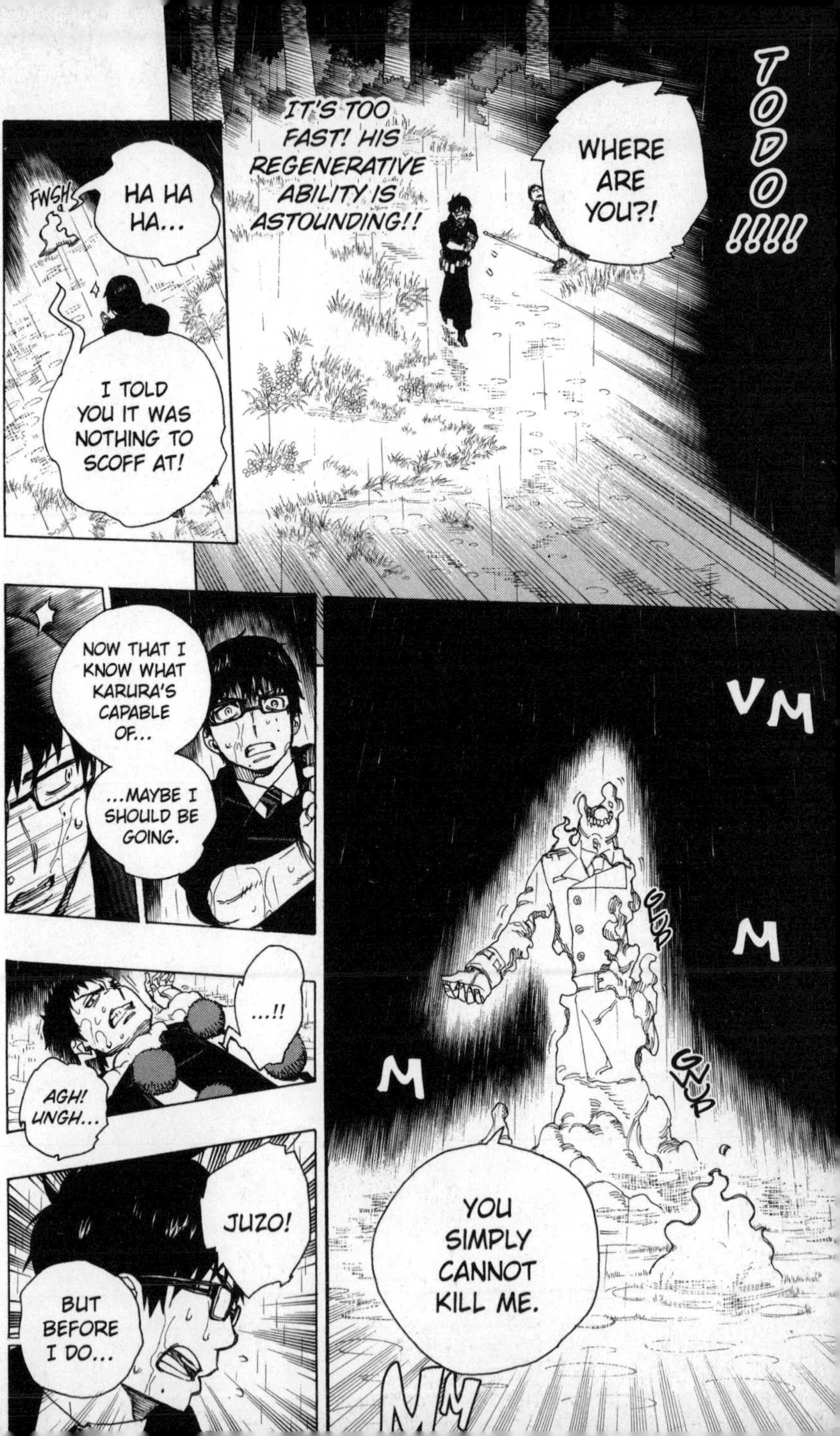
TODO!!!!
WHERE ARE YOU?!
IT'S TOO FAST! HIS REGENERATIVE ABILITY IS ASTOUNDING!!
HA HA HA...
FWSH
I TOLD YOU IT WAS NOTHING TO SCOFF AT!
VM
M
M
MM
YOU SIMPLY CANNOT KILL ME.
NOW THAT I KNOW WHAT KARURA'S CAPABLE OF...
...MAYBE I SHOULD BE GOING.
...!!
AGH! UNGH...
JUZO!
BUT BEFORE I DO...

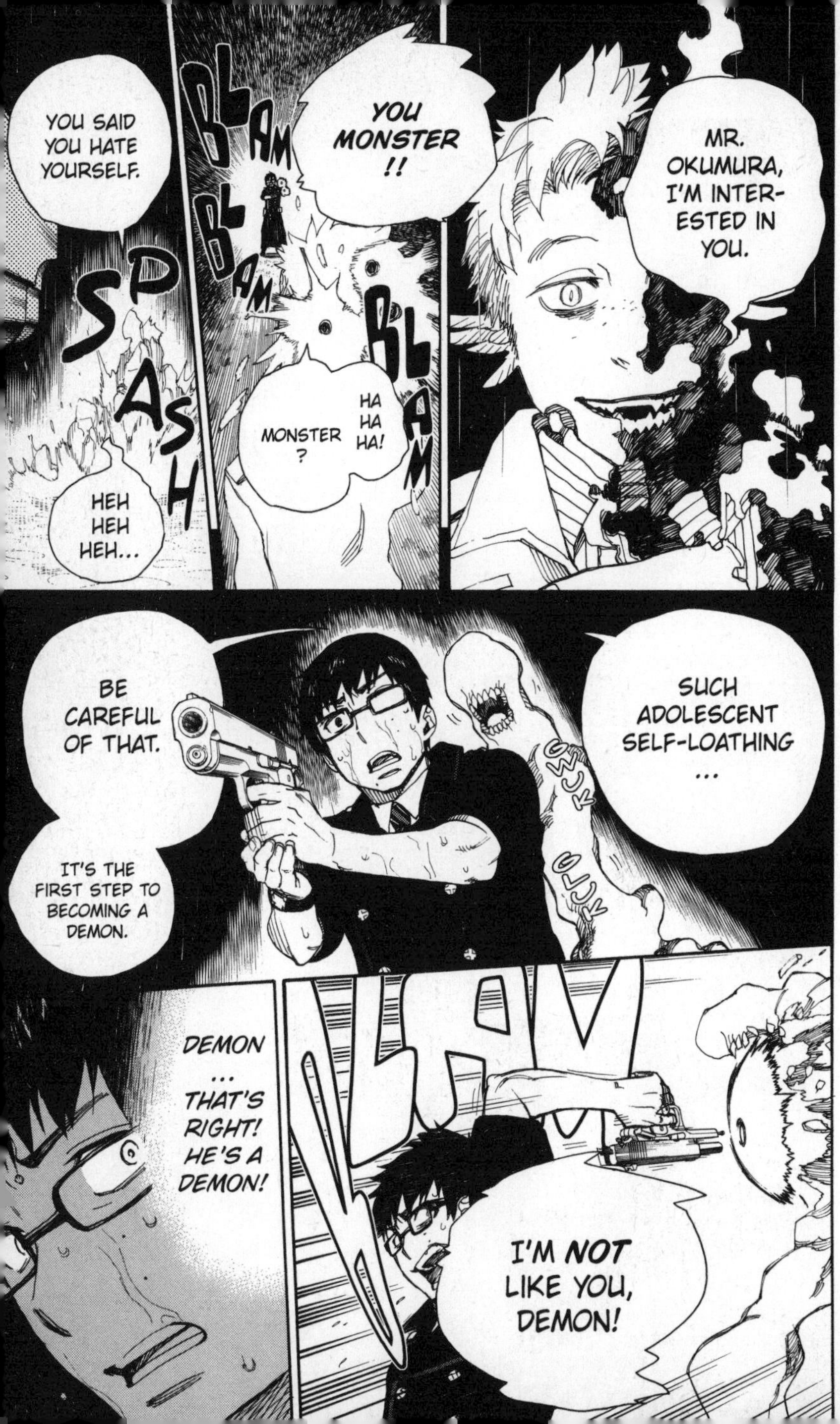
MR. OKUMURA, I'M INTERESTED IN YOU.
YOU MONSTER!!
BLAM
BLAM
BLAM
HA HA HA!
MONSTER?
YOU SAID YOU HATE YOURSELF.
SPLASH
HEH HEH HEH...
SUCH ADOLESCENT SELF-LOATHING...
BE CAREFUL OF THAT.
IT'S THE FIRST STEP TO BECOMING A DEMON.
I'M *NOT* LIKE YOU, DEMON!
DEMON... THAT'S RIGHT! HE'S A DEMON!

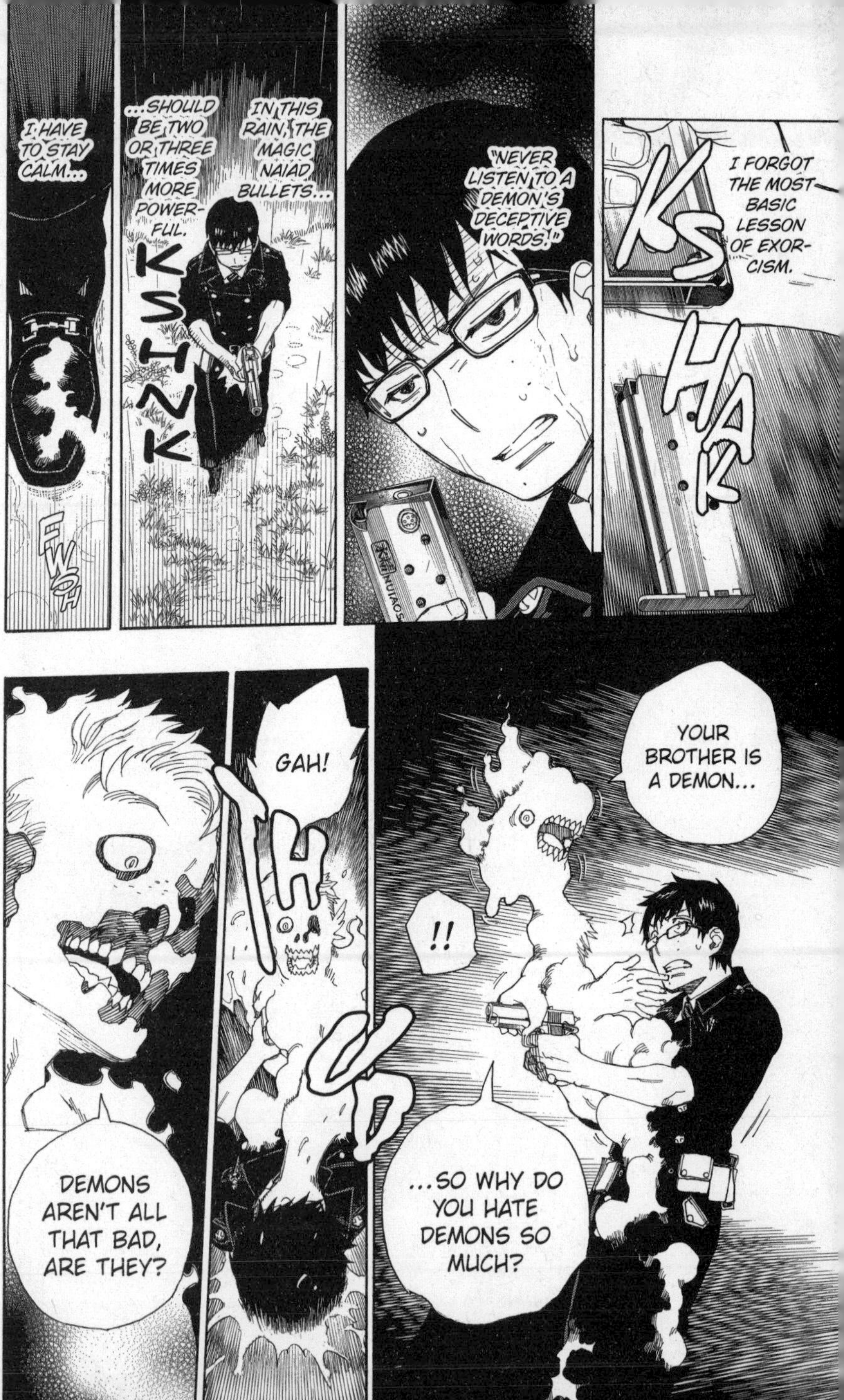
KSHAK
I FORGOT THE MOST BASIC LESSON OF EXORCISM.
"NEVER LISTEN TO A DEMON'S DECEPTIVE WORDS."
IN THIS RAIN, THE MAGIC NAIAD BULLETS...
...SHOULD BE TWO OR THREE TIMES MORE POWERFUL.
KSHNK
I HAVE TO STAY CALM...
FWSH
YOUR BROTHER IS A DEMON...
!!
...SO WHY DO YOU HATE DEMONS SO MUCH?
GAH!
THUD
DEMONS AREN'T ALL THAT BAD, ARE THEY?

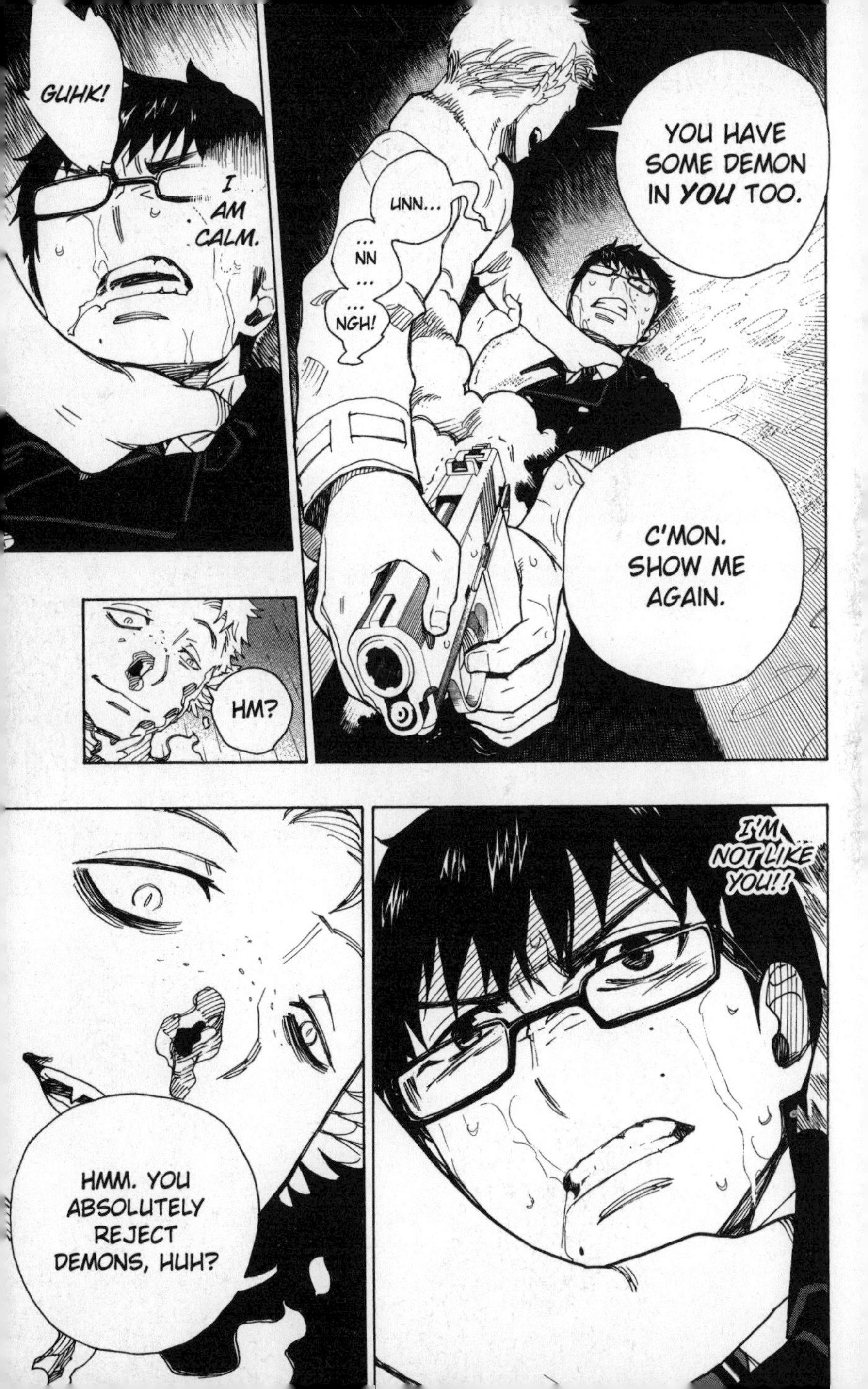
YOU HAVE SOME DEMON IN *YOU* TOO.
UNN...
...NN... ...NGH!
C'MON. SHOW ME AGAIN.
GUHK!
I AM CALM.
HM?
I'M NOT LIKE YOU!!
HMM. YOU ABSOLUTELY REJECT DEMONS, HUH?

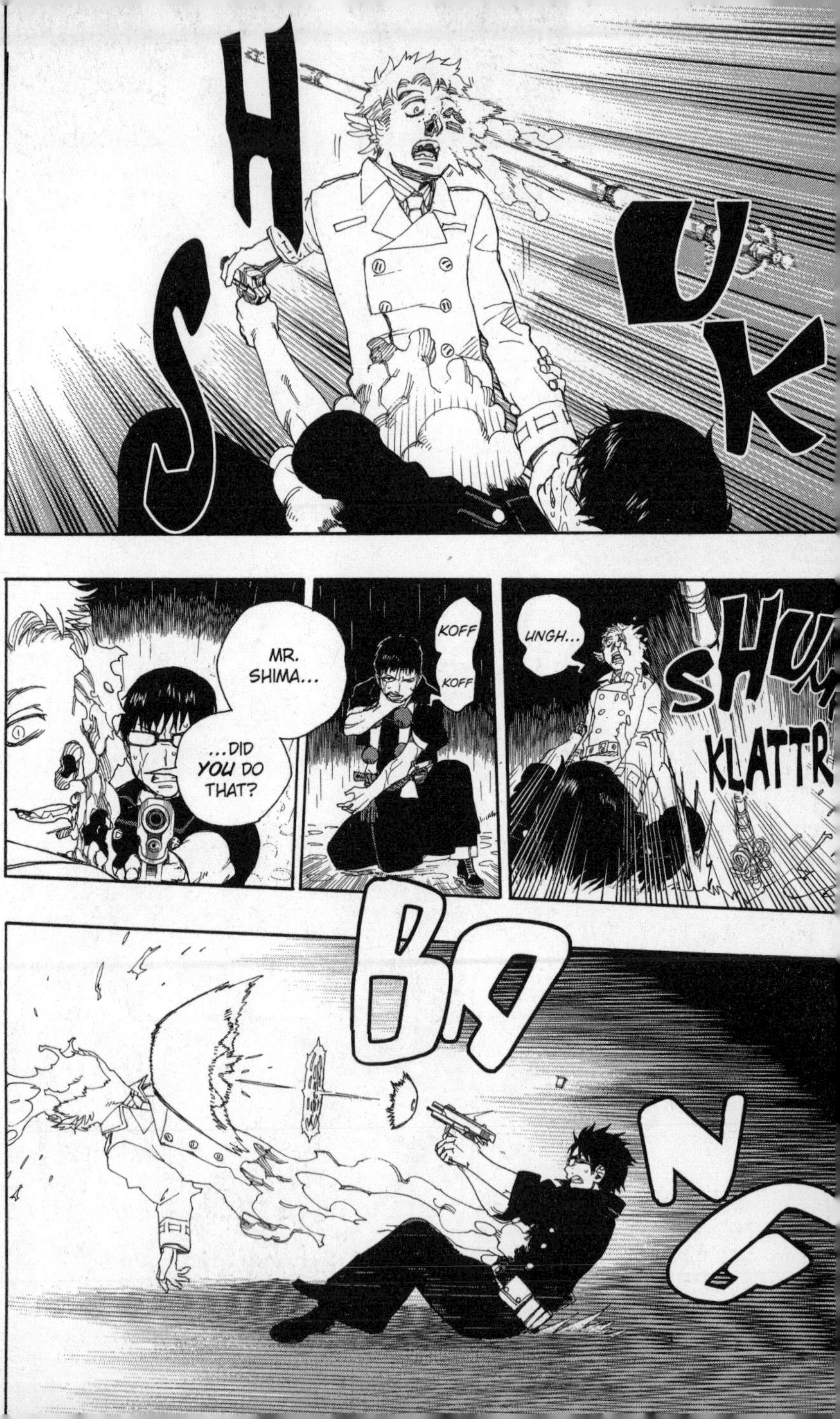
SHUK
UNGH...
SHU
KLATTR
KOFF
KOFF
MR. SHIMA...
...DID *YOU* DO THAT?
BANG

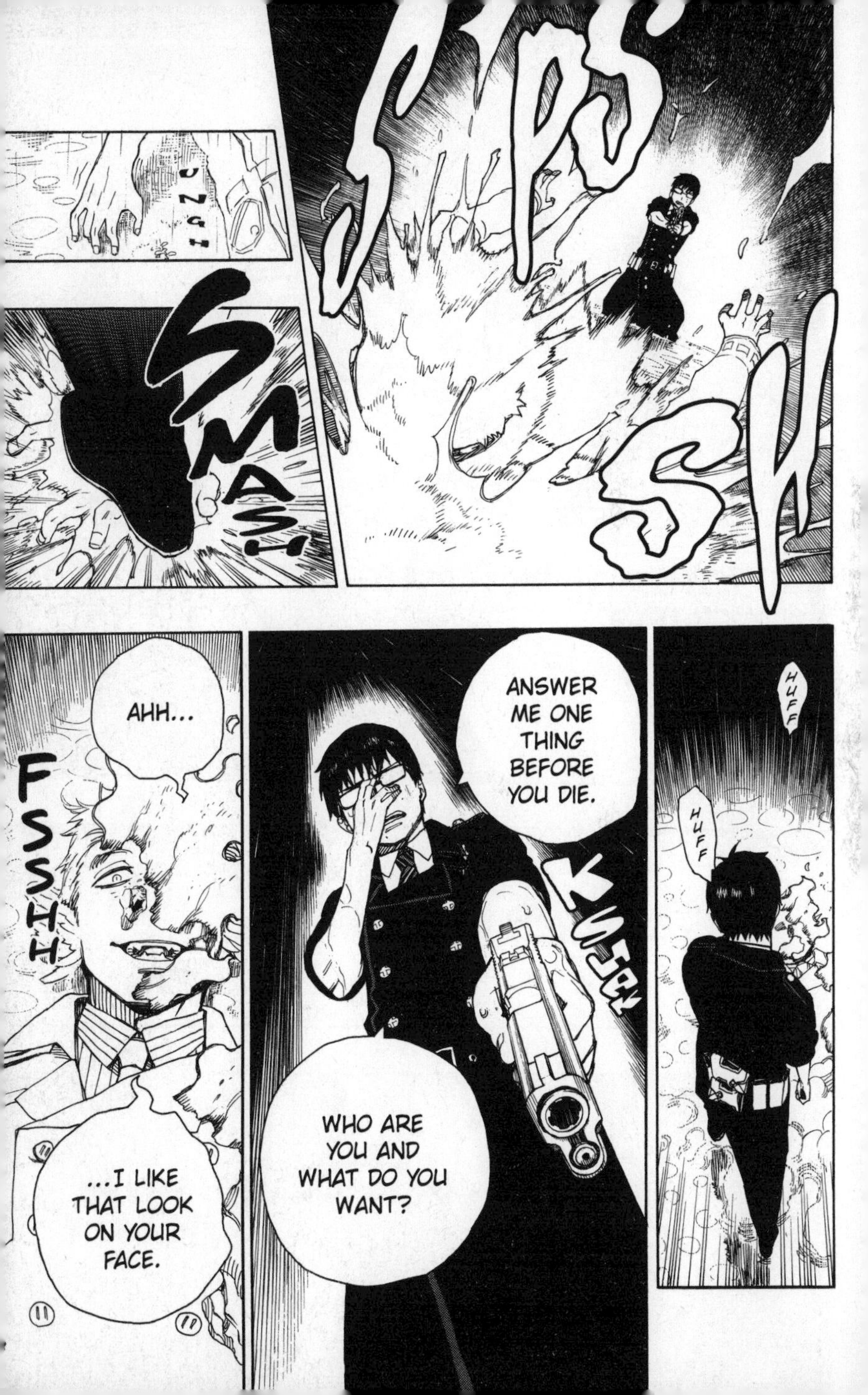
UNGH
SMASH!!
HUFF
HUFF
ANSWER ME ONE THING BEFORE YOU DIE.
WHO ARE YOU AND WHAT DO YOU WANT?
AHH...
FSSHH
...I LIKE THAT LOOK ON YOUR FACE.

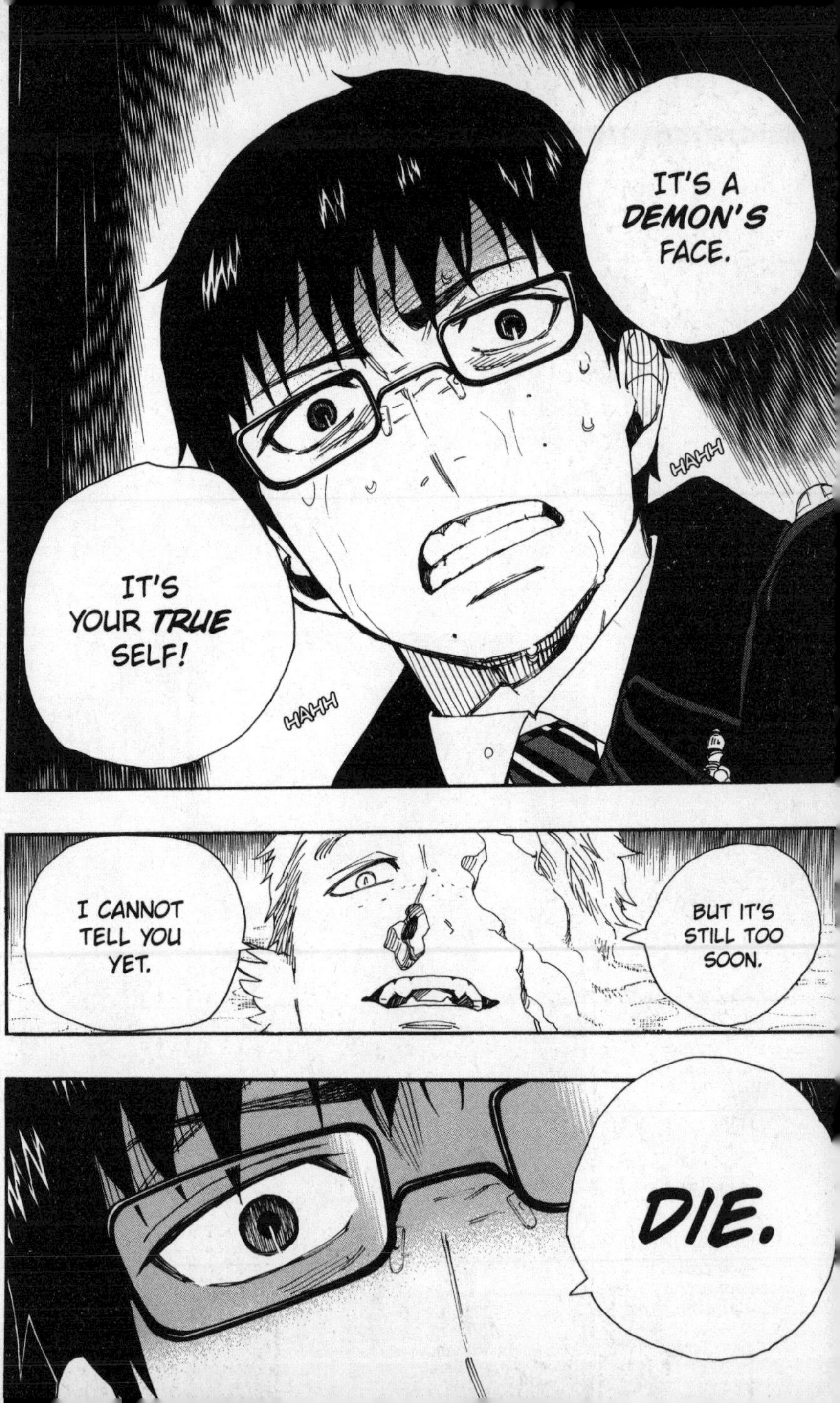
IT'S A DEMON'S FACE.
HAHH
IT'S YOUR TRUE SELF!
HAHH
BUT IT'S STILL TOO SOON.
I CANNOT TELL YOU YET.
DIE.

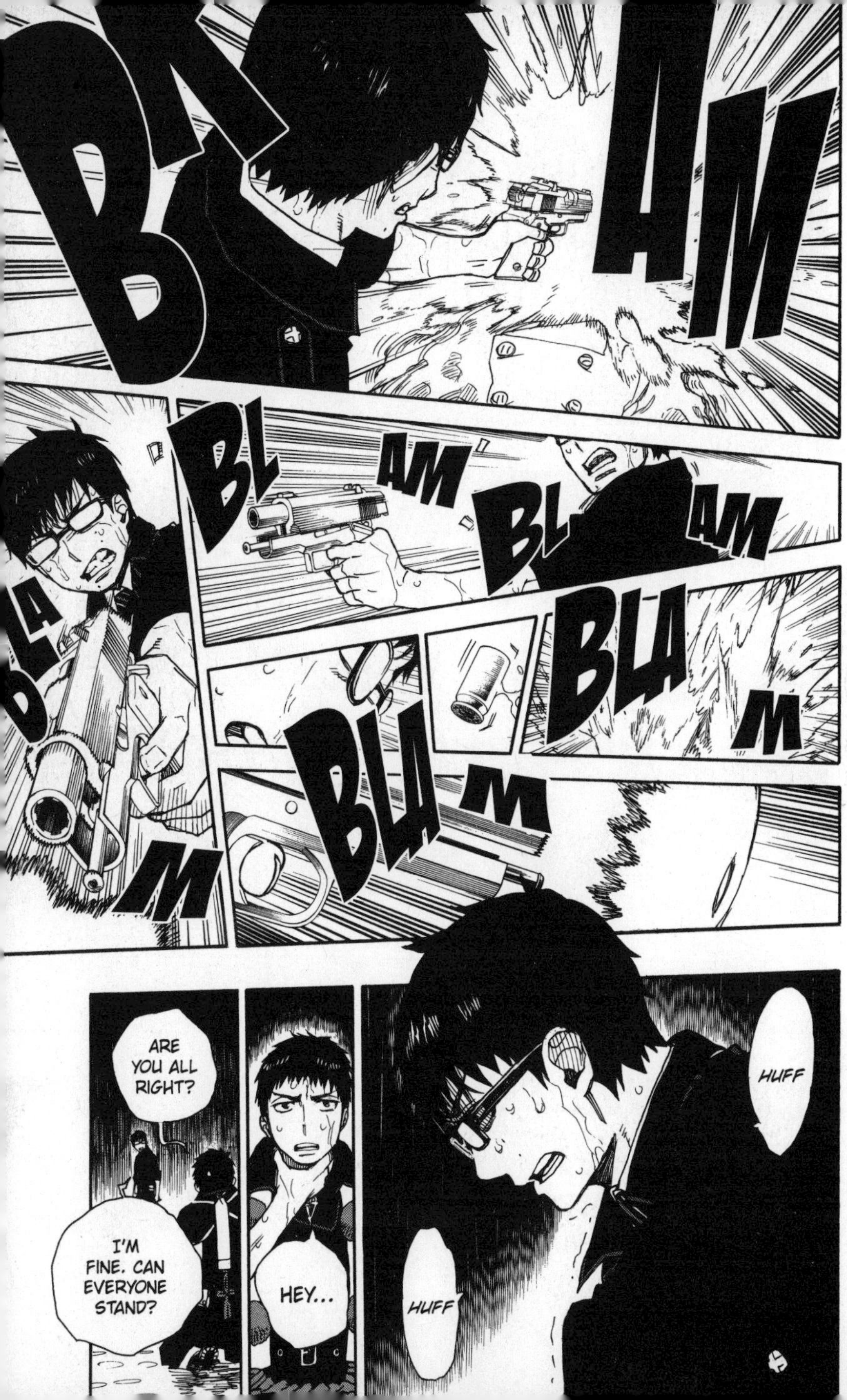
BLAM
BLAM
BLAM
BLAM
BLAM
BLAM
HUFF
HUFF
HEY...
ARE YOU ALL RIGHT?
I'M FINE. CAN EVERYONE STAND?

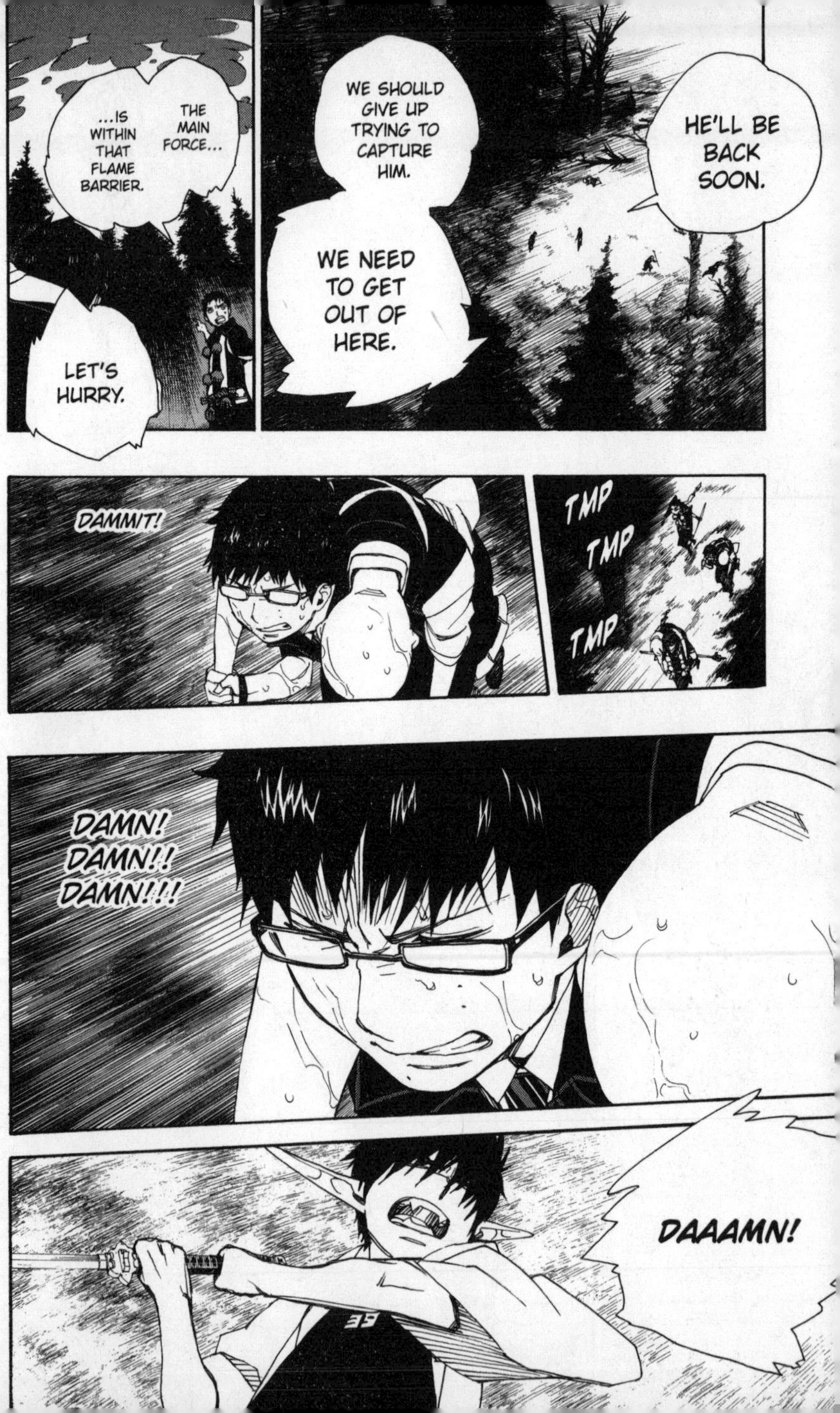
HE'LL BE BACK SOON.
WE SHOULD GIVE UP TRYING TO CAPTURE HIM.
WE NEED TO GET OUT OF HERE.
THE MAIN FORCE...
...IS WITHIN THAT FLAME BARRIER.
LET'S HURRY.
TMP TMP TMP
DAMMIT!
DAMN! DAMN!! DAMN!!!
DAAAMN!

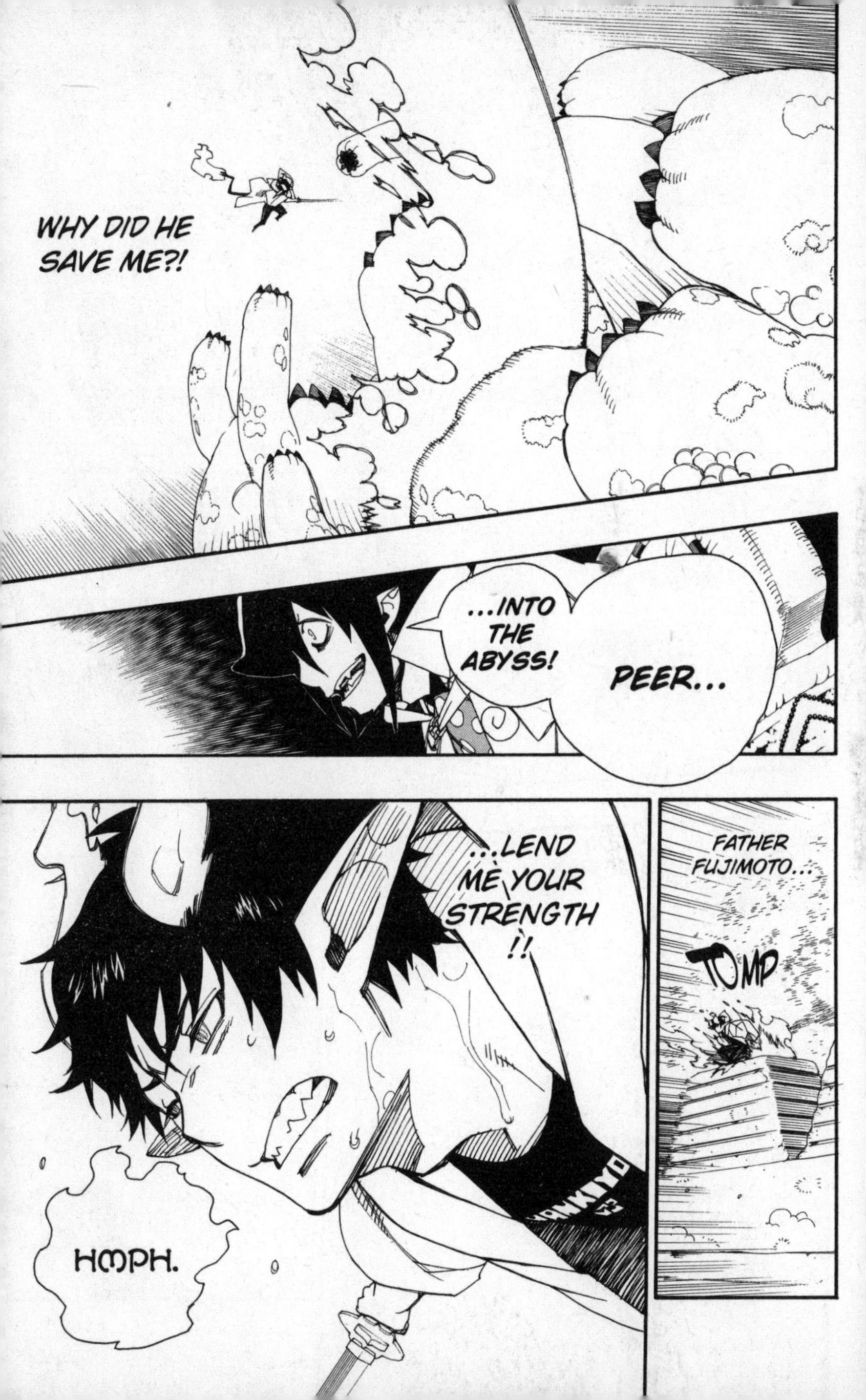
WHY DID HE SAVE ME?!
PEER...
...INTO THE ABYSS!
FATHER FUJIMOTO...
TOMP
...LEND ME YOUR STRENGTH!!
HMPH.

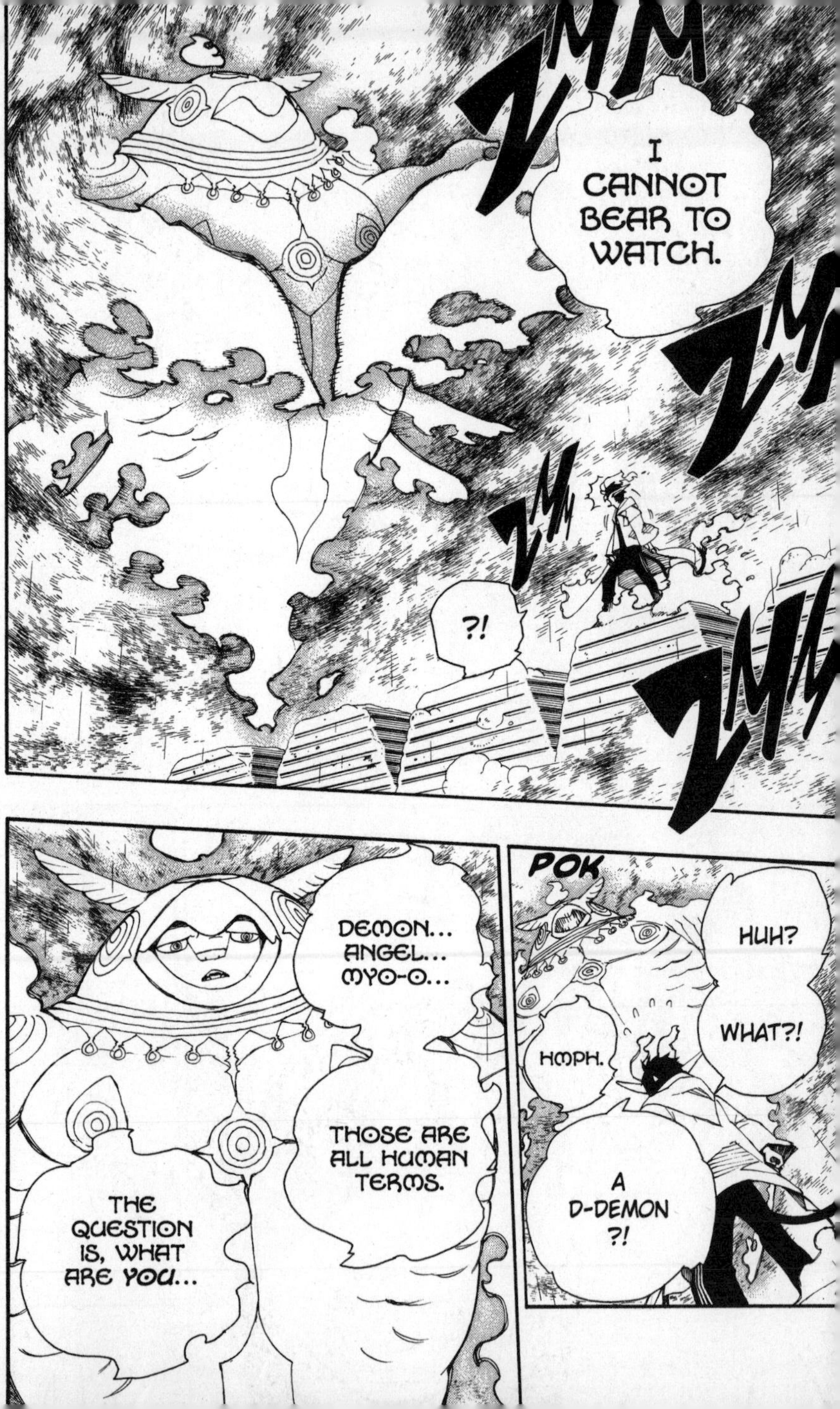
ZMM
I CANNOT BEAR TO WATCH.
ZMM
ZMM
ZMM
?!
POK
HUH?
WHAT?!
HMPH.
A D-DEMON ?!
DEMON... ANGEL... MYO-O...
THOSE ARE ALL HUMAN TERMS.
THE QUESTION IS, WHAT ARE YOU...

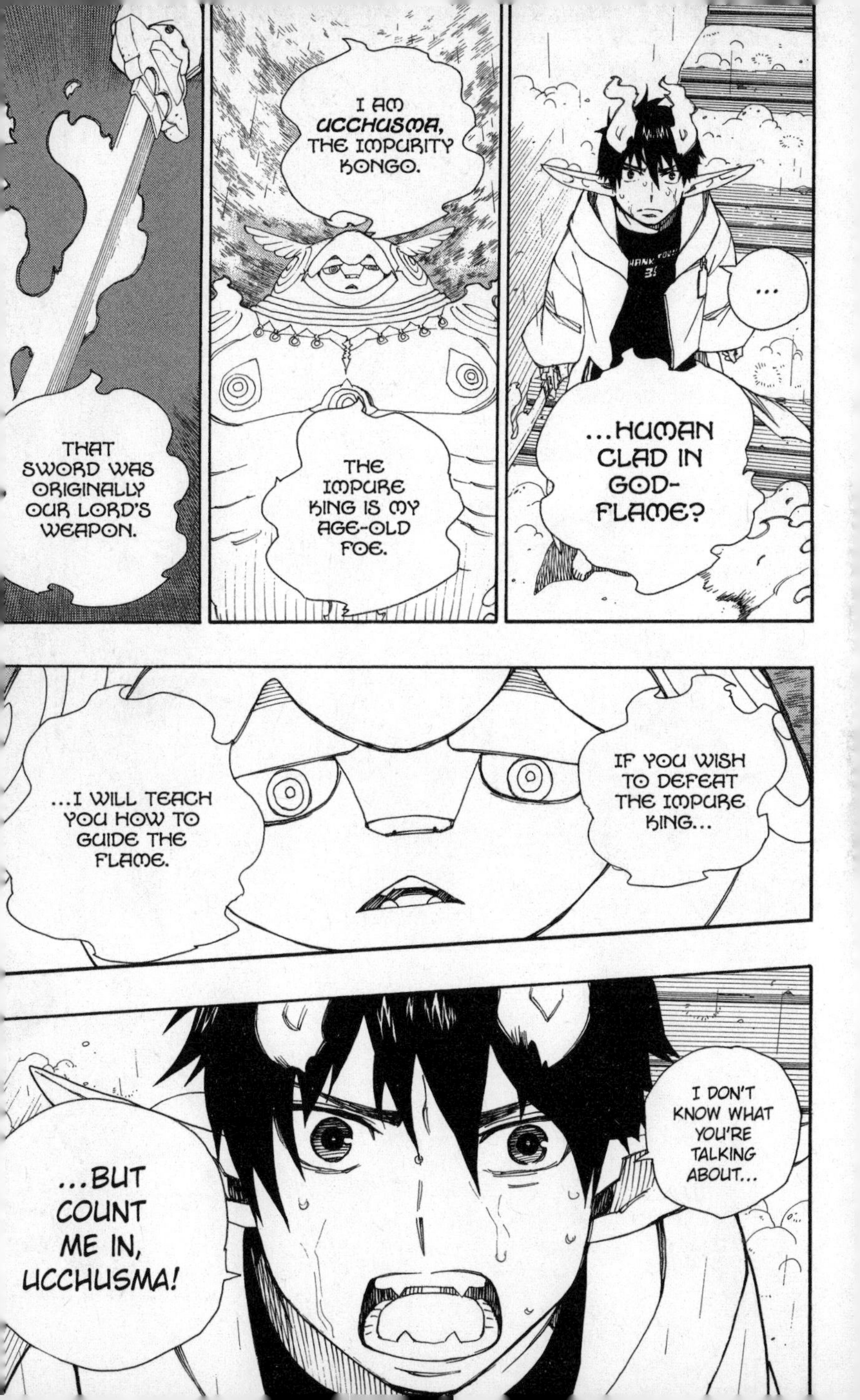
...
...HUMAN CLAD IN GOD-FLAME?
I AM UCCHUSMA, THE IMPURITY KONGO.
THE IMPURE KING IS MY AGE-OLD FOE.
THAT SWORD WAS ORIGINALLY OUR LORD'S WEAPON.
IF YOU WISH TO DEFEAT THE IMPURE KING...
...I WILL TEACH YOU HOW TO GUIDE THE FLAME.
I DON'T KNOW WHAT YOU'RE TALKING ABOUT...
...BUT COUNT ME IN, UCCHUSMA!

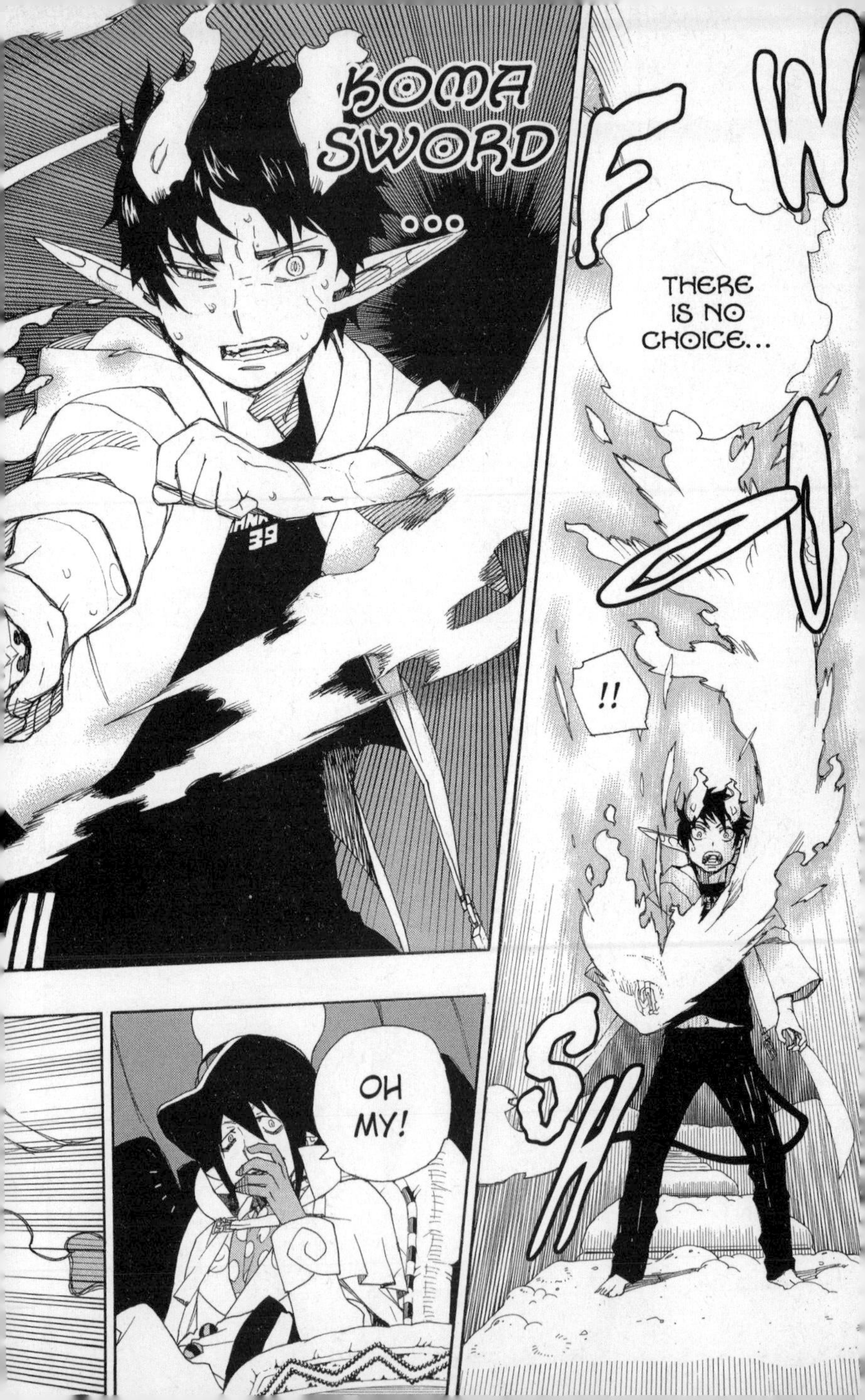
FWOOSH
THERE IS NO CHOICE...
!!
KOMA SWORD
...
OH MY!

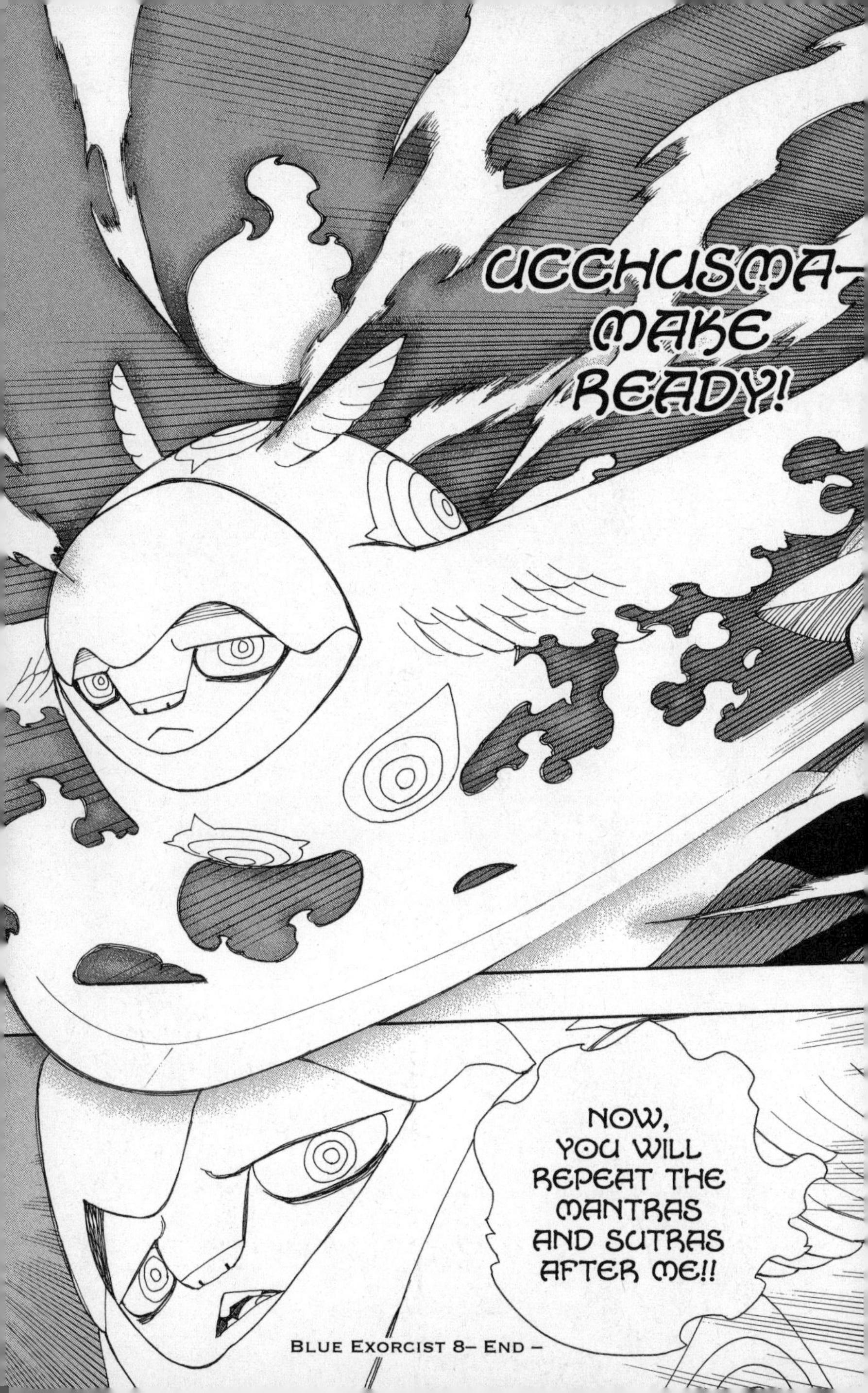
UCCHUSMA-MAKE READY!
NOW, YOU WILL REPEAT THE MANTRAS AND SUTRAS AFTER ME!!

BLUE EXORCIST 8– END –

Blue Exorcist Chapter 32: Abyss

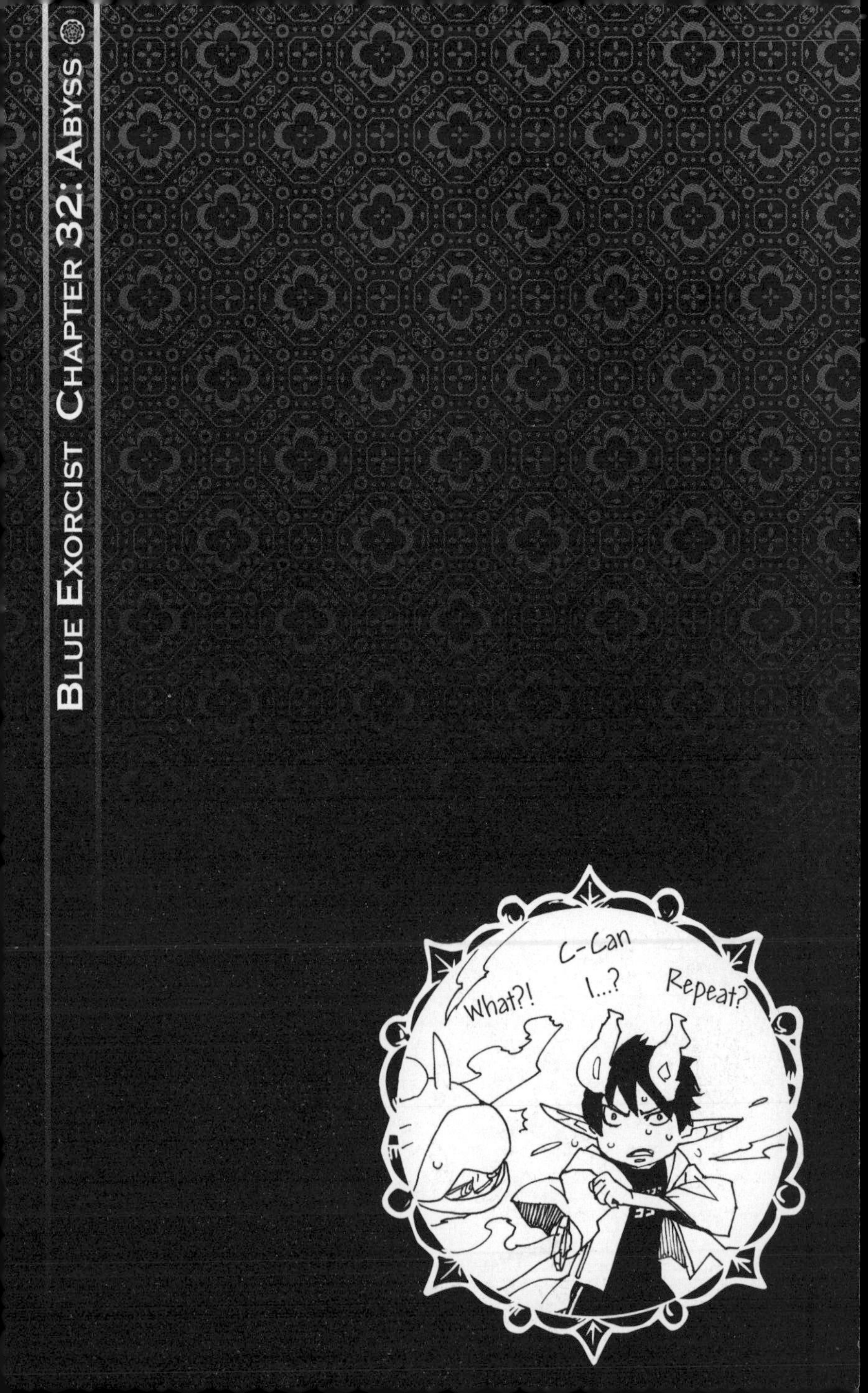
C-Can I..?
Repeat?
What?!

BONUS

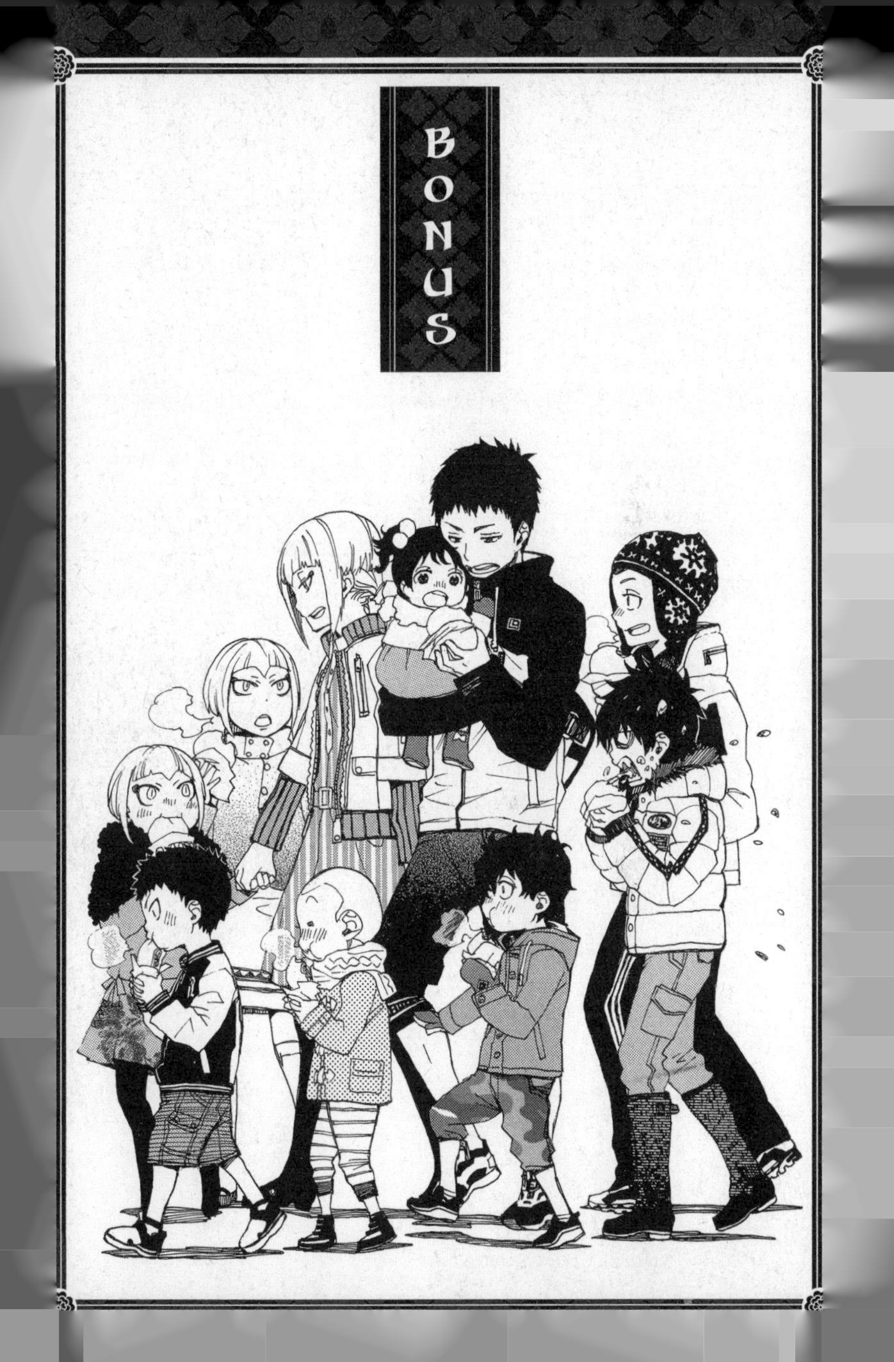

Question Corner β

ALL RIGHT, LET'S BEGIN THE QUESTION CORNER!!

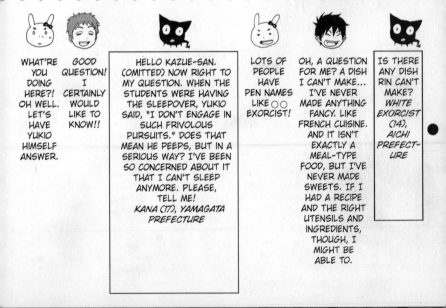

THIS IS A QUESTION FOR KONEKO!! WHEN I WAS READING VOLUME 2, I THOUGHT THE SWEATSHIRT THAT KONEKO WAS WEARING WAS TOO BIG. WHEN I TOOK A CLOSER LOOK, I SAW IT HAD THE NAME "MURAI" ON IT. DID HE GET IT FROM SOMEONE? (IF I DIDN'T SEE IT CORRECTLY, SORRY!)
CHIKIKO (17), TOKYO PREFECTURE

WHOA! I CAN'T BELIEVE YOU NOTICED! IT'S A LITTLE EMBARRASSING TO KNOW THAT YOU'RE LOOKING SO CLOSELY... BUT YOU'RE RIGHT!! TRUE CROSS ACADEMY HIGH SCHOOL IS EXPENSIVE. SINCE MY PARENTS ARE GONE, I GO WITH ASSISTANCE, JUST LIKE BON DOES. TO SAVE MONEY, I BOUGHT MY SWEATSHIRT USED. THEY DIDN'T HAVE MY EXACT SIZE, SO IT'S BAGGY...BUT I MIGHT GROW INTO IT!

I'M SO HAPPY YOU NOTICED THAT!

IS THERE ANY DISH RIN CAN'T MAKE?
WHITE EXORCIST (14), AICHI PREFECTURE

OH, A QUESTION FOR ME? A DISH I CAN'T MAKE... I'VE NEVER MADE ANYTHING FANCY. LIKE FRENCH CUISINE. AND IT ISN'T EXACTLY A MEAL-TYPE FOOD, BUT I'VE NEVER MADE SWEETS. IF I HAD A RECIPE AND THE RIGHT UTENSILS AND INGREDIENTS, THOUGH, I MIGHT BE ABLE TO.

LOTS OF PEOPLE HAVE PEN NAMES LIKE ○○ EXORCIST!

HELLO KAZUE-SAN. (OMITTED) NOW RIGHT TO MY QUESTION. WHEN THE STUDENTS WERE HAVING THE SLEEPOVER, YUKIO SAID, "I DON'T ENGAGE IN SUCH FRIVOLOUS PURSUITS." DOES THAT MEAN HE PEEPS, BUT IN A SERIOUS WAY? I'VE BEEN SO CONCERNED ABOUT IT THAT I CAN'T SLEEP ANYMORE. PLEASE, TELL ME!
KANA (17), YAMAGATA PREFECTURE

GOOD QUESTION! I CERTAINLY WOULD LIKE TO KNOW!!

WHAT'RE YOU DOING HERE?! OH WELL. LET'S HAVE YUKIO HIMSELF ANSWER.

UM... (WHY ARE THE QUESTIONS FOR ME ALWAYS HARD TO ANSWER?) WELL, PEEPING IS A CRIME. I WOULD NEVER DO SOMETHING SO RISKY!

HE'S GETTING FLUSTERED!! HE'S FLUSTERED!!

HUH?!

PEEPING MEANS OVERCOMING YOUR FEAR OF GETTING CAUGHT IN ORDER TO FEAST YOUR EYES UPON THE NAKED FEMALE FORM! IT'S A RITE OF PASSAGE FOR BOYS TO BECOME MEN!! IF YOU DON'T PEEP, YOU'RE INCOMPLETE AS A MAN! IT'S LIKE PROCLAIMING YOUR SMALLNESS AS A MAN!!!

...!!

NO, IT'S JUST THAT PEEPING IS A SEX CRIME.

URGH. WELL, IF I WERE TO PEEP, I WOULDN'T MERELY PLAN IT THEN, I WOULD AIM FOR THE PERFECT CRIME!

WELL SAID, TEACH!! YOU STILL SOUND NERVOUS, BUT IT'S GOOD ENOUGH!! THAT'S A REAL MAN!!

THESE GUYS ARE IDIOTS.

NO! I'D NEVER ACTUALLY DO IT!!

WHEN SABUROTA TODO FORCED KARURA TO POSSESS HIM, HOW MANY YEARS YOUNGER DID HE GET? *MATATABI DAISUKI, OITA PREFECTURE*

OH! THANKS FOR SENDING A QUESTION TO ME! LET'S SEE... LOOKING AT THE SHAPE I'M IN, I'D SAY I LOOK ABOUT LIKE I DID WHEN I WAS 22 OR 23, WHEN I WAS IN MY MENTAL AND PHYSICAL PRIME. I STILL HAD FRECKLES THEN. HA HA HA! HOW EMBARRASSING.

SABUROTA, YOU'RE SCARY.

IN THE MANGA, KURO HAS ONE BIG FANG, SO WHY DOESN'T HE HAVE ONE IN THE ANIME? KURO'S FANG IS CUTE AND I REALLY LOVE IT, SO I'VE BEEN WONDERING ABOUT THAT. *NEKOGORO, NARA PREFECTURE*

THIS IS THE MOST COMMON QUESTION FOR KURO. EVEN ASIDE FROM KURO, SOME OF THE DESIGNS ARE QUITE DIFFERENT BETWEEN THE MANGA AND ANIME. KURO IS MISSING HIS FANG RIGHT FROM THE START IN THE ANIME. I GUESS THAT'S BECAUSE IT'S EASIER TO MAKE HIM MOVE THAT WAY.

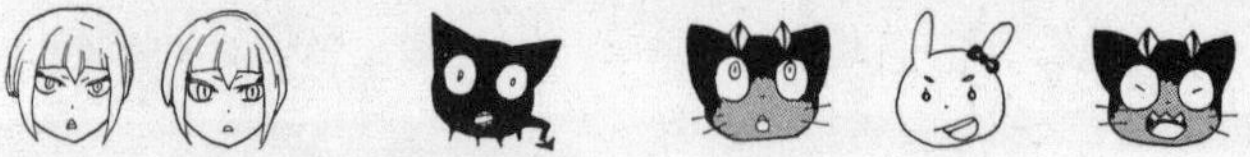

HE HAS A FANG WHEN HE FIRST APPEARS IN THE MANGA, BUT WHEN HE REAPPEARS IN VOLUME 5, IT'S GONE. AS FOR WHY...

WELL, ABOUT THAT...

IT'S A BIT OF A STORY, SO I'VE EXPLAINED IT ELSE-WHERE—NOT HERE! I WONDER WHERE? TAKE A GOOD LOOK AROUND VOLUME 8!

HUH? WHERE IS IT?

I'VE BEEN THINKING ABOUT MAMUSHI, NISHIKI AND AO, THE THREE HOJO SISTERS. I KNOW MAMUSHI IS THE OLDEST, BUT WHICH OF THE OTHER TWO IS OLDER? PLEASE, TELL ME.
RUNA (?), HIROSHIMA PREFECTURE

PEOPLE SAY WE LOOK ALIKE. I'M MAMUSHI, THE ELDEST.

AND THE SECOND ELDEST IS ME. I'M NISHIKI. PEOPLE SAY I HAVE THE HARSHEST GLARE OF THE THREE OF US. IS IT TRUE?

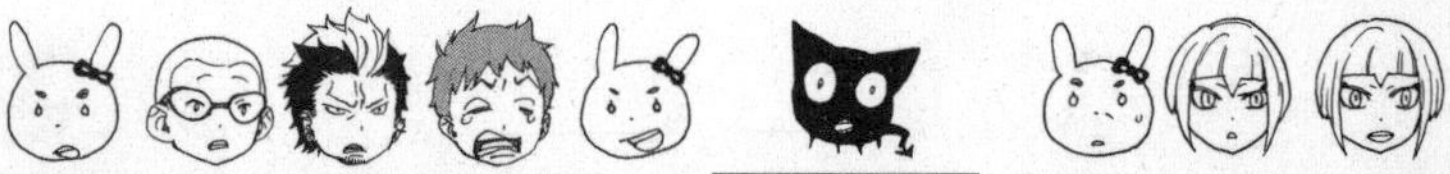

AND I'M AO, THE YOUNG-EST. I LOVE MY BIG SISTERS!

CAN YOU TELL US APART NOW?

UH... CAN YOU?

SUGURO AND KONE-KOMARU ADDRESS JUZO AND KINZO BY THEIR FIRST NAMES, BUT THEY CALL SHIMA, WHO'S WITH THEM ALL THE TIME, BY HIS LAST NAME?
ASARINGO (15), AOMORI PREFECTURE

A LOT OF PEOPLE ASKED THIS ONE, TOO!

THEY'RE RIGHT!! WHY AM I ALWAYS SHIMA?! WE'RE CLOSE ENOUGH FOR YOU TO CALL ME RENZO!

I'M USED TO CALLING YOU SHIMA.

YEAH, YOU JUST DON'T FEEL LIKE A RENZO.

WHY DID YOU START CALLING HIM SHIMA?

WHEN WE WERE IN KINDERGARTEN, HE USED TO WEAR HIS MOM'S UNDERPANTS ON HIS HEAD AND SHOUT "THE MASKED PERVERT!!" AS HE CHASED GIRLS AROUND ...BUCK NAKED.

...

MAYBE IT WAS AN INSTINCT OF SELF-PRESERVATION—LIKE, EVEN AS CHILDREN WE THOUGHT WE SHOULDN'T REVEAL THAT WE WERE CLOSE TO HIM. WHEN WE'RE AROUND OTHER PEOPLE, WE JUST NATURALLY CALLED HIM SHIMA-SAN.

...

HE WAS PRETTY BAD IN ELEMENTARY SCHOOL AND JUNIOR HIGH, TOO.

STOP IT!! DON'T SAY ANY MORE!! YOU'LL DESTROY THE COOL IMAGE I HAVE IN HIGH SCHOOL!!

OKAY, I SEE. SO HE REALLY IS AN EROTIC DEMON!

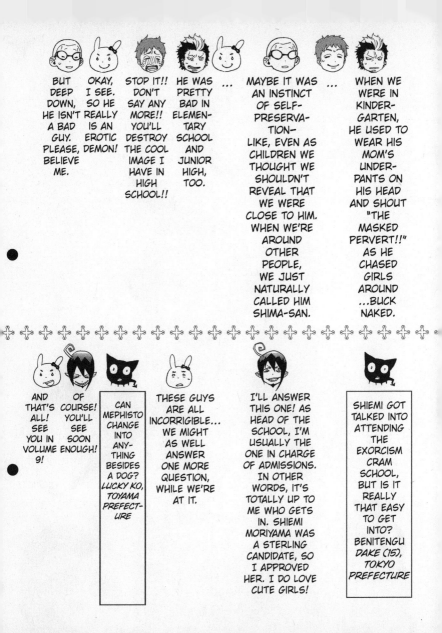

BUT DEEP DOWN, HE ISN'T A BAD GUY. PLEASE, BELIEVE ME.

SHIEMI GOT TALKED INTO ATTENDING THE EXORCISM CRAM SCHOOL, BUT IS IT REALLY THAT EASY TO GET INTO? *BENITENGU DAKE (15), TOKYO PREFECTURE*

I'LL ANSWER THIS ONE! AS HEAD OF THE SCHOOL, I'M USUALLY THE ONE IN CHARGE OF ADMISSIONS. IN OTHER WORDS, IT'S TOTALLY UP TO ME WHO GETS IN. SHIEMI MORIYAMA WAS A STERLING CANDIDATE, SO I APPROVED HER. I DO LOVE CUTE GIRLS!

THESE GUYS ARE ALL INCORRIGIBLE... WE MIGHT AS WELL ANSWER ONE MORE QUESTION, WHILE WE'RE AT IT.

CAN MEPHISTO CHANGE INTO ANYTHING BESIDES A DOG? *LUCKY KO, TOYAMA PREFECTURE*

OF COURSE! YOU'LL SEE SOON ENOUGH!

AND THAT'S ALL! SEE YOU IN VOLUME 9!

QUESTION CORNER β

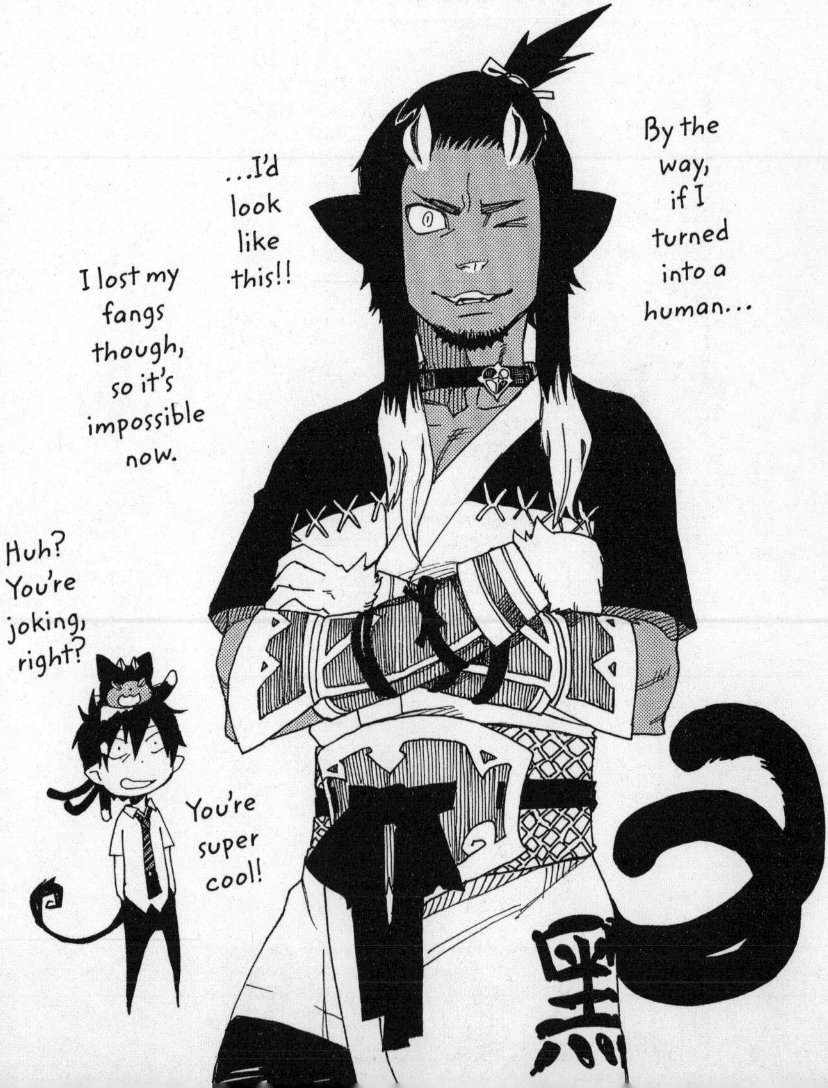
By the way, if I turned into a human...
...I'd look like this!!
I lost my fangs though, so it's impossible now.
Huh? You're joking, right?
You're super cool!
黒

I'm answering the most common question about Kuro here. Sorry.

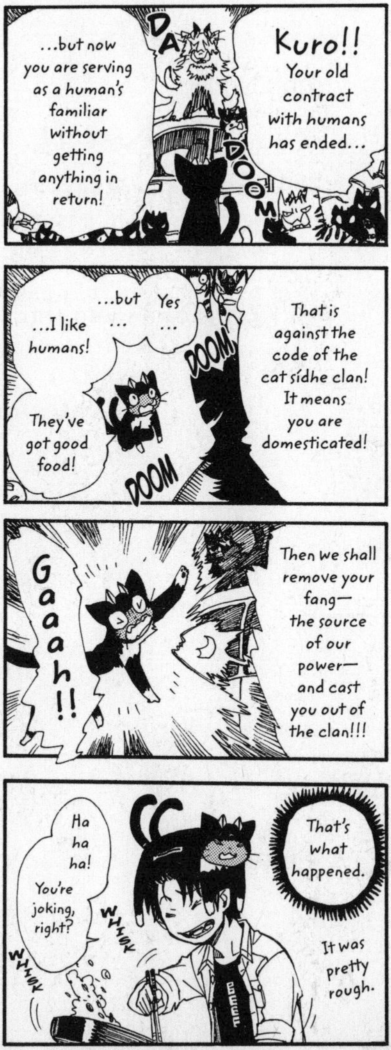
Kuro!! Your old contract with humans has ended...
DA
DOOM
...but now you are serving as a human's familiar without getting anything in return!
That is against the code of the cat sídhe clan! It means you are domesticated!
DOOM
DOOM
Yes ...
...but ...
...I like humans!
They've got good food!
Then we shall remove your fang— the source of our power— and cast you out of the clan!!!
Gaaah!!
That's what happened.
It was pretty rough.
WHISK
Ha ha ha! You're joking, right?
WHISK

Huh? I didn't come up with it later! I thought of it before! It's true! It's true!

...I'm tall and cool lookin'!

This time...

Kazue Kato

This volume features the battle that takes place in the latter half of this long story arc.

Everyone's running around like crazy!

On to volume 8!

BLUE EXORCIST

BLUE EXORCIST VOL. 8
SHONEN JUMP ADVANCED Manga Edition

STORY & ART BY KAZUE KATO

Translation & English Adaptation/John Werry
Touch-up Art & Lettering/John Hunt, Primary Graphix
Cover & Interior Design/Sam Elzway
Editor/Mike Montesa

Printed in the U.S.A.

Published by VIZ Media, LLC
P.O. Box 77010
San Francisco, CA 94107

10 9 8 7 6 5 4 3 2
First printing, November 2012
Second printing, May 2014

In the next volume...

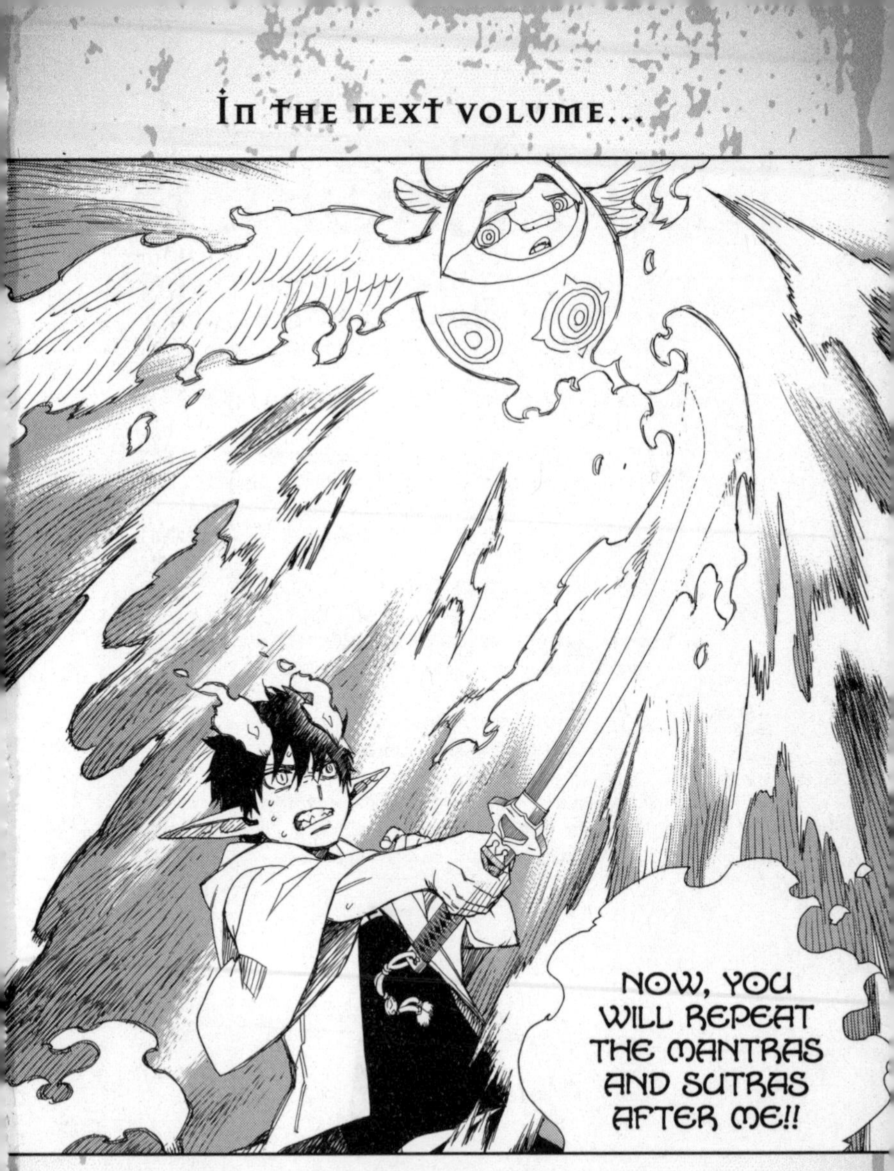
NOW, YOU WILL REPEAT THE MANTRAS AND SUTRAS AFTER ME!!

Rin's friends are doing everything they can to hold off the deadly Impure King so Rin can confront it. But although Rin has drawn his sword and found his confidence, that alone may not be enough to defeat the Impure King!

Available now!